www.wadsworth.com

www.wadsworth.com is the World Wide Web site for
Wadsworth and is your direct source to dozens of online
resources.

At *www.wadsworth.com* you can find out about
supplements, demonstration software, and student
resources. You can also send email to many of our
authors and preview new publications and exciting new
technologies.

www.wadsworth.com
Changing the way the world learns®

THE GLOBAL FUTURE

A Brief Introduction to World Politics

CHARLES W. KEGLEY, JR.
University of South Carolina

GREGORY A. RAYMOND
Boise State University

THOMSON

™

WADSWORTH

Australia • Canada • Mexico • Singapore • Spain
United Kingdom • United States

DEDICATION

To our wives, Debbie and Christine, for their understanding and support.

Publisher: *Clark Baxter*
Executive Editor: *David Tatom*
Senior Development Editor: *Stacey Sims*
Assistant Editor: *Rebecca Green*
Editorial Assistant: *Reena Thomas*
Technology Project Manager: *Michelle Vardeman*
Senior Marketing Manager: *Janise Fry*
Marketing Assistant: *Teresa Jessen*
Advertising Project Manager: *Kelley McAllister*
Project Manager, Editorial Production: *Cheri Palmer*
Art Director: *Maria Epes*
Print/Media Buyer: *Lisa Claudeanos*

Permissions Editor: *Chelsea Junget*
Production Service/Compositor: *Shepherd, Inc.*
Text Designer: *Diane Beasley*
Photo Researcher: *Suzie Wright*
Copy Editor: *Terri Winsor*
Cover Designer: *Brian Salisbury*
Cover Images: *top left: EPA Photo/Kim Ludbrook; top right: Corbis; bottom left: AP Photo/Lefteris Pitarakis; bottom middle: Bernhard Lang/gettyimages; bottom right: AP Photo/Stephen Shaver*
Printer: *Quebecor World/Taunton*

Printed in the United States of America
1 2 3 4 5 6 7 09 08 07 06 05

For more information about our products,
contact us at:
Thomson Learning Academic Resource Center
1-800-423-0563
For permission to use material from this text or product, submit a request online at
http://www.thomsonrights.com.
Any additional questions about permissions can be submitted by email to
thomsonrights@thomson.com.

Library of Congress Control Number: 2004111824

Student Edition: ISBN 0-534-53693-X
Instructor's Edition: ISBN 0-534-53699-9

Thomson Higher Education
10 Davis Drive
Belmont, CA 94002-3098
USA

Asia (including India)
Thomson Learning
5 Shenton Way
#01-01 UIC Building
Singapore 068808

Australia/New Zealand
Thomson Learning Australia
102 Dodds Street
Southbank, Victoria 3006
Australia

Canada
Thomson Nelson
1120 Birchmount Road
Toronto, Ontario M1K 5G4
Canada

UK/Europe/Middle East/Africa
Thomson Learning
High Holborn House
50–51 Bedford Road
London WC1R 4LR
United Kingdom

Latin America
Thomson Learning
Seneca, 53
Colonia Polanco
11560 Mexico
D.F. Mexico

Spain (including Portugal)
Thomson Paraninfo
Calle Magallanes, 25
28015 Madrid, Spain

Brief Table of Contents

Contents

PART II   THE ACTORS IN WORLD POLITICS   42

CHAPTER 3
Foreign Policy Decision Making   44

CHAPTER 4
Great-Power Rivalry and the Lure of Hegemony: Cycles of War and Peace in Modern World History   64

CHAPTER 5
Rich and Poor in World Politics: The Plight of the Global South   89

CHAPTER 6
Nonstate Actors and the Challenge of Global Governance   117

PART III THE POLITICS OF GLOBAL SECURITY 148

CHAPTER 7
Armed Conflict in the Twenty-First Century 150

CHAPTER 8
Military Power and National Security in a Turbulent World 174

CHAPTER 9
Realist Paths to Peace: Alliances, Arms Control, and the Balance of Power
202

CHAPTER 10
Liberal Paths to Peace: International Law and Organization
225

Maps

Preface

In all likelihood, you are enrolled in your first course on world politics (or international relations, as it is called in some college catalogues). Like most students in introductory courses, you probably have a few questions about the relevance of this subject for your education. In particular, you may be wondering why you should study world politics, and when it became part of the typical college curriculum. Since we have written this textbook with students in mind, a good place to begin our exploration of world politics is by addressing these preliminary questions.

Why should I study world politics?

World politics is an endless source of mystery and surprise. As you will see throughout this book, common sense is not sufficient for understanding international events. All too often, our intuition is wrong about why certain things happened. Albert Einstein once hinted at the challenge of explaining world politics when he was asked, "Why is it that when the mind of man has stretched so far as to discover the structure of the atom we have been unable to devise the political means to keep the atom from destroying us?" He replied, "This is simple, my friend, it is because politics is more difficult than physics."

In recent years, the world has experienced many unsettling changes that have made world politics even more difficult than in Einstein's day. The destructive power of military force has increased, terrorism has become a serious global threat, the economic gap between rich and poor nations has widened, and the global environment has suffered from the combined pressures of population growth, resource depletion, and pollution. Further complicating matters is the interconnectedness of nations. Pressing military, social, economic, and environmental problems now spill across national borders, affecting the security and personal well-being of all of us. In more ways than we realize, our lives are affected by world politics.

Since events in distant parts of the world touch our daily lives, we should not leave crucial decisions about international issues to others. In a democracy, every citizen has an opportunity to influence policies on these issues by voting in elections, lobbying government officials, writing letters to newspapers, or joining protest demonstrations. To make the most of these opportunities, we need to understand world politics. This text introduces a set of concepts and analytic tools that will help you better understand the nature of world politics. The effort that you make in learning these concepts and tools will strengthen your ability to think critically about international issues, and enhance your capability to advocate effectively for foreign policies you believe will improve the human condition.

When did world politics become an academic subject?

Although philosophers, theologians, historians, and statesmen have written about war and diplomacy since antiquity, the formal study of world politics began at the dawn of the twentieth century. Prior to the onset of World War I, many people believed that progress toward a more peaceful and prosperous world was inevitable. The great powers had not fought one another for decades, industrial development and international commerce were expanding at astonishing rates, and scientists seemed to be solving the deepest mysteries of the universe. By some accounts, it was the most optimistic period in history. Peace conferences held in The Hague during 1899 and 1907 inspired hope that future generations would settle their differences without resorting to arms. In 1910, the British writer Norman Angell declared that war had become obsolete because it was no longer profitable. Three years later, at the dedication of the building that would house the Permanent Court of Arbitration, the Scottish-American industrialist Andrew Carnegie wrote in his diary: "Looking back a hundred years, or less perchance, from today, the future historian is to pronounce the opening [of the Court] . . . the greatest one step forward ever taken by man, in his long and checkered march upward from barbarism."

In those tranquil, confident times, students of world politics surveyed current events to glean insight on the international issues of the day. The study of world politics consisted mainly of commentary about personalities and interesting incidents, past and present. Rarely did scholars seek to generalize about patterns of behavior that might account for international events.

The gruesome toll extracted by World War I destroyed the sense of security that made this approach popular. However interesting descriptions of current events might be, they were of doubtful use to a world in search of ways to prevent future wars. International relations as a field of academic study emerged as scholars began searching for the underlying causes of the First World War. Not long after the guns had fallen silent, the Royal Institute of International Affairs was established in London, the Council of Foreign Relations was set up in New York, and the first university chair in International Relations was created at the University College of Wales, Aberystwyth. Soon institutions of higher learning throughout Britain and the United States began offering courses on world politics. Since then, the academic study of international affairs has spread to virtually every region of the world.

Overview of the Book

Now that you have some idea about the relevance of studying world politics, let's briefly look at how *The Global Future* is organized and what you can do to take advantage of its features.

Organization and Content

To help you make sense of world politics, *The Global Future* is divided into four parts. Part I introduces the central issues and major theories in the study of international relations. Part II identifies the primary actors in the global arena and discusses the processes by which these actors make decisions. Part III looks at global security, focusing on the problems of war and terrorism as well as rival approaches to preserving peace. Finally, Part IV examines issues of global welfare. Following an analysis of the process of globalization, it addresses the topics of international economic relations, human rights, and the linkage between population dynamics and the environment.

Design and Pedagogy

The Global Future contains a variety of learning aids to help you understand the complexities of world politics.

- **Chapter outlines.** The first item in every chapter is an outline of the material that will be covered.
- **Introductory case studies.** To encourage you to think critically about the topics covered in the book, the narrative section of each chapter begins with a vignette that introduces its underlying theme.
- **Marginal glosses for all key terms.** Whenever we use a technical term for the first time, we highlight it in the text and define it in the margin. Pay close attention to these terms, because they are part of the vocabulary scholars, journalists, and policymakers use when discussing world politics.
- **Controversy boxes presenting essential debates.** We use "controversy" boxes to portray ongoing debates within the field of international relations, and to encourage you to weigh the arguments on each side as you develop your own opinion.
- **Photographs.** To amplify the main points in the text, we have included photographs with captions that explain each image's relationship to key concepts and themes.
- **Tables, figures, and maps.** Visual aids are excellent tools for communicating complex material. When it would reinforce an explanation in the text, we have displayed important information in graphic form.
- **Chapter summaries.** Each chapter concludes with a summary of its main themes.
- **"Where on the World Wide Web?" listings.** At the end of every chapter, we show how to access more information on the World Wide Web. Each web listing is accompanied by an annotation describing the site's content.
- **InfoTrac® College Edition.** Four months of FREE anywhere, anytime access to InfoTrac College Edition, an online library, is automatically packaged with this book, putting cutting edge research and the latest headlines at your fingertips. This fully searchable database offers more than 10 million articles from almost 4,000 sources, ranging from academic journals to periodicals.

Supplements

To enhance teaching and learning, *The Global Future* is accompanied by an extensive ancillary package:

International Relations Interactive CD-ROM

Automatically packaged with every new copy of Kegley and Raymond's *The Global Future,* the CD-ROM gives students access to historical maps, data, and critical thinking services.

The Interactive Book Companion Website
http://politicalscience.wadsworth.com/kegleybrief01/

Correlated chapter by chapter with Kegley and Raymond's *The Global Future,* the website includes chapter outlines, chapter summaries, glossary, tutorial quizzing, book-specific content/boxed features, key terms, and PowerPoint® transparencies. The site is just a mouse click away from Wadsworth's *Political Science Resource Center,* which offers even more resources for students and instructors.

NEW! Multimedia Manager with Instructor Resources: A Microsoft® PowerPoint® Link Tool

Including presentation tools and electronic instructor resources, this book-specific tool is a one-stop source that allows you to most effectively prepare for your course in a timely fashion. The CD-ROM contains Microsoft® Power-Point® images (lecture outlines, illustrations, charts, and graphs from the text itself); *CNN Today* video clips; the *Instructor's Manual* and *Test Bank;* the *Resource Integration Guide;* the *Video Case Studies Instructor's Manual,* and *ExamView®* computerized testing—an easy-to-use assessment program, which allows you to create, deliver, and customize tests and study guides (both print and online) in minutes.

Instructor's Edition—Featuring the Resource Integration Guide!

In addition to a visual walkthrough of the text's ancillaries, the Instructor's Edition includes the *Resource Integration Guide,* an essential course preparation tool—featuring grids that link each chapter of the text to instructional ideas and corresponding supplemental resources. At a glance, you can see which selections from the text's teaching and learning ancillaries are appropriate for each key chapter topic. For your convenience, the *Resource Integration Guide* is also included in the *Multimedia Manager with Instructor Resource* CD-ROM.

CNN® Today Video: *International Relations and Comparative Politics,* 2004 Edition

Short clips to launch your lectures! This engaging video includes 15 three- to five-minute high-interest news stories that will spark classroom discussion and tie current world events to your international relations and comparative politics courses. Topics include the International Criminal Court, oil politics, the Earth Summit, the worldwide AIDS crisis, India–Pakistan relations, and much more.

Launch your lectures with riveting footage from CNN, the world's leading 24-hour global news television network.

America's New War: CNN® Looks at Terrorism, Volume II

This great discussion starter includes 16 two- to five-minute segments featuring CNN news footage, commentator remarks, and speeches dealing with terrorist attacks on U.S. targets throughout the world.

Innovative Student Resources

InfoTrac College Edition . . . FREE access to nearly 5,000 publications!

Adopters and their students have the option of receiving four months of FREE access to InfoTrac College Edition with every new copy of this book. Opening the door to the complete articles (not just abstracts) from nearly 5,000 top journals and popular publications, this online library is expertly indexed, linking users to topic-relevant articles for every chapter in Kegley and Raymond's text. Also included: *InfoWrite*—quick access to critical thinking and paper-writing tutorials.

Opposing Viewpoints Resource Center . . . for pro and con debates

Expose your students to various sides of today's most compelling issues with this dynamic online library of current event topics—the facts, as well as the arguments of each topic's proponents and detractors. For a nominal fee, the *Opposing Viewpoints Resource Center* is available for convenient packaging with each copy of this book. For a demonstration, please visit http://www.gale.com/opposingviewpoints/.

International Relations: Using MicroCase® ExplorIt
by James C. Roberts of Towson University and Alan Rosenblatt of Stateside Associates.

Available for packaging with every copy of Kegley and Raymond's text, this workbook utilizes real data sets to explore important concepts, theories, and phenomena in international relations. Each chapter is organized around examples that focus on a set of concepts or theories. The workbook contains 12 computer-based assignments and includes software and nine data sets.

Also available for convenient packaging with every student text:

- *Wadsworth Atlas of International Relations:* 0-534-61793-X
- *Regime Change: Origins, Execution, and Aftermath of the Iraq War:* 0-534-64337-X
- *Conflict and Cooperation: Evolving Theories of International Relations,* Second Edition: 0-534-50690-9
- *Beyond Sovereignty: Issues for a Global Agenda,* Second Edition: 0-534-60893-0

- *Why Nations Go to War,* Eighth Edition: 0-312-25660-4
- *InfoTrac College Edition Student Guide for Political Science:* 0-534-24728-8
- *From War to Peace: Fateful Decisions in International Politics,* Second Edition: 0-312-39468-3
- *9–11: The Giant Awakens,* Eighth Edition: 0-534-61659-3

Acknowledgments

Many people have contributed to making this book. We greatly appreciate the constructive comments and suggestions offered by reviewers. In particular, we express our gratitude to the professional scholars who provided blind reviews of the manuscript, including Damian Fernandez, Florida International University; William E. Hoehne, Jr., Georgia Institute of Technology; Ian Hurd, Northwestern University; George Kent, University of Hawaii; William W. Lamkin, Glendale Community College; John Mercurio, San Diego State University; Meike Mittelstadt, Spokane Falls Community College; and David Schrupp, Montana State University.

Deserving of special gratitude are our highly skilled, dedicated, and helpful editors at Wadsworth: Senior Developmental Editor Stacey Sims and Executive Editor David Tatom who exercised extraordinary professionalism in guiding the process that brought this edition into print, assisted by the project management of Cheri Palmer and the support of Reena Thomas and Chelsea Junget. Assistant Editor Rebecca Green and Technology Project Manager Michelle Vardeman worked diligently together in developing the CD-ROM that accompanies the new edition. In addition, Peggy Francomb and the staff at Shepherd, Inc., as well as Terri Winsor, our copyeditor, contributed immeasurably to the preparation, polish, and production of the book.

About the Authors

Charles W. Kegley, Jr. is the Pearce Professor of International Relations at the University of South Carolina. A graduate of American University and Syracuse University, and a Pew Faculty Fellow at Harvard University, Kegley serves on the Board of Trustees of the Carnegie Council on Ethics and International Affairs and is a past president of the International Studies Association (1993–1994). Kegley has held faculty appointments at Georgetown University, the University of Texas, the People's University of China, and the Graduate Institute of International Studies, Geneva. Recently published among his four dozen books are *World Politics: Trend and Transformation* (ninth edition with Eugene R. Wittkopf, 2004), *The New Global Terrorism* (2003), and *Controversies in International Relations Theory* (1995). He has also published his primary research in many scholarly journals.

Gregory A. Raymond is the Frank Church Professor of International Relations at Boise State University, where he is also director of the Honors College. A graduate of Park College and the University of South Carolina, and a Pew Faculty Fellow at Harvard University, Raymond was selected in 1994 as the Idaho Professor of the Year by the Carnegie Foundation for the Advancement of Teaching. Raymond has published extensively in scholarly journals and has spoken on international issues at universities and research institutes in 22 countries. He is the author of *Conflict Resolution and the Structure of the State System* (1980), coauthor of *The Other Western Europe: A Comparative Analysis of the Smaller Democracies* (1983), and coeditor of *Third World Policies of Industrialized Nations* (1982), which received an Outstanding Academic Book Award from the American Library Association.

Together Kegley and Raymond have coauthored *The Imperiled Imperium: America's Changing Role on the World Stage* (2005), *From War to Peace: Fateful Decisions in International Politics* (2002), *Exorcising the Ghost of Westphalia: Building International Peace in the New Millennium* (2002), *How Nations Make Peace* (1999), *A Multipolar Peace? Great-Power Politics in the Twenty-First Century* (1994), and *When Trust Breaks Down: Alliance Norms and World Politics* (1990). They have also coedited *International Events and the Comparative Analysis of Foreign Policy* (1975) and coauthored over two dozen articles in such periodicals as the *International Studies Quarterly*, the *Journal of Conflict Resolution*, the *Journal of Politics*, the *Journal of Peace Research*, *International Interactions*, and the *Harvard International Review*.

THE GLOBAL FUTURE

Trend and Transformation in World Politics

In his speech accepting the 2001 Nobel Peace Prize, United Nations secretary-general Kofi Annan lamented that humanity had entered the new millennium through "a gate of fire." Wars, terrorist attacks, and civil strife regularly intrude on our daily lives. A gnawing sense of insecurity torments many of us, regardless of gender, ethnicity, or nationality. Anxious about what might happen next, we struggle to divine our collective fate. What lies ahead? Can we create a better world? How are we to think about the global future?

This book examines the impact of world politics on the global future. Of course, no one can foresee the future precisely. We can, however, identify emerging trends and imagine how they might coalesce in different ways to produce alternative global futures. According to engineer and social policy analyst Willis Harman (1976), thinking about trends is important because "our view of the future shapes the kind of decisions we make in the present." Almost every action we take "involves some view of the future—as we expect it to be, or as we desire it to be, or as we fear it may be." The goals of Part I of this book are to encourage you to begin thinking about the integrative and disintegrative trends in world politics, and consider how the actions we take in response to our image of their impact will influence which alternative global future we will eventually inhabit.

A first step in thinking about the global future is to recognize that the events and trends we observe are not seen in all innocence. They are filtered

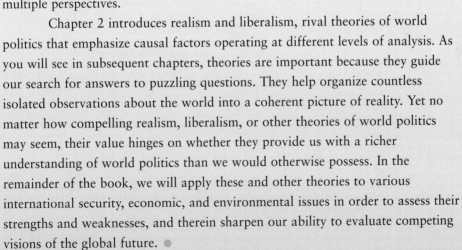

PART I

through a lens of values and beliefs born from previous experiences. Chapter 1 shows how this lens can distort our perception of international affairs. It also demonstrates how viewing things from the individual, state, and systemic levels of analysis can help reduce distortions by providing an explicit, orderly way of examining world politics from multiple perspectives.

Chapter 2 introduces realism and liberalism, rival theories of world politics that emphasize causal factors operating at different levels of analysis. As you will see in subsequent chapters, theories are important because they guide our search for answers to puzzling questions. They help organize countless isolated observations about the world into a coherent picture of reality. Yet no matter how compelling realism, liberalism, or other theories of world politics may seem, their value hinges on whether they provide us with a richer understanding of world politics than we would otherwise possess. In the remainder of the book, we will apply these and other theories to various international security, economic, and environmental issues in order to assess their strengths and weaknesses, and therein sharpen our ability to evaluate competing visions of the global future. ●

CHAPTER 1

Exploring Twenty-First-Century World Politics

At bottom our troubled state of mind reflects an inability to see the future in an historic context. If current events strike us as all surprise and shock it is because we cannot see these events in a meaningful framework. If the future seems to us a kind of limbo, a repository of endless surprises, it is because we no longer see it as the expected culmination of the past, as the growing edge of the present.

ROBERT L. HEILBRONER, economist

When people use the term *international relations,* they usually are referring to interactions among autonomous, territorial **states** that have no higher authority governing their behavior. Our earliest records of such states come from ancient Mesopotamia, where some two dozen rival city-states flourished on the flood plains between the Tigris and Euphrates Rivers. Archaeologists believe that civilization began in Sumeria, the region's southern edge, which borders the coastline of what we now call the Persian Gulf. Here they find evidence of the first wheel and plow, the first extensive use of writing and metallurgy, the first legal codes and business contracts, as well as the first production of beer, of which there were nineteen varieties (Fields, Barber, and Riggs 1998; Durant 1954).

• **state** an organized political entity with a permanent population, a well-defined territory, and a government.

By roughly 2500 BCE, the typical Sumerian city-state possessed several thousand inhabitants, with most living within the city's high mud-brick walls. Fortifications were necessary because the flat terrain of southern Mesopotamia left city-states vulnerable to attack, and frequent conflict over water rights, grazing lands, and trade routes made war an ever-present threat. Sumerian armies were composed of an infantry supported by archers and four-wheeled war carts. Soldiers wore copper helmets and rudimentary armored kilts, carried large rectangular shields, and were armed with spears, swords, and axes (Keegan 1993). Fighting occurred at close quarters. Victors in these brutal contests subjugated the defeated, plundering their land and enslaving their population.

The conflict between the city-states of Lagash and Umma exemplified the harsh nature of Sumerian warfare. After generations of sporadic hostilities, an army led by King Lugal-Zaggisi of Umma finally overwhelmed Lagash (circa 2350 BCE). He sacked the city, massacred many of its citizens, and, in a gesture of contempt, placed statues of their gods in bondage. In one of humanity's earliest works of literature, the poet Dingiraddamu mourned for the patron goddess of Lagash: "O Lady of my city, desolated, when wilt thou return?"

War continued to plague Mesopotamia long after the tragic clash between Lagash and Umma. Over the millennia, many armies marched into the region. When seen through the prism of history, the military campaign led by the United States during the spring of 2003 against Iraqi leader Saddam Hussein was simply the latest outbreak of war in this ancient land. Yet it was a war unlike any other. Touted as the world's first digital war, it used networked communications to merge data from multiple sources to coordinate precision air strikes with swarming ground attacks. Unlike the chaos that cloaked ancient battlefields, American commanders hundreds of miles from the fighting could monitor developments as they happened. Whereas scouts might relay sporadic reports on enemy defenses to Lugal-Zaggisi, Predator drones, Airborne Warning and Control System (AWACS) planes, and special operations units inserted behind enemy lines by helicopter fed General Tommy Franks a continual stream of intelligence. Whereas Sumerian warriors unleashed a volley of arrows and javelins before closing with the enemy, U.S. troops could expect a devastating barrage of cruise missile, stealth fighter, and heavy bomber strikes to begin a campaign. In short, speed and mobility now substitutes for mass; information and firepower, for sheer numbers.

Art Resource

Werner Forman/Art Resource, NY, British Museum, London, Great Britain; Photo
courtesy of the U.S. Army/Staff Sgt. Klaus Baesu

War in Human History "The story of the human race is War," British Prime Minister Winston
Churchill once lamented. As shown in the depiction of an ancient Sumerian war cart and the
photograph of a modern American M1-A1 Abrams tank, although war has been a constant
feature of international relations, the means by which it has been waged has changed over
time. Rapid advances in military technology over the past century and a half have made armed
forces more lethal than ever before. A single American B-52 bomber, for example, can carry
more explosive power than that used in all of the wars fought throughout recorded history.

• **politics** the exercise
of influence to affect
the distribution of val-
ues, such as power,
prestige, and wealth;
to Harold Lasswell, the
process that determines
"who gets what, when,
how and why."

What can we learn by comparing warfare in ancient Mesopotamia and modern
Iraq? Quite simply, it reminds us that **politics** among territorial states is a mixture of
continuity and change. On the one hand, states have lived under what political
scientist Kenneth Waltz (1979) calls the "brooding shadow of violence" since
antiquity. On the other hand, the way armed forces wield violence has changed
profoundly. Change is riveting; it captures our attention. Still, we must be mindful
that some features of world politics are relatively permanent. When considering how
world politics might affect the global future, we need to be attentive to entrenched
continuities as well as the sources of drastic change. As Robert Heilbroner suggests in
the epigraph of this chapter, much of our current uncertainty about the future stems
from an inability to grasp our historic situation.

Continuity and Change in World Politics

How can we best understand the political convulsions that confront the world's
more than six billion people almost daily? How can we anticipate their significance? At the beginning of a new century, people often speculate about the global
future. What will the new world be like? Will it be different? As international
conditions change, will humanity benefit? Or will it suffer?

Looking beyond the confines of our immediate time is difficult. It requires an appreciation of the interaction of previous ideas and events with current realities. As philosopher George Santayana cautioned, "Those who cannot remember the past are condemned to repeat it." Thus, to understand the dramatic changes in world politics today and to predict how they will shape the future, we will view them in the context of a long-term perspective that examines how the international political **system**—the patterns of interaction among world political actors—has changed and how some of its fundamental characteristics have resisted change.

> • **system** a set of interconnected parts that function as a unitary whole. In world politics, the parts consist primarily of states, corporations, and other organizations that interact in the global arena.

What do evolving diplomatic practices suggest about the current state of world politics? Are the episodic shock waves throughout the world clearing the way for a truly new twenty-first-century world order? Or will many of today's dramatic disruptions ultimately prove temporary, mere spikes on the seismograph of history? We invite you to explore these questions with us. To begin our search, let us explore how the differences between continuities and changes in world history can help us orient our effort.

Every historical period is marked to some extent by change. Now, however, the pace of change seems more rapid and its consequences more profound than ever. To many observers, the cascade of events at the start of the twenty-first century implies a revolutionary restructuring of world politics. Numerous *integrative* trends point to that possibility. The countries of the world are drawing closer together in communications and trade, as the linkages among diverse national economies have produced a globalized market. Yet at the same time, *disintegrative* trends paint a less sanguine picture. Weapons proliferation, global environmental deterioration, and the resurgence of nationalism and ethnic conflict all portend a restructuring fraught with disorder. To predict which forces will dominate the future, we must recognize that no trend stands alone. The future is influenced by many determinants, each connected to others in a complex web of linkages. Collectively, these trends may produce stability by limiting the impact of any single disruptive force. It is also possible for them to accelerate the pace of change, moving world politics in directions not possible otherwise.

The opposing forces of integration and disintegration point toward a transformation in world politics, but what will be its long-term ramifications? Distinguishing true historical watersheds from temporary changes is difficult. The moment of transformation from one system to another is not immediately obvious. Nevertheless, certain times are especially likely candidates. Major turning points in world politics usually have occurred at the conclusion of major wars, which typically disrupt or destroy preexisting international arrangements. In the twentieth century, World Wars I and II and the Cold War caused fundamental breaks with the past and set in motion major transformations, providing countries with incentives to rethink the premises underlying their interests, purposes, and priorities. Similarly, many people concluded that the terrorist attacks on September 11, 2001 (9/11) produced a fundamental transformation in world affairs. Indeed, many felt that 9/11 changed everything, perhaps forever: In U.S. president George W. Bush's words, "Night fell on a different world," adding later "This is our life now. . . . The battle's just begun."

Was September 11, 2001, a Transforming Event in World Politics? The terrorist attack on the World Trade Center's twin towers on 9/11 is regarded by many as a watershed event in world history. Time will tell whether this act of terrorism will, as the years go by and the stark pain fades from memory, rank alongside the birth of the nuclear age on August 6, 1945, when the United States bombed Hiroshima, or the November 1989 dismantling of the Berlin Wall that signaled the end of the Cold War, as an event that truly changes the world.

Despite all that appears radically different since the 9/11 terrorist attacks, much also remains the same in world politics. As political journalist Robert J. Samuelson noted on the first anniversary of 9/11, "What is most striking about the past year is how little has changed." We often expect dramatic events to alter our lives forever and later are surprised to discover that certain patterns from the past have reappeared. Given the rapid changes that are occurring in the world alongside enduring continuities, these are uncertain times. Because some aspects of the future are likely to mirror the past, asserting that a major transformation in world politics is under way requires us to define what constitutes a new world order.

How can we determine when an existing pattern of relationships gives way to a completely new international system? Following Stanley Hoffmann (1961), we will proceed by assuming that we have a new international system when we have a new answer to one of three questions: (1) What are the system's basic units? (e.g., states or other type of international actor); (2) What are the predominant foreign policy goals that these units seek with respect to one another? (e.g., territorial conquest or material gain through trade); and (3) What can these units do to one another with their military and economic capabilities?

These criteria might lead us to conclude that a new system has now emerged. First, new trade partnerships have been forged in Europe, the cone of South America, North America, and the Pacific Rim, and these economic blocs may behave as independent actors as they compete with one another. Moreover, international organizations, such as the World Trade Organization and the International Monetary Fund, now sometimes flex their political muscles in contests with individual states, as do some transnational religious movements, such as Islamic fundamentalism. At the same time, some states have disintegrated into smaller units. In 1991, the Soviet Union splintered into a welter of fractious political entities, each searching for national identity and political stability. Other states could disintegrate as well—peacefully, like the former Czechoslovakia, or violently, like the former Yugoslavia.

Second, territorial conquest is no longer the predominant goal of most states' foreign policies. Instead, their emphasis has shifted from traditional military methods of exercising influence to economic means. Meanwhile, the Cold War's ideological contest between capitalism and communism no longer comprises the primary cleavage in international politics, and a major new axis has yet to become clear, even though many conclude that 9/11 marked the beginning of a new age dominated by a global war between terrorists and those who resist them.

Third, the proliferation of deadly weapons has profoundly altered the damage that states can inflict on one another. Great powers alone no longer control the world's most lethal armaments. Even more frightening, advanced weaponry is no longer necessary for a small, elusive group of fanatics to inflict catastrophic damage. Ingenuity and box cutters allowed the 9/11 terrorists to kill thousands of people.

The profound changes in the types of units, goals, and capabilities of recent years have dramatically altered the power rankings of state and **nonstate actors** on the world stage. Still, the hierarchies themselves endure. The economic hierarchy that divides the rich from the poor, the political hierarchy that separates the rulers from the ruled, the resource hierarchy that makes some suppliers and others dependents, and the military hierarchy that pits the strong against the weak all still shape the relations among states, as they have in the past. Similarly, the absence of institutions to govern the globe conspires with chronic national insecurity to encourage the use of force without international mandate. Thus change and continuity coexist, with both forces simultaneously shaping contemporary world politics.

• **nonstate actors** all transnationally active groups other than states, such as international organizations whose members are states (IGOs) and non-governmental organizations (NGOs) whose members are individuals and private groups from more than one state.

The challenge, then, is to observe unfolding global realities carefully in order to describe and explain their character. This requires that we understand how our images of reality shape our expectations. It also requires a set of tools for analyzing the forces of constancy and change that affect our world. Hence, the remainder of this chapter will briefly examine the role that images of reality play in our understanding of world politics, and then will describe some of the tools we will use in this book to interpret trends and transformations in world politics.

How Perceptions Influence Images of Reality

We all carry mental images of world politics—explicit or implicit, conscious or subconscious. But whatever our level of awareness, our images simplify "reality" by exaggerating some features of our environment while ignoring others. Thus we live in a world defined by our expectations and images.

These mental pictures, or perceptions, are inevitably distortions, as they cannot fully capture the complexity and configurations of even physical objects, such as the globe itself (see Controversy: Should We Believe What We See?).

Many of our images of the world politics are built on illusions and misconceptions. And even images that are now accurate can easily become outdated if we fail to recognize changes in the world. Indeed, the world's future will be determined not only by changes in the "objective" facts of world politics but also by the meaning that people ascribe to those facts, the assumptions on which they base their interpretations, and the actions that flow from these assumptions and interpretations—however accurate or inaccurate they might be.

The Nature and Sources of Images

The effort to simplify one's view of the world is inevitable and even necessary. Just as cartographers' projections simplify complex geophysical space so we can better understand the world, each of us inevitably creates a "mental map"—a habitual way of organizing information—to make sense of a confusing abundance of information. Although mental maps are neither inherently right nor wrong, they are important because we tend to react according to the way the world appears to us rather than the way it is. Political leaders, too, are captives of this tendency. As Richard Ned Lebow (1981) warns, "Policymakers are prone to distort reality in accord with their needs even in situations that appear . . . relatively unambiguous."

Most of us—policymakers included—look for information that reinforces our preexisting beliefs about the world, assimilate new data into familiar images, mistakenly equate what we believe with what we know, and deny information that contradicts our expectations. In addition, while we emphasize the push and pull of external forces and constraints when explaining our own actions, we generally attribute the behavior of others to their character traits. Research in cognitive psychology suggests that we are "categorizers" who attempt to understand the world by **schematic reasoning**—matching what we see with images in our memories of prototypical events and people. The absentminded professor, the shady lawyer, and the kindly grandmother are examples of "stock" images that

• **schematic reasoning** the process by which new information is interpreted by comparing it to generic concepts stored in memory about certain stereotypical situations, sequences of events, and characters.

many of us have of certain types of people. Although the professors, lawyers, and grandmothers that we meet may bear only a superficial resemblance to these stereotypical images, when we know little about someone our expectations will be shaped by presumed similarities to these characters (Larson 1994).

Many factors shape our images, including how we were socialized as children, traumatic events we may have experienced growing up, and exposure to the ideas of people whose expertise we respect (Jervis 1976). Once we have acquired an image, it seems self-evident. Accordingly, we try to keep it consistent with our other beliefs and, through a psychological process known as **cognitive dissonance** (Festinger 1957), reject information that contradicts how it portrays the world. In short, our mind selects, screens, and filters information; consequently, our perceptions depend not only on what happens in daily life but also on how we interpret and internalize those events.

Of course, tolerance of ambiguity and receptivity to new ways of thinking vary among individuals. Some people are better able than others to revise perceptual habits to accommodate new realities. Nonetheless, to some extent, we are all prisoners of our perceptions.

• **cognitive dissonance** the psychological tendency to deny or rationalize away discrepancies between one's preexisting beliefs and new information.

The Role of Images in World Politics

We must be careful not to assume automatically that what applies to individuals applies to entire countries. Still, leaders' images of historical circumstances often predispose them to behave in particular ways toward others, regardless of "objective" facts. For instance, the loss of 26 million Soviet lives in the "Great Patriotic War" (as the Russians refer to World War II) reinforced a longstanding fear of foreign invasion, which caused a generation of Soviet policymakers to perceive U.S. military moves with suspicion and often alarm. Similarly, the founders of the United States viewed eighteenth-century European power politics as corrupt, contributing to two seemingly contradictory tendencies later evident in U.S. foreign policy: (1) America's disposition to isolate itself from world affairs, and (2) its determination to reform the world whenever acute problems appeared on the diplomatic horizon. The former led the country to reject membership in the League of Nations after World War I; the latter gave rise to the U.S. globalist foreign policy after World War II, which committed the country to active involvement nearly everywhere on nearly every issue. Most Americans failed to recognize that others might regard such a far-reaching international policy position as arrogant or threatening; they saw in active U.S. interventionism only good intentions. As President Jimmy Carter once lamented, "The hardest thing for Americans to understand is that they are not better than other people."

Because leaders and citizens are prone to ignore or reinterpret information that runs counter to their beliefs and values, mutual misperceptions often fuel discord in world politics, especially when relations between countries are hostile. Distrust and suspicion arise as conflicting parties view each other in the same negative light. This so-called **mirror image** phenomenon occurred in Moscow and Washington during the Cold War. Each side viewed its own actions as constructive but its adversary's responses as hostile. When this occurs, conflict resolution is extraordinarily difficult. Thus fostering peace is not simply a matter of

• **mirror image** the tendency of people in competitive interaction to perceive each other similarly—to see an adversary the same way as the adversary sees them.

Should We Believe What We See? The Organization of Observations and Projections of Global Realities

Many people assume that "seeing is believing" without questioning whether their perceptions are accurate. But is there more to seeing than meets the eye? When looking at the world, do we perceive it in ways that produce distortions? Students of perceptual psychology think so. They maintain that seeing is not a strictly passive act: What we observe is partially influenced by our pre-existing values and expectations. Two observers looking at the same object might easily perceive different realities. To illustrate this, perceptual psychologists are fond of displaying the drawing here, which, depending on how the viewer looks at it, can be seen as either a goblet or two faces opposing each other.

This principle has great importance for students of world politics. Depending on one's perspective, people can vary greatly on how they view international events, actors, and issues. To appreciate the disagreements that can result from the fact that different people can easily see different realities when they look at the same thing, consider something as basic as viewing objectively the location and size of the continents in the world. There exists a long-standing controversy among cartographers about the "right" way to map the globe, that is, how to make an accurate projection of the Earth's surface. All maps of the globe are distorted, because it is impossible to perfectly represent the three-dimensional globe on a two-dimensional piece of paper. The difficulty cartographers face can be appreciated by trying to flatten an orange peel. You can only flatten it by separating pieces of the peel that were joined when it was spherical. Cartographers who try to flatten the globe on paper, without "ripping it" into separate pieces, face the same problem. Although there are a variety of ways to represent the three-dimensional object on paper, all of them involve some kind of distortion. Thus cartographers must choose among the imperfect ways of representing the globe by selecting those aspects of the world's geography they consider most important to describe accurately, while making adjustments to other parts.

Cartographers' ideas of what is most important in world geography have varied according to their own global perspectives. These three maps (Maps 1.1, 1.2, and 1.3) depict the distribution of the earth's land surfaces, but each portrays a different image. Each is a model of reality, an abstraction that highlights some features of the globe while ignoring others. What a map highlights is significant politically because it shapes how people view what is important. In examining these three ways of viewing and interpreting the globe, evaluate which projection you think is best. Which features of global reality are most worthy of emphasizing to capture an accurate picture? What does your answer reveal about your values and view of the world? •

Click on Theories of International Relations to access interactive version of these maps and related critical thinking quesitons.

M A P 1 . 1
Mercator Projection

This Mercator projection, popular in sixteenth-century Europe, is a classic Eurocentric view of the world. It retained direction accurately, making it useful for navigators, but placed Europe at the center of the world and exaggerated the continent's importance relative to other landmasses. Europe appears larger than South America, which is twice Europe's size, and two-thirds of the map is used to represent the northern half of the world and only one-third the southern half. Because lines of longitude were represented as parallel rather than convergent, it also greatly exaggerates the size of Greenland and Antarctica.

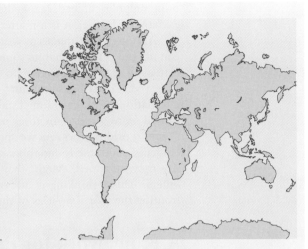

M A P 1 . 2
Peter's Projection

In the Peter's projection, each landmass appears in correct proportion in relation to all others, but it distorts the shape and position of landmasses. In contrast with most geographic representations, it draws attention to the countries of Africa, Asia, and Latin America where more than three-quarters of the world's population live today.

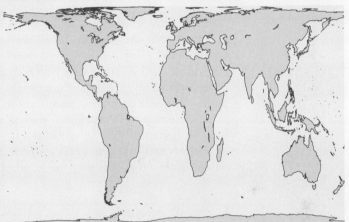

M A P 1 . 3
Orthographic Projection

The orthographic projection, centering on the mid-Atlantic, conveys some sense of the curvature of the Earth by using rounded edges. The sizes and shapes of continents toward the outer edges of the circle are distorted to give a sense of spherical perspective.

bringing political leaders together in international summits or expanding cultural exchanges. Rather, it is a matter of changing deeply entrenched beliefs.

Although our images of world politics are resistant, change is possible. Overcoming old thinking habits sometimes occurs when we experience acute discomfort as a result of clinging to false assumptions. As Benjamin Franklin once observed, "The things that hurt, instruct." Dramatic events in particular can alter international images, sometimes drastically. The Vietnam War, for example, caused many Americans to change their ideas about the use of force in contemporary world politics. As we speculate about the global future, we need to think critically about the foundations on which our perceptions rest. Are they accurate? Are they informed? Might they be adjusted to gain a greater understanding of others? This rethinking is one of the most important challenges we face in confronting the world politics of the twenty-first century.

A Framework for Examining World Politics

If people exaggerate the accuracy of their perceptions and seek information that confirms what they believe, how can we escape the biases created by our preconceptions? How can we avoid overlooking or dismissing evidence that runs counter to our intuition? One way is to use an analytical framework to discipline our observations. Analytic frameworks suggest where to look for information pertinent to some puzzling phenomenon, and how to organize it in an inventory of possible causes. Although no analytical framework can guarantee that we will have an impartial view of world politics, social scientists frequently build levels of analysis and time sequences in the frameworks they use in an effort to illuminate causal factors that they might otherwise neglect.

Levels of Analysis

At the heart of almost every international event lies a puzzle. Someone is perplexed over why an event happened, or is curious about what would have happened if a different action had been taken by one of the participants. The first step in solving the puzzle is to ask: "Of what larger pattern is this event an instance?" (Rosenau and Durfee 1995; Lave and March 1975). Visualizing an event as part of a larger pattern invites us to imagine that the pattern is the end result of some unknown process, and encourages us to think about the causal mechanisms that might have produced the pattern.

Many scholars organize the list of possible causal mechanisms behind an event according to three levels of analysis: the individual, the state, and the entire global system. The **individual level of analysis** refers to the distinctive personality traits, experiences, and behavior of those responsible for making important decisions on behalf of state and nonstate actors, as well as ordinary citizens whose behavior has important political consequences. Here, for example, we may properly locate the impact of a leader's political beliefs, attitudes, and opinions on his or her behavior, and explore questions such as why presidents Bill Clinton and George W. Bush dealt with Saddam Hussein in different ways.

• individual level of analysis an analytical approach to the study of world politics that emphasizes the psychological factors motivating people who make foreign policy decisions on behalf of states and other global actors.

The **state level of analysis** consists of the domestic attributes of nation-states, including their type of government, level of economic development, characteristics of their societies, and so on. The processes by which governments make decisions regarding war and peace, for instance, fall within the state level of analysis. A common example can be found in the argument that authoritarian governments are more bellicose than democracies because their leaders are not constrained by competitive elections or political cultures grounded in norms of tolerance and compromise.

The **systemic level of analysis** provides the most comprehensive view of world politics, focusing on the distribution of resources and pattern of interaction among the political actors on the global stage. The dispersion of military capabilities, the density of alliance networks, and the level of economic interdependence among state and nonstate actors are all characteristics of the international system as a whole. Explanations of international events that are framed at the systemic level contend that the behavior of global actors stems from their placement within the international system. Different actors behave similarly when they have similar positions of power and wealth within the system.

To sum up, categorizing possible causes of an event according to levels of analysis is useful because it encourages us to look beyond our preconceived images. It helps guard against single-factor explanations that hinge on one decisive cause. Like a telescopic camera lens, it allows us to zoom in and examine fine-grained details at the individual level, and then move back to the state and systemic levels to see things from a broader perspective. Moving from one level to another, looking at parts as well as the whole, suggests different questions to ask and what kinds of evidence would be necessary to arrive at meaningful answers.

• **state level of analysis** an analytical approach to the study of world politics that emphasizes how the internal attributes of states influence their foreign policy behavior.

• **systemic level of analysis** an analytical approach to the study of world politics that emphasizes the impact of international structures and processes on the behavior of global actors.

Time Sequences

Once we have identified factors from different levels of analysis that may combine to produce some outcome, it is useful to place them in a sequence. Anyone who owns a combination lock knows that the correct numbers must be entered in their proper order to open the lock. Similarly, to explain why something happened in world politics, we must determine how various individual, state, and systemic-level factors fit together in a configuration that unfolds over time.

People rarely have difficulty grasping configurations in space, writes psychologist Dietrich Dörner (1996). If shown a significant part of some larger spatial form such as a car or a house, they usually recognize it as fragmentary and often have a good idea on how it should be completed. Time configurations are different. People tend to treat successive steps in a temporal development as independent, not as parts of a dynamic pattern. When given part of a larger temporal form, such as a sequence of notes from a melody, they frequently have difficulty predicting what comes next.

One way to build time into our analytic framework is to consider how close each individual, state, or systemic factor was to the occurrence of the event in question. We could do this in several different ways, but for illustrative purposes we will simply distinguish between remote and proximate causes. *Remote causes* are deep, underlying factors whose impact develops over a lengthy time span. *Proximate causes* are those with more immediate effects. By examining a puzzling event from multiple levels of analysis across time, we guard against having our perceptual biases unnecessarily constrict our frame of reference. To illustrate, let us apply our analytical framework to the puzzle of why the Cold War ended peacefully.

Applying the Framework to the Cold War's End

During the Second World War, the United States and the Soviet Union aligned against Nazi Germany. In the waning months of the conflict mutual suspicions in Moscow and Washington hardened into policy disagreements over the future of the postwar world. The day before his suicide, Adolph Hitler predicted that the "laws of both history and geography" would compel the Soviet Union and the United States to engage in "a trial of strength" (Bullock 1962). As Soviet–American relations plummeted in a downward spiral of charges and counter-charges, it seemed as if Hitler's ominous prediction would come to pass.

But fighting did not ensue. Despite over forty years of intense rivalry in what was called the Cold War, the Soviet Union and the United States avoided a trial of strength. Moreover, much to everyone's surprise, the Cold War ended without bloodshed when the Soviet Union collapsed in 1991.

Some people argue that the American military buildup during the Reagan administration drove the Soviet Union into submission. The Cold War ended due to "the Reagan policy of firmness," insisted Richard Perle, one of the former president's military advisors. Our policy was "peace through strength," added George Bush, Reagan's vice president and immediate successor in the White House, "It worked."

This argument sounds persuasive because the collapse of the Soviet Union occurred alongside a massive weapons-building program in the United States. Furthermore, the argument fit a set of preconceptions derived from America's experience with Nazi Germany: Dictators cannot be appeased; the language of military might is the only language they understand. Soviet leaders, many Americans believed, were demagogic and rapacious like Hitler. Whereas British and French vacillation in the 1930s emboldened Hitler, Reagan's steadfastness allegedly brought the Soviets to heel.

Vivid historical images are seductive. They frame how we see the present, often in ways that inhibit dissecting analogies to past events. Rather than patiently examining an issue from every angle, we draw parallels with a memorable incident and stop searching for additional information. For example, the assertion that "Ronald Reagan won the Cold War by being tough on the communists" (Glynn 1993) animates such powerful imagery that seeking other explanations might seem unnecessary. But by not evaluating plausible, rival explanations, we can be misled. The prominent Russian scholar Georgi Arbatov contends that rather than convincing Kremlin hardliners to give up, Reagan's "tough" policy actually stiffened their resolve, thereby prolonging the Cold War (see Kegley and Raymond 1994, 29).

Analytical frameworks help prevent us from giving easily recalled analogies more weight than they deserve by widening the search for additional insights and information. Table 1.1 shows how looking at different levels of analysis and time

TABLE 1.1

Contending Images of the Cold War's End

Level of Analysis	Time Sequence	
	Remote Causes	Proximate Causes
Individual		*The leaders as movers of history* "Ronald Reagan won the Cold War by being tough on the communists." —Patrick Glynn "[The end of the Cold War was possible] primarily because of one man—Mikhail Gorbachev. The transformations we are dealing with now would not have begun were it not for him." —James A. Baker III
State	*Political inertia* "Given communism's inherent unworkability . . . the Soviet empire was doomed in the long run." —Arthur Schlesinger, Jr. *Economic mismanagement* "No other industrialized state [than the Soviet Union] in the world for so long spent so much of its national wealth on armaments and military forces. Soviet militarism, in harness with communism, destroyed the Soviet economy and thus hastened the self-destruction of the Soviet empire." —Fred Charles Iklé	*Media attention* "It was the moral reassessment of the seventy-odd years of this socialist experiment that shook the nation. . . . It was the flood of publications of the Soviet Union's human rights record and its tremendous distortions of moral and ethical principles that discredited the system, especially when introduced into the everyday lives of its individual citizens through the popular media." —Vladimir Benevolenski and Andrei Kortunov *Grassroots movements* "The changes wrought by thousands of people serving in the trenches [were] essential to events in recent years and at least partially responsible for [ending the Cold War]." —David Cortright *Ethnonationalism* "In less tha two years, communism collapsed everywhere. . . . The causes [were] the national communities. —Hélèbe Carrère d'Encausse
Systemic	*Containment* "The U.S. and our allies deserve great credit for maintaining the military and economic power to resist and turn back the Soviet aggression." —Richard Nixon	*Imperial overstretch* "The acute phase of the fall of communism started outside of the Soviet Union and spread to the Soviet Union itself. By 1987, Gorbachev made it clear that he would not interfere with internal experiments in Soviet bloc countries . . . Once communism fell in Eastern Europe, the alternative in the Soviet Union became civil war or dissolution." —Daniel Klenbort

SOURCES: Kegley (1994), Kegley and Raymond (1994: 42–44).

sequences can assist in identifying alternative explanations of why the Cold War ended peacefully. At the individual level, a case could be made that Mikhail Gorbachev's sweeping reforms, not Ronald Reagan's toughness, played the key role. At the state level of analysis, political inertia and economic mismanagement may have gradually weakened the Soviet Union, while social discontent, grassroots protest movements, and the explosive growth of **nationalism** among non-Russian ethnic groups in the Baltic republics and elsewhere accelerated the downfall of the communist regime. Finally, at the systemic level, the long-term U.S. policy of **containment** and the eventual disintegration of the Soviet position in Eastern Europe may have been critical to ending the Cold War.

• **nationalism** the belief that political loyalty lies with a body of people who share ethnicity, linguistic, or cultural affinity, and perceive themselves to be members of the same group.

• **containment** a term coined by U.S. policymaker George Kennan for deterring expansion by the Soviet Union, which has since been used to describe a strategy aimed at preventing a state from using force to increase its territory or sphere of influence.

It is also useful to examine chains of causation that run between levels. For example, political inertia and economic deterioration within the Soviet Union (state level) may have engendered Gorbachev's reforms (individual level), which fractured the network Soviet military alliances (systemic level) by providing an opportunity for Eastern Europeans to chart a new course in the foreign affairs. Another possibility is that Gorbachev's political reforms gave non-Russian ethnic groups in various Soviet republics (state level) the opportunity to express nationalist sentiments and break away from the Soviet Union. We could hypothesize other chains of cause and effect. Determining which ones best account for the collapse of the Soviet Union and the end of the Cold War is a task for subsequent research. Our purpose here is merely to demonstrate how preconceived mental images limit a person's field of vision. We get a richer, more nuanced perspective by studying world politics from multiple levels of analysis across time.

The Book's Approach: Actors, Issues, and Their Interactions

Because world politics is complex and our images of it are often discordant, scholars differ in their approaches to understanding the contemporary world. In this book, we adopt a multilevel, multi-issue perspective that focuses on: (1) the characteristics, capabilities, and interests of the principal *actors* in world politics (states and various nonstate participants in international affairs); (2) the principal welfare and security *issues* on the global agenda; and (3) the patterns of cooperation and contention that influence the *interactions* between and among actors and issues.

A multilevel, multi-issue perspective is useful, not only because it takes into account the forces of constancy and change, but also because it avoids dwelling on particular events, countries, individuals, or transitory phenomena whose long-term significance is likely to diminish. Instead, the perspective seeks to identify behaviors that cohere into general global patterns—trends and transformations that measurably affect global living conditions. Thus we explore the nature of world politics from a perspective that places historical and contemporary events into a larger, lasting theoretical context, providing the conceptual tools that will enable us to interpret subsequent developments.

Our journey begins in Chapter 2 with an overview of the realist and liberal theoretical traditions that scholars and policymakers use most often to interpret world politics. This provides the intellectual background for the description and explanation of the issues and developments that are treated in the remaining chapters.

Chapter 3 begins the analysis of actors, issues, and their interactions with a close examination of foreign policy decision-making processes *within* nation-states, which remain the principal actors in world politics. It also considers the role of leaders in making foreign policy, and how various external and domestic forces can constrain the impact of political leaders.

We will then turn our attention to each of the types of actors in world politics and examine how their characteristics and capabilities affect their interests and influence in the world. Great powers (those wealthy countries with the most powerful militaries) are the focus of attention in Chapter 4. In Chapter 5, we turn our attention to the weaker, less economically developed countries, explaining how the fate of this group of states is shaped by their relations with great powers. Then, in Chapter 6, we cover two groups of nonstate actors, intergovernmental organizations (IGOs) and nongovernmental organizations (NGOs), and demonstrate how they interact with nation-states and increasingly challenge even the great powers.

The next group of chapters shifts attention to how the characteristics, capabilities, and interests of the principal actors in world politics affect security and welfare issues on the global agenda. Security issues are addressed in Chapters 7 through 10. Finally, in Chapters 11 through 14, we examine problems relating to globalization, international political economy, human rights, and the environment.

Understanding today's world requires a willingness to confront complexity. A true but complicated idea always has less chance of success than a simple but false one, the French political sociologist Alexis de Tocqueville (1969) cautioned almost two centuries ago. The challenge is difficult but the payoff warrants the effort. Humankind's ability to chart a more rewarding future is contingent on its ability to entertain complex ideas, to free itself from the sometimes paralyzing grip of prevailing orthodoxies, and to develop a healthy, questioning attitude about rival perspectives on international realities. On that hopeful yet introspective note, we begin our exploration of world politics.

Chapter Summary

- To understand the global future, one must examine the ways in which the contemporary international system has changed and the ways in which its fundamental characteristics have resisted change.
- Trends in world politics rarely unfold in a constant, linear direction. Moreover, no trend stands alone. The path to the future is influenced by multiple determinants, some integrative and others disintegrative.
- Everyone has some kind of "mental model" of world politics that simplifies reality by exaggerating some features of international affairs and ignoring others.

- The shape of the world's future will be determined not only by changes in the objective conditions of world politics, but also by the meanings that people ascribe to those conditions.
- Although most people are prone to look for information that reinforces their beliefs, dramatic events can alter an individual's mental model of world politics.
- An adequate account of continuities and changes in world politics requires examining a variety of causal factors flowing from the individual, state, and systemic levels of analysis.
- Causal factors operating at the individual level of analysis explain international events by focusing on the personal characteristics of humans; those at the state level, by looking at the national attributes of states; and those at the systemic level, by concentrating on the structure and processes of the global system as a whole.

KEY TERMS

cognitive dissonance
containment
individual level of analysis
mirror image

nationalism
nonstate actors
politics
state

schematic reasoning
state level of analysis
system
systemic level of analysis

 ## WHERE ON THE WORLD WIDE WEB?

The World Wide Web's (WWW or web) features make it a powerful tool for providing access to global information sources. Using the web, you have instant access to documentation of important international events and agreements. Online information is current and often more complex than traditional sources. It quickly reflects the changing nature of international events. The web's international reach also permits users to locate opinions and perspectives from individuals across the United States and around the world. Every day more sources become available online as individuals and institutions discover the wonders of the web.

The "Where on the World Wide Web?" sections that accompany each chapter provide you with interesting web links to explore. By examining these links, you will be able to keep abreast of

international events and gain a greater understanding of the concepts and terms discussed in *The Global Future*.

American Journalism Review News Link

http://www.newslink.org/news.html

If you are interested in "going to the source" for your news, check out the *American Journalism Review*'s website. This site provides links to electronic newspapers from the United States or anywhere in the world. Even campus papers are accessible through this site. You can read the news in a foreign language or try to find an English version. You may want to compare the same news story found in different newspapers around the world to see how different countries interpret the same event.

CNN Interactive World News

http://www.cnn.com/WORLD/

Surf the website of the news organization that changed the way world news is reported by providing constant, minute-by-minute coverage of breaking news stories from around the world. CNN's World News main page is divided according to world region and reports the top stories in each area. Over the course of a week, compare and contrast the content of the top stories from each region. Do you see a pattern concerning the type of news stories reported for each area?

Foreign Affairs Online

http://www.people.virginia.edu/~rjb3v/rjb.html

This comprehensive website has been specifically designed to assist students and other individuals interested in international law, international relations, and U.S. foreign policy. It has links to general references, map resources, foreign states, the United Nations system, international organizations, international legal entities, think tanks, and media resources. This is an important gateway to numerous international affairs resources on the web, so you may want to bookmark it.

The National Geographic Society

http://www.nationalgeographic.com/maps

Publisher of the popular *National Geographic* magazine, the society has created an impressive web tool called the MapMachine Online Atlas, one of the best interactive map sets on the web. Viewers can choose many different types of interactive maps. For instance, the Dynamic Maps, which use geographic information systems (GIS), display population densities, ecoregions, weather patterns, earthquake fault lines, mineral deposits, and other features anywhere in the world. The Atlas Maps identify 191 independent states and provide a brief overview of each state. A quick click anywhere on the map gives key geographic, demographic, and economic data. As this chapter explains, all maps focus on specific features while ignoring other features, which leads to distortions. Compare the MapMachine maps with those found in the box, Controversy: Should We Believe What We See? in this chapter. Are the "dynamic" maps more accurate representations of reality? What distortions do they depict?

INFOTRAC® COLLEGE EDITION

Search for the following articles in the InfoTrac College Edition database.

George, Alexander L. "Knowledge for Statecraft," *International Security* Summer 1997.

Hoffmann, Stanley. "Clash of Globalizations," *Foreign Affairs* July–August 2002.

Rothkopf, David J. "Cyberpolitik: The Changing Nature of Power in the Information Age," *Journal of International Affairs* Spring 1998.

Selle, Robert R. "Yen for Adventure—Geopolitics," *World and I* April 2002.

For more articles, enter:

"political science" in the Subject Guide, and then go to subdivision "analysis."

"international relations" in the Subject Guide, and then go to subdivision "analysis."

ADDITIONAL CD-ROM RESOURCES

Click on Theories of International Relations and History of World Politics to access additional resources related to this chapter.

Theories of World Politics

CHAPTER OUTLINE

There is nothing so practical as a good theory.

KURT LEWIN, psychologist

Although the academic study of international relations is relatively new, attempts to theorize about state behavior date back to antiquity. Perhaps the best example can be found in Thucydides, the Greek historian who analyzed the Peloponnesian War (431–404 BCE) between ancient Sparta and Athens. Thucydides believed "knowledge of the past" would be "an aid to the interpretation of the future" and therefore undertook his analysis "not to win the applause of the moment, but as a possession for all time."

Greece in Thucydides's day was not unified; it contained a welter of small, autonomous city-states scattered throughout the Balkan Peninsula, the Aegean Archipelago, and what is today western Turkey. Sparta and Athens were the strongest of these fiercely independent states. The former was a cautious, conservative land power; the latter, a bold, innovative sea power. Relations between them were contentious. When their rivalry eventually escalated to war in 431 BCE, they became trapped in a long, debilitating military stalemate.

With no immediate victory in sight, each side sought allies in the hope of gaining a decisive advantage over the other. In 416 BCE, Athens sent a force of approximately three thousand soldiers to Melos, a city-state that wished to remain nonaligned during the war. The Athenians declared that if Melos did not agree to become their ally, it would be obliterated. The Melians argued that such a brutal attack would be unjust since they had not harmed Athens. Moreover, it was in Athens's self-interest to show restraint: destroying Melos would drive other neutral city-states into the Spartan camp. Finally, the Melians pointed out that it would be unreasonable to surrender while there was still hope of being rescued by the Spartans. Scornful of these appeals to justice, expedience, and reasonableness, the Athenians proclaimed that in interstate relations "the strong do what they can and the weak suffer what they must." Regardless of the merits of the Melian argument, Athens had the strength to subjugate Melos if it so desired. Ultimately, the Melians chose to resist and were destroyed. The Athenians killed all adult men and sold the women and children into slavery.

The Athenian practice of raw power politics raises timeless questions about world politics. What factors explain state behavior? How can states achieve security in an anarchic international system? In the absence of a central authority to resolve the disputes among states, are there limits to the use of military power? What role should ethical considerations play in the conduct of foreign policy? This chapter will focus on the two schools of thought that have most influenced how policymakers and scholars think about these kinds of questions: realism and liberalism.

Contending Theories of World Politics

Imagine yourself the newly elected president of the United States. You are scheduled to deliver the State of the Union address on your views of the current world situation. Your task is to identify those international issues most worthy of attention and explain how you plan to deal with them. To convince citizens these issues are important, you must present them as part of a larger picture of the world, showing how the situation you face may be part of a pattern. You must, in short, think *theoretically*. The success of your effort to explain the causes of current problems, predict their long-term consequences, and persuade others that you have a viable policy to address them will hinge on how well you understand the way the world works.

When leaders face these kinds of intellectual challenges, they fortunately benefit from the existence of several theories of world politics from which they can draw guidance. A **theory** is a set of statements that purports to explain a particular phenomenon. In essence, it provides a map, or frame of reference, that makes the complex, puzzling world around us intelligible. Choosing which theory to heed is an important decision, because each rests on different assumptions about the nature of international politics, each advances different causal claims, and each offers a different set of foreign policy recommendations. Our aim in this chapter is to compare the assumptions, causal claims, and policy prescriptions of realism and liberalism, the two most common theoretical perspectives policymakers and scholars use to interpret international relations. We begin with realism, the oldest of these contending schools of thought.

Realist Theory

Political realism has a long, distinguished history that dates back to the writings of Thucydides about the Peloponnesian War. Other influential figures that contributed to realist thought include the sixteenth-century Italian philosopher Niccolò Machiavelli and the seventeenth-century English philosopher Thomas Hobbes. Realism deserves careful examination because its worldview continues to guide much thought about international politics.

The Realist Worldview

Realism, as applied to contemporary international politics, views the nation-state as the most important actor on the world stage since it answers to no higher political authority. States are sovereign: they have supreme power over their territory and populace, and no one stands above them wielding the legitimacy and coercive capability to govern the international system. Given the absence of a higher authority to which states can turn to for protection and to resolve disputes, realists depict world politics as a ceaseless, repetitive struggle for **power** where, like in the Melian episode described by Thucydides, the strong dominate the weak. Because each state is ultimately responsible for its own survival and feels uncertain about its neighbors' intentions, realism claims that prudent political leaders seek arms and allies to enhance national security. In other words, the anarchic structure of the international system leads even well-intentioned leaders to practice **self-help**, increasing military strength and aligning with others to deter potential threats. Realist theory does not preclude the possibility that rival powers will cooperate on arms control or on other security issues of common inter-

---

• **theory** a set of interrelated propositions that explains an observed regularity.

Click on Theories of International Relations to access an interactive case study that examines the end of the Cold War from a traditional realist perspective.

• **power** the ability to make someone continue a course of action, change what he or she is doing, or refrain from acting.

• **self-help** the principle that in anarchy actors must rely on themselves.

Realist Pioneers of Power Politics In *The Prince* (1532) and *The Leviathan* (1651) Niccolò Machiavelli and Thomas Hobbes, respectively, emphasized a political calculus based on interest, prudence, power, and expediency above all other considerations. This formed the foundation of what became a growing body of modern realist thinking that accepts the drive for power over others as necessary and wise statecraft.

est. Rather it asserts that cooperation will be rare because states worry about the distribution of **relative gains** emanating from cooperation and the possibility that the other side will cheat on agreements.

Realists, with their emphasis on the ruthless nature of international life, tend to be skeptical about the role of ethical considerations in foreign policy deliberations. As they see it, some policies are driven by strategic imperatives that may require national leaders to contravene moral norms. Embedded in this "philosophy of necessity" is a distinction between private morality, which guides the behavior of ordinary people in their daily lives, and reason of state *(raison d'état)*, which governs the conduct of leaders responsible for the security and survival of the state. Whatever actions that are in the interest of state security must be carried out no matter how repugnant they might seem in the light of private morality. "Ignoring one's interests, squandering one's resources in fits of altruism," argues a prominent realist, "is the fastest road to national disaster." For a national leader, "thinking with one's heart is a serious offense. Foreign policy is not social work" (Krauthammer 1993).

• **relative gains** a measure of how much one side in an agreement benefits in comparison with the other's side.

The Evolution of Realist Thought

We have seen how the intellectual roots of political realism reach back to ancient Greece. They also extend beyond the western world to India and China. Discussions of "power politics" abound in the *Arthashastra,* an ancient Indian treatise on statecraft written by Kautilya, as well as in works written by Shang Yang and Han Fei in ancient China.

Modern realism emerged on the eve of the Second World War, when the prevailing belief in a natural harmony of interests among nations came under attack. Just a decade earlier, this belief had led numerous countries to sign the 1928 Kellogg-Briand Pact, which renounced war as an instrument of national policy. Now, with Nazi Germany, Fascist Italy, and Imperial Japan all violating the treaty, British historian and diplomat E. H. Carr (1939) complained that the assumption of a universal interest in peace had allowed too many people to "evade the unpalatable fact of a fundamental divergence of interest between nations desirous of maintaining the *status quo* and nations desirous of changing it."

In an effort to counter what they saw as a utopian, legalistic approach to foreign affairs, Reinhold Niebuhr (1947), Hans J. Morgenthau (1985), and other realists articulated a pessimistic view of human nature. Echoing the seventeenth-century philosopher Baruch Spinoza, many of them pointed to an innate conflict between passion and reason; furthermore, in the tradition of St. Augustine, they stressed that material appetites enabled passion to overwhelm reason. For them, the human condition was such that the forces of light and darkness would perpetually vie for control.

The realists' picture of international life appeared particularly persuasive after World War II. The onset of rivalry between the United States and the Soviet Union, the expansion of the Cold War into a wider struggle between East and West, and the periodic crises that threatened to erupt into global violence all supported the realists' emphasis on the inevitability of conflict, the poor prospects for cooperation, and the divergence of national interests among incorrigibly selfish, power-seeking states.

Whereas these so-called "classical" realists sought to explain state behavior by drawing upon explanatory factors located at the individual level of analysis, the next wave of realist theorizing emphasized the systemic level of analysis. Kenneth Waltz (1979), the leading proponent of what has come to be called "structural" realism, proposed that international anarchy—not some allegedly evil side of human nature—explained why states were locked in fierce competition with one another. The absence of a central arbiter was the defining structural feature of the international system. Vulnerable and insecure, states behaved defensively by forming alliances against looming threats. According to Waltz, balances of power form automatically in anarchic environments. Even when they are disrupted, they are soon restored.

The most recent variant of realist theory also resides at the systemic level of analysis, but asserts that the ultimate goal of states is to achieve military supremacy, not merely a balance of power. For John Mearsheimer (2001) and other exponents of "offensive" realism, the anarchic structure of the international system encourages states to maximize their share of world power in order to improve the odds of surviving the competition for relative advantage. A state with an edge over everyone else has insurance against the possibility that a predatory state might someday pose a grave threat. To quote the old cliche: The best defense is a good offense.

The Limitations of Realism

However persuasive the realists' image of the essential properties of international politics, their policy recommendations suffered from a lack of precision in the way they used such key terms as *power* and *national interest*. Thus, once analysis moved beyond the assertion that national leaders should acquire power to serve the national interest, important questions remained: What were the key elements of national power? What uses of power best served the national interest? Did arms furnish protection or provoke costly arms races? Did alliances enhance one's defenses or encourage threatening counteralliances? From the perspective of realism's critics, seeking security by amassing power was self-defeating. The quest for absolute security by one state would be perceived as creating absolute insecurity for other members of the system, with the result that everyone would become locked in an upward spiral of countermeasures that jeopardized the security of all (Vasquez 1998, 1993).

Because much of realist theorizing was vague, it began to be questioned. Realism offered no criteria for determining what historical data were significant in evaluating its claims and what epistemological rules to follow when interpreting relevant information (Vasquez and Elman 2003). Even the policy recommendations that purportedly flowed from its logic were often divergent. Realists themselves, for example, were sharply divided as to whether U.S. intervention in Vietnam served American national interests and whether nuclear weapons contributed to international security.

A growing number of critics also pointed out that realism did not account for significant new developments in world politics. For instance, it could not explain the creation of new liberal trade and political institutions in Western Europe in the 1950s and 1960s, where the cooperative pursuit of mutual advantage led Europeans away from the unbridled power politics that brought them incessant warfare since the birth of the nation-state some three centuries earlier. Other critics began to worry about realism's tendency to disregard ethical principles and about the material and social costs that some of its policy prescriptions seemed to impose, such as retarded economic growth resulting from unrestrained military expenditures.

Despite realism's shortcomings, many people continue to think about world politics in the language constructed by realists, especially in times of global tension. This happened, for example, in the early 1980s when the Cold War between the United States and the Soviet Union entered a new round of contention. Because realism provides insight into the drive for security through military means, it is frequently used to explain such phenomena as the outbreak of bloody wars during the 1990s in the former Yugoslavia.

Liberal Theory

Liberalism has been called the "strongest contemporary challenge to realism" (Caporaso 1993). Like realism, it has a distinguished pedigree, with philosophical roots extending back to the political thought of John Locke, Immanuel Kant, and Adam Smith. Liberalism warrants our attention because it speaks to issues realism disregards, including the impact of domestic politics on state behavior, the implications of economic interdependence, and the role of international norms and institutions in facilitating international cooperation.

The Liberal Worldview

There are several distinct schools of thought within the liberal tradition. Drawing broad conclusions from such a diverse body of theory risks misrepresenting the position of any given author. Nevertheless, there are sufficient commonalities to abstract some general themes.

The Granger Collection, NY

Pioneers in the Liberal Quest for World Order Immanuel Kant (left) in *Perpetual Peace* (1795) helped to redefine modern liberal theory by advocating global (not state) citizenship, free trade, and a federation of democracies as a means to peace. Richard Cobden (right) primarily foresaw the possibility of peace across borders; in his view, if contact and communication among people could expand through free trade, so too would international friendship and peace, secured by prosperity that would create interdependence and eliminate the need for military forces to pursue rivalries.

As shown in Table 2.1, liberals differ from realists in several important ways. At the core of liberalism is a belief in reason and the possibility of progress. Liberals view the individual as the seat of moral value and assert that human beings should be treated as ends rather than means. Whereas realists counsel decision makers to seek the lesser evil rather than the absolute good, liberals emphasize ethical principle over the pursuit of power, and institutions over military capabilities (see Doyle 1997, Howard 1978, and Zacher and Matthew 1995). Politics at the international level is more of a struggle for consensus and mutual gain than a struggle for power and prestige.

Instead of blaming international conflict on an inherent lust for power, liberals fault the conditions that people live under. Reforming those conditions, they argue, will enhance the prospects for peace. The first element common to various strands of liberal thought is an emphasis undertaking political reforms to establish stable democracies. Woodrow Wilson, for example, proclaimed that "democratic government will make wars less likely." Franklin Roosevelt later reflected this view when he asserted "the continued maintenance and improvement of democracy constitute the most important guarantee of international peace." Based on tolerance, accommodation, and procedural rights, democratic political cultures are said to shun lethal force as a means of settling disagreements. Politics is not seen as a **zero-sum game,** so that the use of persuasion rather than coercion, and a reliance on judicial avenues to settle rival claims are the primary means of dealing with conflict.

According to liberal theory, conflict resolution practices used at home are also employed when dealing with international disputes. Leaders socialized within democratic cultures share a common outlook. Viewing international politics as an extension of domestic politics, they externalize their norms of

• **zero-sum game**
a situation in which what one side wins, the other side loses.

TABLE 2.1		
A Comparison of Realist and Liberal Theories		
Feature	Realism	Liberalism
Philosophical outlook	Pessimistic	Optimistic
View of human nature	Competitive	Cooperative
Key political units	States	State and nonstate actors
Core concern	Increase military power	Promote policy coordination
Structure of global system	Anarchy	Anarchy among states and transnational networks linking nonstate actors
Approach to peace	Balance of power	Collective security
Vision of the future	Continuity: great-power competition for power	Change: cooperation as democratic regimes, open markets, and international institutions spread

regulated competition. Disputes with kindred governments rarely escalate to war because each side accepts the other's legitimacy and expects it to rely on peaceful means of conflict resolution. These expectations are reinforced by the transparent nature of democracies. The inner workings of open polities can be scrutinized by anyone; hence, it is difficult to demonize them as scheming adversaries.

The second thrust common to liberal theorizing is an emphasis on free trade. The idea that commerce helps promote conflict resolution has roots in the work of Montesquieu, Adam Smith, and various Enlightenment thinkers. "Nothing is more favourable to the rise of politeness and learning," noted the philosopher David Hume (1817), "than a number of neighboring and independent states, connected by commerce." This view was later embraced by the Manchester School of political economy and formed the basis for Norman Angell's (1910) famous rebuttal of the assertion that military conquest yields economic prosperity.

The doctrine that unfettered trade helps prevent disputes from escalating to wars rests on several propositions. First, commercial intercourse creates a material incentive to resolve disputes peacefully: War reduces profits by interrupting vital economic exchanges. Second, cosmopolitan business elites who benefit most from these exchanges comprise a powerful transnational interest group with a stake in promoting amicable solutions to festering disagreements. Finally, the web of trade between nations increases communication, erodes parochialism, and encourages both sides to avoid ruinous clashes. In the words of Richard Cobden, an opponent of the protectionist Corn Laws that once regulated British international grain trade: "Free Trade! What is it? Why, breaking down the barriers that separate nations; those barriers, behind which nestle the feelings of pride, revenge, hatred, and jealousy, which every now and then burst their bounds, and deluge whole countries with blood" (cited in Wolfers and Martin 1956).

Finally, the third commonality in liberal theorizing is an advocacy of international institutions. Liberals recommend replacing cut-throat, balance-of-power politics with organizations based on the principle that a threat to peace anywhere is a common concern to everyone. They see foreign policy as unfolding in a nascent global society populated by actors who recognize the cost of conflict, share significant interests, and can realize those interests by using institutions to mediate disputes whenever misconceptions, wounded sensibilities, or aroused national passions threaten their relations.

The Evolution of Liberal Thought

Contemporary liberal theory rose to prominence in the wake of the First World War. Not only had the war involved more participants over a wider geographic area than any previous war, but modern science and technology made it a war of machinery: Old weapons were improved and produced in great quantities, new and far more deadly weapons were rapidly developed and deployed. By the time the carnage was over, nearly twenty million people were dead.

For liberals like U.S. President Woodrow Wilson, World War I was "the war to end all wars." Convinced that another horrific war would erupt if states resumed practicing power politics, liberals set out to reform the international system. These "idealists," as they were called by hard-boiled realists, generally fell into one of three groups (Herz 1951). The first group advocated creating international institutions to mitigate the raw struggle for power between egoistic, mutually suspicious states. The League of Nations was the embodiment of this strain of liberal thought. Its founders hoped to prevent future wars by organizing a system of **collective security** that would mobilize the entire international community against would-be aggressors. The League's founders declared that peace was indivisible: An attack on one member of the League would be considered an attack on all. Since no state was more powerful than the combination of all other states, aggressors would be deterred and war averted.

A second group called for the use of legal procedures to adjudicate disputes before they escalated to armed conflict. Adjudication is a judicial procedure for resolving conflicts by referring them to a standing court for a binding decision. Immediately after the war, several governments drafted a statute to establish a Permanent Court of International Justice (PCIJ). Hailed by Bernard C. J. Loder, the court's first president, as the harbinger of a new era of civilization, the PCIJ held its inaugural public meeting in early 1922 and rendered its first judgment on a contentious case the following year. Liberal champions of the court insisted that the PCIJ would replace military retaliation with a judicial body capable of bringing the facts of a dispute to light and issuing a just verdict.

A third group of liberal thinkers followed the biblical injunction that states should beat their swords into plowshares and sought disarmament as a means of avoiding war. Their efforts were exemplified between 1921 and 1922 by the Washington naval conference, which tried to curtail maritime competition among the United States, Great Britain, Japan, France, and Italy by placing limits on battleships. The ultimate goal of this group was to reduce international tensions by promoting general disarmament, which led them to convene the Geneva Disarmament Conference in 1932.

Although a tone of idealism dominated policy rhetoric and academic discussions during the interwar period, little of the liberal reform program was ever seriously attempted, and even less of it was achieved. The League of Nations failed to prevent the Japanese invasion of Manchuria (1931) or the Italian invasion of Ethiopia (1935); major disputes were rarely submitted to the Permanent Court of International Justice; and the 1932 Geneva Disarmament Conference ended in failure. When the threat of war began gathering over Europe and Asia in the late 1930s, enthusiasm for liberal idealism receded.

The next surge in liberal theorizing arose decades later in response to realism's neglect of **transnational relations** (see Keohane and Nye 1971). Although realists continued to focus on the state, the events surrounding the 1973 oil crisis revealed that nonstate actors could affect the course of international events, and occasionally compete with states. This insight led to the realization that **complex interdependence** (Keohane and Nye 1977) sometimes offered a better description of world politics than realism, especially on international economic and environmental matters. Rather than contacts between countries being limited to high-level governmental officials, multiple communication channels connected societies. Rather than security dominating foreign policy considerations, issues on national agendas did not always have a fixed priority. Rather than military force serving as the primary instrument of statecraft, other means frequently were

• **collective security** a security regime based on the principle that an act of aggression by any state will be met by a collective response from the rest.

• **transnational relations** interactions across state boundaries that involve at least one actor that is not the agent of a government or intergovernmental organization.

• **complex interdependence** a model of world politics based on the assumptions that states are not the only important actors, security is not the dominant national goal, and military force is not the only significant instrument of foreign policy.

more effective when bargaining occurred between economically interconnected nations. In short, the realist preoccupation with government-to-government relations ignored the complex network of public and private exchanges criss-crossing national boundaries. States were becoming increasingly interdependent; that is, mutually dependent on, sensitive about, and vulnerable to one another in ways that were not captured by realist theory.

While interdependence was not new, its growth during the last quarter of the twentieth century led many liberal theorists to challenge the realist conception of anarchy. Though agreeing that the international system was anarchic, they suggested that it was more properly conceptualized as an "ordered" anarchy because most states followed commonly acknowledged normative standards, even in the absence of hierarchical enforcement. When a body of norms fosters shared expectations that guide a regularized pattern of cooperation on a specific issue, we call it an **international regime** (see Hansenclever, Mayer, and Rittberger 1996). Various types of regimes have been devised to govern behavior in trade and monetary affairs, as well as to manage access to common resources like fisheries and river water. By the turn of the century, as pressing economic and environmental issues crowded national agendas, a large body of liberal "institutionalist" scholarship delved into how regimes developed and what led states to comply with their injunctions.

• **international regime** a set of principles, norms, and rules governing behavior within a specified issue area.

The Limitations of Liberalism

Liberal theorists share an interest in probing the conditions under which the convergent and overlapping interests among otherwise sovereign political actors may result in cooperation. Taking heart in the international prohibition, through community consensus, of such previously entrenched practices as slavery, piracy, dueling, and colonialism, they emphasize the prospects for progress through institutional reform. Studies of European integration during the 1950s and 1960s paved the way for the liberal institutionalist theories that emerged in the 1990s. The expansion of trade, communication, information, technology, and immigrant labor propelled Europeans to sacrifice portions of their sovereign independence to create a new political and economic union out of previously separate units. These developments were outside of realism's worldview, creating conditions that made the call for a theory grounded in the liberal tradition convincing to many who had previously questioned realism. In the words of former U.S. president Bill Clinton, "In a world where freedom, not tyranny, is on the march, the cynical calculus of pure power politics simply does not compute. It is ill-suited to the new era."

Yet as compelling as contemporary liberal institutionalism may seem at the onset of the twenty-first century, many realists complain that it has not transcended its idealist heritage. They charge that just like the League of Nations and the Permanent Court of International Justice, institutions today exert minimal influence on state behavior. International organizations cannot stop states from behaving according to balance-of-power logic, calculating how each move they make affects their relative position in a world of relentless competition (Mearsheimer 1994/95, 1995).

Critics of liberalism further contend that most studies supportive of international institutions appear in the **low politics** arena of commercial, financial, and environmental affairs, not in the **high politics** arena of national defense. While it may be difficult to draw a clear line between economic and security issues, some scholars note that "different institutional arrangements" exist in each realm, with the prospects for cooperation among self-interested states greater in the former than the latter (Lipson 1984). National survival hinges on the effective management of security issues, insist realists. Collective security organizations naively assume that all members perceive threats in the same way, and are willing to run the risks and pay the costs of countering those threats (Kissinger 1992). Because avaricious states are unlikely to see their vital interests in this light, international institutions cannot provide timely, muscular responses to aggression. On security issues, conclude realists, states will trust in their own power, not in the promises of international institutions.

• **low politics** the category of global issues related to the economic, social, and environmental aspects of relations between governments and people.

• **high politics** the category of global issues related to military and security aspects of relations between governments and people.

A final realist complaint lodged against liberalism is an alleged tendency to turn foreign policy into a moral crusade. Whereas realists claim that heads of state are driven by strategic necessities, many liberals believe moral necessities impose categorical imperatives on leaders. Consider the 1999 war in Kosovo, which pitted the North Atlantic Treaty Organization (NATO) against the Federal Republic of Yugoslavia. Pointing to Yugoslav leader Slobodan Milosevic's repression of ethnic Albanians living in the province of Kosovo, NATO Secretary General Javier Solana, British Prime Minister Tony Blair, and U.S. President Bill Clinton all argued that humanitarian intervention was a moral imperative. Although nonintervention into the internal affairs of other states had long been a cardinal principle of international law, they saw military action against Yugoslavia as a duty because human rights were an international entitlement and governments that violated them forfeited the protection of international law. Sovereignty, according to many liberal thinkers, is not sacrosanct. The international community has an obligation to use armed force to stop flagrant violations of human rights.

To sum up, realists remain skeptical about liberal claims of moral necessity. On the one hand, they deny the universal applicability of any single moral standard in a culturally pluralistic world. On the other hand, they worry that adopting such a standard will breed a self-righteous, messianic foreign policy. Realists embrace **consequentialism**. If there are no universal standards covering the many situations in which moral choice must occur, then policy decisions can only be judged in terms of their consequences in particular circumstances. Prudent leaders recognize that competing moral values may be at stake in any given situation, and they must weigh the trade-offs among these values, as well as how pursuing them might impinge on national security and other important interests. As the former U.S. diplomat and celebrated realist scholar George Kennan (1985) once put it, the primary obligation of government "is to the *interests* of the national society it represents, not to the moral impulses that individual elements of that society may experience."

• **consequentialism** an approach to evaluating moral choices on the basis of the results of the action taken.

Alternative Theories of World Politics

Although realism and liberalism dominate thinking about international relations in the academic and policy communities, both schools of thought have been challenged by other schools of thought. Three of the most significant challenges have come from socialism, feminism, and constructivism.

Socialism

For much of the twentieth century, socialism was the primary radical alternative to mainstream realist and liberal theorizing. Although there are many strands of socialist thought, most have been influenced by Karl Marx's (1818–1883) argument that explaining events in contemporary world affairs requires understanding capitalism as a global phenomenon. Whereas realists emphasized state security and liberals accentuated individual freedom, socialists focused on class conflict and the material interests embodied by each class (Doyle 1997).

"The history of all hitherto existing society," proclaim Marx and his coauthor Friedrich Engels (1820–1895) in the *Communist Manifesto*, "is the history of class struggles." Capitalism, they argue, has given rise to two antagonistic classes: a ruling class (bourgeoisie) that owns the means of production, and a subordinate class (proletariat) that sells its labor, but receives little compensation. According to Marx and Engels, "The need of a constantly expanding market for its products chases the bourgeoisie over the whole surface of the globe." By expanding worldwide, the bourgeoisie gives "a cosmopolitan character to production and consumption in every country."

Vladimir Ilyich Lenin (1870–1924) extended Marx's analysis to the study of imperialism, which he interpreted as a stage in the development of capitalism where monopolies supplant free-market competition. Drawing from the work of British economist John Hobson (1858–1940), Lenin maintained that advanced capitalist states eventually face the twin problems of overproduction and underconsumption. They respond by seeking foreign markets and investments for their surplus goods and capital, and by dividing the world into spheres of influence that they can exploit. While his assertions have been heavily criticized on conceptual and empirical grounds (see Dougherty and Pfaltzgraff 2001, 437–442), the attention given to social classes and uneven development engendered several new waves of theorizing about capitalism as a global phenomenon.

One prominent example is dependency theory. As expressed in the writings of André Gunder Frank (1969), Amir Samin (1976), and others (see Dos Santos 1970; Cardoso and Faletto 1979), dependency theorists claimed that much of the poverty in Asia, Africa, and Latin America stemmed from the exploitative structure of the capitalist world economy. As they saw it, the economies of less developed countries had become dependent upon exporting inexpensive raw materials and agricultural commodities to advanced industrial states, while simultaneously importing expensive manufactured goods from them. Raúl Prebisch, an Argentinian economist who directed the United Nations Economic Commission for Latin America, feared that these producers of primary products would find it difficult to develop, because the price of their products would fall over time relative to the price of manufactured goods. Dependency theory was criticized for recommending withdrawal from the world economy (Shannon 1989; also Packenham 1992), and was eventually superceded by efforts to trace the economic ascent and decline of individual countries as part of long-run, system-wide change.

World-system theory, which was influenced by both Marxist and dependency theorists, represents the most recent effort to interpret world politics in terms of an integrated capitalist division of labor (see Wallerstein 1988; Chase-Dunn 1989). The capitalist world economy, which emerged in sixteenth-century Europe and ultimately expanded to encompass the entire globe, is viewed as containing three structural positions: a *core* (strong, well-integrated states whose economic activities are diversified and capital-intensive), a *periphery* (areas lacking strong state machinery and engaged in producing relatively few unfinished goods by unskilled, low-wage labor), and a *semi-periphery* (states embodying elements of both core and peripheral production). Within the core, a state may gain economic primacy by achieving productive, commercial, and financial superiority over its rivals. Primacy is difficult to sustain, however. The diffusion of technological innovations and the flow of capital to competitors, plus the massive costs of maintaining global order, all erode the dominant state's economic advantage. Thus in addition to underscoring the exploitation of the periphery by the core, world-system theory calls attention to the cyclical rise and fall of hegemonic core powers.

Whereas the various socialist challenges to realism and liberalism enhance our understanding of world politics by highlighting the roles played by corporations, transnational movements, and other nonstate actors, they overemphasize economic interpretations of international events and consequently omit other potentially important explanatory factors. According to feminist theorists, one such factor is gender.

Feminism

During the last quarter of the twentieth century, feminism began challenging conventional international relations theory (see Controversy: What's Missing in Mainstream Theories of Interstate Relations?). In particular, feminist theory attacked the exclusion of women in discussions about international affairs as well as the injustice and unequal treatment of women this prejudice caused. The mainstream literature on world politics dismissed the plight and contributions of women, treating differences in men's and women's status, beliefs, and behaviors as unimportant. As feminist theory evolved over time, it moved away from focusing on a history of discrimination and began to explore how gender identity shapes foreign policy decision making and how gendered hierarchies reinforced practices that perpetuated inequalities between men and women (see Tickner 2002; Enloe 2001; Beckman and D'Amico 1994; Peterson and Runyan 1993).

Although all feminists stress the importance of gender in studying international relations, there are several contending schools of thought within feminist scholarship. Some feminists assert that on average there are no significant differences in the capabilities of men and women; others claim differences exist, with each gender being more capable than the other in certain endeavors; still others insist that the meaning ascribed to a person's gender is an arbitrary cultural construct that varies from one time or place to another (Goldstein 2002). Regardless of the position taken on the issue of gender differences, feminist scholars emphasize the relevance of women's experiences in international affairs and the contributions they

What's Missing in Mainstream Theories of Interstate Relations? The Feminist Critique

Many scholars are dissatisfied with existing theories of world politics because nearly all fail, in their opinion, to give sufficient attention to certain important factors and forces. No theory can possibly cover everything comprehensively; however, if a theory ignores a key variable or issue in the effort to simplify the essential features of world politics, it will fail to capture the true dynamics of international relations. Determining which features should be emphasized is controversial, because certain questions are more interesting to some people than others.

Does realist theory ignore any crucial factors in world politics? To stimulate your thinking about what is essential and what has potentially been ignored, consider the following six principles of realism described by Hans Morgenthau (1985):

1. Political realism believes that politics, like society in general, is governed by objective laws that have their roots in human nature. . . .
2. The main signpost that helps political realism to find its way through the landscape of international politics is the concept of interest defined in terms of power. . . . [Realists draw] a sharp distinction between the desirable and the possible—between what

is desirable everywhere and at all times and what is possible under the concrete circumstances of time and place. . . .
3. Realism does not endow its key concept of interest defined as power with a meaning that is fixed once and for all. . . . The kind of interest determining political action in a particular period of history depends upon the political and cultural context within which foreign policy is formulated. . . .
4. Political realism is aware of the moral significance of political action. It is also aware of the ineluctable tension between the moral command and the requirements of successful political action. . . . Ethics in the abstract judges action by its conformity with the moral law; political ethics judges action by its political consequences. . . .
5. Political realism refuses to identify the moral aspirations of a particular nation with the moral laws that govern the universe. . . .
6. The difference, then, between political realism and other schools of thought is real and it is profound. . . . Intellectually, the political realist maintains the autonomy of the political sphere, as the economist, the lawyer, the moralist maintain theirs. He thinks in terms of interest defined as power, as the

have made. More than simply acknowledging the impact of female leaders such as Margaret Thatcher of Great Britain, Megawati Sukarnoputri of Indonesia, Golda Meir of Israel, or Corazón Aquino of the Philippines, they urge us to examine events from the personal perspectives of the countless women who have been involved in international affairs as caregivers, grassroots activists, and participants in the informal labor force. "Women have never been *absent* in world politics," writes Franke Wilmer (2000). They have, for the most part, remained "*invisible* within the discourse conducted by men" about world politics.

Constructivism

Since the end of the Cold War, many students of international relations have turned to social constructivism in order to understand world politics. Strictly speaking, "constructivism is not a theory of international politics"; rather, it helps to "clarify the differences and relative virtues" of alternative theories by economist thinks in terms of interest defined as wealth; the lawyer, of the conformity of action with legal rules; the moralist, of conformity of action with moral principles. . . . And he parts company with other schools when they impose standards of thought appropriate to other spheres upon the political sphere.

Morgenthau's perspective on politics among nations was highly influential in the aftermath of the Second World War. But do his six principles help us understand the dynamics of contemporary international relations? Some scholars and policymakers think so; others are doubtful. One skeptic, J. Ann Tickner (1988), draws upon feminist theory to reformulate Morgenthau's principles in an effort to provide an alternative to the conventional realist approach to the study of international relations:

1. A feminist perspective believes that objectivity, as it is culturally defined, is associated with masculinity. Therefore, supposedly "objective" laws of human nature are based on a partial, masculine view of human nature. Human nature is both masculine and feminine; it contains elements of social reproduction and development as well as political domination. . . .
2. A feminine perspective believes that the national interest is multidimensional and contextually contingent. Therefore, it cannot be defined solely in terms of power. . . .
3. Power cannot be infused with meaning that is universally valid. Power as domination and control privileges masculinity and ignores the possibility of collective empowerment. . . .
4. A feminist perspective rejects the possibility of separating moral command from political action. . . .
5. While recognizing that the moral aspirations of particular nations cannot be equated with universal moral principles, a feminist perspective seeks to find common moral elements in human aspirations which could become the basis for de-escalating international conflict and building international community.
6. A feminist perspective denies the autonomy of the political. Since autonomy is associated with masculinity in Western culture, disciplinary efforts to construct a world view which does not have a pluralistic conception of human nature are partial and masculine. Building boundaries around a narrowly defined political realm defines political in a way that excludes the concerns and contributions of women.

For some people, Tickner's reformulation of Morgenthau's principles represents an advance in international relations theorizing; for others, it does not. What do you think? Does feminism offer a fruitful new approach to the study of international relations? ●

critically examining the assumptions that underpin them (Wendt 2000). Its practitioners believe that world politics is socially constructed. That is to say, material resources only acquire meaning for human action through the structure of shared knowledge in which they are embedded. The social structure of a system makes actions possible by constituting actors with certain identities and interests, and material capabilities with certain meanings (see Checkel 1998; Hopf 1998; Onuf 1989; S. Smith 1997). Hence the meaning of "anarchy" or "power" depends on the underlying structure of shared knowledge. The absence of a higher authority above allied states, for example, entails a different meaning than an anarchy composed of bitter rivals. Thus, British nuclear weapons are less threatening to the United States than the same weapons in North Korean hands, because the British are allies and shared Anglo-American expectations about one another differ from those between Washington and Pyongyang (Wendt 1995).

As discussed in the previous chapter, international reality is defined by our images of the world. Constructivists remind us of the intersubjective quality of these images. We are all influenced by collective conceptions of world politics, which are reinforced by social pressures from the reference groups to which we belong. Awareness of how our understandings of the world are socially constructed, and of how prevailing ideas mold our beliefs about what is immutable and what can be reformed, allow us to see theories of world politics in a new, critical light.

Forecasting the Global Future with Theories of World Politics

As we seek to understand the global future, we must recognize the limitations of our knowledge of world politics. The world is complex, and our understanding of its workings remains incomplete. As one scholar suggests, comprehending world politics is like trying to make sense of a disassembled jigsaw puzzle (Puchala 1994). Each piece shows a part of the whole picture, but it's unclear how they fit together. Some pieces depict a struggle for power among self-interested states; others reveal countries pooling their sovereignty to create a supranational union. Some pieces portray wrenching ethnonationalist conflicts; others reveal an absence of war between democracies. Some pieces show an upsurge in parochialism; others describe an emerging global civil society. One of the difficulties of forecasting the global future is that disintegrative trends are splintering the political landscape at the very time that integrative trends are shrinking the planet. Whereas some countries seem mired in a dog-eat-dog world of international anarchy and self-help, others appear to live in a world of international institutions and interdependence.

Theories are maps. They guide us in fitting the seemingly incompatible pieces of complex puzzles together to reveal the complete picture. But just as some maps are more accurate than others, some theories are more useful than others. "There is nothing so practical as a good theory," Kurt Lewin declares in the epigraph that opened this chapter. But what makes a "good" theory? The following are some of the criteria that social scientists use when judging the quality of a theory (see Van Evera 1997):

- *Clarity.* A good theory is clearly framed: Its concepts are precisely defined, cause and effect relationships governing observed patterns are adequately specified, and the argument underpinning those hypothesized relationships is logically coherent.
- *Parsimony.* A good theory simplifies reality: It focuses on an important phenomenon and contains all of the factors relevant for explaining it without becoming excessively complex.
- *Explanatory power.* A good theory has empirical support: It deepens our understanding of a phenomenon, and explains things about it that are not accounted for by rival theories.
- *Prescriptive richness.* A good theory provides policy recommendations: It describes how problems can be avoided or mitigated through timely countermeasures.
- *Falsifiability.* A good theory can be proven wrong: It indicates what evidence would refute its claims.

Although realism and liberalism are the two dominant ways of thinking about world politics today, neither theory completely satisfies all of the criteria listed above. Recall that realism is frequently criticized for relying upon ambiguous concepts, while liberalism is charged with making naive policy recommendations based on idealistic assumptions. Moreover, as the challenges mounted by socialism, feminism, and constructivism suggest, both theories overlook seemingly important aspects of world politics, which limits their explanatory power. Despite these drawbacks, "each has a comparative advantage in explaining certain kinds of international events and the foreign policy of different types of actors" (Doyle 1997). Because we lack a single overarching theory able to account for all facets of world politics, we will draw on both realist and liberal thought in subsequent chapters. Moreover, we will supplement them with insights from socialism, feminism, and constructivism where these alternative theoretical traditions can best help to interpret the topic covered.

Chapter Summary

- A theory is a set of interrelated propositions that explains why certain events occurred. Two overarching theories have dominated the study of world politics: realism and liberalism.
- Several strains of realist theory exist. At the risk of oversimplification, the realist worldview can be summarized as follows:
  1. People are by nature selfish, competitive, and domineering. Changing human nature is a utopian aspiration.
  2. The international system is anarchic. Without the support and protection of a higher authority, states strive for autarchy and engage in self-help.
  3. Under such conditions, international politics is a struggle for power, "a war of all against all," as the sixteenth-century English philosopher Thomas Hobbes put it. The primary obligation of every state in this environment—the goal to which all other objectives should be subordinated—is to follow its "national interest" defined in terms of acquiring power.
  4. Security is a function of power, and power is a function of military capability. States should procure the military capability to deter or subdue any potential rival. They should not entrust their security to the good will of allies or to the promises of international law and organizations.
  5. International stability results from maintaining a balance of power among contending states.
- Various forms of liberal theory also exist. The liberal worldview can be summarized as follows:
  1. People are capable of collaboration and mutual aid. Malicious behavior is the product of an environment that encourages people to act selfishly. Reason enables people to change the conditions they live under, and therefore makes progress possible.
  2. The first important change needed to reduce the probability of war is to promote national self-determination and democratic governance. The domestic

characteristics of states vary, and these variations affect state behavior. Democracies are more peaceful than autocratic governments.

3. The second important change is to promote international commerce. Economic interdependence leads states to develop mechanisms to resolve conflict, which reinforces the material incentive to avoid wars that inhibit business opportunities.

4. The third change is to replace secret diplomacy and the shifting, rival military alliances characteristic of balance-of-power politics with international institutions based on collective security. Competitive, self-interested behavior need not be arbitrary and disorderly. By encouraging reciprocity, reducing uncertainty, and shaping expectations, international institutions help states coordinate their behavior and achieve collective gains.

5. World politics is increasingly shaped by transnational networks, in which states are enmeshed in complex webs that include multinational corporations, international organizations, and nongovernmental organizations.

- The explanation of world politics cannot be reduced to any one simple yet compelling account. While realism and liberalism each explain certain types of international phenomena well, neither adequately captures all facets of world politics. As a result, rival interpretations of world politics have periodically challenged these two mainstream theories. In recent years, theorists belonging to the socialist, feminist, and constructivist schools of thought have voiced some of the most prominent criticisms of conventional international relations theory.

KEY TERMS

theory	zero-sum game	international regime
power	collective security	low politics
self-help	transnational relations	high politics
relative gains	complex interdependence	consequentialism

WHERE ON THE WORLD WIDE WEB?

Contemporary Philosophy, Critical Theory, and Postmodern Thought

http://www.cudenver.edu/~mryder/itc_data/postmodern.html

The University of Colorado at Denver's School of Education has created a website that helps students understand the ideas behind critical theory and postmodern thought. Read about the main authors of postmodern thought and then access their works.

Data on the Net

http://odwin.ucsd.edu/idata/

Try your hand at being a behavioral social scientist. The University of California at San Diego has created a gateway website from which you can browse the collection of several hundred Internet sites of numerous social science statistical data. On the home page, type in a topic that interests you, and receive data that is relevant to your topic.

Feminist Theory Website

http://www.cddc.vt.edu/feminism/

The Center for Digital Discourse and Culture at Virginia Tech University hosts the award-winning Feminist Theory Website. This site provides one of the most extensive lists of research materials and information for students, activists, and scholars interested in women's conditions and struggles around the world, with a staggering 5,425 bibliographical entries and 593 links to other Internet sites. Its stated goals are to encourage research and dialogue between individuals in different countries around the world. True to its international focus, the site can be accessed in English, Spanish, or French. Those interested can read complete bibliographies from various fields as well as obtain information on women's movements and activities anywhere in the world. As noted in this chapter, much literature on world politics has ignored the plight and contributions of women. This website will undoubtedly contribute to remedying this situation.

Niccolò Machiavelli

http://www.philosophypages.com/ph/macv.htm

The writings of Niccolò Machiavelli (1469–1527) are often cited as the base of realist thinking in international relations. As this chapter explains, the realist worldview is primarily concerned with a state's drive for power. Visit this site for a complete informational resource on Machiavelli's life and times. There is also a link to his famous book on how to rule, *The Prince,* which you can read online.

President Woodrow Wilson's Fourteen Points

http://www.yale.edu/lawweb/avalon/wilson14.htm

Woodrow Wilson's celebrated Fourteen Points speech before a joint session of Congress on January 8, 1918, "expressed the sentiments of the liberal world view and program." Take a moment to read the Fourteen Points. In retrospect, did Wilson's speech aim to prevent another war or establish American international dominance in a new world order? Which philosophy do you think underlies current U.S. foreign policy, liberalism or realism?

INFOTRAC® COLLEGE EDITION

Search for the following articles in the InfoTrac College Edition database.

Hoffmann, Stanley. "The Crisis of Liberal Internationalism," *Foreign Policy* Spring 1995.

Jervis, Robert. "Realism, Neoliberalism, and Cooperation," *International Security* Summer 1999.

Kurth, James. "Inside the Cave: The Banality of I.R. Studies," *The National Interest* Fall 1998.

Legro, Jeffrey W., and Andrew Moravcsik. "Is Anybody Still a Realist?" *International Security* Fall 1999.

For more articles, enter:

"liberalism" in the Subject Guide, and then go to subdivision "international aspects."

"neorealism" in Keywords.

"realism theory" in Keywords.

ADDITIONAL CD-ROM RESOURCES

Click on Theories of International Relations to access additional resources related to this chapter.

The Actors in World Politics

In studying world politics we typically use the term *actor* to refer to the agents who participate in world politics. They include countries (for example, the United States and Japan), international organizations (the United Nations and the Nordic Council), multinational corporations (General Motors and Sony), nongovernmental organizations (Greenpeace and the World Wildlife Federation), indigenous nationalities (the Kurds in Iran, Iraq, and Turkey), and terrorist networks (al Qaeda).

Part II identifies the major actors in world politics today and describes the roles they perform and the policies they pursue. We begin in Chapter 3 with an analysis of countries, usually called "states." In Chapter 4 special attention is given to states with the greatest military and economic capabilities—the great powers. Next, in Chapter 5, we examine the weaker, economically less-developed countries known collectively as the Global South, because the majority of them are located on the earth's southern hemisphere. Finally, Chapter 6 deals with the growing role of nonstate actors, which include intergovernmental organizations such as the European Union as well as nongovernmental organizations ranging from multinational corporations to transnational religious movements. ●

Foreign Policy Decision Making

We must recognize that the elimination of conflict [in foreign policymaking] is an idle dream. Conflict is bound to exist whenever a number of individuals are engaged in a decision-making process, whenever a number of institutions project different institutional perspectives.

ZBIGNIEW BRZEZINSKI, former U.S. assistant to the president for national security affairs

F ollowing the attacks of September 11, 2001 on the World Trade Center and the Pentagon, U.S. president George W. Bush and his national security advisors began formulating a new strategy for striking terrorist organizations and the states that harbor them. "We must take the battle to the enemy, disrupt his plans, and confront the worst threats before they emerge," the president insisted during a commencement speech at West Point in June 2002. He promised that his administration would be patient, focused, and methodical in choosing where and when to apply the strategy. As the president explained in an interview with journalist Bob Woodward (2002), teamwork was necessary for the decision-making process to operate effectively.

By the fall of 2002, however, the national security decision-making process looked more messy than methodical, as serious divisions emerged within the Bush administration over whether to wage war against Saddam Hussein's regime in Iraq. On one side stood Vice President Dick Cheney and Deputy Secretary of Defense Paul Wolfowitz, supported by Richard Perle, chair of the Pentagon Defense Policy Board. Arguing that Saddam Hussein possessed weapons of mass destruction that could be used against the United States, they urged the president to invade Iraq, even if America had little international support for launching a preventive war.

Opposing an invasion were Secretary of State Colin Powell and an unlikely coalition of officials from the first Bush administration, including trusted national

Courtesy of the White House/Getty Images

Collective Decision Making During crises that threaten a country's national security, decisions usually are made by the head of state and a small group of advisers rather than by large-scale bureaucracies. George W. Bush and advisors in the White House Situation Room make plans for war against Iraq in October 2002.

security advisors Brent Scowcroft and James A. Baker III, as well as former secretary of state Larry Eagleburger. In one way or another, those questioning a military strike all reflected Powell's qualms about the costs of undertaking such a war with few allies and uncertain domestic support. Although they agreed that Saddam Hussein was a menace, they counseled against military action until it could be proven that the Iraqi dictator possessed weapons of mass destruction. A retired general and the only combat veteran among Bush's senior aides, Powell wrote in *My American Journey*, "Many of my generation, the career captains, majors, and lieutenant colonels seasoned in . . . [the Vietnam War], vowed that when our turn came to call the shots, we would not acquiesce in half-hearted warfare for half-baked reasons that the American people could not understand or support."

As rumors of war spread and the debate between these two groups intensified, the national security policy-making process fell into disarray. While the president had promised to craft a clear, coherent strategy for dealing with Iraq, discord among the members of his foreign policy team suggested otherwise. Deep fissures within the administration soon became public as key advisors quarreled over whether they should obtain United Nations backing for an American attack. Whereas one side stressed the immediate threat posed by Saddam Hussein and advocated acting unilaterally if necessary, the other side emphasized the long-term risks of removing him by force without UN Security Council approval and multilateral assistance. Disagreement over this issue so strained relations between Vice President Cheney and Secretary of State Powell that it "pulled apart the last fraying threads of what had connected them for so many years" (Woodward 2004).

What explains the disarray in the Bush policy-making process? National leaders often describe their foreign policies as the result of neat, orderly, and rational procedures. By their account, they carefully define emerging problems, specify the goals they wish to achieve, identify all the alternative ways of attaining these goals, weigh the costs, benefits, and risks associated with each alternative, and then select the option with the best chance of attaining the desired goals. Yet, promises to the contrary, the Bush policy-making process hardly followed these procedures. Despite the president's desire to have his administration function as a unified body, the process of deciding how to deal with Iraq was contentious and turbulent. Was this deviation from **procedural rationality** unique to the Bush administration's handling of the Iraq situation? Or, was it typical of how foreign policy is made generally? To put it another way, is rational choice more an idealized standard than an accurate description of real-world behavior?

To answer these questions, this chapter will investigate how states make foreign policy. Drawing upon the levels of analysis framework introduced in Chapter 1, we will examine how the properties of the international system, various national attributes, and the personal characteristics of political leaders combine to shape foreign policy. After considering factors at the systemic, state, and individual levels of analysis that influence foreign policy, we will conclude by exploring how they create impediments to rational decision making.

• **procedural rationality** a method of decision making based on having perfect information with which all possible courses of action are carefully evaluated.

Explaining Foreign Policy

When we speak about foreign policy and the decision-making processes that produce it, we mean the goals that officials heading states (or other international actors) seek abroad, the values that underlie those goals, and the means or instruments used to pursue them. Although the state is not the only actor on the world stage, due to its preeminence we begin our examination of foreign policy making by looking back to the origins of the modern system of autonomous, territorial states.

The Emergence of the Modern State System

The modern state system was born with the Peace of Westphalia in 1648, which ended the Thirty Years' War. A complex, multidimensional conflict, the Thirty Years' War originated from a welter of intellectual, cultural, political, and economic crosscurrents that swept through Europe in the wake of the Reformation. One dimension of the war was religious, involving a clash between Catholics and Protestants. Another dimension was governmental, consisting of a civil war over the issue of imperial authority within the Holy Roman Empire (a territory stretching from France to Poland, composed of numerous principalities united through marriages to the Hapsburg dynasty). A third dimension was geostrategic, pitting the Austrian and Spanish thrones of the House of Hapsburg against the Danish, Swedish, Dutch, and French thrones (see Kegley and Raymond 2002a).

When the belligerents in this horrific war finally reached a peace agreement, they provided world politics with a new, decentralized structure. Throughout the Middle Ages, Europeans thought of themselves as part of an all-pervading Christian commonwealth, despite living in a galaxy of bishoprics, duchies, fiefdoms, and other principalities. Now the hierarchical medieval system of papal governance was replaced with geographically and politically separate states that recognized no superior authority. Under the terms of the Peace of Westphalia (so named because it was negotiated at concurrent conferences in the German cities of Münster and Osanbrück in Westphalia), these newly independent states were all given the same legal rights: territory under their sole jurisdiction, unrestricted control of their domestic affairs, and the freedom to conduct foreign relations and negotiate treaties with other states. The concept of **sovereignty**—that no political entity is above the state—captures these legal rights.

• **sovereignty** under international law, the principle that no higher authority is above the state.

The Westphalian system still colors every dimension of world politics and provides the terminology used to describe the primary units in international affairs. Although the term *nation-state* is often used interchangeably with *state* and *nation,* technically the three are different. As noted in Chapter 1, a *state* is a legal entity that possesses a permanent population, a well-defined territory, and a government capable of exercising sovereignty. A *nation* is a collection of people who, on the basis of ethnic, linguistic, or cultural affinity, perceive themselves to be members of the same group. Thus the term *nation-state* implies a convergence between territorial states and the psychological identification of people within them. However, in employing this familiar terminology, we should exercise caution. As we shall explain in Chapter 5, most states are populated by many nations, and some nations are not states. These "nonstate nations" are ethnic groups, such as Native American tribes in the United States, Sikhs in India, or Basques in Spain, composed of people without sovereign power over the territory in which they live.

The Determinants of States' Foreign Policy Behavior

Many factors affect the opportunity, capacity, and willingness of states to make foreign policy choices. Due to the diversity of states, as well as their different positions within the contemporary global system, it is difficult to generalize about the influence of any one factor or combination of factors.

To determine the relative impact of specific factors under different circumstances, we must first distinguish between different types of influences on policy choices. In classifying the determinants of foreign policies, the levels-of-analysis framework introduced in Chapter 1 and displayed in Figure 3.1 helps to describe the multiple influences on states' decision-making processes. Recall that the systemic influences on foreign policy include all activities occurring beyond a state's borders that structure the choices its officials make. Such factors as the number

FIGURE 3.1

The Major Sources of States' Foreign Policy Decisions: Influences at Three Levels

The factors that shape states' foreign policies can be categorized at three basic levels. At the systemic level are those features of the global system such as the prevalence of alliances and the extent of trade interdependence. At the state level are domestic influences such as the state's type of government or the opinions of its citizens. At the individual level are the characteristics of the leader—his or her personal beliefs, values, and personality. All three levels simultaneously affect decisions, but their relative weight usually depends on the issues and circumstances at the time of decision.

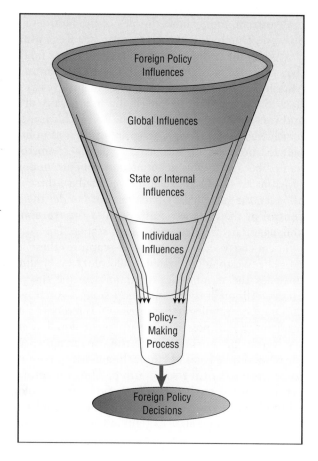

of great powers and the pattern of alliances sometimes profoundly affect the choices of decision makers. State-level influences focus on variations in military capabilities, level of economic development, type of government, and organizational processes. Finally, individual-level influences give attention to the personal characteristics of the leaders who govern different states. Let us examine each of these three types of foreign policy determinants in turn.

International Sources of Foreign Policy

The international environment within which states and nonstate actors operate shapes *opportunities* for action. It sets an ecological context that limits some foreign policy choices but facilitates others (Sprout and Sprout 1965; Starr 1978). Among the most significant facets of the international environment that make possible certain courses of action but not others are the distribution of power among states and the pattern of the alliances around the most powerful.

Polarity and Polarization

Power can be distributed in many ways. It can be concentrated in the hands of one preponderant state, as in the ancient Mediterranean world at the zenith of the Roman Empire, or it may be diffused among several rival states, as it was during the Italian Renaissance when Venice, Florence, Milan, Naples, and the papal states possessed approximately equal strength. Scholars use the term *polarity* to describe the distribution of power among members of the state system. *Unipolar* systems have one dominant power center, *bipolar* systems contain two centers of power, and *multipolar* systems possess more than two such centers.

Closely related to the distribution of power is the pattern of alignments among states. The term *polarization* refers to the degree to which states cluster around the powerful. For instance, a highly bipolarized system is one in which small and medium-sized states form alliances with one of the two dominant powers. The network of alliances around the United States and Soviet Union during the Cold War exemplified such a system.

Polarity and alliance polarization influence foreign policy by affecting the decision latitude possessed by states. To illustrate this point, let's consider two examples. Our first example pertains to polarity and great powers. When power is concentrated in the hands of a single state in a unipolar system, it has more latitude to use military force and intervene in the affairs of others than it would in a system characterized by a diffuse distribution of power, where rivals might obstruct its actions. Our second example focuses on polarization and smaller states. When alliances are tight military blocs, the members of each alliance will feel compelled to conform with the dictates of the alliance's leader. Conversely, when alliances are loosely structured and their membership is fluid, smaller states will have greater latitude to craft foreign policies that are independent of the wishes of the powerful. Of course, we could think of other examples to show how the structural properties of the international system affect decision latitude. What they would show is that the foreign policy impact of polarity and polarization hinges on the geostrategic position of a given state.

• **polarity** the degree to which military and economic capabilities are concentrated among the major powers in the state system.

• **polarization** the degree to which states cluster in alliances around the most powerful members of the state system.

Geostrategic Position

Click on States and International Relations for an interactive map illustrating geographic influences on foreign policy and for related critical thinking questions.

Some of the most important influences on a state's foreign policy behavior are its location and physical terrain. The presence of natural frontiers, for example, may profoundly guide policymakers' choices. Consider the United States, which has prospered because vast oceans separate it from Europe and Asia. The advantage of having oceans as barriers to foreign intervention, combined with the absence of militarily powerful neighbors, permitted the United States to develop into an industrial giant and to practice safely an isolationist foreign policy for over one hundred and fifty years. Consider also mountainous Switzerland, whose easily defended topography has made neutrality a viable foreign policy option.

Similarly, maintaining autonomy from continental politics has been an enduring theme in the foreign policy of Great Britain, an island country whose physical detachment from Europe long served as a buffer separating it from entanglement in major power disputes on the Continent. Preserving this protective shield has been a priority for Britain throughout its history, and helps to explain why London has been so hesitant in the past 20 years to accept full integration in the European Union (EU).

Most countries are not insular, however; they have many states on their borders, denying them the option of noninvolvement in world affairs. Germany, which sits in the geographic center of Europe, historically has found its domestic political system and foreign policy preferences shaped by its geostrategic position. In the twentieth century, for example, Germany struggled through no less than six major radical changes in governing institutions, each of which pursued very different foreign policies: (1) the empire of Kaiser Wilhelm II; (2) the Weimar Republic; (3) Adolf Hitler's dictatorship; its two post–World War II successors, (4) the capitalist Federal Republic in West Germany, (5) the communist German Democratic Republic in East Germany; and, finally, (6) a reunited Germany after the end of the Cold War, now committed to liberal democracy and full integration in the European Union. Each of these governments was preoccupied with its relations with neighbors, but responded to the opportunities and challenges presented by Germany's position in the middle of the European continent with very different foreign policy goals. In no case, however, was isolationistic withdrawal from involvement in continental affairs a practical geostrategic option.

History is replete with other examples of geography's influence on states' foreign policy goals, which is why geopolitical theories have a venerable place in the field of international relations. **Geopolitics** stresses the influence of geographic factors on state power and international conduct. Illustrative of early geopolitical thinking is Alfred Thayer Mahan's (1890) *The Influence of Sea Power in History*, which maintained that control of the seas shaped national power. Thus states with extensive coastlines and ports enjoyed a competitive advantage. Later geopoliticians, such as Sir Halford Mackinder (1919) and Nicholas Spykman (1944), stressed that not only location but also topography, size (territory and population), climate, and distance between states are powerful determinants of the foreign policies of individual countries. The underlying principle behind the geopolitical perspective is self-evident: Leaders' perceptions of available foreign policy options are influenced by the geopolitical circumstances that define their states' places on the world stage.

• **geopolitics** a school of thought claiming that states' foreign policies are determined by their location, natural resources, and physical environment.

System structure and geostrategic position are only two aspects of the global environment that may influence foreign policy. In other chapters we will discuss additional factors. Next, we comment briefly on four internal attributes of states that influence their foreign policies: military capabilities, level of economic development, type of government, and organizational processes.

Domestic Sources of Foreign Policy

Whereas the structure of the international system and a state's geostratic position within it influence the opportunities for state action, various domestic factors affect the *capacity* of states to act when opportunities arise (East 1978). While scholars have investigated many national attributes that determine the amount of resources available to states and the ability to use them, we will concentrate on four prominent factors: military capability, level of economic development, type of government, and organizational structures and processes.

Military Capabilities

The proposition that states' internal capabilities shape their foreign policy priorities is supported by the fact that states' preparations for war strongly influence their later use of force (Levy 2001). Thus, while most states may seek similar goals, their ability to realize them will vary according to their military capabilities.

Because military capabilities limit a state's range of prudent policy choices, they act as a mediating factor on leaders' national security decisions. For instance, in the 1980s, Libyan leader Muammar Qaddafi repeatedly provoked the United States through anti-American and anti-Israeli rhetoric and by supporting various terrorist activities. Qaddafi was able to act as he did largely because neither bureaucratic organizations nor a mobilized public existed in Libya to constrain his personal whims. However, Qaddafi was doubtlessly more highly constrained by the outside world than were the leaders in the more militarily capable countries toward whom his anger was directed. Limited military muscle compared with the United States precluded the kinds of belligerent behaviors he threatened to practice.

Conversely, Saddam Hussein made strenuous efforts to build Iraq's military might (partly with the help of U.S. arms sales) and by 1990 had built the fourth-largest army in the world. Thus, invading Kuwait to seize its oil fields became a feasible foreign policy option. In the end, however, even Iraq's impressive military power proved ineffective against a vastly superior coalition of military forces, headed by the United States. The 1991 Persian Gulf War forced Saddam Hussein to capitulate and withdraw from the conquered territory. Twelve years thereafter, the United States invaded Iraq and finally ousted Saddam Hussein from office.

Economic Conditions

The level of economic and industrial development a state enjoys also affects the foreign policy goals it can pursue. Generally, the more economically developed a state, the more likely it is to play an activist role in the global political economy. Rich states have interests that extend far beyond their borders and typically possess the means to pursue and protect them. Not coincidentally, states that enjoy industrial capabilities and extensive involvement in international trade also tend to be militarily powerful—in part because military might is a function of economic capabilities.

Although economically advanced states are more active globally, this does not mean that their privileged circumstances dictate adventuresome policies. Rich states are often "satisfied" ones that have much to lose from revolutionary change and global instability (Wolfers 1962). As a result, they usually perceive the status quo as serving their interests and often forge international economic policies to protect and expand their envied position at the pinnacle of the global hierarchy.

Levels of productivity and prosperity also affect the foreign policies of the poor states at the bottom of the hierarchy. Some economically weak states respond to their situation by complying subserviently with the wishes of the rich on whom they depend. Others rebel defiantly, sometimes succeeding (despite their disadvantaged bargaining position) in resisting the efforts by great powers and powerful international organizations to control their behavior.

Thus, generalizations about the economic foundations of states' international political behavior often prove inaccurate. Although levels of economic development vary widely among states in the global system, they alone do not determine foreign policies. Instead, leaders' perceptions of the opportunities and constraints that their states' economic resources provide may more powerfully influence their foreign policy choices.

Type of Government

A third important attribute affecting states' international behavior is their political system. Although realism predicts that all states will act similarly to protect their interests, a state's type of government demonstrably constrains important choices, including whether threats to use military force are carried out. Here the important distinction is between **constitutional democracy** (representative government) on one end of the spectrum and **autocratic rule** (authoritarian or totalitarian) on the other.

In neither democratic (sometimes called "open") nor autocratic ("closed") political systems can political leaders survive long without the support of organized domestic political interests, and sometimes the mass citizenry. But in democratic systems those interests are likely to spread beyond the government itself. Public opinion, interest groups, and the mass media are a more visible part of the policy-making process in democratic systems. Similarly, the electoral process in democratic societies more meaningfully frames choices and produces results about who will lead than the process used in authoritarian regimes, where the real choices are made by a few elites behind closed doors. In a democracy, public opinion and preferences may matter and, therefore, differences in who is allowed to participate and how much they exercise their right to participate are critical determinants of foreign policy choices.

The proposition that domestic stimuli, and not simply international events, are a source of foreign policy is not novel. In ancient Greece, for instance, the historian

• **constitutional democracy** a governmental system in which political leaders' power is limited by a body of fundamental principles, and leaders are held accountable to citizens through regular, fair, and competitive elections.

• **autocratic rule** a governmental system where unlimited power is concentrated in the hands of a single person.

Thucydides observed that what happened within the Greek city-states often did more to shape their external behavior than what each did to the others. He added that Greek leaders frequently concentrated their efforts on influencing the political climate within their own polities. Similarly, leaders today sometimes make foreign policy decisions for domestic political purposes—as, for example, when bold or aggressive acts abroad are intended to influence election outcomes at home or to divert public attention from economic woes. This is sometimes called the "scapegoat" phenomenon or the **diversionary theory of war** (Levy 1989b).

Some see the intrusion of domestic politics into foreign policy making as a disadvantage of democratic political systems that undermines their ability to deal decisively with crises or to bargain effectively with less democratic adversaries and allies. Democracies are subject to inertia. They move slowly on issues, because so many disparate elements are involved in decision making and because officials in democracies are accountable to public opinion and must respond to pressure from a variety of domestic interest groups. A crisis sufficient enough to arouse the attention and activity of a large proportion of the population may need to erupt in order for large changes in policy to come about. In contrast, authoritarian governments can "make decisions more rapidly, ensure domestic compliance with their decisions, and perhaps be more consistent in their foreign policy" (Jensen 1982). But there is a cost: Nondemocracies "often are less effective in developing an innovative foreign policy because of subordinates' pervasive fear of raising questions." In short, the concentration of power and the suppression of public opposition can be dangerous as well as advantageous.

The impact of government type on foreign policy choice has taken on great significance following the rapid conversion of many dictatorships to democratic rule. These liberal government conversions have occurred in three successive "waves" since the 1800s (Huntington 1991b). The first wave occurred between 1878 and 1926, and the second between 1943 and 1962. The third wave began in the 1970s when a large number of nondemocratic countries began to convert their governments to democratic rule. In a remarkable global transformation from past world history, the once radical idea that democracy is the ideal form of decision making has triumphed. According to Freedom House, three-fourths of the world's countries are now fully or partially democratic (see Map 3.1).

This recent growth of democracy has emboldened many liberals to predict that the twenty-first century will be safer than its predecessor. Their reasons for predicting the onset of a **democratic peace** vary, but rely on the logic that Immanuel Kant outlined in his 1795 treatise *Perpetual Peace*. Kant believed that because democratic leaders are accountable to the public, and that because ordinary citizens have to supply the soldiers and bear the human and financial cost of aggressive policies, they would constrain leaders from initiating foreign wars (especially against other liberal democracies similarly constrained by norms and institutions that respect compromise and civil liberties).

A considerable body of empirical evidence supports the proposition that liberal democracies do not wage war against each other (Russett 2001; Ray 1995; Raymond 1994). Contrary to realist arguments, the type of government and, more specifically, whether leaders are accountable to opposition groups through multiparty elections, strongly influence foreign policy goals (see Kegley and Hermann 2002).

• **diversionary theory of war** the contention that leaders initiate conflict abroad as a way of steering public opinion at home away from controversial domestic issues.

• **democratic peace** the theory that although democratic states sometimes wage wars against other states, they do not fight each other.

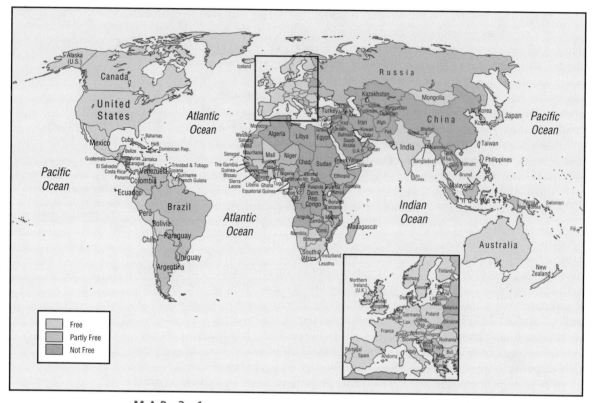

M A P 3 . 1

The Map of Freedom: The Location of Democratically Governed Countries

Throughout history, most states were ruled autocratically and the people living in them were not free. However, since the mid-1970s, an increasing number of states have undertaken political reforms leading to democratic governance and civil liberties. This map shows the location in 2003 of (1) the 85 "free" countries whose governments provide their citizens with a high degree of political and economic freedom and safeguard basic civil liberties, (2) the 59 "partly free" electoral democracies, and (3) the 48 "not free" states, where citizens' human rights and liberties are systematically abused or denied. Democratic peace theory predicts that if the trend toward the spread of liberty worldwide continues, peaceful relations among the growing community of the liberal democracies will exist.

SOURCE: Adapted from "Liberty's Ebb and Flow" by Michael Kilborn in *The Christian Science Monitor,* May 9, 1997, pp. 18–19. Reproduced with permission. Copyright © 1997 *The Christian Science Monitor* (www.csmonitor.com). All rights reserved. Data originally reported on Freedom House website at www.freedomhouse.com.

Organizational Processes

In today's world, leaders turn to large-scale organizations for information and advice when they face critical foreign policy choices. Although this is more true of major powers than of small states, even those without large budgets and complex foreign policy bureaucracies seldom make decisions without the advice and assistance of many individuals and administrative agencies (Korany 1986). Bureaucratic organizations perform vital services, enhancing the state's capacity to cope with changing global circumstances.

In the United States, for instance, the State Department, Defense Department, and Central Intelligence Agency are all key participants in the foreign policy machinery. Other agencies also bear responsibility for specialized aspects of U.S. foreign relations, such as the Treasury, Commerce, and Agriculture Departments. Similar agencies characterize the foreign affairs machinery of most other major powers, whose governments face many of the same foreign policy management challenges as the United States.

Bureaucracies increase efficiency by assigning responsibility for different tasks to different people. They define **standard operating procedures (SOPs)** that specify how tasks are to be performed; they rely on record systems to gather and store information; and they engage in forward planning to anticipate long-term needs and prepare the means to attain them.

• **standard operating procedures (SOPs)** rules for reaching decisions about particular types of situations.

Before jumping to the conclusion that bureaucracies are a blessing, we should emphasize that decision making by and within large organizations sometimes compromises rather than facilitates rational choice. According to what is commonly called **bureaucratic politics** (see Allison and Zelikow 1999; Caldwell 1977), government agencies tend to see each other as rivals. Every administrative unit within a state's foreign policy-making bureaucracy seeks to promote its own purposes and power. Organizational needs, such as larger staffs and budgets, sometimes become equated with the nation's needs, as bureaucrats come to see their own interests as the national interest. Far from being impartial managers, desiring only to carry out orders from the head of state, bureaucratic organizations frequently take policy positions designed to increase their own influence relative to that of other agencies. "Where you stand depends on where you sit" is an aphorism that reflects the nature of bureaucratic politics. Where someone stands on a policy issue may depend on which department he or she sits within.

• **bureaucratic politics model** a description of decision making that sees foreign policy choices as based on bargaining and compromises among government agencies.

Fighting among insiders within an administration and the formation of factions to carry on battles over the direction of foreign policy decisions are chronic in nearly every country (but especially in democracies accepting of participation by many people in the policy-making process). Consider the United States. Splits among key advisors over important foreign policy choices have been frequent. For example, under presidents Nixon and Ford, Secretary of State Henry Kissinger fought often with James Schlesinger and Donald Rumsfeld, who headed the Department of Defense, over strategy regarding the Vietnam War; Jimmy Carter's national security advisor, Zbigniew Brzezinski, repeatedly engaged in conflicts with Secretary of State Cyrus Vance over the Iran hostage crisis; and under Ronald Reagan, Caspar Weinberger at Defense and George Shultz at State were famous for butting heads on most policy issues. Such conflicts are not necessarily bad because they force each side to better explain its viewpoint, and this allows heads of state the opportunity to weigh their competing advice before making decisions. However, battles among advisors can lead to paralysis and to rash decisions that produce poor results.

The tragic events of September 11, 2001 provide a telling example of what can go wrong when bureaucratic politics contaminate the policy-making process. The terrorist attacks on the World Trade Center and the Pentagon were regarded by many as the worst intelligence failure since Pearl Harbor. U.S. intelligence agencies, it was later discovered, received information before hand that terrorists were likely to attack the United States with hijacked airliners as weapons. Why weren't the warnings acted upon in time to prevent the disaster? Why weren't the dots connected? The answer accepted by most analysts was that America's system of intelligence was hampered by turf-protecting bureaucracies that did not share the vital information with each other. More than fifty units of government are involved with national security policy, and agencies like the CIA, the FBI, and the INS in the State Department are habitually loath to share information with each other for fear of compromising "sources and methods." Moreover, as FBI Special Agent Coleen Rowley testified in June 2002, "There's a mutual-protection pact in bureaucracies. Mid-level managers avoid decisions out of fear a mistake will sidetrack their careers while a rigid hierarchy discourages agents from challenging superiors. There is a saying: 'Big cases, big problems; little cases, little problems; no cases, no problems.' The idea that inaction is the key to success manifests itself repeatedly" (Toner 2002). These types of problems are difficult to control, and few students of public administration believe that they can automatically be overcome through massive reorganization and restructuring. That is why critics of President George W. Bush's plan to create a new Department of Homeland Security were doubtful about its prospects for infusing greater rationality into national security policy in general and counterterrorism in particular. Sympathizing with the fact that "Mr. Bush is somewhat in the position of trying to steer an 80,000-ton supertanker with nothing more substantial than a sail boat rudder," George Melloan (2002a) noted that through creation of a homeland security department, President Bush was "no doubt hoping that in the process he could rationalize some of those [decision-making] efforts [but that] given the national tendency of bureaucrats to expand their remits, he will be lucky if he doesn't end up with more duplication and dead-weight than he has now. As Ronald Reagan once commented, 'a government bureau is the nearest thing to eternal life we'll ever see on this earth.' "

Individual Sources of Foreign Policy

In addition to examining the opportunities for state action presented by the international environment and the capacity of states to act based on their national attributes, it is also necessary to consider the *willingness* of political leaders to act when they have the opportunity and capacity. Ultimately, leaders and the kind of leadership they exert shape the way in which foreign policies are made and the consequent behavior of states in world politics. "There is properly no history, only biography" is the way Ralph Waldo Emerson expressed the view that individual leaders move history.

Leaders as the Makers of the Global Future

We expect leaders to lead, and we assume new leaders will make a difference. Moreover, leaders themselves seek to create impressions of their own self-importance while attributing extraordinary powers to other leaders. The assumptions they make about the personalities of their counterparts, consciously or unconsciously, in turn influence their own behavior (Wendzel 1980), as political psychologists who study the impact of leaders' perceptions and personalities on their foreign policy preferences demonstrate (see Kelman 1965).

Nevertheless, we must be wary of ascribing too much importance to individual leaders. Their influence is likely to be subtler, as U.S. president Bill Clinton suggested in 1998 when he observed, "Great presidents don't do great things. Great presidents get a lot of other people to do great things." Most leaders operate under a variety of pressures that limit what they can accomplish. The question at issue is not whether political elites lead or whether they can make a difference. They clearly do both. The relevant question is under what conditions leaders' personal characteristics are influential.

Factors Affecting the Capacity to Lead

The impact of leaders' personal characteristics on their state's foreign policy generally increases when their authority and legitimacy are widely accepted by citizens or, in authoritarian or totalitarian regimes, when leaders are protected from broad public criticism. Moreover, certain circumstances enhance individuals' potential influence. Among them are new situations that free leaders from conventional approaches to defining the situation; complex situations involving many different factors; and situations without social sanctions, which permit freedom of choice because norms defining the range of permissible options are unclear (DiRenzo 1974).

A leader's **political efficacy,** or self-image, combined with the citizenry's relative desire for leadership, will also influence the degree to which personal values and psychological needs govern decision making (DeRivera 1968). For example, when public opinion strongly favors a powerful leader, and when the head of state has an exceptional need for admiration, foreign policy will more likely reflect that leader's inner needs. Thus, Kaiser Wilhelm II's narcissistic personality allegedly met the German people's desire for a symbolically powerful leader, and German public preferences in turn influenced the foreign policy that Germany pursued during Wilhelm's reign, ending in World War I (Baron and Pletsch 1985).

Other factors undoubtedly influence how much leaders can shape their states' choices. For instance, when leaders believe that their own interests and welfare are at stake, they tend to respond in terms of their private needs and psychological drives. When circumstances are stable, however, and when leaders' egos are not entangled with policy outcomes, the influence of their personal characteristics is less apparent.

The amount of information available about a particular situation is also important. Without pertinent information, policy is likely to be based on leaders' personal likes or dislikes. Conversely, the more information leaders have about international affairs, the more likely they are to engage in rational decision making (Verba 1969).

Similarly, the timing of a leader's assumption of power is significant. When an individual first assumes a leadership position, the formal requirements of that role are least likely to restrict what he or she can do. That is especially true throughout the "honeymoon" period routinely given to new heads of state,

• **political efficacy**
the extent to which a policymaker believes in his or her ability to control events politically.

CONTROVERSY

Policy and Personality: Do Leaders Make a Difference?

Some theorists assume that any leader will respond to a choice in the same way, given the same costs and benefits. But does this assumption square with the facts? What do we know about the impact of people's perceptions and values on the way they view choices? Political psychology tells us that the same option is likely to have different value to different leaders. Does this mean that different leaders would respond differently to similar situations?

Consider the example of Richard Nixon. In 1971, Americans took to the streets outside the White House to protest Nixon's massive bombing of Vietnam. His reaction was to shield himself from the voice of the people, without success, as it happened. Nixon complained that "nobody can know what it means for a president to be sitting in that White House working late at night and to have hundreds of thousands of demonstrators charging through the streets. Not even earplugs could block the noise."

Earlier, on a rainy afternoon in 1962, John F. Kennedy faced a similar citizen protest. Americans had gathered in front of the White House for a Ban the Bomb demonstration. His response was to send out urns of coffee and doughnuts and invite the leaders of the protest to come inside to state their case, believing that a democracy should encourage dissent and debate.

Nixon saw protesters as a threat; Kennedy saw them as an opportunity. This comparison suggests that the type of leader can make a difference in determining the kinds of choices likely to be made in response to similar situations. More important than each president's treatment of the protesters, however, was whether he actually changed his policy decisions based on the protests. Although Kennedy was hospitable to protesters, he did not ban nuclear weapons; in fact, military spending under Kennedy grew to consume half of the federal budget. Many would insist that Kennedy alone could not be expected to eliminate nuclear weapons—that this period of history was dominated by fear of the Soviet Union and intense concern for national security. The protesters in 1971, however, were more in keeping with the spirit of the times. Although they alone may not have persuaded Nixon to alter his policies in Vietnam, widespread protest and discontentment with the war, as well as America's inability to win, eventually prompted Nixon to order the gradual withdrawal of U.S. troops, ending American participation in the Vietnam War. These outcomes suggest that leaders are captive to the larger forces that drive international relations in their times.

What do you think? Did Kennedy and Nixon choose courses of action that reflected who they were as individuals? Or would any president in their respective eras have made similar choices? ●

during which time they are relatively free of criticism and excessive pressure. Moreover, when a leader assumes office following a dramatic event (a landslide election, for example, or the assassination of a predecessor), he or she can institute policies almost with a free hand, as "constituency criticism is held in abeyance during this time" (Hermann 1976).

A national crisis is a potent circumstance that increases a leader's control over foreign policy making. Decision making during crises is typically centralized and handled exclusively by the top leadership. Crucial information is often unavailable, and leaders see themselves as responsible for outcomes. Not surprisingly, great leaders (e.g., Napoleon Bonaparte, Winston Churchill, and Franklin D. Roosevelt) customarily emerge during periods of extreme tumult. A crisis can liberate a leader from the constraints that normally would inhibit his or her capacity to control events or engineer foreign policy change.

History abounds with examples of the importance of political leaders who emerge in different times and places and under different circumstances to play critical roles in shaping world history. Mikhail Gorbachev dramatically illustrates an individual's capacity to change the course of history. As noted in Chapter 1, many scholars believe that the Cold War could not have been brought to an end, nor Communist Party rule in Moscow terminated and the Soviet state set on a path toward democracy and free enterprise, had it not been for Gorbachev's vision, courage, and commitment to engineering these revolutionary, system-transforming changes. Ironically, those reforms led to his loss of power when the Soviet Union imploded in 1991.

Having said that the influence of individual leaders can sometimes be significant, we must be cautious and remember that leaders are not all-powerful determinants of states' foreign policy behavior. Rather, their personal influence varies with the context, and often the context is more influential than the leader (see Controversy: Policy and Personality: Do Leaders Make a Difference?). Of course, this ultimately leaves us with the question of whether famous leaders would have an impact whenever and wherever they lived (see Greenstein 1987). That question may be unanswerable but it reminds us at least that multiple factors affect states' foreign policy decisions.

Constraints on the Foreign Policy-Making Process

As we saw in the previous chapter, realists maintain that the primary goal of foreign policy is to ensure state survival. From their perspective, strategic calculations are the primary determinants of policymakers' choices; domestic politics and the process of policy making itself are of secondary concern.

Because realism assumes that leaders' goals and their corresponding approach to foreign policy choices are the same, realists tend to view states as if they were **unitary actors**—homogenous or monolithic units with few or no important internal differences that affect their choices. One way to picture this is to think of states as billiard balls and the table on which they interact as the state system. The balls (states) continuously clash and collide with one another, and the actions of each are determined by its interactions with the others, not by what occurs inside it. According to this view, the leaders who make foreign policy, the types of governments they head, and the characteristics of their societies are unimportant in explaining foreign policy behavior.

In contrast to realism's tendency to concentrate on international interactions, Robert Putnam (1988) argues that national leaders actually play **two-level games.** Besides making moves on an international game board, they also maneuver on a domestic board to obtain support at home for their initiatives abroad. Because moves on one game board affect play on the other, neither level can be ignored. Indeed, astute players recognize that the right move on one level can affect the outcome on the other level. Foreign policies, in other words, have domestic consequences, and actions aimed at domestic constituencies frequently reverberate beyond national borders. As a result, it is often difficult to know where foreign policy ends and domestic policy begins.

• **unitary actor** an agent in world politics (usually a sovereign state) assumed to be internally united, so that changes in its internal circumstances do not influence its foreign policy as much as do the decisions that actor's leaders make to cope with changes in its global environment.

• **two-level games** a concept that refers to the interaction between international bargaining and domestic politics.

Putnam's two-level game metaphor reminds us that foreign policy making occurs in an environment of multiple, competing international and domestic interests. On occasion, it also occurs in situations when national values are threatened, policymakers are caught by surprise, and a quick decision is needed. The stress produced by these factors impairs leaders' cognitive abilities and may cause them to rely on various psychological coping techniques. First, owing to the process of cognitive dissonance described in Chapter 1, policymakers may try to cope with stress by denying a problem exists, blocking out negative information, and looking instead for data that justifies their optimistic viewpoint. A second common coping technique is procrastination. Here they recognize that a problem exists, but hope that it will go away by itself. Finally, a third technique for dealing with stress is **satisficing** (Simon 1957). Because policymakers work in an environment of uncertainty, incomplete information, and short deadlines, their evaluation of alternative policy options is seldom exhaustive. Rather than finding the option with the best chance of success, they may end their evaluation as soon as an alternative appears that seems superior to those already considered.

Thus, despite the image of procedural rationality that policymakers seek to project, the actual practice of foreign policy decision making contains many impediments to **rational choice.** Compounding the cognitive constraints just mentioned are organizational constraints. During a crisis, national leaders typically bypass the standard operating procedures of their foreign affairs bureaucracies and rely on a small, ad hoc group of amiable advisers. When these groups contain people with similar backgrounds who are insulated from outside opinions and surmise their leader's preferred course of action, they often exhibit excessive concurrence-seeking, or what Irving Janis (1982) calls **groupthink.** In the interest of group cohesion, they place extraordinarily high values on conformity and consensus. In addition to stifling dissent, group members adopt stereotypes of their opponents, ignore the full range of possible options, suppress personal reservations about the moral consequences of their recommendations, and fail to develop contingency plans to deal with potential setbacks.

Although policymakers can sometimes absorb new information quickly under great pressure and launch creative policy initiatives based on careful planning, the cognitive and organizational impediments to procedural rationality in foreign policy making are substantial. Table 3.1 compares how the decision process *should* ideally work with how it usually works. It suggests that many policymakers just muddle through; rather than formulating policies with bold, innovative strokes, they make incremental policy changes through trial-and-error adjustments (Lindblom 1979). As one former U.S. official put it, "Rather than through grand decisions or grand alternatives, policy changes seem to come through a series of slight modifications of existing policy, with new policy emerging slowly and haltingly by small and usually tentative steps, a process of trial and error in which policy zigs and zags, reverses itself, and then moves forward" (Hilsman 1967).

The trends currently unfolding in world politics are the products of countless decisions made daily throughout the world. Some decisions are more consequential than others, and some actors are more important than others. Throughout history, great powers such as the United States have at times stood at the center of the world political stage, possessing the combination of natural resources, mil-

• **satisficing** the tendency for decision makers to choose the first available alternative that meets minimally acceptable standards.

• **rational choice** decision-making procedures guided by careful definition of problems, specification of goals, weighing the costs, risks, and benefits of all alternatives, and selection of the optimal alternative.

• **groupthink** the propensity for members of small, cohesive groups to accept the group's prevailing attitudes in the interest of group harmony, rather than speak out for what they believe.

TABLE 3.1	
Foreign Policy Decision Making in Theory and Practice	
Ideal Process	Actual Practice
Accurate, comprehensive information	Distorted, incomplete information
Clear definition of national interests and goals	Personal motivations and organizational interests bias national goals
Exhaustive analysis of all options	Limited number of options considered; none thoroughly analyzed
Selection of optimal course of action for producing desired results	Course of action selected by political bargaining and compromise
Effective statement of decision and its rationale to mobilize domestic support	Confusing and contradictory statements of decision, often framed for media consumption
Careful monitoring of the decision's implementation by foreign affairs bureaucracies	Neglect of the tedious task of managing the decision's implementation by foreign affairs bureaucracies
Instantaneous evaluation of consequences followed by correction of errors	Superficial policy evaluation, imperfect detection of errors, and delayed correction

itary might, and the means to project power worldwide that earned them their lofty status. How great powers have responded to one another has had profound consequences throughout international history. To better understand this, we turn our attention next to the dynamics of great-power rivalry.

Chapter Summary

- Actors on the world stage are many and varied. States demand special attention because they are the principal repositories of economic and military capabilities in world affairs, and they alone possess the legal right to use force.
- The modern system of sovereign territorial states dates back to the Peace of Westphalia (1648) that ended the Thirty Years' War in Europe.
- The foreign policies of states consist of purposeful acts aimed at achieving international goals. Foreign policy making is a complex process that occurs in an environment of multiple, competing international and domestic interests.
- Foreign policy behavior is shaped by a combination of factors operating at different levels of analysis. At the systemic level, polarity, alliance polarization, and geostrategic position influence the opportunity for states to act in certain ways. At the state level, military might, economic strength, the type of government and its organizational processes influence the capacity to act on available opportunities. At the individual level, a leader's personality and the situation surrounding his or her ascension to power influence the willingness or motivation to act.

- Scholars describe rationality as a sequence of decision-making activities involving the following intellectual steps: (1) problem recognition and definition; (2) goal specification; (3) identification and evaluation of alternatives for attaining the desired goals; and (4) selection of the option that maximizes benefits and minimizes costs and risks.
- Although national leaders often claim that they follow procedural rationality when formulating their foreign policies, rational choice is more of an idealized standard than an accurate description of real-world behavior. Many cognitive and organizational factors interfere with effective problem solving. Rather than choosing the course of action with the best chance of success, decision makers may end their analysis of policy options as soon as an alternative appears that seems better than those already considered.

KEY TERMS

procedural rationality
sovereignty
polarity
polarization
geopolitics
constitutional democracy

autocratic rule
diversionary theory of war
democratic peace
standard operating procedures (SOPs)
bureaucratic politics model

political efficacy
unitary actor
two-level games
satisficing
rational choice
groupthink

WHERE ON THE WORLD WIDE WEB?

Cuban Missile Crisis

http://www.hpol.org/jfk/cuban/

The Cuban Missile Crisis is a classic example of crisis decision making. This site provides an in-depth account and analysis of the crisis and the actors and issues involved. It also contains an audio archive of President John F. Kennedy's meetings during the crisis.

Freedom, Democracy, Peace; Power, Democide, and War

http://www2.hawaii.edu/~rummel/

The democratic peace theory presented in this chapter contends that although democratic states sometimes wage wars against other states, they do not fight each other. Political scientist Rudolph J. Rummel has devoted his career to research on the

causes and conditions of collective violence and war with a view toward helping bring about their resolution or elimination; he supports the democratic peace proposition. Visit his website to analyze his work. What evidence do you think supports the democratic peace proposition? How persuasive are his arguments? *Caution:* Some of the pictures on the site contain graphic violence.

Freedom House

http://www.freedomhouse.org/

Founded by Eleanor Roosevelt and Wendell Willkie, this nonprofit organization focuses on threats to peace and democracy. Each year since 1972, Freedom House has published comparative ratings for countries and territories around the world, evaluating levels of political rights and civil liberties. Map 3.1 in this textbook uses data on the spread of democratic liberty throughout the world provided by Freedom House. Examine specific countries' freedom records. Which have radically improved? Why do you think this is so?

The Presidents: PBS's *The American Experience*

http://www.pbs.org/wgbh/amex/presidents/

This inclusive website features some of the most prominent U.S. presidents of the twentieth century, including Theodore Roosevelt, Franklin Roosevelt, Dwight Eisenhower, Harry Truman, John Kennedy, Lyndon Johnson, Richard Nixon, and Ronald Reagan. Sections focus on the U.S. foreign policy achievements of each president. This chapter describes the influence of individuals on world politics. To what extent does foreign policy reflect the preferences and initiatives of the highest government officials? Familiarize yourself with the foreign policy achievements of some U.S. presidents. Do you believe that individual leaders are the most important factor shaping a country's foreign policy?

INFOTRAC® COLLEGE EDITION

Search for the following articles in the InfoTrac College Edition database.

Hoekstra, Douglas J. "Presidential Beliefs and the Reagan Paradox," *Presidential Studies Quarterly* Summer 1997.

Meagher, Michael R. "In an Atmosphere of National Peril: The Development of John F. Kennedy's World View," *Presidential Studies Quarterly* Summer 1997.

Pious, Richard M. "The Cuban Missile Crisis and the Limits of Crisis Management," *Political Science Quarterly* Spring 2001.

Rhodes, Edward. "Do Bureaucratic Politics Matter? Some Discomforting Findings from the Case of the U.S. Navy," *World Politics* October 1994.

For more articles, enter:

"bureaucratic politics" in Keywords.

"John F. Kennedy" in the Subject Guide, and then go to subdivision "military policy."

"Ronald Reagan" in the Subject Guide, and then go to subdivision "military policy."

ADDITIONAL CD-ROM RESOURCES

Click on States and International Relations to access additional resources related to this chapter.

CHAPTER 4

Great-Power Rivalry and the Lure of Hegemony

Cycles of War and Peace in Modern World History

The most emphatic punctuation in . . . one repetitive [historical] cycle after another is the outbreak of a great war in which one power that has forged ahead of all its rivals makes so formidable a bid for world domination that it evokes an opposing coalition of all the other powers.

ARNOLD J. TOYNBEE, historian

O n November 9, 1799, a young, ambitious general named Napoleon Bonaparte rose to power in France after leading a military coup against the ruling government. A man with remarkable persuasive and intellectual abilities, he was also coarse, temperamental, and unscrupulous. Claiming to be following a star of destiny, he gradually turned the French Republic into a personal dictatorship.

In foreign affairs, Napoleon's strategy was to win quick, decisive military victories in an incessant pursuit of territorial gain. Deftly maneuvering his formidable army against the weakest point in an opponent's lines, he won a series of triumphs that gave him dominion over most of Europe. His ultimate objective was to establish a new, vertical international order, one that would replace the horizontal Westphalian system of sovereign autonomous states with a hierarchy of subservient territories presided over by the French emperor.

Napoleon's quest for hegemony stalled after 1811. British naval power thwarted his forays beyond the Continent, an interminable guerrilla war in Spain drained precious resources, and an invasion of Russia ended in disaster, with roughly two-thirds of his forces succumbing in the cold darkness of the Russian winter. Heartened by Napoleon's setbacks, a coalition consisting of Great Britain, Russia, Prussia, and Austria moved against France. Napoleon's dream of "universal monarchy" was finally crushed at Waterloo in 1815. Though distrustful of one another's intentions, the victors met at the Congress of Vienna to craft a peace settlement that would restore the decentralized Westphalian system of sovereign equals, and prevent any single great power from becoming strong enough to threaten the others.

The Napoleonic Wars and the Congress of Vienna highlight a common pattern in world politics. The ascendancy of one great power relative to its principal rivals eventually prompts opposition from the rest. If this hegemonic struggle escalates to global war, the victors will try to design a security regime aimed at preventing the recurrence of such a catastrophic conflict by staving off future challenges to the new international order they have constructed.

This general pattern has colored twentieth-century world politics, with three global wars breaking out. World Wars I and II were fought with fire and blood; the Cold War was fought by less destructive means but with equal intensity. Like the Napoleonic Wars, each of these wars triggered major transformations in world politics. In this chapter we explore their causes and consequences in order to uncover the dynamics of great-power rivalries. By understanding the origins and impact of these struggles over world leadership, we will be in a better position to anticipate whether in the twenty-first century the great powers will be able to avoid yet another global war.

Long Cycles of World Leadership

"All history shows," political scientist Hans J. Morgenthau (1985) once remarked, "that nations active in international politics are continuously preparing for, actively involved in, or recovering from organized violence in the form of

AP/Wide World Photos

The Price of Superpower Predominance? Throughout history, hegemonic states have been feared, envied, and hated by both great-power rivals and subordinate states. Shown here in 2002 is one example: Arabs displaying their intense dislike of the United States and its post–9/11 foreign policies.

• **long-cycle theory** a theory that focuses on the rise and fall of the leading global power as the central political process of the modern world system.

• **hegemon** a single, overwhelmingly powerful state that exercises predominate influence over the global system.

war." Recently, many scholars have become intrigued with the possibility that this process is cyclical and unfolds through a series of distinct phases. According to **long-cycle theory,** over the past five centuries periods of global war have been followed by periods of international rule-making and institution-building, with shifts in the cycle usually occurring in concert with changes in the major states' relative power (see Modelski and Thompson 1999). Each global war led to the emergence of a **hegemon,** a preponderant state capable of dominating the conduct of international political and economic relations (see Nye 2001). With its unrivaled power, the hegemon reshapes the rules and institutions of the state system to preserve its preeminent position.

Hegemony imposes an extraordinary burden on the world leader, which must bear the costs of maintaining political and economic order while protecting its position and upholding its dominion. Over time, as the weight of global engagement takes its toll: The hegemon overextends itself, challengers arise, and the security regime so carefully crafted after the last global war comes under attack. Historically, this struggle for power has set the stage for another global war, the demise of one hegemon and the ascent of another. Table 4.1 summarizes 500 years of the cyclical rise and fall of great powers, their global wars, and their subsequent efforts to restore order.

TABLE 4.1

The Evolution of Great-Power Rivalry for World Leadership, 1495–2025

Dates	Preponderant State(s) Seeking Hegemony	Other Powers Resisting Domination	Global War	New Order after Global War
1495–1540	Portugal	Spain, Valois, France, Burgundy, England, Venice	Wars of Italy and the Indian Ocean, 1494–1517	Treaty of Tordesillas, 1517
1560–1609	Spain	The Netherlands, France, England	Spanish-Dutch Wars, 1580–1608	Truce of 1609; Evangelical Union and the Catholic League formed
1610–1648	Holy Roman Empire (Hapsburg dynasty in Spain and Austria-Hungary)	Shifting ad hoc coalitions of mostly Protestant states (Sweden, Holland) and German principalities as well as Catholic France against remnants of papal rule	Thirty Years' War 1618–1648	Peace of Westphalia, 1648
1650–1713	France (Louis XIV)	The United Provinces, England, the Hapsburg Empire, Spain, major German states, Russia	Wars of the Grand Alliance, 1688–1713	Treaty of Utrecht, 1713
1792–1815	France (Napoleon)	Great Britain, Prussia, Austria, Russia	Napoleonic Wars, 1792–1815	Congress of Vienna and Concert of Europe, 1815
1871–1914	Germany, Austria-Hungary, Turkey	Great Britain, France, Russia, United States	World War I, 1914–1918	Treaty of Versailles creating League of Nations, 1919
1933–1945	Germany, Japan, Italy	Great Britain, France, Soviet Union, United States	World War II, 1939–1945	Bretton Woods, 1944; United Nations, 1945; Potsdam, 1945
1945–2010	United States, Soviet Union	Great Britain, France, China, Japan	Cold War, 1945–1991	NATO/Parter, Partnerships for Peace, 1995; World Trade Organization, 1995
2010–2025	United States	China, European Union, Japan, Russia	A cold peace or hegemonic war, 2010–2025?	A new security regime to preserve world order?

Critics note that long-cycle theorists disagree on whether economic, military, or domestic factors produce these cycles. They also express frustration with the deterministic tone of the theory, which to them implies that global destiny is beyond policymakers' control. Still, long-cycle theory invites us to consider how shifts in the relative strength of great powers affect world politics. It rivets our attention on hegemonic transitions, the rise and fall of leading states in the international system. To underscore the importance of struggles over world leadership in understanding world politics, this chapter inspects the three great-power wars of the twentieth century, as well as the lessons these clashes suggest for the twenty-first century.

The First World War

World War I profoundly altered the world's geopolitical map. By the time it ended, nearly ten million people had died, three empires had crumbled, and a generation of Europeans had become disillusioned with foreign policies grounded in political realism. How can such a catastrophic war be explained? Many scholars believe that World War I was inadvertent, not the result of anyone's master plan. It was a war bred by uncertainty and circumstances beyond the control of those involved, one that people neither wanted nor expected. Other scholars regard the war as a product of calculated choices. It was "a tragic and unnecessary conflict . . . because the train of events that led to its outbreak might have been broken at any point during the five weeks of crisis that preceded the first clash of arms, had prudence or common goodwill found a voice" (Keegan 1999). As we shall see, each of these interpretations captures a different dimension of the war's origins. Although none of Europe's great powers deliberately sought a general war, prevailing conditions made such an outcome highly probable, though not inevitable.

To explain how this long, grueling war happened, let us return to the analytic framework introduced in Chapter 1. We can piece together an understanding about the war's origins by looking for causal mechanisms operating at different levels of analysis, and placing them in a time sequence. By examining World War I from multiple levels across time, we can inoculate ourselves against naive, single-factor explanations of this complex event.

The Causes of World War I

The proximate causes of World War I can be found at the individual level of analysis. A Serbian nationalist seeking to free Slavs in the Balkans from Austrian rule assassinated Archduke Franz Ferdinand, heir to the Hapsburg throne of the Austrian-Hungarian Empire, at Sarajevo on June 28, 1914. This incident sparked a series of moves and countermoves by political leaders in Austria, Germany, and Russia, who held virtuous images of themselves and diabolical images of their adversaries. Rather than take the time to carefully craft policies that did not risk war, they made reactive, fatalistic decisions that seized upon the first suitable option (Williamson 1988). Their impulsive behavior over the next few weeks turned what had been a local dispute between Austria and Serbia into a horrific conflagration.

The archduke's assassination offered Austria an opportunity to weaken Serbia, which Vienna perceived as the source of separatist agitation that was undermining Hapsburg authority within the empire's large Slavic population. On July 25, Serbia rejected an Austrian ultimatum demanding its officials be allowed to participate in Serbia's investigation of the assassination plot, as well as in the punishment of the perpetrators. Serbia's refusal prompted the Austrians to declare war and bombard Belgrade. Responding to Serbian pleas for help, Russia mobilized its forces along the Austrian and German frontiers. In turn, Germany declared war on Russia and its ally, France. When German troops swept into Belgium on August 4 in order to outflank France, Britain declared war on Germany. Eventually, 32 countries on six continents became enmeshed in the conflict.

As this rapid, almost mechanical sequence of moves suggests, a combination of deeper, more remote causes had created an explosive situation that the clumsy statesmen in Vienna, Berlin, and St. Petersburg ignited. At the state level of analysis, many historians view the growth of nationalism, especially in southeastern Europe, as having created a climate of opinion that made war likely. Groups that glorified the distinctiveness of their national heritage began championing their own country above all others. Long-suppressed ethnic prejudices soon emerged, even among political leaders. Russian foreign minister Sergei Sazonov, for example, claimed to "despise" Austria, and Kaiser Wilhelm II of Germany asserted: "I hate the Slavs" (Tuchman 1962).

Domestic unrest inflamed these passions, making it hard to see things from another point of view. Believing that they were upholding their national honor, the Austrians could not comprehend why Russians insisted they were aggressors. German insensitivity to others' feelings prevented them from understanding "the strength of the Russians' pride, their fear of humiliation if they allowed the Germans and Austrians to destroy their little protégé, Serbia, and the intensity of Russian anger" (White 1990). With each side denigrating the character of the other, diplomatic alternatives to war evaporated.

At the systemic level of analysis, a web of rigid alliances and interlocking war plans quickly spread the fighting from one end of the Continent to the other. During the decade before Franz Ferdinand's assassination, European military alignments had become polarized, pitting the Triple Alliance of Germany, Austria-Hungary, and the Ottoman Empire against the Triple Entente of France, Britain, and Russia. Once Russia mobilized in response to Austria's attack on Serbia, alliance commitments pulled one European great power after another into the war.

Another factor underlying the outbreak of the First World War was the rise of German power and the challenge it posed to the British. Although Germany did not become a unified country until 1871, it prospered and used its growing wealth to create an awesome military machine. As the leader of the Continent's foremost industrial and military power, Kaiser Wilhelm II proclaimed in 1898 that Germany had "great tasks outside the narrow boundaries of old Europe." Under the concept of *weltpolitik* (world policy), Germany began building a strong navy to command respect around the globe. Britain, alarmed by the threat this might present to its maritime interests, established formal ties with France and Russia. Convinced that the British, French, and Russians were trying to encircle Germany, Wilhelm sought more armaments and closer relations with Austria-Hungary.

Germany was not the only rising great power at the turn of the century. Russia was also expanding, and becoming a threat to Germany. The decline in power of the Austrian-Hungarian Empire, Germany's only ally, heightened Berlin's anxieties. Hence Germany reacted strongly to Archduke Ferdinand's assassination. Confident that a short, localized, and victorious Balkan war would shore up

Austria-Hungary and weaken Russia's influence in Europe, Wilhelm gave the Austrians a "blank check" to crush Serbia.

Germany's unconditional support for Austria-Hungary proved to be a serious miscalculation, as it solidified the bonds between France and Russia, the two allied powers on Germany's western and eastern borders. Under the so-called Schlieffen Plan, Germany's generals had long based their military preparations on the premise that in the event of war with both France and Russia, German troops would first defeat the French and then turn against the larger but slower-moving Russian army. The quickest way to crush the French, they reasoned, was to swing through neutral Belgium in a vast arcing movement and attack France from the north, where its defenses were the weakest. But when the Germans stormed through Belgium, Britain entered the war on the side of France and Russia. Recognizing the magnitude of the unfolding catastrophe, British foreign secretary Sir Edward Grey lamented: "The lamps are going out all over Europe; we shall not see them lit again in our lifetime."

The Consequences of World War I

Click on History of World Politics to access an interactive map illustrating the geographical consequences of World War I and for related critical thinking questions.

World War I transformed the face of Europe. In its wake, three empires—the Austrian-Hungarian, Russian, and Ottoman (Turkish)—collapsed, and in their place the independent states of Poland, Czechoslovakia, and Yugoslavia emerged. In addition, the countries of Finland, Estonia, Latvia, and Lithuania were born (see Map 4.1). The war also contributed to the overthrow of the Russian czar in 1917 by the Bolsheviks, a change in government and ideology that would have consequences for another 70 years.

World War I evoked revulsion for war and theories of political realism that justified armaments, secret alliances, and power politics. The staggering human and material costs of the previous four years led many of the delegates to the 1919 peace conference convened at Versailles, outside Paris, to reevaluate their convictions about statecraft. The time was ripe for a new approach to building world order. Disillusioned with realism, many turned to liberalism for guidance on how to manage the global future.

The decade following World War I was the high point of liberal idealism. Woodrow Wilson's ideas about world order, as expressed in his January 1917 "Fourteen Points" speech, were anchored in a belief that by reordering the international system according to liberal principles, the Great War (as World War I was then called) would be "the war to end all wars." Wilson's chief proposal was to construct a League of Nations that allegedly would guarantee the independence and territorial integrity of all states. His other recommendations included strengthening international law, settling territorial claims on the basis of self-determination, and promoting democracy, disarmament, and free trade.

However, once the delegates to the peace conference began their work, the knives of parochial national interest began whittling away at the liberal philosophy underpinning Wilson's proposals. Many European leaders had been offended by the pontificating American president. "God was content with Ten Commandments," growled Georges Clemenceau, the cynical French prime minister. "Wilson must have fourteen."

MAP 4.1

Territorial Changes in Europe following World War I

World War I redrew the boundaries of Europe. The map on the left shows state boundaries on the eve of the war in 1914, as well as the members of the two major opposing coalitions that formed. After the war, the victors met at Versailles in France and drafted a punitive peace settlement that stripped vast territories from the defeated German and Austrian-Hungarian Empires as well as from the western front of the Russian Empire, which had been superseded in 1917 by the Union of Soviet Socialist Republics (USSR). The map on the right shows the new borders in 1920, with the nine new states that emerged from the war.

SOURCE: From *Strategic Atlas, Comparative Geopolitics of the World's Powers,* revised edition, by Gerard Chaliand and Jean-Pierre Ragau. Copyright © 1990 by Gerard Chaliand and Jean-Pierre Rageau. Reprinted by permission of HarperCollins Publishers, Inc.

As negotiations at the conference proceeded, hard-boiled power politics prevailed. Ultimately, the delegates were only willing to support those elements in the Fourteen Points that served their national interests. After considerable wrangling, Wilson's League of Nations was written into the peace treaty with Germany as the first of 440 articles. The rest of the treaty was punitive, aimed at stripping the country of its great-power status. Similar treaties were later forced upon Austria-Hungary and Germany's other wartime allies.

The Treaty of Versailles grew out of a desire for retribution. In brief, Germany's military was drastically cut; it was forbidden to possess heavy artillery, military aircraft, or submarines, and its forces were banned from the Rhineland. Germany also lost territory in the west to France and Belgium, in the south to the new state of Czechoslovakia, and in the east to the new states of Poland and Lithuania. Overseas, Germany lost all its colonies. Finally, in the most humiliating clause of the treaty, Germany was assigned responsibility for the war and charged with paying reparations for the damages. On learning of the treaty's harsh provisions, the exiled German kaiser is said to have declared that "the war to end wars has resulted in a peace to end peace."

The Second World War

Germany's defeat in the First World War and its humiliation under the Treaty of Versailles did not extinguish its hegemonic aspirations. On the contrary, they intensified them. Thus conditions were ripe for the second great-power war of the twentieth century, which pitted the Axis trio of Germany, Japan, and Italy against an unlikely "grand alliance" of four great powers who united despite their incompatible ideologies—communism in the case of the Soviet Union and democratic capitalism in the case of Britain, France, and the United States.

The world's fate hinged on the outcome of this massive effort to defeat the Axis. The Allied powers achieved success, but at a terrible cost: 53 million people died during six years of gruesome fighting (see Murray and Millett 2000). To understand the origins of this grisly conflict, we will once again examine how causal factors operating at different levels of analysis fit into a time sequence.

The Causes of World War II

Following Germany's capitulation in 1918, a democratic constitution was drafted by a constituent assembly meeting in the city of Weimar. Many Germans had little enthusiasm for the Weimar Republic. Not only was the new government linked in their minds to the humiliating Versailles Treaty, but it also suffered from the 1923 French occupation of the industrial Ruhr district, various political rebellions, and the ruinous economic collapse of 1929. By the parliamentary elections of 1932, over half of the electorate supported extremist parties that disdained democratic governance. The largest of these was the Nazi, or National Socialist German Workers party.

On January 30, 1933, the Nazi leader, Adolf Hitler, was appointed chancellor of Germany. Less than a month later, the Reichstag (Parliament) building burned down under mysterious circumstances. Hitler used the fire to justify an emergency edict allowing him to suspend civil liberties and move against communists and other political adversaries. Once all meaningful parliamentary opposition had been eliminated, Nazi legislators passed an enabling act that suspended the constitution and granted Hitler dictatorial power.

In his 1924 book *Mein Kampf* ("My Struggle"), Hitler urged Germany to recover territories taken by the Treaty of Versailles, absorb Germans living in neighboring lands, and colonize Eastern Europe. During his first year in power, however, he cultivated a pacific image, signing a nonaggression pact with Poland in 1934. The following year, the goals originally outlined in *Mein Kampf* climbed to the top of Hitler's foreign policy agenda: In 1935, he repudiated the military clauses of the Versailles Treaty; in 1936, he ordered troops into the demilitarized Rhineland; in March 1938 he annexed Austria; and in September 1938, he demanded control over the Sudetenland, a region of Czechoslovakia containing ethnic Germans (see Map 4.2). To address the Sudeten German question, a conference was convened in Munich, attended by Hitler, British prime minister Neville Chamberlain, and leaders of France and Italy (ironically, Czechoslovakia was not invited). Convinced that **appeasement** would halt further German expansionism, Chamberlain and the others agreed to Hitler's demands.

• **appeasement**
a strategy of making concessions to another state in the hope that, satisfied, it will not make additional claims.

Instead of satisfying Germany, appeasement encouraged Hitler to press for further revisions in the international status quo. He was joined in this effort by Japan and Italy. The former invaded Manchuria in 1931 and China proper in 1937; the latter attacked Ethiopia in 1935 and Albania in 1939. Furthermore, both Germany and Italy intervened in the Spanish civil war on the side of the fascists, headed by General Francisco Franco.

These acts of aggression paved the way for the century's second massive war. After Germany occupied the rest of Czechoslovakia in March 1939, Britain and France formed an alliance to protect the next likely victim, Poland. They also opened negotiations with Moscow in hopes of enticing the Soviet Union to join the alliance. Then, on August 23, 1939, Hitler and the Soviet leader Joseph Stalin stunned the world by signing a nonaggression pact. Certain that the Western democracies would not intervene without Soviet assistance, Hitler invaded Poland on September 1, 1939. Britain and France, honoring their pledge to defend the Poles, declared war on Germany two days later.

The war expanded rapidly. Hitler next turned his forces loose on the Balkans, North Africa, and westward. Powerful mechanized German units invaded Norway and marched through Denmark, Belgium, Luxembourg, and the Netherlands. They swept around France's defensive barrier, the Maginot line, and forced the British to evacuate an expeditionary force from the French beaches at Dunkirk. Paris itself fell in June 1940, and in the months that followed, the German air force pounded Britain in an attempt to force it into submission. Instead of invading Britain, in June 1941 Nazi troops attacked the Soviet Union, Hitler's former ally.

Germany's military successes provided an opportunity for Japan to move against British, French, and Dutch colonies in Asia, with the aim of replacing Western influence with a Greater East Asian Co-Prosperity Sphere under Tokyo's leadership. Japan followed its earlier conquests of Manchuria and eastern China with pressure on the Vichy French government to allow Japanese military bases in Indochina (now Vietnam, Laos, and Cambodia), from which the vital petroleum and mineral resources of Southeast Asia could be threatened. Concerned that the United States would try to thwart its ambitions, Japan launched a surprise attack on the U.S. naval base at Pearl Harbor, Hawaii, on December 7, 1941. Almost immediately, Germany declared war on the United States. Over the next six months, Japan occupied the Philippines, Malaya, Burma, and the Dutch East Indies (now Indonesia). The military challenges posed by the Japanese and

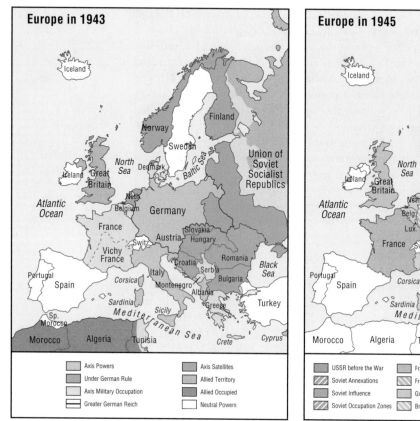

MAP 4.2
World War II Redraws the Map of Europe

The Axis coalition, composed of Germany, Italy, and Japan, sought to conquer and divide the world and almost succeeded. The map on the left shows the height of German expansion in 1943, when it occupied Europe from the Atlantic Ocean and Baltic Sea to the gates of Moscow in the Soviet Union. The map on the right shows the new configuration of Europe after the "Grand Coalition" of Allied forces—Great Britain, the United States, and the Soviet Union—defeated the Axis' bid for supremacy. The Allies partitioned Germany into four sections occupied by British, French, Russian, and American troops, and carved out other territorial changes that returned to the Soviet Union most of the land that it had lost at the end of World War I. Later, Germany was restructured into two independent countries, the Federal Republic of Germany (West Germany) and the German Democratic Republic (East Germany), which united after the Cold War.

SOURCE: Europe in 1945 from *Strategic Atlas, Comparative Geopolitics of the World's Powers,* revised edition, by Gerard Chaliand and Jean-Pierre Rageau. Copyright © 1990 by Gerard Chaliand and Jean-Pierre Ragau. Reprinted by permission of HarperCollins Publishers, Inc.

Topham/Image Works

The Rise of Hitler and German Nationalism In the 1930s the ideologies of national socialism and fascism—belief systems that regarded the state as supreme, justified dictatorship, and mobilized society for aggression—took root in Germany and Italy. Adolf Hitler's propaganda experts staged dramatic political rallies to glorify the Führer (leader), condemn the Jews, and call for the acquisition of Lebensraum (living space) for the German race.

Germans ended U.S. **isolationism,** enabling President Franklin Roosevelt to forge a coalition with Britain and the Soviet Union to oppose the Axis powers.

    The proximate cause of the war lies at the individual level of analysis. Adolf Hitler's truculent personality and aggressive schemes triggered the Second World War. Other more remote factors exerted significant impacts as well. At the state level of analysis, hypernationalism, domestic economic crises, and the demise of democratic governance in Germany provided an environment where Hitler could rise to power (Van Evera 1990–91). In addition, a belief in the dominance of defense over offense held by military establishments that had experienced the First World War made some states complacent in the face of German rearmament. Governments who remembered the rapid escalation of events during the summer of 1914 were also hesitant to respond to German actions in ways that might precipitate an upward spiral of conflict. Recalling the trauma produced by World War I, appeasement seemed preferable to confrontation.

    Finally, at the systemic level of analysis, the vindictive peace settlement constructed at Versailles, U.S. isolationism, and the failure of the League of Nations were crucial factors in explaining the outbreak of the Second World War. Unlike in the aftermath of the Napoleonic Wars, when delegates to the Congress of

• **isolationism**
a policy of withdrawing from active participation with other actors in world affairs and instead concentrating state efforts on managing internal affairs.

Vienna gave France a stake in the new world order, the Versailles Treaty aggravated relations between victor and vanquished. With the United States retreating into isolationism and the League of Nations unable to deter aggression, France and Britain had difficulty coordinating their approaches to Germany. While France wanted to restrain Germany, it was unwilling to act without British support. Britain, in contrast, saw appeasement as the way to prevent a new round of bloodshed with Germany. Meanwhile, Japan saw in Germany's initial military victories an opportunity to expand its control over Chinese territory and move against British, French, and Dutch colonies in Southeast Asia.

The Consequences of World War II

Click on History of World Politics to access an interactive map illustrating the geographical consequences of World War II and for related critical thinking exercises.

By May 1945, Germany lay in ruins. Three months later, the U.S. atomic bombing of Hiroshima and Nagasaki forced Japan to surrender. The Allied victory over the Axis redistributed power and reordered borders. The Soviet Union absorbed nearly six hundred thousand square meters of territory from the Baltic states of Estonia, Latvia, and Lithuania, and from Finland, Czechoslovakia, Poland, and Romania—recovering what Russia had lost in the 1918 Treaty of Brest-Litovsk. Poland, a victim of Soviet expansionism, was compensated with land taken from Germany. Meanwhile, Germany was divided into occupation zones that eventually provided the basis for its partition into East and West Germany. Finally, pro-Soviet regimes assumed power throughout Eastern Europe (see Map 4.2). In the Far East, the Soviet Union took the four Kurile Islands (or Northern Territories) from Japan, and Korea was divided into Soviet and U.S. occupation zones at the thirty-eighth parallel.

With the defeat of the Axis, one global system ended, but the defining characteristics of the new system had not yet become clear. Although the United Nations was created to replace the old, discredited League of Nations, the management of world affairs still rested in the hands of the victors. Yet victory only magnified their distrust of one another's intentions. The "Big Three" leaders—Winston Churchill, Franklin Roosevelt, and Joseph Stalin—had met at the Yalta Conference in February 1945 to design a new world order, but the vague compromises they reached concealed political differences percolating below the surface. Following Germany's unconditional surrender, the Big Three (with the United States now represented by Harry Truman) met again in July 1945 at Potsdam. The meeting ended without agreement, and the façade of Allied unity began to crumble.

• **multipolar** an international system with more than two dominant power centers.

• **bipolar** an international system with two dominant power centers.

Perhaps the most important change in the structure of the international system engendered by the war was the shift from a **multipolar** to a **bipolar** distribution of power. Whereas significant military capabilities previously were spread among several great powers, now they were concentrated in the hands of two superpowers, the United States and the Soviet Union. Great Britain and France, exhausted by the war, fell from the apex of world power. Germany, Italy, and Japan, defeated in war, also slipped from the ranks of the great powers. Thus, as the French political sociologist Alexis de Tocqueville had foreseen over a century earlier, the Americans and Russians would hold sway over the destinies of half of mankind. In what eventually became known as the Cold War, the two giants began the third and last hegemonic struggle of the twentieth century.

The Cold War

Unparalleled in scope and unprecedented in destructiveness, the second great war of the twentieth century brought into being a system dominated by two superpowers, whose nuclear might far surpassed the military capabilities of the rest of the world. Out of these circumstances grew the conflict known as the Cold War, a competition between Washington and Moscow for hegemonic leadership.

The Causes and Evolutionary Course of the Cold War

The origins of the twentieth century's third struggle for world leadership are debated to this day because the historical evidence lends itself to different interpretations (see Gaddis 1997). Several possible causes stand out. The first is advanced by realism: The Cold War stemmed from discordant geostrategic interests. The preeminent status of the United States and the Soviet Union at the top of the international hierarchy made their rivalry inescapable. As direct competitors for global influence who presumed that gains by one side would yield losses for the other, they were mutually suspicious and relentlessly contentious.

A second interpretation holds that the Cold War was simply an extension of the superpowers' mutual disdain for each other's economic beliefs and political system. American animosity toward the Soviet Union arose during the 1917 Bolshevik revolution in Russia, which brought to power a government that embraced the radical ideas of Karl Marx. U.S. fears of Marxism led it to adopt an ideology of anticommunism and embark on a crusade to contain Soviet influence. Under what was popularly known as the **domino theory,** U.S. policymakers assumed that the fall of one country to communism would trigger the fall of its neighbors, and in turn still other countries, until the entire world came under Soviet domination.

Soviet leaders were equally hostile to the United States. Believing that communism could not coexist with capitalism, they tried to stoke revolutionary fires around the world in an effort to encourage communist insurgencies. Thus when viewed through the lens of ideology, diametrically opposed systems of belief precluded compromise between the superpowers, locking them into a long, bitter struggle (see Controversy: Was Ideology the Primary Source of East–West Conflict?).

A third explanation sees the Cold War rooted in psychological factors, particularly in the superpowers' misperceptions of each other's motives. Mistrustful actors are prone to see virtue in their own behavior and malice in those of their adversaries. When such mirror images exist, hostility is inevitable (Bronfenbrenner 1971). Moreover, as perceptions of an adversary's duplicity become accepted, **self-fulfilling prophecies** can arise. Suspicious of the other side, national leaders become fixated upon alleged intrigues, exaggerate the susceptibility of their opponent to coercion, and assume that decisive action will yield a **bandwagon** of support. From this perspective, the Cold War was not simply a product of divergent interests. Nor was it merely attributable to incompatible ideologies. Instead, it was a conflict steeped in reciprocal anxieties bred by the way policymakers on both sides misinterpreted each other's intentions.

• **domino theory** a metaphor popular during the Cold War which predicted that if one state fell to communism, its neighbors would also fall in a chain reaction, like a row of falling dominoes.

• **self-fulfilling prophecy** the tendency for one's expectations to evoke behavior that helps to make the expectations become true.

• **bandwagon** the tendency for weak states to seek alliance with the strongest power, irrespective of that power's ideology or form of government, in order to increase security.

Was Ideology the Primary Source of East–West Conflict?

Cold War America was gripped by a "Great Fear" not simply of the Soviet Union but of communism. Senator Joseph McCarthy led an infamous hunt for communist sympathizers in government, Hollywood production companies blacklisted supposed communist sympathizers, and average American citizens were often required to take loyalty oaths at their offices. Everywhere communism became synonymous with treasonous, un-American activity. As the nuclear arms race escalated and the U.S. government took military action to contain the Soviet Union, its justification was almost always expressed in terms of ideology. The threat, it claimed, was that of an atheistic, inherently expansionistic communist system that challenged America's democratic freedoms. The Soviet Union also couched its Cold War rhetoric in terms of ideology, objecting to the imperialistic, capitalist system that they said Washington planned to impose on the whole world. Indeed, many Soviets echoed former leader Vladimir Lenin's prediction: "As long as capitalism and socialism exist, we cannot live in peace; in the end, either one or the other will triumph—a funeral dirge will be sung either over the Soviet Republic or over world capitalism."

Some would argue that fear of the other side's world dominance may have been more important in the Cold War than pure ideology. Both the American and the Soviet governments may have entered the Cold War to secure their relative power in the world order as much as to protect pure principles. After all, the United States and the Soviet Union had managed to transcend differing ideologies when they allied against the Axis powers in World War II. Following the war, a power vacuum created by the decline of Europe's traditional great powers drew them into conflict with each other, and as they competed, ideological justifications surfaced.

Ideologies fulfill a common human need to simplify and explain a complex and confusing world. But commitment to an ideology may at times cause hatred and hostility. Fervent believers in a particular ideology are prone to perceive other ideologies competitively—as challenges to the truth of their own core beliefs. Ideology can thus become an excuse for violence. Although scholars are still debating the causes of the Cold War, we need to ask whether it was, in fact, an ideological contest over ideas or a more general contest for power—in which the two governments proselytized about communism and capitalism to win peoples' hearts and minds.

What do you think? Was the Cold War really an ideological contest between international communism and democratic capitalism? ●

Additional factors beyond those rooted in conflicting interests, ideologies, and images contributed to the Soviet-American rivalry. To sort out their relative causal influence, scholars have found it useful to trace how the Cold War changed over its 42-year history. We can highlight these changes by dividing the Cold War into the three chronological phases shown in Figure 4.1.

Confrontation, 1945–1962. A brief period of wary friendship preceded the mutual antagonism that developed between the United States and the Soviet Union. In February 1946, Stalin gave a speech in which he spoke of "the inevitability of conflict with the capitalist powers." Shortly thereafter, George F. Kennan, then a diplomat in the American embassy in Moscow, sent to Washington his famous "long telegram" assessing the sources of Soviet conduct. Kennan's ideas were circulated widely in 1947, when the influential journal *Foreign Affairs* published his views in an article signed simply "X." In it, Kennan argued that

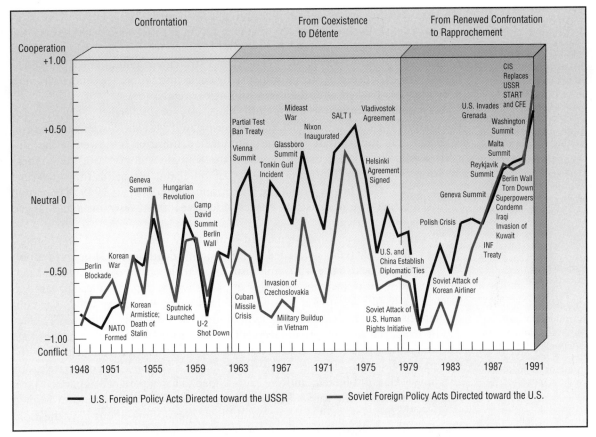

FIGURE 4.1
Key Events in the Evolution of U.S.–Soviet Relations, 1948–1991

The evolution of U.S.–Soviet relations during the Cold War displays a series of shifts between periods of conflict and cooperation. As this figure shows, each superpower's behavior toward the other tended to be reciprocal, and, for most periods prior to 1983, confrontation prevailed over cooperation.

Soviet leaders forever would feel insecure about their political ability to maintain power against forces both within Soviet society and in the outside world. Their insecurity would lead to an activist—and perhaps aggressive—Soviet foreign policy. However, the United States had the power to increase the strains under which the Soviet leadership would have to operate, which could lead to a gradual mellowing or final end of Soviet power. Hence, Kennan concluded: "In these circumstances it is clear that the main element of any United States policy toward the Soviet Union must be that of a long-term, patient but firm and vigilant containment of Russian expansive tendencies" (Kennan 1947).

Soon thereafter, President Harry S. Truman made Kennan's assessment the cornerstone of American postwar foreign policy. Alarmed by domestic turmoil in Turkey and Greece, which he asserted was communist inspired, Truman declared, "I believe that it must be the policy of the United States to support free peoples

• **Truman Doctrine**
the declaration by
President Harry S.
Truman that U.S.
foreign policy would
use intervention to
support peoples who
allied with the United
States against external
subjugation.

• **containment** a
strategy to prevent
another state from
using force to expand
its sphere of influence.

• **peaceful
coexistence** Soviet
leader Nikita
Khrushchev's 1956
doctrine that war
between capitalist and
communist states is not
inevitable and that
interbloc competition
could be peaceful.

• **détente** a strategy
of relaxing tensions
between adversaries to
reduce the possibility
of war.

who are resisting attempted subjugation by armed minorities or by outside pressures." Eventually known as the **Truman Doctrine,** this statement defined the grand strategy that the United States would pursue for the next 40 years, over Kennan's objections (1967, 361). The grand strategy of **containment** sought to prevent the expansion of Soviet influence by encircling the Soviet Union with military alliances backed with the threat of nuclear retaliation.

A seemingly endless series of Cold War crises soon followed. They included the communist coup d'état in Czechoslovakia in 1948; the Soviet blockade of West Berlin in June of that year; the communist acquisition of power on the Chinese mainland in 1949; the outbreak of the Korean War in 1950; the Chinese invasion of Tibet in 1950; and a series of on-again, off-again Taiwan Straits crises. The Soviets finally broke the U.S. atomic monopoly in 1949. Thereafter, the risks of massive destruction of each side necessitated restraint and changed the terms of their rivalry.

Because the Soviet Union remained strategically inferior to the United States, Nikita Khrushchev (who succeeded Stalin upon his death in 1953) pursued a policy of **peaceful coexistence** with capitalism. Nonetheless, the Soviet Union at times cautiously sought to increase its power in places where opportunities appeared to exist. As a result, the period following Stalin's death saw many Cold War confrontations, with Hungary, Cuba, Egypt, and Berlin becoming flash points.

In 1962, the surreptitious placement of Soviet missiles in Cuba set the stage for the greatest test of the superpowers' capacity to manage their disputes—the Cuban Missile Crisis. The superpowers stood eyeball to eyeball. Fortunately, one (the Soviet Union) blinked, and the crisis ended. This experience expanded both side's awareness of the suicidal consequences of a nuclear war, and transformed the way Washington and Moscow would henceforth think about how the Cold War should be waged.

From Coexistence to Détente, 1963–1978. The looming threat of mutual destruction, in conjunction with the growing parity of American and Soviet military capabilities, made coexistence or nonexistence appear to be the only alternatives for political leaders in Washington and Moscow. At the American University commencement exercises in 1963, U.S. president John F. Kennedy warned that the superpowers were "caught up in a vicious and dangerous cycle in which suspicion on one side breeds suspicion of the other and new weapons beget counterweapons." He went on to signal a shift in how the United States hoped thereafter to interact with the Soviet Union, which elicited a positive response from the Kremlin.

Another step forward was taken following Richard Nixon's election in 1968. Coached by his national security adviser, Henry A. Kissinger, President Nixon initiated a new approach to dealing with the Soviet Union that he labeled **détente.** The Soviets also adopted this term to describe their policies toward the United States, and relations between the two countries moved in a more constructive direction. Arms control stood at the center of their activities. The Strategic Arms Limitation Talks (SALT), initiated in 1969, sought to restrain the threatening, expensive, and spiraling arms race by limiting the deployment of antiballistic missiles. As Figure 4.1 shows, cooperative interaction became more commonplace than hostile relations. Visits, cultural exchanges, trade agreements, and joint technological ventures replaced threats, warnings, and confrontations.

From Renewed Confrontation to Rapprochement, 1979–1991. Despite the careful nurturing of détente, it did not endure. When the Soviet Union invaded Afghanistan in 1979, President Jimmy Carter defined the situation as "the most serious strategic challenge since the Cold War began." He promptly declared America's willingness to use military force to protect its access to oil supplies from the Persian Gulf. In addition, he suspended grain exports to the Soviet Union, and attempted to organize a worldwide boycott of the 1980 Moscow Olympics.

Relations deteriorated dramatically thereafter. Carter's successor in the White House, Ronald Reagan, described the Soviet Union as "the focus of evil in the modern world." His counterparts in the Kremlin (first Yuri Andropov and then Konstantin Chernenko) responded with equally scathing criticisms of the United States. As the rhetorical salvos became increasingly harsh, the arms race resumed. Some American leaders hinted that a nuclear war could be "winnable," and advocated a military strategy that included the threat of a "first use" of nuclear weapons in the event of a conventional attack by the Soviets. Under the **Reagan Doctrine** the United States pledged support for anticommunist insurgents who sought to overthrow Soviet-supported governments in Afghanistan, Angola, and Nicaragua.

• **Reagan Doctrine** a pledge of U.S. backing for anti-communist insurgents who sought to overthrow Soviet-supported governments.

By 1985, superpower relations had deteriorated to the point that Mikhail Gorbachev, the new Soviet leader, characterized the situation as "explosive." Further complicating matters for the Soviet Union, its economy was buckling under the weight of exorbitant military expenditures, estimated at roughly a quarter of the country's gross domestic product. Faced with economic stagnation and declining civic morale, Gorbachev implemented a series of far-reaching domestic reforms to promote democratization and a market system. Meanwhile, in an effort to reduce the suffocating level of military expenditures, he sought a **rapprochement** or reconciliation with the West, and proclaimed his desire to end the Cold War. "We realize that we are divided by profound historical, ideological, socioeconomic, and cultural differences," he noted in 1987 during his first visit to the United States. "But the wisdom of politics today lies in not using those differences as a pretext for confrontation, enmity, and the arms race." Soviet spokesperson Georgi Arbatov elaborated, informing the United States that "we are going to do a terrible thing to you—we are going to deprive you of an enemy."

• **rapprochement** in diplomacy, a policy seeking to reestablish normal relations between enemies.

Surprisingly, the Soviets ended their aid to Cuba, withdrew from Afghanistan, and announced unilateral reductions in military spending. Gorbachev also agreed to two new disarmament agreements: the Strategic Arms Reduction Treaty (START) for deep cuts in strategic arsenals, and the Conventional Forces in Europe (CFE) Treaty to reduce the Soviet presence in Europe. Finally, to nearly everyone's astonishment, Moscow acquiesced to the disbanding of the Warsaw Pact and the reunification of Germany. In 1989, the Berlin Wall was dismantled. Long a stark, frightening symbol of the division between East and West, its removal heralded the end of the Cold War. Its peaceful conclusion suggested something quite different from the twentieth century's two world wars: Hegemonic struggles are not doomed to end in violence; sometimes great-power rivals can reconcile their differences without resorting to global war.

The Consequences of the Cold War

Though locked in a geostrategic rivalry exacerbated by antagonistic ideologies and mutual misperceptions, the United States and the Soviet Union avoided a fatal showdown. In accepting the devolution of their empire, Soviet leaders made the most dramatic peaceful retreat from power in history. The end of the Cold War altered the face of world affairs in profound and diverse ways. With the dissolution of the Soviet Union in 1991, no immediate great-power challenger confronted American hegemonic leadership. However, a host of new security threats emerged, ranging from rogue states to terrorist networks. As the turbulent twentieth century wound down, the simple Cold War world of clearly defined adversaries gave way to a shadowy world of elusive foes.

The Future of Great-Power Politics

Rapid, unanticipated changes in world politics often create uncertainty about the global future. To optimists, the tides of change that swept across the world following the collapse of communism signified "the end of mankind's ideological evolution and the universalization of Western liberal democracy as the final form of government" (Fukuyama 1989). To pessimists, these sea changes suggested not history's end, but its resumption. Both groups recognized that Cold War bipolarity had been superseded by a **unipolar** configuration of power that presented new and difficult challenges.

• **unipolar** an international system with one dominant power center.

America's Unipolar Moment

Unipolarity refers to the concentration of power in a single preponderant state. At present, the United States stands alone at the summit of the international hierarchy. It is the only country with the military, economic, and cultural assets to be a decisive player in any part of the world it chooses (Krauthammer 1991). Its military is not just stronger than anybody's—it is stronger than everybody's, with defense expenditures in 2004 estimated to exceed all other countries combined. Complementing America's military might is its economic strength. With 4.7 percent of global population, the United States accounts for more than 31 percent of global gross domestic product, 36 percent of global defense spending, and 40 percent of global spending on research and development (Emmott 2002, 4). What is more, America wields enormous influence as a source of popular culture and the hub of global communications.

This rare confluence of military, economic, and cultural power gives the United States an extraordinary ability to shape the global future. Such overwhelming power can easily tempt national leaders to act in a **unilateral** manner. Rather than working in concert with others, independent action may seem attractive to a strong, self-confident nation worried about being hamstrung by quib-

• **unilateral** a strategy that relies on independent, self-help behavior in foreign policy.

A New Global Hegemon? China is a rising power that many expect to become the world's richest country. In the West this has generated the fear that as China's economic power increases, it will translate its wealth into military power. Shown here are Chinese Peoples' Liberation Army soldiers marching with bayoneted rifles while performing official honor guard duties at a welcoming ceremony in Beijing.

bling lesser powers. Whereas other countries must address international problems through global organizations to be effective, the United States has the capability to "go it alone,"even in the face of strident criticism from abroad.

Unilateralism has its costs, however. Acting alone may appear expedient, but it erodes international support on issues, such as combating global terrorism, where the United States needs cooperation from others. Overwhelming power, observes former secretary of state Henry Kissinger (2001), "evokes nearly automatically a quest by other societies to achieve a greater voice . . . and to reduce the relative position of the strongest." If Washington neglects the politics of compromise and consensus-building, it will find itself isolated at the very time that it requires friends.

While the United States may hold an unrivaled position in the world today, unipolarity will not endure. No state has maintained primacy indefinitely. As Map 4.3 and Figure 4.2 show, long-term economic trajectories based on differential national growth rates point to a world in which China, a united Europe, and

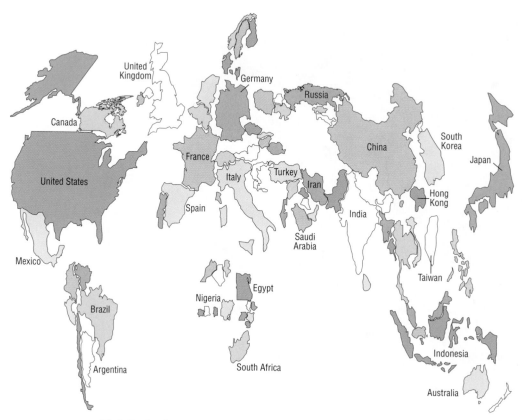

MAP 4.3
Emerging Centers of Power in the Twenty-First Century

To estimate which countries are the most powerful and which are relatively weak, analysts frequently rely on the size of states' economies, because it predicts the power potential of each state (that is, their relative capacity to project power and exercise global influence). This map displays the proportionate economic clout of the leading great powers (measured by purchasing power parities), showing the United States, China, Japan, India, and several European countries as today's economic powerhouses. Figure 4.2 projects their probable rank order by the year 2020, and suggests that the world will look quite different from today, with China at the apex of economic power.
SOURCE: *The Economist* (2002), 24.

perhaps other great powers, will challenge American financial preeminence within the next two decades (see Nye 2002a; Wallerstein 2002). At the same time, the United States will find it costly to maintain military dominance. Aside from major deployments in Afghanistan and Iraq, U.S. forces are positioned along a belt of global instability reaching from the Korean Peninsula through the Gulf of Aden to Latin America. Imperial overstretch, the gap between internal resources and external commitments, has bedeviled every leading great power (Kennedy 1987). Throughout history, hegemons repeatedly have defined their security interests more broadly than other states only to slip from the pinnacle of power by reaching

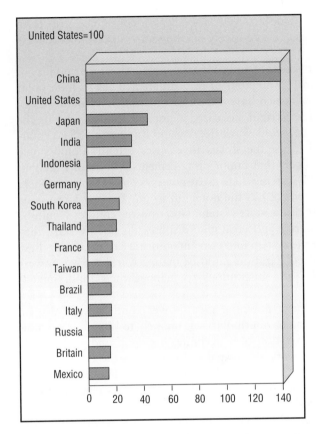

United States=100

China
United States
Japan
India
Indonesia
Germany
South Korea
Thailand
France
Taiwan
Brazil
Italy
Russia
Britain
Mexico

0   20   40   60   80   100   120   140

FIGURE 4.2
Projection of the Fifteen Largest Global Economies by 2020

Using purchasing power parities (PPPs) to account for differences in countries' price levels, the World Bank forecasts the probable size of the largest economies. The projections show that the rank order of these economies by 2020 will be substantially different from today's. The political and military consequences are not predicted, but long-cycle theory postulates that the economic changes will breed political and even military conflict.

SOURCE: McGranahan (1995), 59; see also World Bank (2002b).

beyond their grasp. "The problem in defense spending," former U.S. president Dwight Eisenhower concluded, "is to figure out how far you should go without destroying from within what you are trying to defend from without."

From Unipolarity to Multipolarity?

Many scholars and policymakers believe that today's unipolar system will be replaced by a multipolar one. Some of the states frequently mentioned as potential members of a future multipolar system include the United States, China, the European Union, Japan, and a reinvigorated Russia. Because multipolar systems include several comparatively equal great powers, they are complex. When we take into account the interplay of military and economic factors, such systems are also fraught with uncertainty. Differentiating friend from foe becomes difficult when allies in military security may be rivals in trade relationships.

Predicting what cleavages and partnerships will develop among the great powers in a twenty-first-century multipolar system will be complicated because "it is hard to locate a main axis of conflict" (Jervis 1992). Conflict could emerge between any pair of great powers, but it may be restricted to one sphere of activity. For example, the United States, Japan, and China exhibit conflict in their commercial relations but nevertheless also display continuing efforts to manage their security relations collaboratively (as shown by their cooperation in fighting terrorism).

Such cross-cutting axes of conflict and cooperation will affect the stability of any future multipolar system. Throughout history different types of multipolar systems have existed, some of which have exhibited more stability than others. The most unstable have possessed rigid, polarized alignments, such as during the period prior to the outbreak of World War I (Kegley and Raymond 1994). Polarized systems are dangerous because they focus adversaries' attention on a single threat, thus making it more likely that minor disagreements will become magnified into larger tests of will. A system where great powers compete in one sphere of activity but cooperate elsewhere has the potential to prevent any given issue from polarizing the members of the state system. Great-power conflict would be frequent, but as long as security and economic disputes do not overlap, they would not necessarily divide the system into two antagonistic camps. Under these circumstances, the danger of polarization could be managed if the great powers developed international rules and institutions to manage their fluid, mixed-motive relationships.

Establishing rules to manage potential great-power conflicts will also be important because the transition to multipolarity is unlikely to be smooth. Scholars have found that the combination of a declining hegemon and an unstable hierarchy among the major powers are related to increases in the occurrence of warfare (Geller and Singer 1998). Historically, interstate hostilities have tended to flare up when the principal defender of the status quo loses its relative advantage over other major powers.

Of course, we have no way of knowing whether the future will resemble the past history of multipolar systems. Patterns and practices can change, and it is possible for policymakers to learn from previous mistakes and avoid repeating them. However, we can anticipate that the future will be largely in the hands of the great powers, because "powerful states make the rules" (Keohane and Nye 2001a). What kinds of rules and institutions will they create, and what impact will they have on other states? To explore these questions, in Chapter 5 we will turn our attention from the rich, powerful, and commercially active great powers at the center of the world system and examine the poorer, weaker, and economically dependent states that lie along its periphery.

Chapter Summary

- Great powers possess enormous military and economic capabilities relative to other states. As a result, they play a leading role in world politics, particularly on international security issues.
- Change is endemic to world politics, but one constant stands out: great-power rivalry. World politics tends to be reordered following hegemonic wars among the great powers. In their aftermath, the victors tend to create new international rules and institutions in an effort to prevent a repetition of these horrific conflicts.

- Single-factor theories are inadequate for explaining great-power war. Such conflicts involve causal mechanisms operating on multiple levels of analysis, and a fusion of proximate causes with deeper, more remote structural causes.
- The twentieth century experienced three great-power struggles for world leadership: World Wars I and II, and the Cold War.
- The proximate causes of World War I were the assassination of Franz Ferdinand, and the series of reactive, fatalistic decisions made by political leaders of Austria, Germany, and Russia. Deeper underlying causes included the rise of nationalism in southeastern Europe, the growth of German power, the creation of rigid mobilization plans, and the development of a polarized system of military alliances.
- The proximate causes of World War II can be found in Adolf Hitler's voracious appetite for conquest and domination, and the failed efforts by the internally divided Western democracies to appease the Nazi dictator. The remote causes included German resentment over the Treaty of Versailles, the rise of hypernationalistic ideologies within the Axis countries, the collapse of the international economic system, and the U.S. foreign policy of isolationism.
- The advent of nuclear weapons transformed world politics by radically changing the role that threats of force would henceforth play in international bargaining.
- Scholars disagree about the causes of the Cold War. Some of them see it as the result of a conflict of interests between the United States and the Soviet Union, others point to ideological incompatibilities, and still others emphasize the superpowers' misperceptions of each other's motives.
- Several conspicuous patterns existed throughout the Cold War. While periods of intense conflict alternated with periods of relative cooperation, the United States and the Soviet Union consistently made avoidance of all-out war their highest priority. Reciprocal, action–reaction exchanges were also evident (friendly U.S. initiatives toward the Soviet Union were reciprocated in kind). Both rivals were also willing to disregard their respective ideologies whenever their perceived national interests rationalized such inconsistencies; for example, each backed allies with political systems antithetical to its own when the necessities of power politics seemed to justify doing so.
- Following the collapse of the Soviet Union in 1991, the United States emerged as the preponderant global power. However, many scholars believe that the current unipolar system will not persist. Factors such as uneven economic growth and imperial overstretch will alter the relative positions of the great powers and bring about a multipolar structure.

KEY TERMS

long-cycle theory
hegemon
appeasement
isolationism
multipolar
bipolar

domino theory
self-fulfilling prophecy
bandwagon
Truman Doctrine
containment
peaceful coexistence

détente
Reagan Doctrine
rapprochement
unipolar
unilateral

WHERE ON THE WORLD WIDE WEB?

The World War I Document Archive
http://www.lib.byu.edu/~rdh/wwi/

The World War I Military History List has assembled a group of primary documents from World War I. Read the treaties, scan personal reminiscences, see photos, and access links to other resources.

This chapter describes various factors that contributed to the onset of World War I. Some scholars assert that choices of individual German leaders who wanted to consolidate power led to war. Others claim that state-level factors, such as the rise of nationalism in southeastern Europe, were responsible. And finally, many point to the web of military alliances in Europe. After reading the documents in the archive, which factors do you think best explain the advent of World War I?

The Avalon Project—World War II
http://www.yale.edu/lawweb/avalon/wwii/wwii.htm

Yale Law School has ambitiously undertaken to collect and house digital documents relevant to the fields of law, history, economics, politics, diplomacy, and government. This site links you to documents relating to World War II.

As this chapter explains, the end of World War II generated uncertainty and mistrust. While visiting

the archive, read the text of the agreements reached at the Yalta Conference at which Roosevelt, Churchill, and Stalin tried to resolve territorial issues after World War II. Did the agreements reached at Yalta make the Cold War inevitable?

Cold War
http://www.cnn.com/SPECIALS/cold.war/

Learn more about the most recent great-power rivalry by exploring CNN's award-winning, comprehensive, Cold War website. Navigate interactive maps of the nuclear testing sites in the American Southwest. Learn more about the key players and then play an interactive game to see which Cold War players you recognize. Hear sound bites and match them to the statesman who made them. Tour Cold War capitals through 3-D images. See espionage weapons and hear real-life spy stories.

Senator Joe McCarthy
http://webcorp.com/mccarthy/

A multimedia site where students can see and hear the most famous speeches and hearings given by Joe McCarthy. This is an important site for contemporary students who are unaware of the fear of communism that permeated American society during the early years of the Cold War.

INFOTRAC® COLLEGE EDITION

Search for the following articles in the InfoTrac College Edition database.

Brooks, Stephen G., and William C. Wohlforth. "Power, Globalization, and the End of the Cold War: Reevaluating a Landmark Case for Ideas," *International Security* Winter 2000.

Howard, Michael. "The Great War," *The National Interest* Summer 2001.

Skidelsky, Robert. "Imbalance of Power (History of the Grand Alliance during World War II)," *Foreign Policy* March 2002.

Wallerstein, Immanuel. (2002). "The Eagle Has Crash Landed," *Foreign Policy* 131 (July/August): 60–68.

Waltz, Kenneth N. "Structural Realism after the Cold War," *International Security* Summer 2000.

For more articles, enter:

"cold war" in the Subject Guide.

"World War, 1914–1918" in the Subject Guide.

"World War, 1939–1945" in the Subject Guide.

ADDITIONAL CD-ROM RESOURCES

Click on History of World Politics to access additional resources related to this chapter.

CHAPTER 5

Rich and Poor in World Politics
The Plight of the Global South

A global human society based on poverty for many and prosperity for a few, characterized by islands of wealth surrounded by a sea of poverty, is unsustainable.

THABO MBEKI, president of South Africa

O n September 4, 1970, Chileans went to the polls to elect a new president. To almost everyone's surprise, the candidate who received the most votes was Salvadore Allende, a self-proclaimed Marxist who led a broad but fragile coalition known as Popular Unity. Although Allende consistently pledged to uphold civil liberties if elected, his victory appeared ominous to U.S. president Richard Nixon. Henry Kissinger, then-assistant to the president for National Security Affairs, warned that Argentina, Bolivia, and Peru might follow Chile in forming Marxist governments. Other members of the Nixon administration expressed alarm over the implications of Allende's triumph for U.S. businesses operating in Chile.

Known as a pragmatic politician, Salvadore Allende had served in the Chilean Senate for over two decades. Now, as the country's new president, he was in a position to address what he believed were structural problems within Chile's economy. To begin with, copper exports alone generated more than three-fourths of the country's foreign exchange, and 80 percent of the industry was owned by U.S.-based corporations. U.S. direct private investment in Chile amounted to $1.1 billion out of a total of $1.67 billion. Foreign corporations controlled nearly all of the communication and pharmaceutical industries, 60 percent of chemical production, and roughly half of the output of petroleum products. Chileans, Allende concluded, were not in command of their country's economy.

Among Allende's proposed reforms were nationalizing foreign-owned enterprises and placing critical sectors of the economy under state control. His proposals elicited stiff foreign and domestic opposition; rumors of plots against the government swirled through the capital. As he began implementing his policies, he came under increasing pressure. Frustrated that the Nixon administration and U.S. business interests were aiding his domestic opponents, Allende complained in a 1972 speech delivered before the UN General Assembly that Chile was the victim of foreign intervention. Outside powers, he charged, were attempting to "strangle the economy and paralyze the sale of copper . . . , and keep us from access to sources of international financing." Nine months later, following a series of crippling strikes, the Chilean military launched a coup d'etat that ended with Allende's death, bringing to a close more than four decades of uninterrupted constitutional government.

In the previous chapter we examined the strongest states within the international system, those with the economic and military capabilities to dominate everyone else. The experience of Chile during the Allende years raises important questions about those states that are not great powers. Does being a less wealthy and militarily mighty country place one's future in the hands of others? What accounts for the inequalities that currently divide humanity? Can anything be done to close the gap between the world's rich and poor?

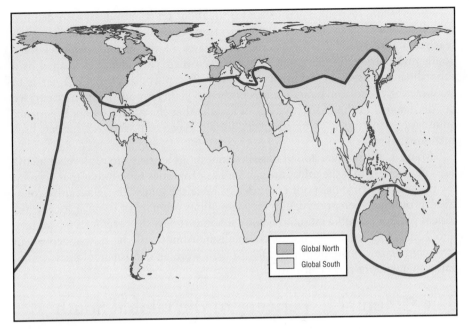

M A P   5 . 1
The Global North and Global South

The countries of the Global North are those that are wealthy, democratic, and technologically innovative, with declining birthrates and aging populations. In contrast, the countries in the Global South are home to 80 percent of the world's population, but the impoverished people living there possess only 15 percent of its wealth.

Global Inequalities

Earth is divided into two hemispheres, north and south, at the equator. This artificial line of demarcation is, of course, meaningless except for use by cartographers to chart distance and location on maps. However, this divide also represents a popular way of describing the inequalities that separate rich and poor states. By and large, these two groups are located on either side of the equator (see Map 5.1).

Life for most people in the Northern Hemisphere is very different from that in the Southern Hemisphere. The disparities are profound, and in many places appear to be growing. The division in power and wealth between the states comprising the **Global North** and **Global South** poses problems for which solutions must be found if the world is to experience a peaceful future. As British prime minister Tony Blair warned: "One illusion has been shattered on September 11: that we [in the Global North] can have the good life . . . irrespective of the state of the rest of the world. . . . The dragon's teeth are planted in the fertile soil of wrongs unrighted, of disputes left to fester for years, of failed states, of poverty and deprivation."

 Click on International Political Economy for an interactive version of this map and related critical thinking questions.

• **Global North** a term used to refer to the world's wealthy, industrialized countries located primarily in the Northern Hemisphere.

• **Global South** a term used to designate the less-developed countries located primarily in the Southern Hemisphere.

Poverty and inequality has existed throughout most periods of recorded history. But today the level of relative deprivation between rich and poor states has reached unprecedented proportions. The states in the less-developed Global South find themselves marginalized, with even their very identities shaped by a subordinate position in the global hierarchy. The purpose of this chapter is to examine the causes and consequences of the inequality among the more than two hundred states in the global system. Why is it that the great powers experience abundance while many other countries seem trapped in poverty? What has bred such inequality?

Many analysts begin addressing these questions at the systemic level of analysis. They believe that the interstate system has properties built into it that account for the inability of most poor countries to close the gap with the wealthy countries. From their perspective, current inequalities are part of a much longer historical pattern. To understand the Global South today, they recommend we take into consideration the legacy of **colonialism.** Almost all the now-independent sovereign states in the Southern Hemisphere were at one time colonies, subjugated by far more powerful states.

• **colonialism** the rule of a region by an external sovereign power.

The Colonial Experience of the Global South

• **Third World** a Cold War term to describe the developing countries of Africa, Asia, and Latin America.

During the Cold War, the term **Third World** was used to describe the economically less-developed states that tended to share a colonial past. They were contrasted with the so-called **First World,** composed of the industrialized democracies in western Europe, North America, and Japan, and the **Second World,** which consisted of the Soviet Union and its allies. Today the communist countries comprising the former Second World have almost totally vanished, thus making the term *Third World* obsolete. Now the terms *Global North* (the wealthy countries located primarily in the Northern Hemisphere) and *Global South* (the less-developed countries in the Southern Hemisphere) are popular.

• **First World** the relatively wealthy industrialized countries that share a commitment to varying forms of democratic political institutions and developed market economies.

Although journalists, policymakers, and scholars frequently generalize about the Global South, considerable diversity exists within this group of states. For example, it includes low-income countries such as Ghana and Haiti, where a majority of the population works in subsistence agriculture; middle-income countries like Brazil and Malaysia, who produce manufactured goods; and a few countries like Kuwait and Qatar, where petroleum exports have generated incomes rivaling those of Global North countries.

• **Second World** during the Cold War, the group of countries, including the Soviet Union and its then-Eastern European allies, that shared a commitment to centrally planned economies.

Global South countries are diverse in other ways as well. Included among their ranks is Indonesia, an archipelago of more than seventeen thousand islands scattered throughout an oceanic expanse larger than the United States, and Burundi, a landlocked state slightly smaller than Maryland. Also included are India, with over one billion inhabitants, and Belize, with under three hundred thousand people. Aside from these geographic and demographic differences, Global South countries also vary politically and culturally, ranging from democratic Costa Rica to autocratic Burma.

Despite this diversity, most Global South countries in Africa, Asia, and Latin America share a set of common problems, which allow us to differentiate them from the countries in the Global North. As displayed in Map 5.2, the Global South is home to more than 85 percent of the world's people but commands less than 15 percent of its wealth. These countries are characterized by low productivity, high rates of population growth, and skewed patterns of income distribution, with large segments of their populations suffering from poverty, illiteracy, and ill health.

The emergence of the Global South as an identifiable group of states is a distinctly contemporary phenomenon. Although most Latin American countries were independent before World War II, not until then did the floodgates of decolonization first open. In 1947, Great Britain granted independence to India and Pakistan, after which **decolonization**—the freeing of colonial peoples from their dependent status—gathered speed. Since then, a profusion of new sovereign states has joined the global community, nearly all carved from the British, Spanish, Portuguese, Dutch, and French empires built under colonialism 400 years ago.

• **decolonization** the achievement of independence by countries that were once colonies of other states.

Today, the decolonization process is complete. However, colonialism's effects persist. Many of the ethnic conflicts now so prevalent in the Global South have colonial roots, as the imperial powers drew borders with little regard for the identities of the indigenous peoples. In addition, the poverty facing most Global South countries is partly a product of their imperial pasts, when they were exploited by European powers. Given colonialism's impact, let us briefly examine how it evolved over the course of the past six centuries.

The First Wave of European Imperialism

The first wave of European empire building began in the late fifteenth century, as the Dutch, English, French, Portuguese, and Spanish used their military power to conquer territories for commercial gain. As scientific innovations made the European explorers' adventures possible, merchants followed in their wake, "quickly seizing upon opportunities to increase their business and profits. In turn, Europe's governments perceived the possibilities for increasing their own power and wealth. Commercial companies were chartered and financed, with military and naval expeditions frequently sent out after them to ensure political control of overseas territories" (Cohen 1973).

The economic strategy underlying the relationship between colonies and colonizers during this era is known as **mercantilism**: an economic philosophy advocating government regulation of economic life to increase state power and security. Early mercantilists believed acquiring gold and silver increased power. Later mercantilists shifted their emphasis to building strong, self-sufficient economies by using royal decrees to launch new industries, subsidize strategically targeted enterprises, protect domestic producers from foreign competition through tariff barriers, and maintain a "favorable" balance of trade by increasing exports and curbing imports.

• **mercantilism** an economic strategy for accumulating state wealth and power by using governmental regulation to encourage exports and curtail imports.

To maximize national power and wealth, European leaders saw the conquest of foreign territory as a natural by-product of active government management of the economy. In addition to providing them with precious metals and other raw materials, colonies were untapped markets, which could be closed to commercial

GROSS NATIONAL INCOME

M A P 5 . 2
The Great North-South Divide in Wealth and Population

If the countries in the globe were redrawn to reflect the size of their economies and populations, as shown here, huge differences would be visible. Most of the wealth is in the Global North, and most of the people are in the Global South. If prevailing trends persist as expected, the disparities will continue to widen the existing division between rich and poor.

SOURCE: Adapted from *World Development Report 1999/2000:* by World Bank, Copyright © 2000 by the International Bank for Reconstruction and Development/The World Bank.

POPULATION

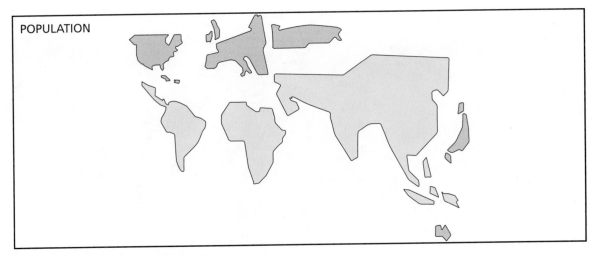

MAP 5.2
(Continued)

competition from other powers. By selling finished goods to their colonies under monopolistic conditions, it was thought that imperial powers could boost domestic employment and keep the profits from these sales at home.

By the end of the eighteenth century the European powers had spread themselves, although thinly, throughout virtually the entire world, but the colonial empires they had built now began to crumble. Britain's 13 North American colonies declared their independence in 1776, and most of Spain's possessions in South America won their freedom in the early nineteenth century. Nearly one hundred colonial relationships worldwide were terminated in the half-century ending in 1825 (Bergesen and Schoenberg 1980).

As the first wave of European colonization waned, belief in the mercantilist philosophy also declined. In 1776, the Scottish political economist Adam Smith published *The Wealth of Nations*, a vigorous critique of mercantilism that called for free trade. While Smith acknowledged that the state should be involved in defending the nation against external aggression, enforcing property rights, upholding contracts, and the like, he denied that it could be more efficient or innovative than an unregulated market. His arguments laid much of the intellectual foundation for **laissez-faire economics**. Henceforth European powers would continue to seek colonies, but the rationale for their imperial policies began to change.

• **laissez-faire economics** a body of thought emphasizing free markets with little governmental regulation.

The Second Wave of European Imperialism

Beginning in the 1870s and extending until the outbreak of World War I, a new wave of imperialism washed over the world as Europe, joined later by the United States and Japan, aggressively colonized new territories. The portion of the globe that Europeans controlled was one-third in 1800, two-thirds by 1878, and four-fifths by 1914 (Fieldhouse 1973, 3). As illustrated in Map 5.3, in the last 20 years of the nineteenth century Africa fell under the control of seven European powers

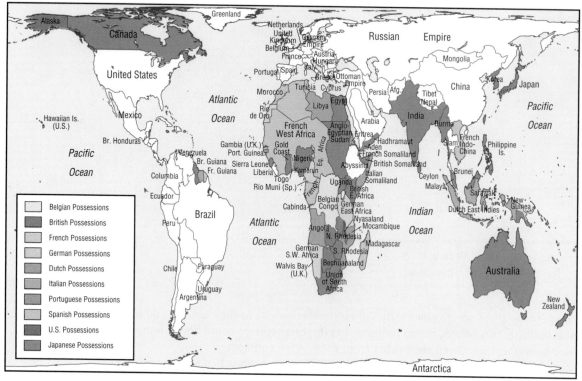

MAP 5.3
Global Imperialism, 1914

The ten major imperial powers competed for colonies throughout the globe in the present-day Global South, and on the eve of World War I their combined territories covered much of the world.

• **sphere of influence** the area dominated by a great power.

(Belgium, Britain, France, Germany, Italy, Portugal, and Spain), and in all of the Far East and the Pacific, only China, Japan, and Siam (Thailand) were not conquered. China, however, was divided into **spheres of influence** by the foreign great powers, and Japan itself occupied Korea and Formosa (Taiwan). Elsewhere, the United States acquired Puerto Rico and the Philippines in the 1898 Spanish–American War, extended its colonial reach westward to Hawaii, leased the Panama Canal Zone "in perpetuity" from the new state of Panama (an American creation), and exercised considerable control over several Caribbean islands, notably Cuba. The preeminent imperial power, Great Britain, in a single generation expanded its empire to cover one-fifth of the earth's land area. As British imperialists were proud to proclaim, it was an empire on which the sun never set.

Why did most of the great powers—and those that aspired to great-power status—engage in this expensive and often vicious competition to control other peoples and territories? What explains the new imperialism? The answers are rooted in economics and politics.

Economic Explanations for the New Imperialism. With the Industrial Revolution, capitalism grew, emphasizing the free market, private ownership of the

Bettman/CORBIS, Bettman/CORBIS

Karl Marx Challenges Imperialism Pictured on the left is the German philosopher Karl Marx (1818–1883), whose revolutionary economic theory argued that "the history of all hitherto existing society is the history of class struggle." Imperial conquest of colonial peoples could only be prevented, Marx warned, by humanity's shift from a capitalist to a socialist economy. Pictured on the right is the kind of imperialistic activity that provoked his wrath: ruthless, aggressive, and bent on acquiring property for profit, Britain's nineteenth-century imperial forces marched into battle to seize foreign territory.

means of production, and the accumulation of wealth. Theorists following Karl Marx, saw imperialism as the result of competition among capitalists for profitable overseas outlets for their surplus capital. One of them was the Soviet leader Vladimir Lenin. In his famous 1916 monograph *Imperialism, The Highest Stage of Capitalism,* Lenin argued that military expansion abroad was produced by the "monopoly stage of capitalism." He concluded that the only way to end imperialism was to abolish capitalism. Liberal economists, on the other hand, regarded the new imperialism not as a product of capitalism as such but rather as a result of maladjustments within the capitalist system, which could be corrected. What the two perspectives shared was the belief that economics explained the new imperialism: "The fundamental problem was the presumed material needs of advanced capitalist societies—the need for cheap raw materials to feed their growing industrial complexes, for additional markets to consume their rising levels of production, and for investment outlets to absorb their rapidly accumulating capital" (Cohen 1973). Thus, from both the Marxist and classical liberal perspectives, the material needs of capitalist societies explained their imperial drive.

Political Explanations for the New Imperialism. Not everyone agreed that economic motives underpinned the second wave of imperial expansion. Political factors were also identified. For example, in his influential 1902 book, *Imperialism,* J. A. Hobson argued that the jockeying for power and prestige between competitive empires had always characterized the great powers' behavior in the European balance-of-power system, and that imperialism through overseas expansion was simply a global extension of this inter-European competition for dominance.

Self-Determination and Decolonization

• **self-determination**
the doctrine that
people should be able
to determine the
government that will
manage their affairs.

Regardless of the causes underlying the second wave of imperialism, world opinion took an anti-imperial turn when the 1917 Versailles peace settlement that ended World War I embraced the principle of national **self-determination** advocated by U.S. president Woodrow Wilson. Self-determination meant that each distinct people would have the right to decide which authority would represent and rule them. Wilson and others who shared his liberal convictions believed that freedom of choice would lead to the creation of states and governments content with their territorial boundaries and therefore less inclined to make war. In practice, however, the attempt to redraw states' borders to separate nationality groups was applied almost exclusively to war-torn Europe, where six new states were created from the territory of the former Austrian-Hungarian Empire (Austria, Czechoslovakia, Hungary, Poland, Romania, and the ethnically divided Yugoslavia). Other territorial adjustments were also made in Europe, but the proposition that self-determination should be extended to Europe's overseas empires did not receive serious support.

Still, the colonial territories of the powers defeated in World War I were not simply parceled out among the victorious allies, as had typically happened in the past. Instead, the territories controlled by Germany and the Ottoman Empire were transferred under League of Nations auspices to countries that would govern them as "mandates" pending their eventual self-rule. The principle implicit in the mandate system was that "colonies were a trust rather than simply a property to be exploited and treated as if its peoples had no rights of their own" (Easton 1964). This set an important precedent for the negotiations after World War II, when territories of the defeated powers placed under the United Nations trusteeship system were not absorbed by others but were promised eventual self-rule, and support for self-determination gained momentum. The decolonization process accelerated in 1947, when the British relinquished political control of India and Pakistan. War eventually erupted between these newly independent states as each sought to gain control over disputed territory in Kashmir. Violence also broke out in Indochina and Algeria in the 1950s and early 1960s as the French sought to regain control over colonial territories they had held before World War II. Similarly, bloodshed followed closely on the heels of independence in the Congo when the Belgians granted their African colony independence in 1960, and it dogged the unsuccessful efforts of Portugal to battle the winds of decolonization that swept over Africa as the 1960s wore on.

Despite these political convulsions, decolonization for the most part was not only extraordinarily rapid but also remarkably peaceful. This may be explained by World War II's having sapped the economic and military vitality of many of the colonial powers. Regardless of the underlying cause, colonialism became less acceptable in a world increasingly dominated by rivalry between East and West. The Cold War competition for political allies and the fear of large-scale warfare gave the superpowers incentives to lobby jointly for the liberation of overseas empires. Decolonization "triumphed," as Inis Claude (1967) explains, "largely because the West [gave] priority to the containment of communism over the perpetuation of colonialism."

With colonialism in retreat, in 1960, Global South states took advantage of their growing numbers in the UN General Assembly to secure passage of the historic Declaration on the Granting of Independence to Colonial Countries and Peoples. "The General Assembly proclaimed that the subjection of any people to alien domination was a denial of fundamental human rights, contrary to the UN Charter, and an impediment to world peace and that all subject peoples had a right to immediate and complete independence. No country cast a vote against this anticolonial manifesto. . . . It was an ideological triumph" (Riggs and Plano 1994).

As the old order crumbled—and as the leaders in the newly emancipated territories discovered that freedom did not translate automatically into autonomy, economic independence, and domestic prosperity—the conflict between the rich Global North and the emerging states of the Global South began.

North and South Today: Worlds Apart

The Global South is sometimes described today as a "zone of turmoil" in large measure because, in contrast with the Global North where "peace, wealth, and democracy" prevail, most of the world's people live amidst "poverty, war, tyranny, and anarchy" (Singer and Wildavsky 1993). Although democracy has spread throughout much of the Global South since the 1980s, the commitments of some of these governments to regular elections and human rights are fragile. Furthermore, many Global South countries lack well-developed domestic market economies based on entrepreneurship and private enterprise. Differences in technological capabilities also separate North and South. Typically, Global South countries have been unable to evolve an indigenous technology appropriate to their own resources and have been dependent on powerful Global North multinational corporations (MNCs) to transfer technical know-how. This means that research and development expenditures are directed toward solutions of the Global North's problems, with technological advances seldom meeting the needs of the Global South. And in the information age, technology has not been distributed equally geographically: The highest density of computer connections to the Internet is in the Global North (see World Bank 2002a).

The fact that 85 percent of the world's population is poor is a reflection of these unequally distributed resources. As Table 5.1 shows, the data on the division between Global North and Global South point to brutal disparities and inequalities. This picture darkens even more when focus is shifted to the plight of the poorest in the low-income developing countries. More than 2.4 billion people (two-fifths of humanity) live in one of the 63 countries at the bottom of the global

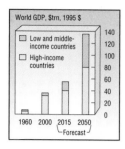

World GDP, $trn, 1995 $

- Low and middle-income countries
- High-income countries

1960 2000 2015 2050
└ Forecast ┘

TABLE 5.1

Two Worlds of Development: An International Class Divide

Characteristic	Developing Global South	Developed Global North
Number of countries	158	50
Population (millions)	5,154	903
Population density (people for each sq. km)	52	29
Women in policy positions (%)	6%	16%
Land area (thousands of sq. km)	101,491	32,315
GNI ($ billions)	$6,356	$24,891
Average growth rate of the domestic economy, 1990–2000	3.5%	2.5%
Foreign direct investment ($ millions)	$185,390	$727,130
Exports ($ billions)	$1,748	$6,350
Exports as percent of GDP	51%	32%
Average years of citizens' schooling	6.5	10
Internet secure servers	5,573	115,650
Life expectancy at birth	64	78
Percent of population living in cities	41%	79%
Percent of roads paved	32%	93%
Number of motor vehicles for each 1,000 people	60	610
Personal computers for each 10,000 people	20	393
Television sets for each 1,000 people	185	641
Mobile phones for each 1,000 people	51	532

Where people live on the earth influences how they live. As this information shows, the quality of life is quite different in the developed countries of the Global North than it is in the developing countries of the Global South. As the World Bank predictions in the attached figure show, global trends indicate that the discrepancy between the rich and the poor will grow considerably by the year 2050.

SOURCES: World Bank (2002a and 2002b); figure on the division of world economies by 2050 from *The Economist*, July 6, 2002, p. 4. Copyright © 2002 by The Economist Newspaper Ltd. All rights reserved. Reprinted with permission. Further reproduction prohibited. www.economist.com.

• **least developed of the less-developed countries (LLDCs)** the most impoverished states in the Global South.

• **barter** the exchange of one good for another rather than the use of currency to buy and sell items.

hierarchy, sometimes called by the International Monetary Fund the **least developed of the less-developed countries (LLDCs),** where, typically, **barter** of one agricultural good for another (rather than money) is used for economic exchanges. These low-income countries are not participants in the global market: they account for less than 0.3 percent of world trade, and their meager exports are largely confined to inexpensive primary products, including food stuffs (cocoa, coffee, and tea), minerals, hides, and timber. Because they consume most of what they produce, theirs is typically a subsistence economy, and the prospects for change are dim, because most of these least-developed countries have been bypassed by direct foreign investment and ignored by foreign aid donors (World Bank 2002b).

High rates of population growth since 1990 have compounded the problems faced by the LLDCs. It will take only 25 years for the LLDCs' total population to double, compared with two and a half centuries for that in the Global North. LLDCs' economic growth rates in the recent past have averaged less than 0.1 percent each year. Growth rates elsewhere have almost uniformly been higher. This is a powerful reason why the rich minority gets richer while the poorest of the poor will likely become even poorer.

For many people living in the Global South, the future is bleak. The aggregate pattern underlying global trends in the last 20 years shows that more than sixty countries today are worse off than they were and are falling ever further behind the levels achieved by the countries in the Global North. This tragic situation raises a basic theoretical question: Why does so much of the Global South suffer from such destitution?

Why Do North-South Disparities Persist?

Why has the Global South lagged so far behind the Global North in its comparative level of well-being and **development**? And why have the development experiences even within the Global South differed so widely?

The diversity evident in the Global South invites the conclusion that underdevelopment is explained by a combination of factors. Some theorists explain underdevelopment by looking primarily at internal causes. Other theorists focus on the position of developing countries in the global political economy. We shall briefly discuss each of these schools of thought, beginning with the interpretation proposed by classical economic development theory.

Internal Factors: Classical Economic Development Theory's Interpretation

Liberal economic development theories of **modernization** emerged in the early post–World War II era. They argued that the major barriers to development were posed by the Global South countries' own internal characteristics. Productivity remained low due to managerial inefficiency, a lack of modern technology, and inadequate transportation and communication infrastructures. To overcome these barriers, most classical theorists recommended that the wealthy countries supply various "missing components" of development, such as investment capital through foreign aid or private foreign direct investment.

Once sufficient capital was accumulated to promote economic growth, these theorists predicted that its benefits would eventually "trickle down" to broad segments of society. In this way, everyone, not just a privileged few, would enjoy the benefits of rising affluence. Walt W. Rostow, an economic historian and U.S. policymaker, formalized this theory in his influential book *The Stages of Economic Growth* (1960). He predicted that traditional societies beginning the path to development would inevitably pass through various stages by means of the free market and would eventually "take off" to become similar to the mass-consumption societies of the capitalist Global North. Even though the rich are likely to get richer, it was argued, as incomes in the world as a whole grow, the

• **development** the processes through which a country increases its capacity to meet its citizens' basic human needs and raise their standard of living.

• **modernization** a view of development that argues that self-sustaining economic growth is created through technological innovation, efficient production, and investments from capital accumulation.

odds increase that a preindustrialized economy will grow faster and eventually reduce the gap between it and richer countries.

That prognosis and the policies on which it was based were ultimately rejected by the Global South. Leaders there did not accept the classical liberal argument that Global North countries became prosperous because they concentrated on work, invention, and skill (see Landes 1998; Thurow 1999). Instead, they were persuaded by a rival theory that attributed the Global South's plight to the structure of the global political economy.

External Factors: Dependence Theory's Interpretation

• dependency theory a view of development asserting that the leading capitalist states dominate and exploit the poorer countries on the periphery of the world economy.

Whereas classical developmental theory pointed to internal factors to explain the plight of the Global South, **dependency theory** emphasized external factors. Although the dependency literature is large and diverse (see Caporaso and Levine 1992; Packenham 1992), all dependence theorists reject Rostow's stages-of-growth thesis, arguing that underdevelopment "is not a stalled stage of linear development, a question of precapitalism, retarded or backward development" (Shannon 1989). As noted in Chapter 2, dependence theory builds on Lenin's critique of imperialism, but goes beyond it to account for changes that have occurred in recent decades. Its central proposition is that the structure of the capitalist world economy is based on a division of labor between a dominant core and a subordinate periphery. As a result of colonialism, the Global South countries that make up the periphery have been forced into an economic role whereby they export raw materials and import finished goods. While classical liberal theorists submit that specialization according to comparative advantage will increase income in an unfettered market and therein help close the gap between the world's haves and have-nots, dependence theorists maintain that global inequalities cannot be reduced so long as developing countries continue to specialize in primary products for which there are often numerous competing suppliers and limited demand.

Dependence theorists also argue that countries in the Global South are vulnerable to cultural penetration by multinational corporations (MNCs) and other outside forces, which saturate them with values alien to their societies. Once such penetration has occurred, the inherently unequal exchanges that bind the exploiters and the exploited are sustained by elites within the penetrated societies, who sacrifice their country's welfare for personal gain.

• dualism the existence of a rural, impoverished, and neglected sector of society alongside an urban, developing, or modernizing sector, with little interaction between the two.

The argument that a privileged few benefit from dependency at the expense of their societies underscores the dual nature of many developing countries. **Dualism** refers to the existence of two separate economic and social sectors operating side by side. Dual societies typically have a rural, impoverished, and neglected sector operating alongside an urban, developing, or advanced sector—but with little interaction between the two. Thus whatever growth occurs in the industrial sector in dual societies "neither initiates a corresponding growth process in the rural sector nor generates sufficient employment to prevent a growing population in the stagnant sectors" (Singer and Ansari 1988). MNCs contribute to dualism by promoting "the interests of the small number of well-paid modern-sector workers against the interests of the rest by widening wage differentials . . . and worsen the imbalance between rural and urban economic opportunities by locating primarily in urban areas and contributing to the flow of rural-urban migration" (Todaro 2000).

Although dependence theory has great appeal within the Global South, it cannot easily explain the emergence of what many people call **newly industrialized countries (NICs)**, members of the Global South that have begun exporting manufactured goods to the Global North. To explain this phenomenon, they sometimes use the term **dependent development** to describe the industrialization of peripheral areas in a system otherwise dominated by the Global North. The term suggests the possibility of either growing or declining prosperity, but not outside the confines of a continuing dominance–dependence relationship between North and South.

Can the Economic Gap Be Closed?

Is it possible for the Global South to escape the vicious cycle of poverty? When we look at the situation from the perspective of the poorest of the poor countries, the prospects appear dismal. However, there is a basis for optimism that can be found if you broaden the picture and see the conspicuous exceptions to the general pattern of persistent poverty. Although many Global South countries appear to be mired in inexorable poverty, some have managed to break the chains of underdevelopment. By pursuing bold paths for growth, they have seen their fortunes rise and are poised to enter the ranks of the advanced industrial economies. The ability for some developing countries to escape the syndrome that still affects the rest of the Global South suggests that others can succeed as well.

Consider the example of the newly industrialized countries, which have moved beyond the export of primary products to the export of manufactured goods. Today the NICs are among the largest exporters of manufactured goods and the most prosperous members of the Global South. In particular, the so-called "Asian Tigers" (South Korea, Singapore, Taiwan, and Hong Kong) have taken advantage of comparatively low wage rates to promote export-led economic growth through "neomercantilist" practices such as protecting infant industries from foreign competition and providing financial incentives for manufacturing industries. Spectacular economic growth has followed. With their population growth generally in check, the Asian Tigers have joined the ranks of the world's wealthiest states, and still other "new tigers" such as India have emerged as exports and foreign investment have stimulated a booming economy.

Neither geography nor current levels of economic performance identify well the emerging markets with the greatest potential. What most distinguishes these countries engineering an economic revolution is that their governments have stabilized the value of their currencies, brought inflation under control, and privatized the businesses once owned by the government. In addition, many opened themselves to foreign investment. This change in philosophy about the causes of and cures for underdevelopment formerly prevalent throughout the Global South was a concession in Global South thinking, stimulated in part by pressure for reforms by such powerful global IGOs as the World Bank and the International Monetary Fund.

• **newly industrialized countries (NICs)** prosperous members of the Global South, which have become important exporters of manufactured goods.

• **dependent development** the industrialization of areas outside of the leading capitalist states within confines set by the dominant capitalist states, which enables the poor to become wealthier without ever catching up to the core Global North countries.

The success of the free-market practices of the Asian NICs in elevating themselves from the rest of the Global South encouraged others to emulate their strategies and heightened cries for additional reforms in the Global South countries in order to remove still other obstacles standing in the way of economic growth. These include pressure by the UN, the IMF, and the World Bank for poor countries to pay more attention to attacking corruption and to move more quickly toward fuller democratic governance.

The achievements of the NICs alongside the plummeting financial fate of the poorest Global South countries provoke policy questions: Despite these differences and the inequalities between Global South states, is there a commonality, a consensus, that unites them as a group? What strategies have they forged to deal with their position of weakness in a world of powers?

The Global South's Foreign Policy Response

The vast political, economic, and social differences separating North and South indicate that the Global South is "weak, vulnerable, and insecure—with these traits being the function of both domestic and external factors" (Ayoob 1995). Coping with this insecurity has long been a primary foreign policy goal of Global South states, and efforts to overcome it have often brought the Global South into contention with the Global North. Ironically, the end of the Cold War reduced the great powers' security interest in providing economic aid to Global South countries. With foreign assistance declining, the Global South is now experiencing new armed conflicts and economic vulnerabilities.

Given these problems, strategies to maximize security and prosperity preoccupy foreign policy thinking in the Global South. Different states have taken different approaches, however. Let us examine how the Global South countries are pursuing their objectives, particularly in their relationships with the Global North.

In Search of Security

The Global South countries emerging after World War II struggled on separate tracks to find a foreign policy approach that could provide them with the security they lacked. Some states aligned themselves with either the United States or Soviet Union; others avoided taking sides in the Cold War. The latter approach gathered momentum in 1955, when 29 Asian and African countries met in Bandung, Indonesia, to devise a strategy to combat colonialism. Six years later, leaders from 25 countries, mostly former colonies, met in Belgrade, Yugoslavia, where they created the Nonaligned Movement (NAM), a political coalition whose membership would later grow to more than one hundred countries.

• **nonalignment** a foreign policy posture that rejects participating in military alliances with rival blocs for fear that formal alignment will entangle the state in an unnecessary war.

Nonalignment. Because many Global South countries feared becoming entrapped in the Cold War, they adopted foreign policies based on **nonalignment.** The strategy energized both the United States and the Soviet Union to renew their efforts to woo the uncommitted Global South countries to their own network of allies, often offering economic and military aid as an inducement. The Cold War's end eroded the bargaining leverage nonalignment had provided the Global South.

The challenge facing the nonaligned states today is how to promote their interests in a world where few listen to their voices. The nonaligned Global South can complain, but its bargaining power to engineer institutional reforms is limited. This weakness is displayed in the UN, where the most influence the Global South has mustered has symbolically been to delay serious proposals to make Germany and Japan permanent members of the Security Council by insisting that one of the larger developing countries (such as Brazil, Indonesia, Mexico, or South Africa) also be given a seat among the mighty. Weak states have some vocal power in numbers, but no clout or control. Thus, the Global South worries that the twenty-first century will witness "the reemergence of a more open and explicit form of imperialism, in which national sovereignty is more readily overridden by a hegemonic power pursuing its own self-defined national interest" (Bienefeld 1994).

Arms Acquisitions.   During the Cold War, many developing countries became battlegrounds on which the superpowers conducted covert activities, paramilitary operations, and proxy wars. More than 90 percent of the inter- and intrastate conflicts and 90 percent of the casualties in the past half-century occurred within the Global South (Gleditsch et al. 2002). Today, the danger of anarchy and violence has reached epidemic proportions, as the Global South contains numerous **failed states** that do not have governments strong enough to preserve domestic order.

• **failed states**
countries whose governments have little or no control over their territory and population.

Faced with seemingly endless conflict at home or abroad, it is not surprising that the Global South has joined the rest of the world's quest to acquire modern weapons of war—including in some cases (China, India, Iraq, North Korea, Pakistan) nuclear weapons. As a result, the burden of military spending (measured by the ratio of military expenditures to GNP) is highest among those least able to bear it. In the Global South military spending typically exceeds expenditures on health and education; impoverished states enmeshed in ethnic or religious strife at home are quite prepared to sacrifice expenditures for economic development in order to acquire weapons.

Few Global South states produce their own weapons. Weak governments, anxious over the possibility of separatist revolts and other forms of civil strife, have invested large proportions of their country's modest national budgets in arms rather than allocating these scarce revenues to social and economic programs aimed at reducing poverty. Ironically, many Global South countries have raised their military spending to purchase arms produced in the Global North at higher rates than their wealthy Global North counterparts do (Grimmett 2002). Thus in responding to its security concerns, the Global South appears to be increasing its dependence for arms purchases on the very same rich states whose military and economic domination they historically have most feared and resented.

In Search of Prosperity

Breaking out of their dependent status and pursuing their own industrial development remains their greatest foreign policy priority for countries in the Global South. To this end, some of them (particularly those in Latin America) have

• **import-substitution industrialization** a strategy for economic development that involves encouraging domestic entrepreneurs to manufacture products traditionally imported from abroad.

pursued development through an **import-substitution industrialization** strategy designed to encourage domestic entrepreneurs to manufacture products traditionally imported from abroad. Governments (often dictatorships) have been heavily involved in managing their economies and in some cases became the owners and operators of industry.

Import-substitution industrialization eventually fell from favor, in part because manufacturers often found that they still had to rely on Global North technology to produce goods for their domestic markets. The preference now is for **export-led industrialization,** based on the realization that "what had enriched the rich was not their insulation from imports (rich countries do, in fact, import massively all sorts of goods) but their success in manufactured exports, where higher prices could be commanded than for [Global South] raw materials" (Sklair 1991).

• **export-led industrialization** a growth strategy that concentrates on developing domestic export industries capable of competing in overseas markets.

As exemplified by the NICs, the shift toward export-led growth strategies has transformed some Global South countries from being suppliers of raw materials into manufacturers of products already available in the Global North. Thus a new international division of labor is emerging as production, capital, labor, and technology are increasingly integrated worldwide and decision making has become transnational. "The old ideas of national autonomy, economic independence, self-reliance, and self-sufficiency have become obsolete as the national economies [have] become increasingly integrated" (Dorraj 1995).

Not all Global South economies are positioned to survive in this highly competitive globalized market. Many of the least-developed countries remain heavily dependent on raw materials and other primary products for their export earnings. While some benefit from such integration and prosper, others remain immune from the alleged benefits of globalization, and are especially vulnerable to recessions in the global economy.

How to cope with dominance and dependence thus remains a key Global South concern. As they search for status and economic security, let us next evaluate the Global South's key strategies in their relations with the Global North.

A New International Economic Order? The emerging Global South countries were born into an international economic order with rules they had no voice in creating. In order to gain control over their economic futures, they began coordinating their efforts within the United Nations where their growing numbers and voting power gave them greater influence than they could otherwise command. In the 1960s, they formed a coalition of the world's poor, the **Group of 77** (known in diplomatic circles simply as the **G-77**) and used their voting power to convene the UN Conference on Trade and Development (UNCTAD). UNCTAD later became a permanent UN organization through which the Global South would express its interests concerning development issues.

• **Group of 77 (G-77)** the coalition of Third World countries that sponsored the 1963 Joint Declaration of Developing Countries calling for reforms to allow greater equity in North–South trade.

• **New International Economic Order (NIEO)** the 1974 policy resolution in the UN that called for a North–South dialogue to open the way for the less-developed countries of the Global South to participate more fully in the making of international economic policy.

A decade later, the G-77 (then numbering more than one hundred twenty countries) again used its UN numerical majority to push for a **New International Economic Order (NIEO)** to replace the international economic regime championed by the United States and the other capitalist powers since World War II. Motivated by the oil-exporting countries' rising bargaining power, the Global

South sought to compel the Global North to abandon practices perceived as perpetuating their dependence. More specifically, the proposals advanced under the banner of the NIEO included:

- Giving preferential, nonreciprocal treatment to Global South exports to industrialized countries;
- Establishing commodity agreements to regulate and stabilize the world market for primary commodities;
- Linking the price of Global South exports to the price of imports from industrialized states;
- Increasing financial resource transfers to Global South countries;
- Reducing the burden of Global South debt through rescheduling, interest subsidization, or cancellation;
- Increasing the participation and voting power of Global South countries in international financial institutions;
- Regulating the activities of multinational corporations in the Global South to promote the reinvestment of profits earned by MNCs in host country economies; and
- Expanding technical assistance programs and reducing the cost of transferring technology to the Global South.

Not surprisingly, the Global North rebuffed many of the South's proposals, although some of the issues that were raised (such as debt relief) remain on the global agenda.

Regional Trade Regimes. With the failure of reform envisioned by the NIEO, the integration of Global South countries into the globalization process will occur according to the rules dictated by the Global North. Are there alternatives? Can regional arrangements enable Global South states to take advantage of growing economic interdependence to achieve their development goals?

To promote growth through regional economic agreements, in the 1990s the global economy began to subdivide into three "trade blocs"—one in Europe, with the European Union (EU) as its hub; a second in the Americas, with the United States at the center; and a third in East Asia, with Japan and China dominant. Consider some recent developments:

- *In the Americas:* The North American Free Trade Agreement (NAFTA), formalized in 1993, brought Canada, Mexico, and the United States into a single free-trade area whose market size rivals that of the EU to create a hemisphere-wide free-trade area, in which tariffs among member countries are eliminated. In addition, the Mercosur agreement, which links Argentina, Brazil, Paraguay, and Uruguay (Latin America's largest trade bloc), hopes to incorporate the Andean Group (Bolivia, Colombia, Ecuador, Peru, and Venezuela) in its free-trade union.
- *In Asia:* The association of Asia-Pacific Economic Cooperation (APEC), an informal forum created in 1989 that has committed itself to creating a free-trade zone during the next 25 years. In addition, the members of the

Association of Southeast Asian Nations (ASEAN), first established in 1967 by Brunei, Indonesia, Malaysia, the Philippines, Singapore, and Thailand and now including Vietnam, agreed to set up a free-trade area.

- *In Africa:* The Southern African Development Community (SADC) formed in 1980 has pledged to develop a free-trade area and common currency.

Will the lofty expectations of these regional politicoeconomic groups be realized? In the past, political will and shared visions have proven to be indispensable elements in successful regional trade regimes. Economic complementarity is another essential component, as the goal is to stimulate greater trade among the members of the free-trade area, not simply between it and others. If one or more members export products that each of the others wants, the chances of the regime's success are greater; if, on the other hand, they all tend to export the same products or to have virtually no trade with one another (typically the case in Africa), failure is more likely.

Prospects for the success of regional trade regimes seem greatest when Global South countries cobble their futures to Global North states—but, complain Global South leaders, on terms that the North dictates. That conclusion hardly bodes well for regional economic agreements as an effective method for balancing the North–South relationship.

Foreign Aid, Investment, and Debt Relief.   The developing countries have long pleaded for greater access to the Global North's markets in order to fuel their economic growth. But many Global South countries have not improved their lot, often for two major reasons. First, market access has become increasingly difficult because domestic pressure groups in Global North countries have lobbied their governments to reduce the imports of other countries' products that compete with their own industries. Trade may be preferred to aid, but political barriers often interfere with free trade.

Second, the character and distribution of foreign aid have changed as criticism of its effectiveness and effects has risen. Economic assistance comes in a variety of forms and is used for a variety of purposes. Some aid consists of outright grants of money, some of loans at concessional rates, and some of shared technical expertise. Although most foreign aid is bilateral and is termed **official development assistance (ODA)**—meaning the money flows directly from one country to another—an increasing portion is now channeled through global institutions such as the World Bank, and hence is known as "multilateral aid." Moreover, the purposes of aid are as varied as its forms. Commonly stated foreign aid goals include not only the reduction of poverty through economic development, but also human development, environmental protection, the development of private enterprise, increased power for women, the promotion of democratic governance and human rights, humanitarian disaster relief, and assistance to refugees. However, security objectives traditionally have figured prominently as motives of donors in the allocation of both economic aid and military assistance, and still do. For example, the United States continues to target Israel and Egypt as major recipients to symbolize friendship, maintain a balance of power, and tilt the scales toward peace in the Middle East.

- **official development assistance (ODA)** grants or loans to countries from other countries, usually channeled through multilateral aid organizations, for the primary purpose of promoting economic development and welfare.

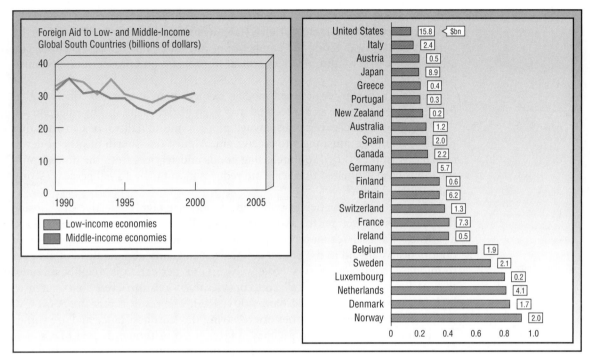

FIGURE 5.1

The Decline of Global North Foreign Aid to the Global South

Official development assistance (ODA) from Global North donors has not grown over the past decade at a pace commensurate with the rate of global economic growth. In 2001 it totaled only $53.7 billion, or less that 0.001 percent of the global economy (*Vital Signs 2002*, 119). As the figure on the left shows, since 1990, "the real value of aid to developing countries has fallen 8 percent," and only half goes to the poorest Global South countries (World Bank 2002a, 14). The bar on the right shows the top 22 Global North foreign aid donors' official aid disbursements, as well as the percent of their income their donation represents. Only five countries (Sweden , Luxembourg, the Netherlands, Denmark, and Norway) meet the UN international target recommending donors to give 0.7 percent of their national income for assistance. In absolute terms, the United States was by far the world's most generous donor, giving over $15.8 billion. But that represented less than 0.2 percent of its GDP, not even half of what the UN would like.
SOURCES: World Bank Atlas: 2002 (paper) by World Bank Staff. Copyright 2002 by World Bank.

Overall global official development assistance has in fact declined since peaking in 1991 (see Figure 5.1). Many aid donors have become frustrated with the slow growth rates of many of the Global South recipients and have grown doubtful of the effectiveness of their aid programs, despite strong evidence that foreign aid has made a positive difference (Easterbrook 2002). Critics particularly resent what they perceive to be a state of mind in many Global South cultures that stands in the way of development, which—while bemoaning poverty—at the same time condemns the profit motive and competition. "The revolution of economic development occurs when people go on working, competing, inventing, and innovating when they no longer need to be rich," argues Mariano Grondona, an Argentinian political scientist, in a statement that expresses the Global North's faith in hard work, economic competition, and individual entrepreneurial creativity as necessary cultural values crucial to progress and prosperity (in Samuelson 2001).

The shift to market-oriented models has led many donors to conclude that foreign aid is no longer as needed and may even be detrimental. The emergent climate of opinion, moreover, has spawned more "conditionality," or demands that recipient countries must meet to receive aid. Almost one-fourth of official development assistance is tied to purchasing goods and services from the donor country. It has been estimated that tying aid reduces its value by 15–30 percent (World Bank 2001, 2000).

On top of this practice of tying aid, donors are highly selective in choosing the countries they target for assistance, especially when they treat foreign aid as a subsidy for their domestic corporations producing exports. Although most donors distribute aid to the poorer countries, "currently about a third of aid goes to middle-income countries, whose average GNP per capita is roughly six times that of low-income countries" and considerable sums are even contributed to high-income countries (World Bank 2001, 196). The result is that the poorest of the poor Global South countries are receiving the least assistance and are suffering the most from the recent declines in foreign aid. Although some LLDCs view aid as repayment for years of unequal exchange perpetuated through colonialism, many Global South leaders have criticized foreign aid, interpreting it as an instrument of neocolonialism imposed by the International Monetary Fund and other multilateral economic institutions.

Rather than calling for additional foreign aid, some Global South countries have encouraged multinational corporations (MNCs) to funnel an increasing share of their **foreign direct investment (FDI)** into developing countries. Of course, this strategy for economic growth has always been the target of critics who question whether the investment of capital by multinational corporations (and, to a lesser extent, private investors) into local or domestic business ventures is really a financial remedy. The strategy has always been controversial, because there are many hidden costs associated with permitting corporations controlled from abroad to set up business within the host state for the purpose of making a profit. What share of the benefits will foreign investors and host countries get from the investments that are made? Considerable risks are entailed, as are a number of trade-offs among competing values (see Controversy: Multinational Corporations in the Global South: Do They Help or Hurt?).

The primary danger with this strategy is the potential for foreign investments to lead to foreign control, the erosion of sovereign governments' capacities to regulate the economy within their borders, and the probability that the multinational foreign investors will not invest their profits locally but channel them abroad for new investments or disburse them as dividends for their wealthy Global North shareholders. However, despite the risks, many developing countries have relaxed restrictions in order to attract foreign investors, with emphasis placed less on liberalizing investment restrictions and encouraging open domestic economic competition than on offering tax and cash enticements and oppor-

• **foreign direct investment (FDI)** an investment in a country involving a long-term relationship and control of an enterprise by nonresidents and including equity capital, reinvestment of earnings, other long-term capital, and short-term capital as shown in balance of payments accounts.

CONTROVERSY

Multinational Corporations in the Global South: Do They Help or Hurt?

Within the Global South, there is widespread concern about the impact of multinational corporations (MNCs) on the economies and societies of the countries in which they operate. Because their record can be evaluated on different criteria, MNCs are praised by some people and condemned by others. The following is a "balance sheet" summarizing the major arguments for and against MNCs. Using this summary of contending interpretations, you can easily see why the role of MNCs is so controversial. What do you think? On balance, do MNCs help or harm the Global South's ability to close the gap in wealth with the Global North? How do you assess their relative benefits and costs for Global South countries?

Positive

- Increase the volume of trade.
- Assist the aggregation of investment capital that can fund development.
- Finance loans and service international debt.
- Lobby for free trade and the removal of barriers to trade, such as tariffs.
- Underwrite research and development that allows technological innovation.
- Introduce and dispense advanced technology to less-developed countries.
- Reduce the costs of goods by encouraging their production according to the principle of comparative advantage.
- Generate employment.
- Encourage the training of workers.
- Produce new goods and expand opportunities for their purchase through the internationalization of production.
- Disseminate marketing expertise and mass advertising methods worldwide.
- Provide investment income to facilitate the modernization of less-developed countries.
- Generate income and wealth.
- Advocate peaceful relations between and among states in order to preserve an orderly environment conducive to trade and profits.

- Break down national barriers and accelerate the globalization of the international economy and culture and the rules that govern international commerce.

Negative

- Give rise to oligopolistic conglomerations that reduce competition and free enterprise.
- Raise capital in host countries (thereby depriving local industries of investment capital) but export profits to home countries.
- Breed debtors and make the poor dependent on those providing loans.
- Limit the availability of commodities by monopolizing their production and controlling their distribution in the world marketplace.
- Create "sanctuary markets" that restrict and channel other investments to give MNCs an unfair advantage.
- Export technology ill-suited to underdeveloped economies.
- Inhibit the growth of infant industries and local technological expertise in less-developed countries while making Global South countries dependent on Global North technology.
- Conspire to create cartels that contribute to inflation.
- Curtail employment by driving labor competition from the market.
- Limit workers' wages.
- Limit the supply of raw materials available in international markets.
- Erode traditional cultures and national differences, leaving in their place a homogenized world culture dominated by consumer-oriented values.
- Widen the gap between rich and poor countries.
- Increase the wealth of local elites at the expense of the poor.
- Support and rationalize repressive regimes in the name of stability and order.
- Challenge national sovereignty and jeopardize the autonomy of the states.
- Create cartels with other MNCs that share markets in order to cut competition. ●

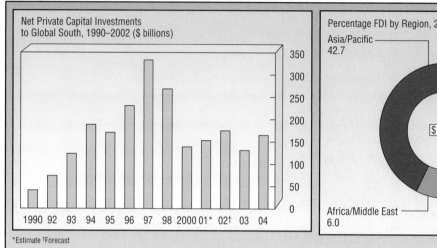

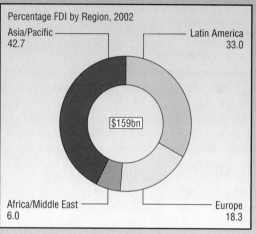

FIGURE 5.2

The Rise and Fall of Capital Investments in the Global South, 1990–2002

Since the early 1990s many Global South countries have competed for capital investments from abroad to stimulate economic growth. As the figure on the left shows, they largely succeeded until 1997, after which private capital inflows have declined. As the chart on the right shows, less than one-fifth of the investments were going in 2002 to the emerging market European countries, with Asia and Latin America as the leading contenders for the rest.

SOURCE: From *The Economist,* May 4, 2002, p. 102. Copyright © 2002 by The Economist Newspaper, Ltd. All rights reserved. Reprinted with permission. Further reproduction prohibited. www.economist.com

tunities for joint ventures. This has stimulated a recent surge in the flow of capital investments to the Global South (see Figure 5.2). However, keep in mind that four-fifths of all FDI is channeled to the Global North, and the poorest Global South countries (the LLCDs) benefit from only 3.4 percent of investments from abroad (World Bank 2002a, 286).

The impact of this new infusion of foreign investments in the developing countries has been substantial, given the relatively small economies of the Global South. It has paved the way for emerging markets in the Global South to expand their rates of economic development despite the resistance of local industries in the Global South threatened by the competition and critics who have complained about the income inequalities that the investments are causing. Such fears and consequences notwithstanding, an intensified push among the Global South developing countries to compete for foreign investment capital in order to liberate themselves from dependence and destitution seems likely.

The prospects for either foreign aid or for foreign direct investments to contribute to the future development of, and relief of poverty in, the Global South will depend on a number of other factors. Foremost is the extent to which the staggering level of debt facing many Global South countries can be managed.

In 2001, the World Bank identified 57 Global South countries, more than 80 percent of them in Africa, as burdened by "unsustainable debt" and in need of

Not the Choice of a New Generation Many nationalists blame multinational corporations for the problems of their countries' economies and social conditions. Foreign firms often face a backlash. In 1995, Hindu nationalists in India—the world's largest democracy—protested economic reforms that would open the country's borders to liberal trade and investment. These and other opponents pledged to drive some of the world's best-known brands out of the Indian market.

Robert Nickelsberg/Getty Images

relief, noting that "many heavily indebted poor countries spend as much as a fifth of their annual budgets on debt service" (World Bank 2001, 201). The financial dilemmas faced by Zambia illustrate the problem. According to the World Bank, Zambia began the new millennium with $5.2 billion in public external debt (net present value), which was roughly equivalent to 60 percent of its GDP and 500 percent of Zambia's exports of goods and nonfactor services. In 1999, merely servicing this debt (paying the interest and principal) amounted to 24.5 percent of the central government's revenues. Obviously, such a staggering amount of debt poses an enormous constraint on the government's ability to improve the quality of life of the 70 percent of its citizens that live in poverty.

Debt relief—slashing the amount owed by Zambia and the other heavily indebted poor countries—is reflective of the changing attitudes toward the Global South by the great powers and multilateral institutions, such as the World Bank. They have distributed more than $56 billion in relief to financially distressed Global South countries (World Bank 2002a, 362), partly out of compassion but also due to the economic self-interest of the Global North, which sees in debt relief a pragmatic method for preventing an economic collapse that could threaten the entire world economy in the age of interdependent globalization.

• Heavily Indebted Poor Countries (HIPCs) the subset of countries identified by the World Bank's Debtor Reporting System whose ratios of government debt to gross national product are so substantial that they cannot meet their payment obligations without experiencing political instability and economic collapse.

The World Bank's "Enhanced **HIPC (Heavily Indebted Poor Country)** initiative" and the International Monetary Fund's "Enhanced Structural Adjustment Facility," are the primary products of this attempt to reduce the widening disparities between the Global North and Global South. Whether these programs will succeed will depend on the degree to which the Global South countries can undertake, with minimal corruption, the often painful liberalizing political reforms for democratic governance that are widely seen as a requirement for sustained economic growth (Kim and Wolfensohn 1999).

The Future of the Global South

It is useful to remember the historic trends underlying the problems faced by the countries of the Global South. Most were colonized by people of another race, experienced varying degrees of poverty, and felt powerless in a world system dominated by the affluent countries that once controlled them and perhaps still do. Considerable change occurred as post–World War II decolonization proceeded, but much also remained the same.

The relationships between the world's developed and developing countries will no doubt continue to change, but exactly how remains uncertain. A turn inward, toward isolationist foreign policies, in the Global North could lead to a posture of "benign neglect" of the Global South. Conversely, a new era of North–South cooperation could commence, dedicated to finding solutions to common problems ranging from commercial to environmental and security concerns. Elements of both approaches are already evident. Although the fate of the Global North remains to be determined, it is clear that the Global South is, for the time being, in a world dominated by the most powerful state and nonstate actors, and the choices of the powerful will strongly influence its fate. "Development was—and continues to be for the most part—a top-down, ethnocentric, and technocratic approach that treats people and cultures as abstract concepts, statistical figures to be moved up and down in the charts of 'progress.' . . . It comes as no surprise that development became a force so destructive to cultures [throughout the Global South], ironically in the name of people's interests" (Escobar 2000).

Chapter Summary

- The term *Global South* refers to the world's poorer, economically less developed countries, most of which lie in the Southern Hemisphere and were once colonies of other states. Significant inequalities exist between these countries and those industrialized states that comprise the Global North. Whereas the Global South contains more than 85 percent of the world's population, it commands less than 15 percent of its wealth.
- Considerable diversity exists among Global South countries: some are big, others are small; some possess vast quantities of oil and natural gas; others lack significant natural resources; some have subsistence economies, others export

manufactured goods; some are democracies, others are autocracies. Despite these and other differences, most Global South countries share a set of common problems related to their poverty and vulnerability.

- Between the fifteenth and twentieth centuries, two waves of European imperialism resulted in the colonization of the Global South. Decolonization began in earnest after World War II and is now complete. For the most part, it was not only extraordinarily rapid but also remarkably peaceful. Still, the vestiges of colonialism remain, and they have important consequences for the shape of the global future.

- Although the debate over how to eliminate the disparities between the Global North and South focuses on the economic development of impoverished countries, these issues are intensely political. They derive from the struggle by those at the bottom of the international hierarchy to improve their position in the global pecking order.

- The development process is complex because the problems faced by the Global South are characterized by a series of intertwined vicious circles, none of which seems capable of being broken without addressing the others.

- Classical economic development theory claims that the causes of underdevelopment are internal. Among the factors it identifies are low rates of productivity, a lack of sufficient investment capital, and inadequate communication and transportation systems.

- Dependence theory holds that the causes of underdevelopment are external. Less developed countries are vulnerable to penetration by outside forces. According to dependence theory, the Global South has been exploited by wealthier, more powerful members of the world capitalist system.

- Global South states have tried various strategies to overcome their weakness and insecurity. To cope with the threat of separatist movements, many of them have sought to acquire modern weaponry, even if that meant sacrificing funds for health, education, and welfare programs. To promote economic growth, many have tried to forge regional free-trade groups, encourage foreign direct investment, and seek relief from staggering levels of debt.

KEY TERMS

barter
colonialism
decolonization
dependency theory
dependent development
development
dualism
export-led industrialization
failed states
First World
foreign direct investment (FDI)
Global North
Global South

Group of 77 (G-77)
Heavily Indebted Poor
  Countries (HIPCs)
import-substitution
  industrialization
laissez-faire economics
least developed of the less-
  developed countries (LLDCs)
mercantilism
modernization
New International Economic
  Order (NIEO)

newly industrialized countries
  (NICs)
nonalignment
official development assistance
  (ODA)
Second World
self-determination
sphere of influence
Third World

WHERE ON THE WORLD WIDE WEB?

Many U.S. citizens have trouble understanding the plight of the Global South. Use the following websites to familiarize yourself with the diverse array of Global South countries and the common problems they face. Each site has links to country-specific information that will allow you to make social, political, and economic comparisons.

African Studies
http://www.sas.upenn.edu/African_Studies/AS.html

Asian Studies
http://coombs.anu.edu.au/WWWVL-AsianStudies. html

Latin American Studies
http://www.georgetown.edu/pdba/

Middle Eastern Studies
http://menic.utexas.edu/menic/

United Nations Conference on Trade and Development (UNCTAD)
http://www.unctad.org/Templates/
Page.asp?intItemID=1676&lang=1

From the UNCTAD homepage, go to the Least Developed Countries subsite and investigate the backgrounds of the countries that the United Nations has deemed the poorest countries in the world. Examine the various policies UNCTAD has for helping the Least Developed Countries. Which do you think have the best chance of succeeding? Why?

United Nations Development Program (UNDP)
http://www.undp.org/

This United Nations branch helps countries in their efforts to achieve sustainable human development. As discussed in this chapter, the fulfillment of basic human needs (food, water, clothing, shelter, sanitation, health care, employment, and dignity) are important measures of a country's development level. The UNDP focuses its efforts on assisting countries in the Global South to design and carry out national development programs. Examine the various projects of the UNDP. Which have had the greatest impact on development?

U.S. Agency for International Development (USAID)
http://www.usaid.gov/

USAID is the federal government agency that implements foreign economic and humanitarian assistance programs to advance the political and economic interests of the United States. It assists countries recovering from disaster, trying to escape poverty, and engaging in democratic reforms. On the homepage you can choose regions from the "Where" section and examine U.S. aid efforts in each country of the world. Based on your comparison, what do you see as the U.S. aid priorities in each region?

INFOTRAC® COLLEGE EDITION

Search for the following articles in the InfoTrac College Edition database.

Bhagwati, Jagdish. "The Poor's Best Hope—Trading for Development," *The Economist* (US) June 22, 2002.

Blinder, Alan S. "Eight Steps to a New Financial Order," *Foreign Affairs* September–October 1999.

Goldman, Michael. "Constructing an Environmental State: Eco-Governmentality and other Transnational Practices of a 'Green' World Bank," *Social Problems* November 2001.

Streeten, Paul. "Beyond the Six Veils: Conceptualizing and Measuring Poverty," *Journal of International Affairs* Fall 1998.

For more articles, enter:

"developing countries" in the Subject Guide.

"International Monetary Fund" in the Subject Guide, and then go to subdivision "evaluation."

"World Bank" in the Subject Guide, and then go to subdivision "economic policy."

ADDITIONAL CD-ROM RESOURCES

Click on International Political Economy to access additional resources related to this chapter.

CHAPTER 6

Nonstate Actors and the Challenge of Global Governance

A novel redistribution of power among states, markets, and civil society is underway, ending the steady accumulation of power in the hands of states that began with the Peace of Westphalia in 1648.

JESSICA T. MATHEWS, president of the Carnegie Endowment for International Peace

On Saturday, October 4, 2003, a young Palestinian woman from the West Bank town of Jenin entered a bustling seaside restaurant in the northern Israeli city of Haifa. A few seconds later, she detonated explosives strapped to her body, killing herself and 19 other people. The Israeli government immediately held the Palestinian Authority responsible, charging that its security forces failed to curb a suicide bombing campaign that had been targeting Israeli busses, cafes, and markets for over a decade. When asked whether Israel would retaliate against Yasser Arafat, the president of the Palestinian Authority, a spokesman for Prime Minister Ariel Sharon declared "Everyone who has had a hand in this attack should worry."

Several hours later, Israeli aircraft struck the Ein Saher training camp northwest of Damascus, Syria. According to the Israelis, the camp had been used by several terrorist organizations, including Palestinian Islamic Jihad, the group claiming responsibility for the Haifa bombing. Unable to mount a military response to the airstrike deep within its territory, Syria sought external support. At an emergency session of the Arab League, Syrian foreign minister Farouq al-Sharaa called for measures to deter future Israeli attacks. Meanwhile, at a meeting of the United Nations Security Council, Syria's UN ambassador Fayssal Mekdad presented a draft resolution condemning Israel's actions.

As the Syrians and Israelis exchanged threats, diplomats from other countries worried about an escalation of the Arab-Israeli conflict. They feared militant groups like Hamas, Hezbollah, and the al-Aqsa Martyrs Brigade would step up their attacks, prompting the Israelis to lash out against neighboring states perceived to be supporting terrorism. In response, the Arab League would call for the United Nations to impose sanctions against Israel, with the result that the fragile Middle East peace process would grind to a halt.

As this episode illustrates, the political dynamics of the Middle East involve more than the interactions of nation-states such as Israel and Syria. Nonstate entities ranging from global and regional intergovernmental organizations to ethnic and religious nongovernmental organizations are important actors as well. Indeed, it would be impossible to make sense of contemporary Middle Eastern affairs without devoting attention to nonstate actors. In view of their importance, the aims of this chapter are to describe the various types of nonstate actors in world politics, and to explain when and how they exert their influence.

Types of Nonstate Actors

The history of world politics for the past 350 years has largely been a chronicle of interactions among sovereign, territorial states. Today, however, world affairs are also being shaped by organizations that transcend national boundaries. In addition to the United Nations and regional bodies such as the Arab League, the course of world affairs is affected by groups of people who band together for ethnic, religious, or other reasons. The Islamic Jihad, Hamas, the al-Aqsa Martyrs

Brigade, and Hezbollah exemplify such groups. Diverse in scope and purpose, these nonstate actors push their own agendas and increasingly exert international influence.

There are two principal types of nonstate actors: **intergovernmental organizations (IGOs)**, whose members are states, and **nongovernmental organizations (NGOs)**, whose members are private individuals and groups. Both types existed prior to the twentieth century and both are now pervasive. The Union of International Organizations, which maintains comprehensive, up-to-date information on such organizations, records that their numbers increased sharply during the nineteenth century, as international commerce and communications grew alongside industrialization. In 1909, there were 37 IGOs and 176 NGOs. By 1960, there were 154 IGOs and 1,255 NGOs, and by 2003, these numbers had risen to 243 and 28,775, respectively (see Figure 6.1).

IGOs are created by states to solve shared problems. As shown in Table 6.1, they vary widely in size and purpose. The North Atlantic Treaty Organization

• **intergovernmental organizations (IGOs)** institutions created and joined by states' governments, which give them authority to make collective decisions to manage particular problem(s) on the global agenda.

• **nongovernmental organizations (NGOs)** transnational organizations of private citizens that include foundations, professional associations, multinational corporations, or groups in different countries joined together to work toward common interests.

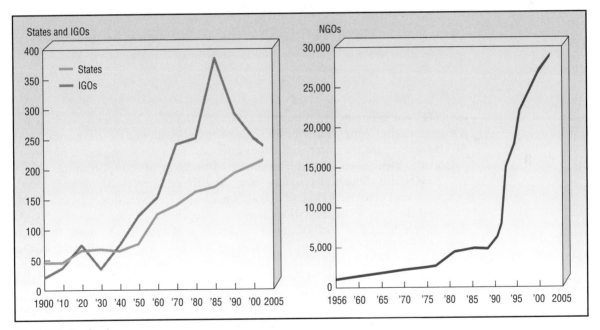

FIGURE 6.1
The Number of States, IGOs, and NGOs since 1900

The number of independent states increased greatly in the twentieth century—especially since the decolonization movement began after World War II—but the number of intergovernmental organizations (IGOs) and especially nongovernmental organizations (NGOs) has grown even more rapidly.

SOURCES: Figures for states are based on the Correlates of War (COW) project at the University of Michigan under the direction of J. David Singer; States, Polity III data (Jaggers and Gurr 1995); IGOs and NGOs from *Yearbook of International Organizations 1993/1994* (1993, p. 1699); http://www.uia.org/statistics/pub.php; and moving averages from selected prior volumes.

TABLE 6.1

A Simple Classification of Intergovernmental Organizations (IGOs)

| | *Range of Stated Purpose* | |
Geographic Scope of Membership	Multiple Purposes	Single Purpose
Global	United Nations	World Health Organization
	World Trade Organization	International Labor Organization
	UNESCO	International Monetary Fund
	Organization of the Islamic Conference	Universal Postal Union
Interregional, regional subregional	European Union	European Space Agency
	Organization for Security and Cooperation in Europe	Nordic Council
	Organization of American States	North Atlantic Treaty Organization
	Organization of African Unity	International Olive Oil Council
	League of Arab States	International North Pacific Coffee Organization
	Association of Southeast Asian Nations	African Groundnut Council

---

(NATO), for example, is primarily a military alliance, while others, such as the Organization of American States (OAS), promote economic development. Most IGOs concentrate their activities on specific economic or social issues of special concern to them, such as the management of trade, or of transportation.

NGOs also differ widely. They span virtually every facet of political, social, and economic activity, including science, health care, culture, theology, law, security, and defense. As organizations that are independent of governments, NGOs link people from different societies in transnational networks in order to advocate specific policies. For this purpose, many NGOs interact formally with IGOs. More than one thousand NGOs actively consult with various agencies of the extensive UN system, maintain offices in hundreds of cities, and hold parallel conferences with IGO meetings to which states send representatives. Such partnerships between NGOs and IGOs enable both types of organizations to work (and lobby) together in pursuit of common policies and programs.

In this chapter, we will begin our analysis of nonstate actors by discussing some prominent and representative IGOs, including the United Nations (UN) and the European Union (EU). Next, we will turn our attention to NGOs, examining the impact of ethnopolitical groups, religious movements, multinational corporations, transnational banks, and issue-advocacy groups. Finally, we will ask whether the activities of nonstate actors are undermining the position of the nation-state in world politics.

Global Intergovernmental Organizations

The United Nations

The United Nations is the best-known global organization. What distinguishes it from most other IGOs is its nearly universal membership, including today 191 independent states from every region (see Figure 6.2). The UN's nearly fourfold growth from the 51 states that joined it in 1945 has been spectacular, but the admission process has from the start been governed by political conflicts that show the extent to which the organization reflects the relationships of the five great powers that shape its direction through their veto authority in the Security Council.

Purposes and Agenda. In addition to possessing nearly universal membership, the UN is also a multipurpose organization. As Article 1 of the UN Charter states, its objectives are to:

- Maintain international peace and security
- Develop friendly relations among nations based on respect for the principle of equal rights and self determination of peoples
- Achieve international cooperation in solving international problems of an economic, social, cultural, or humanitarian character and in promoting and encouraging respect for human rights and for fundamental freedoms for all
- Function as a center for harmonizing the actions of nations in the attainment of these common ends

Peace and security figured prominently in the thinking of those responsible for creating the United Nations at the end of the Second World War to replace the League of Nations. However, the ambitions that the UN's founders had in the security realm were soon frustrated by the Cold War between the United States and the Soviet Union. Though unable to make headway on security issues, work toward the goal of improving the quality of life for humanity carried the UN into nearly every corner of the world.

The history of the UN reflects the fact that both rich countries and developing countries have successfully used the organization to promote their own foreign policy objectives, and this record has bred hopes throughout the world that the UN will be able to manage an ever changing and growing agenda. However, ambitions for the UN may exceed its meager resources. Since the end of the Cold War, the organization has been asked to address an expanding set of military and nonmilitary problems. Consider the wide array of world conferences that the organization has sponsored over the past three and a half decades: human environment (1972, 2002), law of the sea (1973–1982), population (1974, 1984, 1994, 1999), food (1974, 1976), women (1975, 1980, 1985, 1995), human settlements (1976), basic human needs (1976), water (1977, 2002), desertification (1977), disarmament (1978, 1982, 1988), racism and racial discrimination (1978, 2002), technical cooperation among developing countries (1978), agrarian reform and rural development (1974, 1979), science and technology for

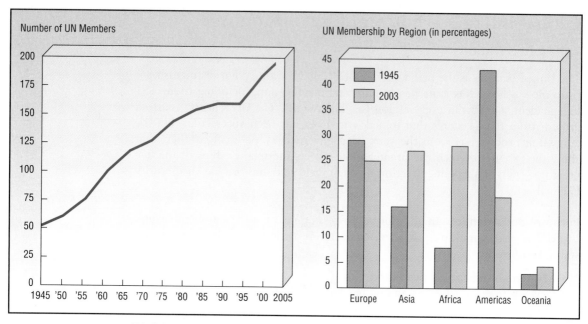

FIGURE 6.2

The Changing Membership of the United Nations, 1945–2005

As the figure on the left shows, the UN's membership has seen episodic bursts of growth from 51 states in 1945 to 191 in 2003 with the admission of Switzerland and newly independent East Timor (the world's two hundred eighth sovereign state). Over nearly six decades of expansion, the United Nations has increasingly included Global South countries (see figure on right). This shift has influenced the kinds of issues the UN has confronted, expanding the global agenda from the priorities of the great powers in the Global North to include those important to the developing states in the Global South.
SOURCE: United Nations.

development (1979), new and renewable sources of energy (1981), least-developed countries (1981), aging (1982), the peaceful uses of outer space (1982), Palestine (1947, 1982), the peaceful uses of nuclear energy (1983), the prevention of crime and the treatment of offenders (1985), drug abuse and illicit trafficking in drugs (1987, 1990, 1998), the protection of children (1990), the environment and economic development (1992, 2002), transnational corporations (1992), indigenous peoples (1992, 1994), internationally organized crime (1994), social development (1995), housing (1996), human rights (1993, 1997), global warming (1992, 1997, 2002), international trafficking of children for prostitution (2000), and principles for world order (2000). These conferences, in effect, comprise a list of "the most vital issues of present world conditions," and "represent a beginning in a long and evolving process of keeping within manageable proportions the major problems of humanity" (Bennett 1988).

In response to the demands that have been placed upon it, the United Nations has developed a vast administrative structure, with offices not only in the

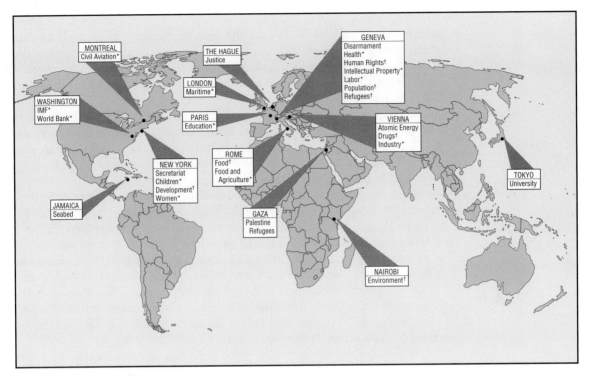

MAP 6.1
The UN's Headquarters and Global Network

The United Nations has sought, since its creation, to address the continuously expanding problems on the global agenda. As shown on this map, the United Nations has spread its administrative arm to every corner of the globe in order to serve what Secretary-General Kofi Annan has called "a noble experiment in human cooperation."

*Specialized agencies.
†Funds and programs.
SOURCE: *The UN Handbook*.

UN Headquarters in New York but also in centers spread throughout the world (see Map 6.1). To evaluate the capacity of the United Nations to shoulder the huge burdens that it has been asked to carry, let us examine how it is organized.

Organizational Structure. The UN's limitations are perhaps rooted in the ways it is organized for its wide-ranging purposes. According to the Charter, the UN structure contains the following six major organs:

- *General Assembly.* Established as the main deliberative body of the United Nations, all members are equally represented according to a one-state/one-vote formula. Decisions are reached by a simple majority vote, except on so-called "important questions," which require a two-thirds majority. The resolutions it passes, however, are only recommendations.

- *Security Council.* Given primary responsibility by the Charter for dealing with threats to international peace and security, the Security Council consists of five permanent members with the power to veto substantive decisions (the United States, the United Kingdom, France, Russia, and the People's Republic of China), and ten nonpermanent members elected by the General Assembly for staggered two-year terms.
- *Economic and Social Council.* Responsible for coordinating the UN's social and economic programs, functional commissions, and specialized agencies, its 54 members are elected by the General Assembly for staggered three-year terms. This body has been particularly active addressing economic development and human rights issues.
- *Trusteeship Council.* Charged with supervising the administration of territories that had not achieved self-rule, the Trusteeship Council suspended operation in 1994, when the last remaining trust territory gained independence.
- *International Court of Justice.* The principal judicial organ of the United Nations, the International Court of Justice is composed of 15 independent judges who are elected for nine-year terms by the General Assembly and Security Council. The competence of the Court is restricted to disputes between states, and its jurisdiction is based on the consent of the disputants. The Court may also give nonbinding advisory opinions on legal questions raised by the General Assembly, Security Council, or other UN agencies.
- *Secretariat.* Led by the secretary-general, the Secretariat contains the international civil servants who perform the administrative and secretarial functions of the UN.

The founders of the UN expected the Security Council to become the organization's primary body, since it was designed to maintain peace and its permanent members were the victorious great powers who had been allied during the Second World War. With the onset of the Cold War, however, frequent use of the veto power—initially by the Soviet Union and later by the United States—prevented the Council from acting on many security problems. As a result, the General Assembly gradually assumed wider responsibilities, and has now become the chief body for addressing security as well as social and economic problems.

The United Nations has changed in other ways not envisioned by its founders, evolving into an extraordinarily complex network of overlapping institutions, some of which (the UN Children's Fund or the United Nations University, for example) fulfill their mission in part through NGOs. The UN has also increasingly come to rely on the many NGOs that are not under its formal authority. This collaboration blurs the line between governmental and nongovernmental functions, but UN-NGO cooperation helps the UN's mission. In the process, the UN has become not one organization but a decentralized conglomerate of countless committees, bureaus, boards, commissions, centers, institutes, offices, and agencies scattered around the globe, with each of its many specialized activities managed from offices in various cities.

Many of the UN's changes have come in response to concerns voiced by Global South countries, who seized the advantage of their growing numbers under the one-state/one-vote rules of the General Assembly to push the UN in new directions. Today, a coalition of the less-developed Global South countries comprising three-fourths of the UN and led by the **Group of 77,** attempt to steer the organization's programs toward the needs of its poorer members.

North-South differences over perceived priorities are most clearly exhibited in the heated debate over the UN's budget. This controversy centers on how members should interpret the organization's charter, which states that "expenses of the Organization shall be borne by the members as apportioned by the General Assembly."

The UN budget consists of three distinct elements: the core budget, the peacekeeping budget, and the budget for voluntary programs. States contribute to the voluntary programs and some of the peacekeeping activities as they see fit. The core budget and other peacekeeping activities are subject to assessments.

The precise mechanism by which assessments have been determined is complicated, but, historically, assessments were allocated according to states' capacity to pay. Although this formula is under attack in many wealthy states, it still governs. Thus the United States, which has the greatest resources, contributes 22 percent of the core UN budget (and is also the primary contributor to UN peacekeeping and voluntary programs), whereas the poorest 70 percent of the UN's members pay the minimum (0.01 percent) and contribute only $13,000 annually. By this agreement, the richest states paid more than three-fourths toward the UN's $1.2 billion budget in the fiscal year 2003.

Resistance to this budgetary formula for funding UN activities has always existed. But it has grown progressively worse, in large part because when the General Assembly apportions expenses, it does so according to majority rule. The problem is that those with the most votes (the Global South countries) do not have the money, and the most prosperous countries do not have the votes. Wide disparities have grown so that by 2002 the ten largest contributors to the UN commanded only ten votes, but were expected to pay 75 percent of its cost. At the other end of the spectrum, the poorest members paid only 25 percent of the cost but commanded 175 votes. This deep imbalance has led to many fierce disputes over the kinds of issues on which the UN's attention and resources should be focused. The wealthy members charge that the existing budget procedures institutionalize a system of taxation without fair representation. The critics counter with the argument that the great-power members should bear financial responsibilities commensurate with their wealth and influence.

At issue, of course, is not simply money, which is paltry (averaging less than eighteen cents for each person in the world each year). Differences in images of what is important and which states should have political influence are the real issues. Poor states argue that needs should determine expenditure levels rather than the other way around. Major contributors, sensitive to the amounts asked of them and the purposes to which the funds are put, do not want to pay for programs they oppose. The United States in particular was historically the most vocal about its dissatisfaction and was still in arrears more than $1.2 billion until the 9/11 terrorist attack, when the United States promptly paid its debt as it sought UN support to wage a global war against terrorism.

Even though the Global South countries have usually managed to set the agenda in the General Assembly, like the United States they also regularly failed

• **Group of 77 (G-77)**
a coalition of the world's poor countries formed in 1964 to press for concessions from wealthy Global North states.

to pay their share of the budget. In fact, in early 2002 about 90 percent of the Global South members were also in arrears, and the unpaid assessments exceeded $3.1 billion.

In response to persisting cash flow problems and rising complaints about the UN's inefficient administration, Secretary-General Kofi Annan undertook what he called "bold reforms—the most extensive and far-reaching reforms in the history of the Organization." His initiative consolidated the programs under his control, reduced costs, corrected corruption and waste, and reassigned administrative responsibilities to different units in order to make the UN more efficient. These massive reforms cut the Secretariat's administrative costs by one-third, from 38 percent of the core budget to 25 percent and put the savings into a development fund for poor countries. The assessments of some Global North members were also adjusted: The United States pays 22 percent of the core budget, and Japan now pays 19.6 percent, Germany 9.8 percent, but France 6.5 percent, Russia only 2.9 percent, and China only 0.9 percent. The reorganization plan merged the score of disparate programs into five categories and created the UN's first deputy secretary-general position. The new budget for the 191 members puts the UN financial house on a firmer, if leaner, foundation.

The future of the UN nonetheless remains uncertain. Still, many supporters feel optimistic about the organization's long-term prospects, because past crises have been overcome and the UN's many important previous contributions to world peace and development have given most countries a large stake in its survival. The great gap between the mandates that the UN's members ordered, and the means they allowed for fulfilling them, may yet be closed. Failure would spell disaster.

In contemplating the UN's future agenda, it is sobering to reflect on Kofi Annan's warning that "The global agenda has never been so varied, so pressing or so complex. It demands of the international community new approaches, new resources and new commitments of political will." The challenges facing the UN are great, because the organization is expected to serve the economic and social development needs of 191 states and 6 billion people with less money than the annual budget for New York City's police department. In the final analysis, the UN can be no more than the mandates and power that the member states give to it. As one high-level UN civil servant, Brian Urquhart, described the world's political dilemma, "Either the UN is vital to a more stable and equitable world and should be given the means to do the job, or peoples and governments should be encouraged to look elsewhere. But is there really an alternative?"

Other Prominent Global IGOs

Beyond the UN, literally hundreds of other IGOs are active internationally. Few are truly global, including as members every independent state. To round out our examples of global IGOs, we look briefly at three of the most significant: the World Trade Organization, the World Bank, and the International Monetary Fund.

The World Trade Organization. Remembering the hardships caused by the Great Depression of 1929, the United States sought to create international economic institutions after World War II that would prevent another depression by

Beth A. Keiser/AP/Wide World Photos

Rage against Institutional Symbols of Globalization In the recent past, the meetings attended by finance ministers at such powerful IGOs as the World Bank or the International Monetary Fund drew little interest or publicity. Now, with increasing criticism of the globalization of national economies, these meetings are convenient targets for protesters. Seen here is one recent outburst, when the meeting of the World Trade Organization mobilized a broad-based coalition of NGOs to criticize the impact of economic globalization.

facilitating the expansion of world trade. One proposed institution was the International Trade Organization (ITO), first conceived as a specialized agency within the overall framework of the UN. While negotiations for the anticipated ITO were dragging on, many people urged immediate action. Meeting in Geneva in 1947, 23 states agreed to a number of **bilateral** tariff concessions that were written into a final act called the General Agreement on Tariffs and Trade (GATT), which originally was thought of as a temporary arrangement until the ITO came into operation.

• **bilateral** relationships or agreements between two states.

When a final agreement on the ITO proved elusive, GATT provided a mechanism for continued multilateral negotiations on reducing tariffs and other barriers to trade. Over the next several decades, eight rounds of negotiations were held to liberalize trade. Under the principle of nondiscrimination, GATT members were to give the same treatment to each other as they gave to their "most favored" trading partner.

On January 1, 1995, GATT was superceded by the World Trade Organization (WTO). Though not exactly the ITO envisaged immediately following World War II, it nevertheless represented the most ambitious undertaking yet launched to regulate world trade. Unlike GATT, which functioned more as a coordinating secretariat, the World Trade Organization is a full-fledged intergovernmental organization with a formal decision-making structure at the ministerial level. Mandated to manage disputes arising from its trading partners, the WTO was given authority for enforcing trading rules and authorizing third parties to adjudicate conflicts among its more than 145 members. In fact "the Dispute Settlement process within the WTO gives it the strongest enforcement capacity of all international organizations" (Smith and Moran 2001).

The present goal of the WTO is to transcend the existing matrix of free-trade agreements between pairs of countries and within particular regions, and replace them with an integrated and comprehensive worldwide system of liberal or free trade. This agenda poses a threat to some states. At the heart of their complaint is the charge that the WTO undermines the traditional rule of law prohibiting interference in sovereign states' domestic affairs, including management of economic practices *within* the states' territorial jurisdiction. However, the WTO, it should be kept in mind, developed as a result of agreements states reached to voluntarily surrender some of their sovereign decision-making freedom, under the conviction that this pooling of sovereignty would produce greater gains than losses. Nonetheless, the WTO seems destined to remain a target for criticism because "there is little evidence of democracy within the WTO operations" (Smith and Moran 2001). Many of its policies are orchestrated by its most powerful members during informal meetings that do not include the full WTO membership.

The World Bank. Created in July 1944 at the United Nations Monetary and Financial Conference held in Bretton Woods, New Hampshire, attended by 44 countries, the World Bank (or International Bank for Reconstruction and Development) was originally established to support reconstruction efforts in Europe after the Second World War. Over the next decade, the Bank shifted its attention from reconstruction to developmental assistance. Because Global South countries often have difficulty borrowing money to finance projects aimed at promoting economic growth, the Bank offers them loans with lower interest rates and longer repayment plans than they could typically obtain from commercial banks. In 2002, the Bank lent $11.5 billion to support 96 developmental projects in 40 countries.

Administratively, ultimate decision-making authority in the World Bank is vested in a board of governors, consisting of a governor and an alternate appointed by each of the Bank's 184 member countries. A governor customarily is a member country's minister of finance, or an equivalent official. The board meets annually in the Bank's Washington, DC headquarters to set policy directions, and delegates responsibility for the routine operations of the Bank to the 24 directors of its executive board. The five countries with the largest number of shares in the World Bank's capital stock (the United States, Germany, Japan,

France, and the United Kingdom) appoint their own executive directors, and the remaining executive directors are either appointed (Saudi Arabia), elected by their states (China, Russia, and Switzerland), or elected by groups of countries.

The World Bank operates according to a system of weighted voting. Each member is entitled to two hundred and fifty votes and receives one additional vote for each share held in the Bank's capital stock. This system recognizes the differences among members' holdings and is intended to protect the interests of the great powers that make more substantial contributions to the World Bank's resources. If a country's economic situation changes over time, its quota is adjusted and its allocation of shares and votes changes accordingly.

Most of the World Bank's loan funds are obtained, not from governments, but from borrowing in private capital markets. Applicants must demonstrate that loans will finance well-planned undertakings that will contribute to the productive and earning capacity of the recipient countries. For many years, the Bank frowned on loans for social projects, like building hospitals and schools or for slum clearance. Historically it also was reluctant to provide general-purpose loans, or loans to meet rising debt or to resolve balance-of-payment problems; but this has declined in recent years. On average, World Bank loans have financed only 25 percent of the cost of projects; to provide the balance, other investors are now required to support the World Bank.

Over the years, both the self-image and operations of the World Bank have changed—from a strictly financial IGO to that of a development agency. Instead of remaining aloof and merely passing judgment on loan applications, the Bank now assists states in their development planning, helps prepare project proposals, and provides training for senior development officials. Its economic survey missions actively monitor the resource and investment potential of member countries and determine priorities for country and regional projects. The World Bank has also participated increasingly in consortium arrangements for financing private lending institutions. It has demonstrated repeatedly that it is also dedicated to the promotion of democratic governance, by its recent insistence on democratic reforms as a condition for economic assistance.

Despite its increased pace of activity, the World Bank has never been able to meet all the needs for financial assistance of the developing states. The repayment of loans in hard currencies has imposed serious burdens on impoverished and indebted borrowing states from the Global South. The deficiencies of the World Bank, however, have been partly offset by the establishment of another lending IGO, the International Monetary Fund.

The International Monetary Fund. Prior to World War II, the international community lacked institutional mechanisms to manage the exchange of money across borders. At the 1944 Bretton Woods Conference, the United States was a prime mover in creating the International Monetary Fund (IMF), a global institution designed to maintain currency-exchange stability by promoting international monetary cooperation and orderly exchange arrangements, and by functioning as a lender of last resort for countries experiencing financial crises.

The IMF is now one of the 16 specialized agencies within the UN system. Each IMF member is represented on its governing board, which meets annually to fix general policy. Day-to-day business is conducted by a 22-member executive board chaired by a managing director, who is also the administrative head of a staff of approximately two thousand employees.

The IMF derives its operating funds from member states. Contributions are based on a quota system set according to a state's national income, gold reserves, and other factors affecting each member's ability to contribute. In this way, the IMF operates like a credit union that requires each participant to contribute to a common pool of funds from which it can borrow when the need arises. The IMF's voting is weighted according to a state's monetary contribution, giving a larger voice to the wealthier states.

The IMF, as a standard practice, usually attaches strict conditions to its loans, which has led to considerable criticism. Some people charge that the IMF imposes austerity measures on countries in financial crises, forcing them to cut government spending on social programs when they are most needed. Others complain that the IMF makes political demands regarding democratization and privatization that exceed the institution's original mandate. Many theorists from radical branches of the socialist tradition argue that IMF conditions are tools for weakening domestic groups opposing the spread of international capitalism. IMF officials retort that they are simply trying to ensure that the problems that produced the crisis are remedied, so foreign investment can flow into the country.

Regional Intergovernmental Organizations

The tug-of-war between states within global IGOs is a reminder that these organizations are run by the states that join them. This severely inhibits the IGOs' ability to rise above interstate competition and pursue their own purposes. Because they cannot act autonomously, universal IGOs are often viewed more as instruments of their state members' foreign policies and arenas for debate than as independent nonstate actors.

When certain states dominate universal international organizations like the UN, the prospects for international cooperation decline because, as realist theorists emphasize, national leaders fear multilateral organizations that may compromise their country's vital interests. Yet, as liberal theorists argue, *regional* cooperation among powerful states is possible, as evidenced by the evolution of the European Union (EU). In many respects the EU is unique, if for no other reason than that it stands as the world's greatest example of peaceful international cooperation producing an integrated **security community** with a single economy and a common currency.

• **security community** a group of states whose high level of noninstitutionalized collaboration results in the settlement of disputes by compromise rather than by force.

The European Union

Click on International Law and Organization for an interactive Case Study on the European Union.

Europe emerged from the Second World War a devastated continent with a demoralized population. Over 35 million Europeans perished during the fighting. Much of the urban landscape was reduced to bomb craters and rubble. Countless buildings were uninhabitable, the transportation infrastructure lay in ruins, and food was scarce. Some Europeans felt that the only way to prevent their countries from squaring off on the battlefield in a generation was through political and economic unification.

The process of European unification began with the creation of the European Coal and Steel Community (ECSC) in 1951. A year earlier, French Foreign Minister Robert Schuman had proposed placing all French and German coal and steel resources under a joint authority, and allowing other European states to take part in the new organization. As part of the ECSC, Germany could revive its heavy industry after the war without alarming its neighbors, who would now possess some degree of control over key German resources by virtue of their representation in the joint authority. Ultimately, France and Germany were joined in the ECSC by Belgium, Luxembourg, The Netherlands, and Italy.

The drive toward further European unity gathered momentum in 1957 with the creation of the European Atomic Energy Community (Euratom), patterned after the ECSC, and the European Economic Community (EEC), a fledgling common market providing for the free movement of goods, people, and capital among member states. These three communities were collectively recognized in the 1992 Maastricht Treaty as the first "pillar" of the EU structure. Two additional pillars have since been under construction: a Common Foreign and Security Policy pillar and a Justice and Homeland Affairs pillar. The former is an attempt to create a single European foreign and defense policy; the latter, common policies on immigration and criminal justice.

During this process of regional institution-building, membership grew in a series of waves to encompass 25 countries: Belgium, France, Germany, Italy, Luxembourg, and the Netherlands (the original "six"); Denmark, Ireland, and the United Kingdom (which joined in 1973); Greece (1981); Portugal and Spain (1986); Austria, Finland, and Sweden (1995); and Poland, the Czech Republic, Slovakia, Hungary, Slovenia, Latvia, Lithuania, Estonia, Malta, and Cyprus (2004). These sequential enlargements have created the world's biggest free-trade bloc, and have transformed the face of Europe by ending the continent's division. The idea of a single Europe remains compelling for many Europeans who are haunted by the specter of European nationalities and states that have been fighting each other ever since the Pax Romana collapsed 1,800 years ago.

The principal institutions for EU governance include a Council of Ministers, the European Commission, a European Parliament, and a Court of Justice. The EU's central administrative unit, the Council of Ministers, consists of cabinet ministers drawn from the EU's member states, who participate in the most important policy decisions. The council also sets general guidelines for the European Commission, which consists of twenty commissioners (two each from Britain, France, Germany, Italy, and Spain, and one each from the remaining member states). Commissioners are nominated by EU member governments and must be approved by the European Parliament. Headquartered in Brussels, the primary functions of the European Commission are to propose new laws for the EU, oversee EU treaties, and execute the decrees of the European Council. A professional staff of 17,000 civil-service "Eurocrats" assist the commission in proposing legislation and implementing EU policies. It also manages the EU's budget, which, in contrast with most international organizations, derives part of its revenues from sources not under the control of member states.

The European Parliament represents the political parties and public opinion within Europe. It has existed from the beginning of Europe's journey toward political unification, although at its creation this legislative body was appointed rather than elected and had very little power. That is no longer the case. The European Parliament is now chosen in a direct election by the citizens of the EU's member states. Its 626 deputies debate issues at the monumental glass headquarters in Brussels and at a lavish Strasbourg palace in the same way that democratic national legislative bodies do. The European Parliament shares authority with the Council of Ministers representing member governments, but the Parliament's influence has increased over time. The deputies elected through universal suffrage pass laws with the council, approve the EU's budget, oversee the European Commission, and can overturn its acts.

The European Court of Justice in Luxembourg has also grown in prominence and power as European integration has gathered depth and breadth. From the start, the court was given responsibility for adjudicating claims and conflicts among EU governments as well as between those governments and the new institutions the EU created. Comprising 15 judges, the court interprets EU law for national courts, rules on legal questions that arise within the EU's institutions, and hears and rules on cases concerning individual citizens. The fact that its decisions are binding distinguishes the European Court of Justice from most other international tribunals.

The political unification of Europe has been built step-by-step as the EU has marched toward ever greater unity. Moving beyond the nation-state toward a single integrated European federation has not been smooth, and disagreement persists over the extent to which the EU should become a single, truly united superstate, a "United States of Europe." Debate continues also over how far and how fast such a process of **pooled sovereignty** should proceed, and about the natural geographical limits of the EU's membership and boundaries. Nevertheless, the EU represents a remarkable success story in the history of international relations. Who would have expected competitive states that have spent most of their national experiences waging war against one another would consolidate, put their clashing ambitions aside, and construct a new European identity built on confederated decision making? The EU has moved above the nation-state as a *supranational* regional organization pledged to giving the EU dominion over its 25 members' internal affairs and control over common foreign and military policies, while at the same time developing a sense of solidarity and belonging among the regions' peoples.

• **pooled sovereignty** legal authority granted to an IGO by its members to make collective decisions regarding specified aspects of public policy heretofore made exclusively by each sovereign government.

Other Regional IGOs

Since Europe's move toward economic and political integration, more than a dozen regional IGOs have been created in various other parts of the world, notably among states in the Global South. Most seek to stimulate regional economic growth, but many have drifted from that original purpose to pursue multiple political and military purposes as well. Africa exemplifies this pattern (See Map 6.2). Although it has a number of small IGOs focused on liberalizing regional trade, it also contains large, multipurpose organizations such as the Eco-

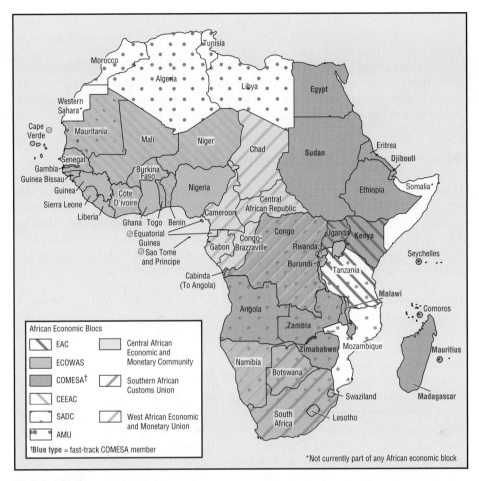

MAP 6.2
Africa's Regional IGOs

Africa contains a network of regional IGOs, with multiple, crosscutting memberships. This map shows its major economic IGOs. Created in the spirit of free trade, they enjoy support from the World Trade Organization, which believes that the improved administrative capabilities of regional IGOs will help prepare Africa for fuller participation in global efforts to reduce trade barriers.

SOURCE: From *The Economist,* Feb. 10, 2001, p. 77. Copyright © 2001 by The Economist Newspaper, Ltd. All rights reserved. Reprinted with permission. Further reproduction prohibited. www.economist.com

nomic Community of Western African States (ECOWAS) and the Common Market for Eastern and Southern Africa (COMESA) (*The Economist.* February 10, 2001, 77).

None of the regional IGOs outside of Europe have managed to collaborate at a level that begins to match the institutionalized collective decision making achieved by the EU. The reasons vary, but in general these regional IGOs are limited by national leaders' reluctance to make politically costly choices that would undermine their personal popularity at home and their governments' sovereignty.

Nonetheless, these attempts at regional cooperation demonstrate many states' acceptance of the fact that they cannot individually resolve many of the problems that confront them collectively.

Another set of nonstate actors on the world stage are NGOs, such as ethnopolitical groups, religious movements, multinational corporations, transnational banks, and issue-advocacy groups. We now turn our attention to their behavior and impact.

Nongovernmental Organizations

If you are like most people, there is at least one problem of concern to you that crosses national borders. You would like to see it resolved, but you probably realize that you cannot engineer global changes all by yourself. Recognizing that collective voices are more likely to be heard, many people have found that by joining nongovernmental organizations (NGOs) they can lobby more effectively for causes they support. NGOs are international actors whose members are not states, but instead are people drawn from the populations of two or more societies who have come together to promote their shared interests. There are almost 30,000 NGOs in existence worldwide, and they tackle global issues ranging from environmental protection to human rights. Most of them pursue objectives that are highly respected and constructive, and therefore do not arouse much opposition. For example, NGOs such as the International Chamber of Commerce, the Red Cross, Save the Children, and the World Wildlife Federation enjoy widespread popular support. Others, however, are more controversial because they push for changes which, were they to succeed, would threaten the interests of those who have a stake in preserving the status quo. At recent UN World Population Conferences, for example, NGOs supporting reproductive rights have clashed with right-to-life groups. Hence, many NGOs work at cross-purposes in a competitive struggle to redefine the global agenda.

What makes NGOs increasingly prominent on the world stage is that their activities are now shaping responses to issues that once were determined exclusively by governments (Runyan 1999). Greenpeace, Amnesty International, and other global issue-advocacy groups have used their technical expertise, organizational flexibility, and grassroots connections to affect every stage of the development of **international regimes,** from problem recognition through policy implementation. Their influence demonstrates that world politics is not merely the interaction of sovereign, territorial states. It also involves complex networks of people, who coalesce in myriad combinations at different times for various purposes. Moreover, as al Qaeda and other transnational terrorist groups remind us, these purposes are not always benign.

As NGOs rise in numbers and influence, it is important to consider how they may transform world politics. Although NGOs comprise a large, heterogeneous group of nonstate actors, a small subset of them receive the most attention and provoke the most controversy. Within this subset, NGOs based on ethnic identity are particularly noteworthy.

• **international regimes** sets of principles, norms, rules, and decision-making procedures agreed to by a group of states to guide their behavior in particular issue-areas.

Ethnopolitical Movements

Although the state remains the most visible actor in world affairs, some people pledge their primary allegiance not to the government that rules them, but rather to an **ethnopolitical group,** whose members share a common nationality, language, cultural tradition, and kinship ties. They view themselves as members of their ethnic group first and of their state only secondarily. Many states are divided, multiethnic societies made up of a variety of politically active groups that seek, if not outright independence, a greater level of regional autonomy and a greater voice in the domestic and foreign policies of the state. "Nearly three quarters of the world's larger countries have politically significant minorities," and 275 minority groups comprising one-sixth of the world's population are at risk from persecution worldwide (Gurr, Ted Robert 2001). Some of these minorities, such as the Kurds in Iraq, Turkey, and Iran, spill across several countries. Thus, images of the state as a unitary actor and of governments as autonomous rulers of integrated nations are not very accurate. These ethnic divisions and the NGOs that often develop around them make thinking of international relations as exclusively interactions between homogeneous states with impermeable, hard-shell boundaries—the realist "billiard ball model"—dubious.

Indigenous peoples are the ethnic and cultural groups that were native to a geographic location now controlled by another state or political group. The world is populated by an estimated six thousand separate indigenous nations, each of which has a unique language and culture and strong, often spiritual, ties to an ancestral homeland. In most cases indigenous people were at one time politically sovereign and economically self-sufficient. Today there are an estimated 300 million indigenous people, more than 5 percent of the world's population, scattered in more than seventy countries (see Map 6.3); some have placed the number as high as 650 million (*The State of Indigenous People* 2002).

It is extremely difficult to classify and count the variety of indigenous ethnopolitical movements struggling for recognition. Perhaps the best way of making a rough estimate is by observing linguistic similarity. A huge number of ethnolinguistic divisions separate cultures. "Measured by spoken languages, the single best indicator of a distinct culture, all the world's people belong to 6,000 cultures; 4,000 to 5,000 of these are indigenous ones" (Durning 1993, 81).

Still, this indicator may be somewhat misleading, since the belief systems and backgrounds that arouse ethnopolitical movements among indigenous peoples are varied and often overlapping. Beyond language, these movements are based on many other cultural traits, which can lead their members to place higher value on ideals other than patriotic loyalty to particular states.

Religion is another force that can create identities and loyalties that transcend national boundaries. To expand our exploration of the role of NGOs in world politics, let us examine religious movements.

Religious Movements

In theory, religion would seem a natural force for global harmony. Yet millions have died in the name of religion. The Crusades between the eleventh and

• **ethnopolitical group** people whose identity is primarily defined by their sense of sharing a common ancestral nationality, language, cultural heritage, and kinship ties.

• **indigenous peoples** the native ethnic and cultural inhabitant populations within countries ruled by a government controlled by others, referred to as the "Fourth World."

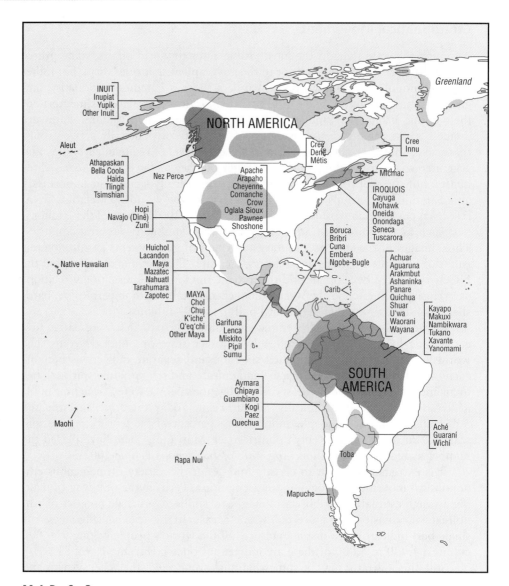

M A P   6 . 3
The Indigenous Cultures of the World

More than 5,000 indigenous peoples live throughout the world. As Julian Burger of the UN's Office of the High Commissioner for Human Rights noted in 1999, many are now "asserting their cultural identity, claiming their right to control their futures, and struggling to regain their ancestral lands." To protect their human rights, they have begun to organize, as can be seen in the 1992 World Conference of Indigenous Peoples held in Rio de Janeiro, Brazil. As a result of their lobbying, the UN named 1993 the International Year of the World's Indigenous Peoples.

NOTE: Colors indicate regional concentrations of indigenous peoples.

SOURCE: Julian Burger, United Nations. Adapted from "Vanishing Cultures" by Wade Davis, *National Geographic,* August 1999, pp. 66–67. NG Maps/NGS Image Collection.

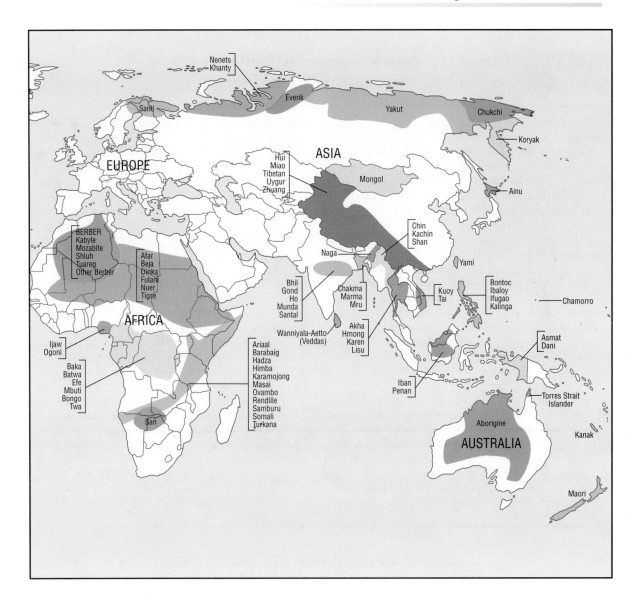

fourteenth centuries left countless Christians and Muslims dead. Similarly, the religious conflicts during the Thirty Years' War (1618–1648) between Catholics and Protestants killed nearly one-fourth of all Europeans.

Many of the world's more than 6 billion people are affiliated in some form with a religious movement—a politically active organization based on strong religious convictions. At the most abstract level, a religion is a system of thought shared by a group that provides its members an object of devotion and a code of behavior by which they can ethically judge their actions. This definition points to commonalities across the great diversity of organized religions in the world, but it fails to capture that diversity. The world's principal religions vary greatly in the

CONTROVERSY

Are Religious Movements Causes of War or Sources of Transnational Harmony?

After September 11, 2001, debate about the impact of religion on international conflict intensified, because many believed that the terrorist attacks on the World Trade Center and the Pentagon were motivated by religious fanatics within the al Qaeda organization. As a result, the religious sources of political violence have received considerable attention, as have religious NGOs more generally.

It is difficult to understand the religious origins of violence because most people equate religion with compassion and forgiveness, not hatred and intolerance. Indeed, many of the principles that the world's major religious movements espouse would seem conducive to peace. They all voice respect and reverence for the sanctity of life and acceptance of all people as equal creations of a deity, regardless of race or ethnicity. These are noble ideals. Religions speak to universal principles, across time and place—to enduring values in changing times.

If all the world's great religious movements espouse pacific ideals, why are those same religions increasingly criticized as sources of international conflict?

In evaluating the role of religious NGOs in international affairs, consider first the view of sociologists of religion who contend that religious hostility results from the fact that universalistic religions are managed by organizations that often adopt a particularistic and dogmatic outlook (see Juergensmeyer 2003). Followers of a religion may conceive the world through a lens that sees outsiders as rivals and other creeds as challenges to their own faith. In a word, religious movements often practice intolerance—disrespect for diversity and the right of people to freely embrace another religion's beliefs. Sometimes the next step is for fanatics to portray these outsiders as evil and call for violence against them. "If you want war," sociologist William Graham Sumner once quipped, "nourish a doctrine."

Does this argument hold up under careful examination? Those who think it doesn't point out that societies recognizing no higher deity also have waged war against others. Meanwhile, many religions perform ably the mission of peace making.

It is important for you to weigh the evidence about the impact of religious NGOs on international affairs. In doing so, take into account the impact of this controversy on theories of world politics. Observing that many wars have been fought in the name of religion, some realists argue that religion can be a serious danger to world order, since it may foster a crusading spirit. Compromise, the mutual accommodation of conflicting claims, is difficult when disputants are the standard-bearers of rival faiths (Morgenthau 1985). What do you think? Does religion transform disputes into wars for total stakes? ●

theological doctrines they embrace. They also differ widely in the size of their followings, in the geographical locations where they are most prevalent, and in the extent to which they engage in political efforts to influence international affairs.

These differences make it risky to generalize about the impact of religious movements on world affairs. Those who study religious movements comparatively note that a system of beliefs provides followers with their main source of identity, and that this identification with and devotion to their religion springs from the natural human need to find a set of values with which to evaluate the meaning of life. Unfortunately, this need sometimes leads believers to perceive the values of their own creed as superior to those of others. Members of many religious movements believe that their religion should be universal, and actively proselytize to convert nonbelievers to their faith. Though conversion is usually sought through persuasion, at times it has been achieved by the sword (see Controversy: Are Religious Movements Causes of War or Sources of Transnational Harmony?).

In evaluating the impact of religious movements, it is important to distinguish carefully the high ideals of doctrines from the activities of the people who head these religious bodies. The two realms are not the same, and each can be judged fairly only against the standards they set for themselves. To condemn what large-scale religious movements sometimes do when they abuse the principles of the religions they manage does not mean that the principles themselves deserve condemnation. Still, many observers maintain that otherwise humanitarian religions sometimes oppose each other violently, despite their professed doctrines of tolerance. When they do, religious movements become sources of international tension.

While not all religious movements are alike, militant movements involved in politics share certain similar characteristics:

1. Militant religious political movements tend to view existing government authority as corrupt and illegitimate because it is secular and not sufficiently rigorous in upholding religious authority or religiously sanctioned social and moral values.
2. They attack the inability of government to address the domestic ills of the society in which the movement exists. In many cases the religious movement substitutes itself for the government at the local level and is involved in education, health, and other social welfare programs.
3. They subscribe to a particular set of behavior and opinions that they believe political authority must reflect, promote, and protect in all governmental and social activities. This generally means that government and all of its domestic and foreign activities must be in the hands of believers or subject to their close oversight.
4. They are universalists: Unlike ethnic movements, they tend to see their views as part of the inheritance of everyone who is a believer. This tends to give them a trans-state motivation, a factor that then translates their views on legitimacy of political authority into a larger context for action. In some cases, this means that international boundaries are not recognized as barriers to the propagation of the faith, even if this means they resort to violence.
5. They are exclusionists: They relegate all conflicting opinions on appropriate political and social order to the margins—if they do not exclude them altogether. This translates as second-class citizenship for any nonbeliever in any society where such a view predominates.
6. Finally, they are militant, willing to use coercion to achieve the only true end. (Shultz and Olson 1994, 9–10)

Although militant religious movements are not the only nonstate actors whose ideologies and activities may contribute to violence, many experts believe that they tend to stimulate five specific types of international activities. The first is **irredentism**—the attempt by a dominant religion or ethnic group to reclaim previously possessed territory in an adjacent region from a foreign state that now controls it. The second is **secession**—the attempt by a religious (or ethnic) minority to break away from an internationally recognized state in a separatist revolt. Third, militant religions tend to incite migration, the departure of religious minorities from their countries of origin to escape persecution. Whether they

• **irredentism** efforts by an ethnonational or religious group to regain control of territory by force so that existing state boundaries will no longer separate the group.

• **secession** the attempt by a religious or ethnic minority to break away from an internationally recognized state.

move by force or by choice, the result—a fourth consequence of militant religion—is the same: The emigrants create diasporas, or communities that live abroad in host countries but maintain economic, political, and emotional ties with their homelands. Finally, a fifth effect of militant religions is international terrorism in the form of support for radical coreligionists abroad.

If we critically inspect the activities of militant religious movements, we come away with the impression that they not only bring people together but also divide them. Religious movements often challenge state authority, and religious-driven strife can tear countries apart.

Multinational Corporations and Transnational Banks

• **multinational corporations (MNCs)** business enterprises headquartered in one state that invest and operate extensively in other states.

In an age of porous borders and growing interdependence, we need to look beyond ethnopolitical groups and religious movements to consider the roles of multinational corporations and transnational banks as nonstate actors. **Multinational corporations (MNCs)** have grown dramatically in scope and influence since World War II. At the beginning of the twenty-first century, the UN estimated that more than 53,000 MNCs and their 450,000 foreign affiliates had global assets in excess of $13 trillion and global sales of more than $9.5 trillion. This financial clout is estimated to account for more than one-fifth of the world's economy, one-third of the world's exports, and one-third of the world's stock of all **foreign direct investment (FDI)**.

• **foreign direct investment (FDI)** ownership of assets in a country by nonresidents in order to control the use of those assets.

MNCs also employ more than 75 million people, although most of the existing MNCs are small and employ fewer than two hundred fifty people (Stopford 2001). Today most multinational corporations are " 'flag planters,' colonial outposts of basically domestic companies with some plant, or mines, or sales organizations in a few foreign lands" (Jain and Chelminski 1999). About twenty percent of all MNC employees work in the developed countries of the Global North, but MNCs penetrate the labor force throughout the world.

• **transnational banks (TNBs)** the world's top banking firms, whose financial activities are concentrated in transactions that cross state borders.

MNC expansion has been facilitated by **transnational banks (TNBs)**, another type of global NGO whose revenues and assets are primarily generated by financial transactions in the international economy. At the start of 2000, the combined assets of the world's 20 largest banks exceeded $425 trillion, a staggering figure attesting to the consolidation of the highly profitable control of financial resources in a highly globalized economy. TNBs funnel trade and help to reduce the meaning of political borders by making each state's economy dependent on other states' economies through the transfer of capital through international loans and investments. Together, TNBs and MNCs redistribute wealth and income throughout the world economy, contributing to the economic development of some states and the stagnation of others. One feared consequence in the Global South is that the TNBs advance the rich Global North at the South's expense, because about four-fifths of foreign direct investment is funneled into the richest countries with the poorest countries typically receiving very little. Like MNCs, therefore, TNBs spread the rewards of globalization unequally and inequitably, increasing wealth for a select group of countries and marginalizing the others.

Through their loans to the private sector, TNBs have made capital highly mobile and expanded the capacity of MNCs to function as the primary agents in the globalization of production. Table 6.2 captures the importance of MNCs in world politics, ranking firms by annual sales and states by GNP. The profile shows that of the world's top 100 economic entities, multinationals account for only 14 of the top 50, but in the next 50, they account for 37. MNCs' financial clout thus rivals or exceeds that of most countries, with the result that many people fear that these corporate giants are undermining the ability of sovereign states to control their own economies and therefore their own fates.

Because of their financial strength and global reach, it is tempting to conclude that MNCs are a threat to state power. Their ability to make decisions on many issues over which national political leaders have little control appears to be eroding state sovereignty, the international system's major organizing principle. However, this interpretation overlooks the fact that at the same time MNCs have grown in size, the regulatory power of states has grown. "Agreements over such things as airline routes, the opening of banking establishments, and the right to sell insurance are not decided by corporate actors who gather around a table; they are determined by diplomats and bureaucrats. Corporations must turn to governments when they have interests to protect or advance" (Kapstein 1991–1992).

Still, controlling the resulting webs of corporate interrelationships, joint ventures, and shared ownership for any particular national purpose is nearly impossible. Part of the reason is that about one-third of world trade in goods and services occurs *within* multinationals, from one branch to another. Joint production and **strategic corporate alliances** to create temporary phantom "virtual corporations" undermine states' ability to identify the MNCs they seek to control. "There is widespread concern that MNCs are becoming truly 'stateless' [as] the explosion of strategic alliances is transforming the corporate landscape" with more than 10,000 strategic alliances estimated to be forged each year recently (Stopford 2001, 74–75). "By acquiring earth-spanning technologies, by developing products that can be produced anywhere and sold everywhere, by spreading credit around the world, and by connecting global channels of communication that can penetrate any village or neighborhood, these institutions we normally think of as economic rather than political, private rather than public, are becoming the world empires of the twenty-first century" (Barnet and Cavanagh 1994, 14).

• **strategic corporate alliances** cooperation between multinational corporations and foreign companies in the same industry, driven by the movement of MNC manufacturing overseas.

Issue-Advocacy Groups and Global Civil Society

A final type of NGO that we will examine is composed of associational interest groups organized around special policy interests, such as environmental protection or upholding human rights. Greenpeace, for example, focuses much of its attention on preventing pollution and maintaining biodiversity through education programs, lobbying, and nonviolent protest demonstrations. Boasting a worldwide membership of 2.8 million and offices in 41 countries, Greenpeace had a total income of over $165 million in 2002, derived largely from individual donations and foundation grants. Included among what it claims as its successes

TABLE 6.2

Countries and Corporations: A Ranking by Size of Economy and Revenues

Rank	County/Corporation	GNP/Revenues (Billions of Dollars)	Rank	County/Corporation	GNP/Revenues (Billions of Dollars)
1	United States	9996.24	51	NIPPON TELEGRAPH & TELEPHONE	103.23
2	Japan	4619.81	52	ENRON	100.79
3	Germany	1921.97	53	Egypt, Arab Rep.	96.17
4	United Kingdom	1434.87	54	Ireland	95.07
5	France	1317.11	55	Singapore	93.49
6	Italy	1080.87	56	AXA	92.78
7	China	1070.72	57	SUMITOMO	91.17
8	Canada	698.79	58	IBM	88.40
9	Brazil	641.95	59	Colombia	87.00
10	Spain	564.67	60	Malaysia	86.13
11	Mexico	563.83	61	MARUBENI	85.35
12	Korea	490.99	62	Iran	82.55
13	India	474.98	63	Philippines	78.87
14	Australia	385.30	64	VOLKSWAGEN	78.85
15	Netherlands	371.35	65	HITACHI	76.13
16	Taiwan, China	320.98	66	SIMENS	74.86
17	Argentina	289.32	67	Chile	74.66
18	Switzerland	242.02	68	ING GROUP	71.20
19	Russia	236.16	69	ALLIANZ	71.02
20	Sweden	235.17	70	MATSUSHITA ELECTRIC INDUSTRIAL	69.48
21	Belgium	229.21	71	E. ON	68.43
22	EXXON MOBIL	210.39	72	NIPPON LIFE INSURANCE	68.05
23	Turkey	197.68	73	DEUTSCHE BANK	67.13
24	WAL-MART STORES	193.30	74	SONY	66.16
25	Austria	192.30	75	AT&T	65.98
26	GENERAL MOTORS	184.63	76	VERIZON COMMUNICATIONS	64.71
27	FORD MOTOR	180.60	77	U.S. POSTAL SERVICE	64.54
28	Saudi Arabia	167.81	78	PHILIP MORRIS	63.28
29	Hong Kong, China	163.25	79	CGNU	61.50
30	Denmark	160.95	80	Pakistan	61.48
31	Indonesia	160.17	81	J. P. MORGAN CHASE	60.07
32	Norway	158.01	82	CARREFOUR	59.89
33	Poland	156.78	83	CREDIT SUISSE	59.32
34	DAIMLERCHRYSLER	150.07	84	NISSHO IWAI	58.56
35	ROYAL DUTCH/SHELL GROUP	149.15	85	HONDA MOTORS	58.46
36	BRITISH PETROLEUM	148.06	86	Peru	58.17
37	GENERAL ELECTRIC	129.85	87	BANK OF AMERICA	57.75
38	Thailand	129.70	88	BNP PARIBAS	57.61
39	South Africa	129.28	89	Algeria	57.02
40	MITSUBISHI	126.58	90	NISSAN MOTOR	55.08
41	Finland	121.76	91	TOSHIBA	53.83
42	TOYOTA MOTOR	121.42	92	PDVSA	53.68
43	MITSUI	118.01	93	ASSICURAZIONI GENERALI	53.33
44	Greece	114.79	94	FIAT	53.19
45	Venezuela	114.73	95	Hungary	52.48
46	CITIGROUP	111.83	96	MIZUHO HOLDINGS	52.07
47	ITOCHU	109.76	97	New Zealand	51.91
48	Portugal	105.91	98	SBC COMMUNICATION	51.48
49	TOTAL FINA ELF	105.87	99	BOEING	51.32
50	Israel	105.70	100	TEXACO	51.13

By integrating production and marketing their products worldwide, MNCs are dominating the global economy. As a result, MNCs rival many countries in wealth and are translating that income into influence as NGO actors. The value of MNC global mergers and acquisitions rose five-fold in the 1990s, to over $3.6 trillion in 2000 (*The Economist*, January 27, 2001, 61). This trend suggests that the "sheer size and power that some of these companies are amassing", leaves few ways to prevent "big monopolies from overwhelming consumers and preventing big business from overwhelming democratic government," observes Thomas Friedman (2000). Four months after these data were reported, Enron filed for bankruptcy.

SOURCE: MNC revenues, *Fortune* August, 2001;
www.fortune.com/indexw.jhtml?channel=/editorial/site_map.html/; countries' GDP, *The World Economic Outlook* (WEO) Database, IMF (May, 2001).

are international prohibitions on large-scale driftnet fishing, dumping of radioactive wastes at sea, and mining in Antarctica.

Issue-oriented NGOs like Greenpeace flourish when governments permit freedom of expression and association, and thus have increased exponentially as the number of democracies worldwide has risen over the past two decades. Their increase has led some scholars to observe that "interest group pluralism is growing" in world politics (Falk and Strauss 2001). NGOs, they argue, are empowering ordinary people, giving them a voice and a means of political leverage. In effect, the proliferation of NGOs is "creating an incipient, albeit imperfect, civil society at the global level" (Keohane and Nye 2001a).

However, not everyone believes that we are witnessing the formation of a global civil society. Skeptics claim that "NGOs have tended to reinforce rather than counter existing power structures, having members and headquarters that are primarily in the rich Global North countries. Some also believe that NGO decision making does not provide for responsible, democratic representation or accountability" (Stephenson 2000). By their account, many NGOs represent vested interests working quietly behind the scenes to lobby for global policies that protect the powerful.

How influential and effective are grassroots NGOs? Research on this question suggests the following conclusions, which cast doubt over whether pressure from NGOs can lead to far-reaching reforms in the conduct of international relations:

- Interest group activity operates as an ever present, if limited, constraint on global policy making, but the impact varies with the issue and their influence is weakest on the most important problems on the global agenda.
- Similarly, the occasions when private NGOs are most influential are rare. The influences are greatest with respect to a particular issue—such as nuclear nonproliferation—when in the interests of the great powers.
- As a general rule, NGOs are relatively weak in the high politics of international security, because states remain in control of defense policy and are relatively unaffected by external NGO pressures. Conversely, the NGOs' clout is highest with respect to issues in low politics, such as protecting endangered species (e.g., whales) or combating global warming, which are of concern to great and small powers alike.
- The influence between state governments and NGOs is reciprocal, but it is more probable that government officials manipulate transnational interest groups than that NGOs exercise influence over governments' foreign policies.
- Single-issue NGO interest groups have more influence than large general-purpose organizations.
- NGOs sometimes seek inaction from governments and maintenance of the status quo; such efforts are generally more successful than efforts to bring about major changes in international relations. For this reason NGOs are often generally seen as agents of policy continuities.

To sum up, the mere presence of NGOs, and the mere fact they are organized with the intent of persuasion, does not guarantee their penetration of the global policy-making process. On the whole, NGOs have participation without real power and involvement without real influence, given that the ability of any *one* to exert influence is offset by the tendency for countervailing powers to materialize over the disposition of major issues. That is, as any particular coalition of NGOs works together on a common cause and begins to be powerful, other groups threatened by the changes advocated spring up to balance it. When an interest group seeks vigorously to push policy in one direction, other nonstate actors—aroused that their established interests are being disturbed—are stimulated to push policy in the opposite direction. Global policy making consequently resembles a taffy pull: Every nonstate actor attempts to yank policy in its own direction, with the result that movement on many global problems fails to proceed consistently in any single direction.

This balance between opposing actors helps to account for the reason why so few global issues are resolved. Competition stands in the way of consensus, and contests of will over international issues are seldom settled. No side can ever claim permanent victory, for each decision that takes international policy in one direction merely sets the stage for the next round of the contest, with the possibility that the losers of the moment will be winners tomorrow. The struggle between those wishing to make protection of the environment a global priority and those placing economic growth ahead of environmental preservation provides one among many examples.

Nonstate Actors and the Global Future

As people, products, and information increasingly move across the planet, IGOs and NGOs will play ever-larger roles in the world. More than at any time since the Peace of Westphalia in 1648, nonstate actors are challenging sovereign, territorial states in the management of international affairs. According to one scholar, states are losing much of their problem-solving credibility (Falk 1998). Not only are they challenged from above by multinational corporations, transnational banks, and global economic IGOs, but they are also being challenged from below by the grassroots NGOs of an emerging global civil society.

"After three and a half centuries," notes Jessica Mathews (1998), president of the Carnegie Endowment for International Peace, "it takes a big mental leap to think of world politics in any terms other than that of occasionally cooperating but usually competing states." Yet in a world characterized by ever-increasing ties among individuals and organizations who see territorial boundaries as anachronisms, nation-states are not the Leviathans described by the seventeenth-century philosopher Thomas Hobbes. Rather than being autonomous entities, they are enmeshed with nonstate actors in complex webs that blur the distinction between foreign and domestic affairs. If the traditional Westphalian worldview could be symbolized by a static two-dimensional map depicting discrete territorial states on a grid of longitude and latitude, then a post-Westphalian worldview might be represented by a dynamic holographic projection of a vast, multilayered network linking states with many other types of actors.

To sum up, IGOs and NGOs are changing the face of international affairs as they seek to reshape the global agenda. The question for the twenty-first century is whether the nation-state system as we know it will survive. States cannot insulate their populations from "the flow of images and ideas that shape human tastes and values. The globalized 'presence' of Madonna, McDonald's, and Mickey Mouse make a mockery of sovereignty as exclusive territorial control" (Falk 2001b). Of course, this does not mean that the era of state dominance is over. States retain a (near) monopoly on the use of coercive force in the world, and they mold the activities of nonstate actors more than their behavior is molded by them. It is also true that "a gain in power by nonstate actors does not necessarily translate into a loss of power for the state" (Slaughter 1997). Nevertheless, we must conclude that whereas it would be premature to abandon the focus on the state in world politics, it would be equally mistaken to exaggerate the state's power as a determinant of the world's fate and dismiss the expanding role of nonstate actors in shaping the global future.

Chapter Summary

- Despite states having an enormous capacity to influence national and global welfare, the state is ill-suited for managing many transnational policy problems; consequently no analysis of world politics would be complete without a treatment of the role played by nonstate actors.
- There are two principle types of nonstate actors in world politics, intergovernmental organizations (IGOs) and nongovernmental organizations (NGOs). Even though the vast majority of nonstate actors are NGOs, IGOs generally wield more influence because their members are states.
- Most IGOs engage in a comparatively narrow range of activities. Given its global membership and purposes, the United Nations (UN) differs from other IGOs. Because the UN is a mirror of world politics, not an alternative to it, the UN reflects the forces outside the organization that have animated world politics since the end of World War II.
- Although the European Union (EU) has some supranational elements, the term *pooled sovereignty* captures its essence, because states remain paramount in its institutional structures and decision-making processes. Regional IGOs outside of Europe have not approached the same level of institution building because of the reluctance of national leaders to make political choices that would undermine their state's sovereignty.
- Many people do not pledge their primary allegiance to the state. Rather, they think of themselves primarily as members of an ethnic nation group and the cultural values it represents. Ethnopolitical groups based on these feelings are among the most important NGOs in contemporary world politics.
- As a force in world politics, religious movements not only bring people together but also divide them. While not all extremist religious NGOs are alike, many of them incite irredentist claims, separatist revolts, migration, and political violence.
- Since World War II, MNCs have grown dramatically in scope and power. To some observers, this growth has undermined the ability of sovereign states to control their own economies; to others, this growth is helping to create a more prosperous world.

- Issue-advocacy NGOs have become influential in the fields of economic development, human rights, and the environment. Although some people see these groups as rabble-rousers, others contend that they provide an avenue for citizens of different countries who have shared interests to associate with one another, lobby collectively, and exert leverage over state policies. Moreover, they believe that these kinds of interactions are creating a rudimentary global civil society.

- The dramatic growth of nonstate actors challenges the traditional state-centric view of world politics. Although some nonstate actors are capable of advancing their interests largely outside the direct control of states, the state still molds the activities of nonstate actors more than its behavior is molded by them.

KEY TERMS

bilateral
ethnopolitical group
foreign direct investment (FDI)
Group of 77 (G-77)
indigenous peoples
intergovernmental
  organizations (IGOs)

international regimes
irredentism
multinational corporations
  (MNCs)
nongovernmental organizations
  (NGOs)

pooled sovereignty
secession
security community
strategic corporate alliances
transnational banks (TNBs)

 ## WHERE ON THE WORLD WIDE WEB?

United Nations

http://www.un.org/

The United Nations (UN) is an IGO with global membership that performs multiple purposes. The UN website is organized according to the organization's primary concerns: peace and security, international law, humanitarian affairs, economic and social development, and human rights.

The World Trade Organization

http://www.wto.org/

The mission of the World Trade Organization (WTO) is to ensure that trade flows between states as smoothly, predictably, and freely as possible. Decision making within the WTO is by consensus among all 145 member countries. Trade agreements are then ratified by members' parliaments. The WTO also uses a dispute settlement process that focuses on interpreting agreements and ensur-

ing that member countries' trade policies follow them. Click on "WTO News" and "Trade Topics." What important issues is the WTO currently addressing?

International Monetary Fund

http://www.imf.org/

The International Monetary Fund (IMF) was created to promote international monetary cooperation and facilitate the expansion and balanced growth of international trade by promoting exchange stability. It does this by making monetary resources temporarily available to its members. Choose two or three countries of interest to you and see how they have interacted with the IMF. Examine the "current topics" section. What are the main issues discussed here? Which countries or groups of countries are affected?

European Union
http://europa.eu.int/index.htm

The EU is an IGO with regional membership and multiple purposes. This chapter characterizes the authority structure of the EU as one of pooled sovereignty, under which the member states grant the EU legal authority to make some collective decisions for them. After entering the Europa website, explore the main institutions of the EU. How does the Court of Justice differ from the UN's International Court of Justice? How many political groupings are represented in the European Parliament? How might these divisions affect the formation of a unified EU foreign policy?

INFOTRAC® COLLEGE EDITION

Search for the following articles in the InfoTrac College Edition database.

Calleo, David. "A Choice of Europes," *The National Interest* Spring 2001.

Huebner, David, and Raja Haddad. "UN-Paid Dues: The Costs of Cooperation," *Harvard International Review* Summer 2002.

Peang-Meth, Abdulgaffar. "The Rights of Indigenous Peoples and Their Fight for Self-Determination," *World Affairs* Winter 2002.

Thiessen, Marc A. "When Worlds Collide," *Foreign Policy* March 2001.

For more articles, enter:

"Europe" in the Subject Guide, and then go to subdivision "politics and government."

"indigenous peoples" in the Subject Guide.

"United Nations" in the Subject Guide, and then go to subdivision "management."

ADDITIONAL CD-ROM RESOURCES

Click on International Law and Organization to access other online resources related to this chapter.

The Politics
of Global
Security

The threat of violence casts a dark cloud over much of the world. Many people live in fear of terrorists attacks, invasion by neighboring states, or repression by their own government, bent on persecuting its citizens because of their ethnicity or religion. Even though the Cold War ended more than a decade ago, global security remains precarious. Millions of people are the victims of aggression, and millions more have had to flee their homelands to seek sanctuary from the ravages of war.

Part III of *The Global Future* examines the quest for security in the twenty-first century. Chapter 7 begins our examination by looking at trends in the incidence of armed conflict since the birth of the modern world system. In addition to analyzing what scholars and policymakers believe are the major causes of war, it traces the evolution of political terrorism into a worldwide threat. Chapter 8 addresses the national security strategies national leaders use to cope with the dangers posed by rival states and global terrorists. Finally, in the last two chapters of Part III, we consider the alternative paths to peace prescribed by the realist and liberal theoretical traditions. Whereas Chapter 9 assesses the use of military alliances to prevent war by creating a balance of power among rival states, Chapter 10 evaluates the use of international law and organization to maintain a system of collective security. ●

Armed Conflict in the Twenty-First Century

War is a continuation of policy by other means.

KARL VON CLAUSEWITZ, Prussian general

O n September 30, 1862, Count Otto von Bismarck, the chief minister of Prussia, addressed a legislative budget committee on the need to expand the country's military. It was a difficult task. Many members of parliament had been resisting tax increases for some time, even to fund reforms of the armed forces.

Prussia was one of 38 Germanic states scattered across central Europe in the mid-nineteenth century. Many people in these states supported unification, but were leery of Prussian ambitions to lead a united Germany. Austria and France were worried as well. A united Germany under Prussian leadership would pose an enormous security threat. They preferred to leave the Germans divided into several dozen small states.

Bismarck recognized these barriers to Prussian aspirations, and feared they might not be overcome without a modern military. "The position of Prussia in Germany," he told the legislative budget committee, "will be determined not by its liberalism but by its power." Prussia must strengthen its military. "Not through speeches and majority decisions are the great questions of the day decided," he thundered, "but through iron and blood."

During the next decade, Bismarck's policy of iron and blood led to wars against Denmark (1864), Austria (1866), and France (1870–1871). Collectively known as the Wars of German Unification, they were won by a combination of Bismarck's uncanny ability to isolate his international opponents, and the training, firepower, and mobility of Prussia's modernized military. Together, they transformed the fragmented German lands into a powerful centralized state, with Bismarck serving as its imperial chancellor.

Bismarck's genius resided in his ability to entertain multiple courses of action, explore all of their permutations, and move on several fronts simultaneously. No single move was an end in itself; each positioned him to advance in another direction. "One cannot play chess," he insisted," if from the outset sixteen of the sixty-four squares are out of bounds." A tenacious advocate of Prussian interests, he could see opportunities presented by different diplomatic configurations on the diplomatic chessboard. To exploit them, he was willing to be disingenuous and, at times, even ruthless. "If it hadn't been for me, there wouldn't have been three great wars, 80,000 men would not have died, and parents, brothers, sisters, and widows would not be in mourning," he once admitted. "But that I have to settle with God."

Like Karl von Clausewitz, the Prussian general who had fought against Napoleon half a century earlier, Bismarck saw war as an extension of foreign policy by other means, a political instrument for attaining one's goals when diplomacy fails to resolve a stalemate. To Clausewitz and Bismarck, conflict was normal, and war was a way to resolve it by compelling an adversary to do one's will.

In international relations, conflict regularly occurs when state and nonstate actors have disputes arising out of incompatible interests. However, its costs can become staggering when disputants readily embrace war as a tool of foreign policy and take up arms to settle their differences. This chapter explores the challenge that armed conflicts pose in world affairs, examining their causes, magnitude, and changing form since the end of the Second World War.

Trends in Armed Conflict

Throughout history, war has destroyed property and devastated lives. Social scientists have attempted to measure the frequency of military conflict in an effort to ascertain if the level of international violence has been increasing, decreasing, or holding steady over time. Figure 7.1 charts the number of armed conflicts globally from two perspectives: The first looks at changes from 1400 to 2000; the second covers the 1950–2001 time period. These trends reveal that the frequency of military conflict has risen significantly during the last 300 years, with the twentieth century being extraordinarily violent. "No other century on record equals the twentieth," notes Ruth Sivard (1996) "in the number of conflicts waged, the hordes of refugees created, [and] the millions of people killed in wars." Estimates suggest that some 130–142 million people died in these violent conflicts (*Vital Signs 2002*, 95).

Les Stone/Zuma; Chris Hondros/Getty Images

War's Human Impact Innocent noncombatants, especially children and women, are often the primary victims of military conflict in the Global South. At the May 2002 World Summit for Children, the United Nations estimated that about 300,000 children under the age of 18 were made soldiers and forced to fight in wars in more than thirty countries (*Newsweek,* May 13, 2002, 28). Shown here (left) is the 10-year-old son of an Afghani police commissioner carrying an assault rifle nearly as tall as him. The protection of children and women from warfare has usually required humanitarian military intervention by an outside power. Shown on the right are a starving Somalian mother and child in 1997 waiting for relief supplies delivered by U.S. military aircraft to a refugee camp in Kenya.

Several patterns in the incidence of militarized disputes emerged during the last half of the twentieth century that have implications for the global future. A total of 225 armed conflicts occurred between 1946 and 2001, with the number peaking in 1992 at 51—a level almost four times that of the 1950s, and nearly three times the yearly average during the 1960s. More than 31 conflicts occurred each year in the 1970s, and more than forty each year in the 1980s and 1990s

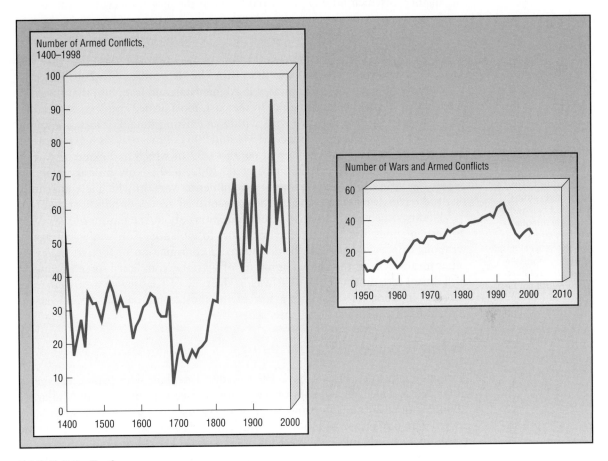

FIGURE 7.1

Two Pictures of the Changing Frequency of Armed Conflicts

Armed conflict between states has been around for as long as sovereign states have existed, as the trend on the left inventorying 2,566 individual wars for each decade since the year 1400 indicates. It shows that the number dropped considerably in the late 1600s in the aftermath of the Thirty Years' War, but has risen sharply in the three centuries since, peaking in the 1960s. The figure on the right captures the ebb and flow of active armed conflicts each year since 1950. Most of these conflicts have occurred in the Global South; of the 38 underway in 2002, the vast majority began years and even decades earlier. In recent years, most armed conflicts have been civil wars within states.

SOURCES: Left: Adapted from "The Characteristics of Violent Conflict since 1400 A.D." by Peter Brecke. Used with permission. Right: University of Hamburg, presented in *Vital Signs 2002*, pp. 94–95.

(Gleditsch et al. 2002). What these frequency counts do not show, however, are important patterns among the participants in late twentieth-century conflicts. Specifically,

- The proportion of countries throughout the world engaged in wars has declined in recent years.
- In particular, wars between the great powers have decreased; since 1945 the world has experienced a long peace—the most prolonged period in modern history in which no wars occurred between the most powerful countries.
- Most wars now occur in the Global South, which is home to the highest number of states, with the largest populations, the least income, and the least stable governments.

These participation patterns, together with the September 11, 2001 terrorist attacks and the wars they precipitated in Afghanistan and Iraq, hint that the character of armed conflict is changing. In the past, most armed conflicts were either between states or involved civil wars within an existing state. For instance, of the 225 armed conflicts fought between 1946 and 2001, 42 were wars between states and an additional 178 were internal conflicts, 32 of which had external participation by other countries (Gleditsch et al. 2002, 620). Now military planners expect the future to include numerous **asymmetric wars**, in which irregular militias and terrorist networks engage the conventional armies of nation-states.

Findings such as these raise several questions about the nature of war. Why do certain states and nonstate actors resort to violence? Can war in an age of weapons of mass destruction be considered a continuation of foreign policy by other means? Given the changing nature of warfare, is military force as much a of political instrument today as it was in the time of Clausewitz and Bismarck? To seek answers, let's examine a few of the most common theories about the sources from which wars originate.

• **asymmetric war** an armed conflict between belligerents of vastly unequal military strength, in which the weaker side is often a nonstate actor that relies on unconventional tactics.

What Causes War?

Throughout history, efforts have been made to explain why people engage in organized violence. Inventories of war's origins (see Cashman 2000; Midlarsky 2000; Vasquez 2000; Geller and Singer 1998) generally agree that hostilities are rooted in multiple sources found at various levels of analysis. Some are proximate causes that directly influence the odds of war; others are remote and indirect, creating explosive background conditions that enable any one of a number of more immediate factors to trigger violence. The most commonly cited sources of war can be classified into three broad categories: (1) aggressive traits found in the human species; (2) pernicious national attributes that beget conflict-prone states; and (3) unstable structures and volatile processes within the international system that encourage disputes to become militarized.

The First Level of Analysis: Human Nature

In a sense, all wars between states originate from the decisions of national leaders, whose choices ultimately determine whether armed conflict will occur (see

Chapter 3). We must therefore begin looking for the causes of war at the individual level of analysis, where questions about human nature are central.

The repeated outbreak of war has led some, such as psychologist Sigmund Freud (1968), to conclude that aggression is an instinctive part of human nature that stems from humans' genetic programming and psychological makeup. Identifying Homo sapiens as the deadliest species, ethologists (those who study animal behavior in order to understand human behavior) such as Konrad Lorenz (1963) similarly argue that humankind is one of the few species practicing intraspecific aggression (routine killing of its own kind), in comparison with most other species, which practice interspecific aggression (killing only other species, except in the most unusual circumstances—cannibalism in certain tropical fishes being one exception). Robert Ardrey (1966) proposes a "territorial imperative" to account for intraspecific violence: Like most animals, humans instinctively defend territory they believe belongs to them. Ethologists are joined in their interpretation by those political realists who assume that the drive for power is innate and cannot be eliminated. Some of them even apply Charles Darwin's ideas about evolution to world politics. For these so-called "social" Darwinists, international life is a struggle for survival of the fittest, where natural selection eliminates traits that interfere with successful competition.

Many scholars question these views on both empirical and logical grounds. If aggression is a deep-seated drive emanating from human nature, then shouldn't all people exhibit this behavior? Most people, of course, do not; they reject killing as evil and neither murder nor excuse homicide committed by others. At some fundamental level, argues Francis Fukuyama (1999a), human beings are built for consensus, not for conflict: "People feel intensely uncomfortable if they live in a society that doesn't have moral rules." Even accepting natural selection as an explanation of human evolution need not lead to the conclusion that aggression is ordained by hereditary. As James Q. Wilson (1993) argues, "the moral sense must have adaptive value; if it did not, natural selection would have worked against people who had such useless traits as sympathy, self-control, or a desire for fairness in favor of those with the opposite tendencies."

Most social scientists now strongly disagree with the premise that humans fight wars because of innate genetic drives. Although conflict among humans is ubiquitous, a compelling body of anthropological evidence indicates that various societies have avoided outright warfare. Some, like the Semi of the Central Malay Peninsula have accomplished this through internalized psychological restraints; others, like the Mehinaku of the Xingu River in Brazil, have done it through external sociocultural constraints (Gregor and Robarcheck 1996). In fact, since 1500, one in five countries has never experienced war (Sivard 1991, 20). For these reasons, the 1986 *Seville Statement,* endorsed by more than a dozen professional scholarly associations, maintains that "it is scientifically incorrect" to say that "we have inherited a tendency to make war from our animal ancestors," "that war or any other violent behavior is genetically programmed into our human nature," or "that war is caused by 'instinct' or any single motivation" (see Somit 1990). In short, the "capacity, but not the need, for violence appears to be biologically entrenched in humans" (Gurr 1970).

If the origins of war do not lie in human nature, where should we turn to uncover its causes? Operating from the premise that war occurs because of the choices people make, not due to inbred aggressive traits, we will shift our attention to those domestic and international factors that affect national security decisions.

The Second Level of Analysis: Internal Characteristics of States

Do different types of states exhibit different amounts of war involvement? Conventional wisdom holds that variations in the geography, culture, society, economy, and government of states influence whether their leaders will initiate war. To evaluate this claim, we need to examine research findings on how the internal characteristics of states affect leaders' choices regarding the use of force.

Geographic Location. Natural resources, transportation routes, strategic borders, and other factors related to a country's territory have long been recognized as important sources of international friction. Following the end of the Cold War, competitions over access to valuable commodities ranging from oil to water "have produced a new geography of conflict, a reconfigured cartography in which resource flows rather than political and ideological divisions constitute the major fault lines" (Klare 2001). Territorial issues can be thought of as remote, underlying causes of war. That is to say, depending on how they are handled, they can set off a chain of events that increases the probability of war (Vasquez 2000). Researchers have found that contiguous states are more likely than geographically distant states to have their disputes escalate to full-scale war (Siverson and Starr 1991; Diehl 1985), especially when they involve territorial issues. Furthermore, states involved in territorial disputes tend to experience recurrent conflict (Hensel 2000).

Click on Global Conflict and International Security to access an interactive Case Study on Civil Strife in Rwanda.

• **xenophobia** a fear of foreigners.

Cultural Values. Human behavior is strongly influenced by culture. Some governments promote political cultures that encourage citizens to accept whatever their leaders declare is necessary for national security, including using military force to resolve international disagreements. The risk of war increases whenever values that sustain **xenophobia** and blind obedience gain wide acceptance.

Nationalism can become a caldron within which these self-glorifying and other-maligning values simmer (Van Evera 1994). "The tendency of the vast majority of people to center their supreme loyalties on the nation-state," Jack Levy (1989a) explains, is a powerful catalyst to war. When people "acquire an intense commitment to the power and prosperity of the state [and] this commitment is strengthened by national myths emphasizing the moral, physical, and political strength of the state and by individuals' feelings of powerlessness and their consequent tendency to seek their identity and fulfillment through the state . . . nationalism contributes to war."

The connection between nationalism and war has a long history and provokes much debate (see Controversy: Does Nationalistic Love of Country Cause War with Foreign Nations?). Critiques of nationalism were especially pronounced in the last century. The English essayist Aldous Huxley once termed nationalism "the religion of the twentieth century." Today nationalist feelings

Hutton Archive by Getty Images; U.S. ARMY/AP/Wide World Photos

Nationalism's Deadly Past Under the fascist dictatorship of Adolf Hitler, shown on the left, the Nazi government glorified the state and claimed that the German people were a superior race. What followed from this extreme form of nationalism was war against Germany's neighbors and the campaign of genocide against the Jews and other ethnic minorities. U.S. troops under the command of General George Patton, shown on the right, are arriving to liberate the concentration camp at Buchenwald in May 1945, but not in time to save the lives of the prisoners the Nazi guards had put to death in the gas chambers.

remain intense in many parts of the world, and continue to arouse violence among stateless nations seeking their own independent states.

While not denying the power of hypernationalism, feminist theory points to another set of cultural values that may lead to war. As pointed out in Chapter 2, some feminists believe that aggression is rooted in the masculine ethos of realism, which prepares people to accept war and to respect the warrior as a hero (see especially Enloe 2000 and Tickner 2002). Celebrating certain gender roles and marginalizing others contributes to society's militarization, they argue. The penchant for warfare does not breed in a vacuum; it is produced by **socialization.** When powerful social institutions promote values that condone organized violence, disputes with other states are more likely to be resolved through force than amicable procedures (Lind 1993).

• **socialization** the processes by which people learn the beliefs, values, and behaviors that are acceptable in a given society.

Civil Strife. Insurgencies resulting in at least one thousand civilian and military deaths per year occurred 242 times between 1816 and 2001 (Small and Singer 1982; Singer 1991, 66–75; Wallensteen and Sollenberg 2001). Their outbreak has been somewhat irregular, but their casualty rates show an alarming growth. Ten of the fifteen most lethal civil wars since 1816 took place in the twentieth century; of those, most transpired after World War II. Civil wars almost constantly

CONTROVERSY

Does Nationalistic Love of Country Cause War with Foreign Nations?

What does *patriotism* mean? The most familiar definition is popularly expressed as "love for one's country." Often, it involves "love for the nation or nationality of the people living in a particular state," especially when the population of that state primarily comprises a single ethnonational racial or linguistic group. Because "love" for valued objects of affection, such as a person's homeland, is widely seen as a virtue, it is understandable why governments everywhere teach young citizens that love for country is a moral duty. Nationalism fosters a sense of political community, and thereby contributes to civic solidarity. On these grounds, nationalism is not controversial. However, critics of nationalism find patriotism to be potentially dangerous in its extreme form. Superpatriots, these critics warn, are hypernationalists who measure their patriotism by the degree of hatred and opposition exhibited toward foreign nations and by the blind approval of every policy and practice of the "patriot's" own nation. In this sense, nationalistic patriotism can ignore transcendent moral principles such as the love for all humanity, even toward one's enemies, as preached by Jesus Christ in the Sermon on the Mount and other religious leaders such as Muhammad, the founder of Islam, and the legendary King Solomon in Judaism. If so, then is nationalistic superpatriotism sometimes a cause of war between nations? What do you think?

In thinking about this controversial issue—about whether nationalism and internationalism are mutually exclusive—consider the view of Karl Deutsch, a German-born immigrant and famous scholar who taught for many years at Harvard University. Deutsch, an authority on nationalism, described nationalism's linkage to armed conflict in these moving words:

Nationalism is an attitude of mind, a pattern of attention and desires. It arises in response to a condition of society and to a particular stage in its development. It is a predisposition to pay far more attention to messages about one's own people, or to messages from its members, than to messages from or about any other people. At the same time, it is a desire to have one's own people get any and all values that are available. The extreme nationalist wants his people to have all the power, all the wealth, and all the well-being for which there is any competition. He wants his people to command all the respect and deference from others; he tends to claim all rectitude and virtue for it, as well as all enlightenment and skill; and he gives it a monopoly of his affection. In short, he totally identifies himself with his nation. Though he may be willing to sacrifice himself for it, his nationalism is a form of egotism written large. . . .

Even if most people are not extreme nationalists, nationalism has altered the world in many ways. Nationalism has not only increased the number of countries on the face of the earth, it has helped to diminish the number of its inhabitants. All major wars in the twentieth century have been fought in its name. . . .

Nationalism is in potential conflict with all philosophies or religions—such as Christianity—which teach universal standards of truth and of right and wrong, regardless of nation, race, or tribe. Early in the nineteenth century a gallant American naval officer, Stephen Decatur, proposed the toast, "Our country! In her intercourse with foreign nations, may she be always in the right, but our country, right or wrong." Nearly 150 years later the United States Third Army, marching into Germany following the collapse of the Nazi regime, liberated the huge concentration camp at Buchenwald. Over the main entrance to that place of torture and death, the Nazi elite guard had thoughtfully written, "My Country, Right or Wrong." (Deutsch 1974, 124–125) ●

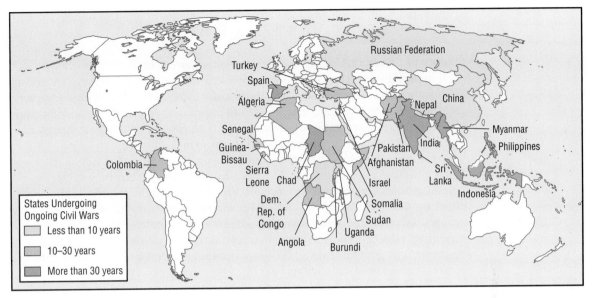

M A P   7 . 1

States Threatening to Collapse in Civil Wars

Civil wars have broken out with increasing frequency since the end of World War II. As failing states splinter and new states emerge, the United Nations predicts that by the year 2025 there could be as many as 500 sovereign states. This map underscores the magnitude of the problem, showing the location in 2002 of 25 long-term civil wars resulting in 1,000 or more deaths. Collectively, these civil wars are estimated to have taken the lives of at least 5 million people.

SOURCES: Copyright © 2002 by *Harper's Magazine*. All rights reserved. Reproduced from the March issue by special permission.

cast their shadow over world politics (see Map 7.1), with roughly one in five since the Second World War involving outside intervention (Gleditsch et al. 2002, 620).

Many analysts believe that civil strife is linked to interstate war because leaders who experience acute opposition at home provoke crises abroad to divert attention from their domestic failures. As mentioned in Chapter 3, this diversionary theory of war stems from sociological research that shows in-group bonds tighten when faced with an out-group threat. War, according to this theory, gives a leader the opportunity to introduce ruthless forms of domestic political control while simultaneously being hailed as a protector (Morris 1969). As John Foster Dulles observed in 1939 before becoming U.S. secretary of state, "The easiest and quickest cure of internal dissension is to portray danger from abroad."

Numerous studies have examined the relationship between internal turmoil and foreign conflict. The evidence does not point to a clear, direct connection between civil strife and interstate war initiation. Perhaps the most compelling reason for these results is that "when domestic conflict becomes extremely intense it would seem more reasonable to argue that there is a greater likelihood that a state will retreat from its foreign engagements in order to handle the situation at home" (Zinnes and Wilkenfeld 1971).

Economic Conditions.   Does a state's economic system affect the probability that it will initiate a war? The question has provoked controversy for centuries. Marxists, for example, claim that capitalism is the primary cause of war. Recall from Chapter 5 that according to Vladimir Lenin's theory of imperialism, the need for capitalist states to export surplus capital spurs military efforts to capture and protect foreign markets. For Marxists, the only way to end war is to end capitalism.

Contrary to Marxist theory is liberalism's conviction that free-market systems promote peace, not war. The reasons are multiple, but they center on the premise that commercial enterprises are natural lobbyists for world peace because their profits depend on it. War interferes with trade, destroys property, causes inflation, consumes scarce resources, and encourages big government and counterproductive controls over business activity. By extension, this reasoning continues, as government regulation of internal markets declines, prosperity will increase and fewer wars will occur.

The debate between Marxists and liberals was at the heart of the ideological contest between East and West during the Cold War, when the relative virtues and vices of socialism and capitalism were uppermost in people's minds. At the time, Marxists cited the record of European colonial wars to support their claim that capitalist states were war-prone. However, they generally omitted references to communist uses of military force, including the Soviet invasion of Finland in 1939, North Korea's attack on South Korea in 1950, and the People's Republic of China's occupation of Tibet in 1959. Nor did they explain the repeated military clashes between communist states, such the Soviet Union with Hungary (1956), Czechoslovakia (1968), and China (1969), and China with Vietnam (1979 and 1987). Simply put, the proposition that communist states were inherently peaceful failed to stand up to empirical evidence.

The end of the Cold War did not end the debate about the relationship between economics and war. It simply moved the discussion away from a preoccupation with capitalism versus communism and riveted people's attention on whether economic interdependence promoted peace. The widening and deepening economic connections among wealthy countries in the Global North led scholars to ask whether openness to the global economy, high amounts of bilateral trade, and economic development reduce the probability of war. The evidence to date supports the liberals' belief that economic openness and high levels of economically important trade are significant constraints on the use of force (Russett and Oneal 2001). In addition, states with highly advanced economies appear less likely to fight one another than pairs of states with less developed economies, or pairs with one advanced and one less developed economy (Bremer 1992).

Before we conclude that poverty always breeds war, however, we must note that the *most* impoverished countries have been the least prone to start wars with their neighbors. The poorest countries cannot vent their frustrations aggressively because they lack the military or economic resources to do so. This does not mean that the poorest countries will always remain peaceful. If the past is a guide to the future, then the impoverished countries that develop economically will be those most likely to acquire arms and eventually go to war. In particular, many studies suggest that states are likely to initiate foreign wars *after* sustained periods of economic growth—that is, during periods of rising prosperity, when they can most afford them (Cashman 2000). This signals danger if rapidly developing countries in the Global South direct their new resources toward armament rather than invest in sustained development.

Political Institutions. As discussed in Chapter 2, liberal theory assigns great weight to the kinds of political institutions that states possess. Furthermore, as pointed out in Chapter 3, researchers have found that although democratic governments use force against nondemocracies, they rarely make war on other democracies. In fact, they hardly ever skirmish. "Pairs of democratic states have been only one-eighth as likely as other kinds of states to threaten to use force against each other, and only one-tenth as likely actually to do so" (Russett 2001, 235).

The capacity of democracies to manage conflict with one another has led scholars to speculate about the consequences of having democratic institutions diffuse around the world. As the proportion of democracies grows, will norms and practices of nonviolent conflict resolution cascade throughout the state system? Some scholars imagine that once a critical mass of democratic states is reached, many other states would be persuaded to adopt democratic institutions, which would prompt another round of adoptions, and so on. A world populated by stable democracies, they predict, would be freed from the curse of war.

As shown in Figure 7.2, the community of liberal democracies has grown over the past two centuries, with the last two decades of the twentieth century experiencing the collapse of autocratic regimes in scores of countries. Just over ten years after the collapse of communism in Eastern Europe and the Soviet Union, 70 percent of the world's countries were holding multiparty elections (UNDP 2002, 1, 14). But the euphoria surrounding this latest wave of democratization has given way to the realization that there is no certainty that liberal democracy will become universal. Nor will halting, erratic moves toward liberalization by the world's remaining autocracies automatically produce a more peaceful global order. Unlike their older, constitutionally secure brethren, fledgling

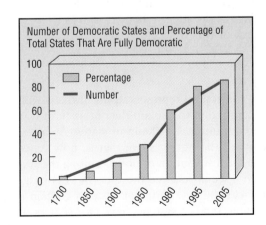

Number of Democratic States and Percentage of Total States That Are Fully Democratic

FIGURE 7.2

The Advance of Democracy, 1700–2005

Throughout the modern era, autocrats of various types have ruled many states and made foreign policy choices about war. As shown in this figure, a global shift from authoritarian to democratic regimes has occurred. According to an index of democratization designed by Ted Robert Gurr, the number of authoritarian countries fell from almost 70 in 1980 to fewer than 30 in 2000. Over the same period, the number of democratic regimes doubled, from 41 to 82 (UNDP 2002, 15).

SOURCES: *Global Trends 2005*, by Michael J. Mazarr, p. 107. Copyright © Michael J. Mazaar.

democracies occasionally resort to force (Mansfield and Snyder 1996). Finally, the fact that leaders in established democracies are accountable to electoral approval does not guarantee that they will moderate the use of force when it is applied. The sensitivity of democratic leaders to casualties "sometimes leads to profligate uses of firepower or violent efforts to end wars quickly" (E. Cohen 1998).

The preceding discussion of the characteristics of states that influence their proclivity for war does not exhaust the subject. Many other state-level causes have been hypothesized. But, however important domestic influences might be as a source of war, many believe that the nature of the international system is even more critical.

The Third Level of Analysis: System Structure and Processes

As we saw in Chapter 2, some political realists see war as a product of the decentralized character of the international system that encourages self-help rather than teamwork. To illustrate how the absence of a central authority affects behavior, the philosopher Jean-Jacques Rousseau suggests we imagine a group of primitive hunters tracking a stag (male deer). The hunters are hungry, and must all cooperate in order to have a chance of trapping an animal large enough to feed the entire group. While stalking the creature, one hunter spots a hare. If he leaves the group to pursue the hare, he would almost certainly bag it and feed himself. But without his help, the remaining hunters could not catch the stag and would go hungry. Rousseau uses this allegory to show how egoistic actors in an anarchic environment are tempted to follow their own short-term interests, which undercuts the opportunity to attain larger goals that benefit everyone. Applying this reasoning to the outbreak of the First World War, the British scholar G. Lowes Dickinson (1926) claimed "whenever and wherever the anarchy of armed states exists, war does become inevitable."

International anarchy may make war likely, but as a constant condition of modern international life it doesn't explain why some periods erupt in violence, while others remain tranquil. To account for variation in the amount of war over time, we need to look at changes in the structure and processes operating within the anarchic international system. More specifically, we need to consider how the distribution of power among the members of the state system, as well as shifts in that distribution, may affect the outbreak of war.

Power Distributions

Theories of world politics are abstract, conjectural representations of the world. Thus far we have examined theories that attempt to explain the outbreak of war by concentrating on human nature and the internal makeup of states. An alternative approach focuses on the structure of the state system; that is, how states are positioned or arranged according to the distribution of power among the system's members (Waltz 1979). In Chapter 3 we introduced the concept of polarity to describe the distribution of material capabilities. Unipolar systems contain a structure with one dominant power center, bipolar systems have two centers of power, and multipolar systems possess more than two such centers. Since periods of uniploarity have been rare and fleeting during the history of the modern state system, scholars have tended to debate whether bipolar or multipolar systems are more likely to experience war.

Advocates of bipolarity assert that a world containing two centers of power that are significantly stronger than the next tier of states will be stable because the dire consequences of war between these giants encourages them to exercise caution when dealing with one another, and to prevent conflicts among their allies from engulfing them in a military maelstrom. Conversely, those favoring multipolarity believe that situations of rough parity among several great powers will be peaceful because a rise in interaction opportunities and a diminution in the share of attention that can be allocated among many potential adversaries reduce the rigidity of conflicts. In rebuttal, the former submit that because of its ambiguous nature, multipolarity will promote war through miscalculation. The latter retort that bipolarity, lacking flexibility and suppleness, will deteriorate into a struggle for supremacy (see Christensen and Snyder 1990; Midlarsky 1988; Deutsch and Singer 1964).

Research into the relative merits of bipolar versus multipolar structures suggests that the distribution of material capabilities within the state system is not related to the onset of war (Kegley and Raymond 1994; Bueno de Mesquita 1981; Ostrom and Aldrich 1978); nevertheless it affects the *amount* of war should armed conflict occur (Levy 1985; Wayman 1985). Wars occur in both bipolar and multipolar systems, but multipolar systems experience larger, more severe wars (Vasquez 2000; 1986).

Although different polarity configurations do not raise or lower the probability of war, alliance polarization makes war more likely. Recall that polarity differs from polarization. As discussed in Chapter 3, polarity concerns the distribution of power; alliance polarization refers to the propensity of lesser powers to cluster around the strongest states. The interstate system can be said to be moving toward greater polarization if its members align in two hostile blocs.

Alliance polarization is hazardous because the structural rigidity it fosters reduces the opportunities for a wide array of multifaceted interactions among states, therein decreasing the chances for **crosscutting cleavages** to emerge. Crosscutting reduces the odds of war, because opponents on one issue may be partners on another. They are not implacable enemies confined to an endless zero-sum struggle. In an international environment of **overlapping cleavages**, adversaries have few interests in common, and thus become fixated on the things that divide them. Under these circumstances, minor disagreements are magnified into bigger tests of will where reputations are thought to be at stake. Tight, polarized blocs of states are thus war-prone; peace is best preserved when there is a moderate amount of flexibility in the structure of alliances (Kim 1989; Kegley and Raymond 1982; Wallace 1973).

Power Trajectories and Transitions

Although the international system is anarchic, possessing no higher authority above the sovereign state, it is nonetheless stratified due to variations in the

• crosscutting cleavages a situation where politically relevant divisions between international actors are contradictory, with their interests pulling them together on some issues and separating them on others.

• overlapping cleavages a situation where politically relevant divisions between international actors are complementary; interests pulling them apart on one issue are reinforced by interests that also separate them on other issues.

• **power transition theory** the contention that war is likely when a dominant great power is threatened by the rapid growth of a rival's capabilities, which reduces the difference in their relative power.

relative power of its members. If the international pecking order is clear, with the dominant state holding a substantial advantage over its nearest potential rival, then efforts to alter the rank order of states by force are unlikely. Conversely, if the capability advantage of the dominant state is small or eroding due to the growth of a challenger, the probability of war increases (Geller 2000).

According to what has been dubbed **power transition theory,** "peace is preserved best when there is an imbalance of national capabilities between disadvantaged and advantaged nations" (Kugler 1993; Organski and Kugler 1980). War, it is argued, often involves "rear-end" collisions between a rapidly rising dissatisfied state and the dominant state, which wishes to preserve the status quo. When the relative strength of the revisionist challenger and the dominant state converge toward rough parity, armed conflict can erupt in two different ways. First, the dominant state may initiate a preventive war so as not to be overtaken by the challenger. Second, and more commonly, the challenger may strike first, confident that it can accelerate its climb to the apex of international power.

• **power cycle theory** the contention that armed conflict is probable when a state passes through certain critical points along a generalized curve of relative power, and wars of enormous magnitude are likely when several great powers pass through critical points at approximately the same time.

Some scholars believe that the trajectory of state power follows a cycle of ascendance, maturation, and decline, based on the ratio of its strength relative to others within the system (Doran 2000; Doran and Parsons 1980). According to **power cycle theory,** war is most likely at certain critical points along this cycle; namely when shifts in the rate of growth or decline in a state's relative power creates discontinuities between prior foreign policy expectations and future realities. Preliminary research indicates that when numerous great powers pass through these critical points at the same time, massive wars ensue (Doran 1989).

Cyclical theories have always provoked discussion. Years ago, for example, Italian historian Luigi da Porto received considerable attention by asserting: "Peace brings riches; riches bring pride; pride brings anger; anger brings war; war brings poverty; poverty brings humanity; humanity brings peace; peace, as I have said, brings riches, and so the world's affairs go round." For many people, assertions like his makes it seem plausible that certain rhythms characterize the tides of history.

As discussed in Chapter 4, various scholars have looked for long cycles in the rise and fall of hegemonic leaders over the past five centuries (see Hopkins and Wallerstein 1996; Modelski and Thompson 1996; Goldstein 1988). However, they have failed to reach a consensus about the existence of periodicities in global war. Their findings diverge, because different definitions of hegemonic leadership and different measures of global war lead to different estimates of the duration of periods of peace and war. Hence the debate continues as to whether the onset of global warfare follows a repeating sequence.

The Changing Face of Warfare

Since the birth of the modern world system some three and a half centuries ago, national leaders have prepared for wars against other countries. Throughout this period, war has been conceived as large-scale organized violence between the regular armies of sovereign states. Although leaders today still ready their nations for such clashes, increasingly they are faced with the prospect of asymmetric warfare—armed conflict between terrorist networks and conventional military forces.

Passions Aroused by Terrorism In reaction to Palestinian suicide bombings in 2002, Israeli prime minister Sharon ordered the construction of an "antiterrorism" fence to keep militant Palestinian terrorists from entering territory controlled by the state of Israel.

Political **terrorism** is the deliberate use or threat of violence against noncombatants, calculated to instill fear, alarm, and ultimately a feeling of helplessness in an audience beyond the immediate victims. Because perpetrators of terrorism often strike symbolic targets in a horrific manner, the psychological impact of an attack can exceed the physical damage. A mixture of drama and dread, political terrorism is not senseless violence; it is a premeditated strategy of extortion that presents people with a danger that seems ubiquitous, unavoidable, and unpredictable.

Terrorism can be employed to support or change the political status quo. Repressive terror, which is wielded to sustain an existing political order, has been utilized by governments as well as by vigilantes. From the Gestapo (secret state police) in Nazi Germany to the death squads in various Latin American states, establishment violence attempts to defend the prevailing political order by eliminating opposition leaders and by intimidating virtually everyone else.

• **terrorism** the premeditated use or threat of violence perpetrated against noncombatants, usually intended to induce fear in a wider audience.

AP/Wide World Photos

Dissidents who use terrorism to change the political status quo vary considerably. Some groups, like the MPLA (Popular Movement for the Liberation of Angola), used terrorism to expel colonial rulers; others, such as ETA (Basque Homeland and Liberty), adopted terrorism as part of an ethnonational separatist struggle; still others, including the Islamic Jihad, the Christian Identity Movement, the Sikh group Babbar Khalsa, and Jewish militants belonging to Kach, placed terror in the service of what they saw as religious imperatives; finally, groups such as the Japanese Red Army and Italian Black Order, turned to terrorism for left- or right-wing ideological reasons. In short, dissident terror may be grounded in anticolonialism, separatism, religion, or secular ideology.

Although the ultimate goals of individuals and groups that employ terrorism differ, they seek similar intermediate objectives as a means of attaining their goals. The following objectives are the most common:

- The *agitational* objectives of terrorism include promoting the dissident group, advertising its agenda, and discrediting rivals. Shocking behavior makes people take heed, especially when performed at a time and place imbued with symbolism. Nineteenth-century anarchists were among the first to emphasize the propaganda value of terrorism. One stunning act, they believed, would draw more attention than a thousand leaflets.

- The *coercive* objectives of terrorism include disorienting a target population, inflating the perceived power of the dissident group, wringing concessions from authorities, and provoking a heavy-handed overreaction from the police and military. Launching vicious, indiscriminate attacks at markets, cafes, and other normally tranquil locations can create a paralyzing sense of foreboding within the general public and goad political leaders into adopting repressive policies, which terrorists hope will drive the population to their side of the struggle.

- The *organizational* objectives of terrorism include acquiring resources, forging group cohesion, and maintaining an underground network of supporters. Robbing banks, obtaining ransom for hostages, and collecting protection money from businesses can finance training and logistical support for field operations. Moreover, since high initiation costs tend to lower group defections, these activities can increase allegiance when recruits are required to participate in violent acts.

To accomplish these objectives, terrorists use a variety of tactics, including bombing, assault, hijacking, and taking hostages. Bombing alone accounts for roughly half of all recorded terrorist incidents. Hijacking and hostage-taking generally involve more complex operations than planting a bomb in a crowded department store or gunning down travelers in an airport lounge. An example of such careful planning can be seen in the coordinated hijacking of five airliners by Palestinians during September 1970, which eventually led to one airliner being blown up in Cairo and three others at Dawson Field in Jordan. To be successful, these kinds of seizures require detailed preparation, vigorous bargaining, and the capacity to guard captives for long periods of time. Among the payoffs of such efforts is the opportunity to articulate the group's grievances. The Lebanese group behind the 1985 hijacking of TWA flight 847, for instance, excelled at using U.S. television networks to articulate their grievances to the American public, which had the effect of circumscribing the options that the Reagan administration entertained while searching for a solution to the crisis.

Beyond the conventional tactics of bombings, assaults, hijacking, and hostage-taking, two other threats could become part of the terrorist repertoire. First, dissidents may acquire weapons of mass destruction to deliver a mortal blow against detested enemies. Nuclear armaments are the ultimate terror weapons, but radiological, chemical, and biological weapons also pose extraordinary dangers. Crude radiological weapons can be fabricated by combining ordinary explosives with nuclear waste or radioactive isotopes, which could be stolen from hospitals, industrial facilities, or research laboratories. Rudimentary chemical weapons can be made from herbicides, pesticides, and other toxic substances that are available commercially. Biological weapons based on viral agents are more difficult to produce, though the dispersal of anthrax spores through the mail during the fall of 2001 illustrated that low-technology attacks with bacterial agents in powder form are a frightening possibility.

The second tactical innovation on the horizon is cyberterrorism. Not only can the Internet be used by extremists as a recruiting tool and a means of coordinating their activities with like-minded groups, but it allows them to case potential targets by hacking into a foe's computer system. Viruses and other weapons of **information warfare** could cause havoc if they disabled financial institutions, power grids, air traffic control systems, and other key elements in country's communication infrastructure.

• **information warfare** attacks on an adversary's telecommunications and computer networks to degrade the technological systems vital to its defense and economic well-being.

Figure 7.3 shows changes in the frequency and severity of contemporary terrorism, as measured by the U.S. Department of State's Office of Counterterrorism. As the data indicate, global terrorist activity increased nearly threefold between 1968 and 1987, after which the number of incidents gradually but erratically declined. International terrorist attacks during 2001 fell to 348 from the prior year of 426 separate terrorist acts. However, in three fateful years—1995, 1999, and 2001—the number of people killed or wounded by terrorism rose dramatically: Nearly 3,000 people were killed as a result of the September 11 attacks, the most deadly terrorist episode since World War II.

The New Global Terrorism

The conventional view of terrorism as a rare and relatively remote threat was challenged by the events of September 11, 2001. The horrors visited upon the World Trade Center and the Pentagon forced the world to confront a grim new reality: Terrorists were capable of executing catastrophic attacks almost anywhere, even without an arsenal of sophisticated weapons. Not only did groups like al Qaeda have global reach, but stealth, ingenuity, and meticulous planning could compensate for their lack of firepower. "America is full of fear," proclaimed a jubilant Osama bin Laden. "Nobody in the United States will feel safe."

What arguably made September 11 a symbolic watershed was that it epitomized a deadly new strain of terrorism. Previously, terrorism was regarded as political theater, a frightening drama where the perpetrators wanted a lot of people watching, not a lot of people dead. Now there seemed to be a desire to kill as

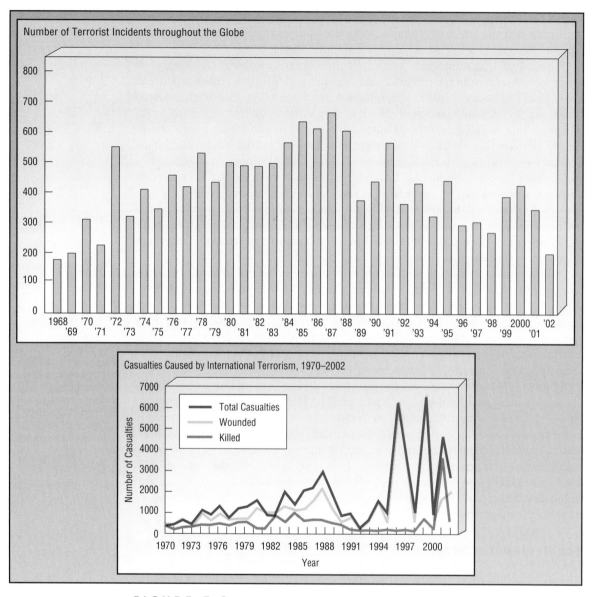

FIGURE 7.3
The Number of Terrorist Incidents and Related Casualties, since the Late 1960s

The frequency of international terrorist activity has changed over time since 1968, with the number of incidents each year fluctuating between 174 (in 1968) and 666 (in 1987). No level of casualties is acceptable, but on average far fewer people die each year from terrorist acts than from the annual toll of U.S. homicides (11,000 Americans were murdered in 2001). Tragically, casualty rates have begun to climb dramatically since 1995, and fears of mass destruction through terrorism have risen since 9/11.

SOURCE: Office of the Coordinator for Counterterrorism, U.S. Department of State, with 2002 a preliminary projection based on the first nine months of that year.

AP/Wide World Photos

Terrorist Mastermind The 9/11 terrorist attacks were coordinated by Osama bin Laden, the wealthy Saudi expatriate, former CIA employee in the Afghan resistance against the Soviet Union, and zealous Islamic revolutionary shown here. He financed the al Qaeda terrorist network, which has been responsible for many other terrorist episodes besides the September 11 attack.

many people as possible. Driven by searing hatred, annihilating enemies appeared more important to these global terrorists than winning sympathy for their cause.

Another feature of this new strain of terrorism is its organizational form. Instead of having a hierarchical command structure, al Qaeda is a shadowy network of semi-autonomous cadres and front organizations, loosely tied together by the Internet, e-mail, and cellular telephones. Rather than serving as a commander,

Osama bin Laden generally functions as a coordinator who provides financial and logistical support to extremist groups fighting those who he perceives as archenemies. However, according to *The 9/11 Commission Report,* in some operations he has also been deeply involved in the planning process.

What makes the new breed of terrorists who belong to organizations such as al Qaeda more lethal than previous terrorists is their religious fanaticism, which allows them to envision acts of terror on two levels. At one level, terrorism is a means to change the political status quo by punishing those culpable for felt wrongs. At another level, terrorism is an end in itself, a sacrament performed for its own sake in an eschatological confrontation between good and evil (Juergensmeyer 2000). Functioning only on the first level, most secular terrorist groups rarely employ suicide missions. Operating on both levels, religious terrorist groups see worldly gain as well as transcendent importance in a martyr's death. Ramadan Shalah of the Palestinian Jihad is reported to have explained the military logic of suicide tactics within asymmetric warfare in the following way: "Our enemy possesses the most sophisticated weapons in the world. . . . We have nothing . . . except the weapon of martyrdom. It is easy and costs us only our lives."

Counterterrorism

The threat facing civilization after September 11, 2001 was described by U.S. president George W. Bush as a network of terrorist groups and rogue states that harbored them. Efforts to combat this threat, he insisted, "will not end until every terrorist group of global reach has been found, stopped, and defeated." In what was subsequently called the **Bush Doctrine,** the president declared that each nation had a choice to make: "Either you are with us, or you are with the terrorists."

Terrorist groups are a type of nonstate actor (or global NGO), distinguished by the fact that they use violence as their primary method of exercising influence. States have often financed, trained, equipped, and provided sanctuary for terrorists whose activities serve their foreign policy goals. The practice of such **state-sponsored terrorism** is among the charges that the United States leveled against Iraq prior to toppling Saddam Hussein in 2003, and continues to apply to countries like Iran, North Korea, Sudan, and Syria. However, disagreement about the character and causes of global terrorism remain pronounced, and, without agreement on these preliminaries, a consensus on the best response is unlikely. Much like a disease that cannot be treated until it is accurately diagnosed, so the plague of the new global terrorism cannot be eradicated until its sources are understood. Those persuaded by one image of terrorism are drawn to certain counterterrorism policies, while those holding a different image recommend contrary policies. As constructivist theorists remind us, what we see depends on what we expect, what we look at, and what we wish to see.

Consider the diametrically opposed views of whether repression or conciliation is the most effective counterterrorist policy. Those advocating repression see terrorism springing from the cold calculations of extremists who should be neutralized by preemptive surgical strikes. As expressed by U.S. secretary of

• **Bush Doctrine** a policy that singles out states that support terrorist groups and advocates military strikes against them to prevent a future attack on the United States.

• **state-sponsored terrorism** formal assistance, training, and arming of foreign terrorists by a state in order to achieve foreign policy goals.

defense Donald Rumsfeld: "If the [United States] learned a single lesson from September 11, it should be that the only way to defeat terrorists is to attack them. There is no choice. You simply cannot defend in every place at every time against every technique."

In contrast to this coercive approach to counterterrorism, those who see terrorism rooted in frustrations with political oppression and **relative deprivation** urge negotiation and compromise. Rather than condoning military strikes aimed at exterminating the perpetrators of terrorism, they endorse conciliatory policies designed to reduce terrorism's appeal.

• **relative deprivation** people's perception that they are unfairly deprived of wealth and status in comparison to others who are advantaged but not more deserving.

The debate about how to deal with the new global terrorism thus revolves around a series of interconnected issues: Are repressive counterterrorist policies ethical? Are they compatible with democratic procedures? Do they require multilateral (international) backing to be legal, or can they be initiated unilaterally? Is conciliation more effective than military coercion? What are its relative costs, risks, and benefits?

Although most experts would agree that whereas "it is not possible to extirpate terrorism from the face of the globe," they share faith in the more modest goal—that "it should be possible to reduce the incidence and effectiveness of terrorism" (Reinares 2002). Accomplishing this goal while maintaining a proper balance between undertaking resolute action and upholding civil liberties will be difficult for several reasons. First, today's relatively open, borderless world makes terrorism easy to practice. Second, numerous **failing states** offer out-of-the-way places for terrorists groups to locate and train. Third, the growing possibility that terrorists will obtain weapons of mass destruction will create unprecedented opportunities for them to commit unspeakable atrocities. Finally, contemporary terrorists have become extremely violent, holding few reservations about inflicting heavy casualties and causing enormous physical destruction (Laqueur 2001).

• **failing states** states in danger of political collapse due to overwhelming internal strife.

An analysis of the history of terrorism indicates that there is no terrorist orthodoxy on strategic questions, no canon with strict precepts running from ultimate political goals to intermediate objectives to specific tactics. Strategic thinking about the use of terrorism in asymmetric warfare has evolved in response to new technologies, new targets of opportunity, and new counterterrorist policies. The perpetrators of political terrorism are not mindless; they have long-term aims and they carefully consider how different operations may facilitate accomplishing their purposes. Indeed, it is their ability to plan, execute, and learn from these operations that makes them so dangerous.

War in all its forms extracts a terrible toll on human life. In this chapter we have briefly examined trends in the frequency and changing character of modern warfare, as well as several prominent theories about its causes. We have seen that wars are not the legacy of what Sigmund Freud once called a "death instinct" embedded within human nature. Neither are they the product of a single cause, such as capitalism or communism. Wars can be brought on by several different causal sequences, each involving a complex combination of factors. In the next chapter, we will explore the national security policies states use to advance their interests in a world where the threat of war abounds.

Chapter Summary

- Force is an instrument that states often use to resolve their conflicts. However, war is not inevitable: some societies have never known the outbreak of war, and some historical periods have not experienced warfare.
- Since the end of World War II, all wars have been between countries in the Global South or have entailed military action by great powers against them. None have occurred between the great powers.
- War is best explained by multiple factors operating at various levels of analysis.
- There is little evidence that human nature is a direct cause of war.
- Evidence pertaining to state-level explanations of war suggests that the probability of militarized conflict is increased by hypernationalism and territorial disputes among contiguous countries. Its probability declines significantly when both parties to a dispute are stable democracies, and they possess open, advanced economies linked by commerce.
- Evidence pertaining to system-level explanations of war suggest that the following conditions increase the probability of militarized conflict: polarized alliances, an unstable hierarchy of states, and the existence of several great powers simultaneously passing through critical points in their cycle of relative power. Whether a system is bipolar or multipolar in structure does not affect the occurrence of war; however, it influences the magnitude and severity of any wars that break out, with multipolarity suffering from larger wars involving more casualties.
- The global future is likely to experience an increasing amount of asymmetric warfare between sovereign states and terrorist networks.
- Political terrorism is the purposeful use or threat of violence against noncombatants, undertaken to intimidate a wider audience. The ultimate goals of those who employ terrorism vary: Some groups employ it to support the political status quo; others, to overthrow the status quo. For both types of groups, terror is used to accomplish agitational, coercive, and organizational objectives.
- Traditionally, terrorist groups have relied on bombing, assault, hijacking, and hostage-taking to intimidate their target audience. Two emerging threats are the use of weapons of mass destruction (nuclear, radiological, chemical, and biological weapons) and cyberterrorism—attacks on an opponent's computer systems.
- Some contemporary terrorist groups have acquired the means to strike targets almost anywhere in the world. Their fanaticism has led to a vigorous debate over counterterrorist policies. Those who see the roots of the new global terrorism in an inextinguishable hatred by extremists generally call for aggressive efforts at military preemption. In contrast, those would attribute terrorism to frustration over oppression and deprivation tend to advocate more conciliatory policies.

KEY TERMS

asymmetric war
Bush Doctrine
crosscutting cleavages
failing states
information warfare

overlapping cleavages
power cycle theory
power transition theory
relative deprivation

socialization
state-sponsored terrorism
terrorism
xenophobia

WHERE ON THE WORLD WIDE WEB?

Incore
http://www.incore.ulst.ac.uk/cds/countries/

The University of Ulster has developed an Internet Guide for the Initiative on Conflict Resolution and Ethnicity that allows you to examine the most recent international conflicts and nationalist movements in detail. Clearly arranged by geographic location, this site offers information about conflict from Kosovo to Ethiopia and Eritrea. There are links to research sources, news sources, maps, nongovernmental organizations, and e-mail lists and newsgroups. You can also gather information according to theme.

Institute for War and Peace Reporting
http://www.iwpr.net/

Students of international relations often have a hard time getting up-to-date information from conflict areas that is not heavily censored by government agencies. The main goal of the Institute for War and Peace Reporting (IWPR) is to bring unbiased information on international conflicts to Internet users. An independent media resource, IWPR informs readers on international conflicts and supports media development in war-torn areas. Special reports provide in-depth analysis of conflict, media, and human rights issues in regions across the globe.

International Crisis Group
http://www.intl-crisis-group.org/

The International Crisis Group (ICG) is a private, multinational organization dedicated to understanding and responding to international crises. The organization's analysts conduct field research and prepare reports about ongoing conflicts that are used to make recommendations to states' decision makers. Currently, ICG has projects in northern and central Africa, the Balkans, and Southeast Asia. Students who are interested in these regional conflicts will find useful overviews of specific countries, reports on developments, and maps.

War, Peace, Security Guide
http://wps.cfc.dnd.ca/

The Canadian Forces College has created an information resource center on war and peace at this website. It contains a clickable map of world conflicts, as well as graphical links to armed forces, peace and disarmament sites, and military information are available.

INFOTRAC® COLLEGE EDITION

Search for the following articles in the InfoTrac College Edition database.

Bennett, D. Scott, and Allan C. Stam III. "The Duration of Interstate Wars, 1816–1985." *American Political Science Review* June 1996.

Kagan, Donald. "A Look at the Great Wars of the Twentieth Century," *Naval War College Review* Autumn 2000.

Serebriannikov, V. V. "On Cold and Hot Wars," *Military Thought* March–April 2002.

Van Evera, Stephen. "Hypotheses on Nationalism and War," *International Security* Spring 1994.

For more articles, enter:

"Persian Gulf War, 1991" in the Subject Guide.

"war" in the Subject Guide, and then go to subdivision "analysis."

"war" in the Subject Guide, and then go to subdivision "causes of."

ADDITIONAL CD-ROM RESOURCES

Click in Global Conflict and International Security to access other online resources related to this chapter.

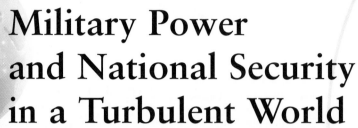

CHAPTER 8
Military Power and National Security in a Turbulent World

If you want peace, prepare for war.

FLAVIUS VEGETIUS RENATUS,
Roman general

E arly on the morning of August 2, 1990, columns of T-72 tanks from Iraq's elite Republican Guard crossed their country's southern border with Kuwait and raced down a six-lane highway toward its capital city. Within hours, resistance to the invasion collapsed. Saddam Hussein, the Iraqi leader who ordered the attack, promptly announced that Kuwait would be annexed. "If anyone tries to stop me," he threatened, "I will chop his arm off at the shoulder."

Although Iraq's invasion of Kuwait caught the United States off guard, President George Bush's response was strong and unequivocal. A pilot whose aircraft was shot down during World War II, Bush saw the crisis through the lens of the 1930s. From his perspective, Saddam Hussein was another Adolf Hitler, a dictator bent on conquering defenseless countries. Great Britain and France failed to deter Nazi aggression, Bush insisted, due to a series of miscalculations about Hitler's character and long-range goals. Anglo-French vacillation in the face of Hitler's remilitarization of the Rhineland, their acquiescence to his annexation of Austria, and their efforts to appease the Nazi leader were among the foreign policy mistakes Bush believed had led to World War II. If London and Paris had stood firm and communicated a credible threat to punish aggression, German expansion would have been contained. Each time the Western democracies failed to show resolve, Hitler was emboldened to make further encroachments on neighboring countries. Bush vowed not to make the same mistake with Saddam Hussein.

Operation Desert Storm, the Bush administration's plan for liberating Kuwait, hinged on what General Colin Powell, then-chairman of the Joint Chiefs of Staff, called the doctrine of invincible force. Powell advocated using all of the resources necessary to overwhelm Iraq in a fast and furious military campaign. In his words, it was the mind-set of a New York street fighter: "Here's my bat, here's my gun, here's my knife, I'm wearing armor. I'm going to kick your ass. . . ."

On January 17, 1991, the United States began a relentless air assault on Iraqi positions, followed a few weeks later by a devastating ground attack. Kuwait was liberated on February 26. Two days later, the president ended offensive military operations. For the Bush administration, the outcome of the Persian Gulf War confirmed the old Roman maxim that national security depends on military power. As Colin Powell explained, "A side that sees an easy victory will go after it."

This chapter examines the role of power in world politics. It begins by analyzing the ambiguous concept of "power." After reviewing the difficulties in measuring a country's power potential, it evaluates states' efforts to amass military capabilities by exploring trends in military spending, the arms trade, and weapons technology. Finally, the chapter concludes by discussing how states use their military and economic resources to exercise influence over other international actors.

Power in World Politics

Throughout history, many leaders have seen the acquisition of power as their primary objective. In their eyes, security is a function of power; therefore increasing power is in the national interest. Yet the meaning of "power" is not self-evident. It is used in different ways by different people. Most scholars define power in relational terms, as the ability of one state to make another continue a course of action, change what it is doing, or refrain from acting. A powerful state, in other words, has the capacity to control others. By exercising power, it can reduce the probability of something it does not want to happen and increase the probability of a preferred outcome (Deutsch 1978; Rothgeb 1993).

The Elements of State Power

Having defined power in terms of control, the question remains as to how we might measure the potential of one international actor to make another do what it otherwise would not. As David Baldwin (1989) points out, "the problem of measuring political power is like the problem of measuring purchasing power in an economy without money." In the absence of a standard unit of account, it is difficult to create a precise ranking of states that would predict who would prevail in a political conflict. Our intuition may suggest that larger countries are more powerful than smaller ones, but size alone does not always determine the outcome of political conflicts. France and, later, the United States were unable to exercise control over Vietnam. Similarly, the Soviet Union could not control Afghanistan. Indeed, history is replete with examples of small countries that won wars or defended their independence against much larger states.

• **power potential**
the relative capabilities or resources held by a state that are considered necessary to its asserting influence over others.

Since we lack a single measuring rod for assessing **power potential**, scholars and policymakers alike try to rank order states according to a combination of capabilities or resources presumed necessary to influence others. Normally, geographic, demographic, economic, and other tangible factors are mixed with intangible factors like leadership and public morale. Though the exact combination may differ from one person to the next, the intention is usually the same: Power is equated with those capabilities that enhance a country's war-making ability.

The importance customarily accorded to military prowess arises from the tendency to regard force as the ultimate arbiter of serious international disputes. Recall from earlier chapters that the anarchical environment of world politics requires states to rely on self-help for protection. No higher authority safeguards their interests. Under such conditions, military strength is seen as the primary source of national security and international influence.

While military strength may be effective in controlling the behavior of friends and foes in some contexts, it is ineffective in others. Power is situationally specific: The capabilities that allow an actor to influence one set of countries on a certain issue may be useless in influencing other countries on a different matter. A state's overall power, therefore, is defined in terms of the kinds of actors that it can control and the types of issues over which it has influence. As discussed in Chapter 4, a great power is a state that is able to exercise control over a wide domain of targets and an extensive scope of issues, usually by having a broad range of rewards and punishments at its disposal.

Globalization and the Changing Nature of State Power

Although military capability is central to most realist conceptions of power and security, some liberal theorists argue that the sources of state power today depend less on military strength than on factors such as information, technology, and trade competitiveness (Nye 1990). Since the end of World War II, a handful of states have increased their relative power by investing their resources in civilian rather than military technology. While the United States spent two-thirds of its research and development budget on military programs since the mid-1980s, European countries spent two-thirds on developing new technologies related to consumer goods, and Japan spent 99 percent in the same area (SIPRI 2002). The growing influence of the European Union and Japan in international affairs has led critics of realism to assert that we are entering a world based on education and human capital, one where creative ideas, product design, financing, and marketing will increasingly become major sources of economic success and political power (Rosecrance 1999).

Critics of the realist emphasis on continually preparing for war also claim that military expenditures extract high **opportunity costs** (see Controversy: Does High Military Spending Lower Human Security?). According to the International Monetary Fund (IMF), "military spending crowds out both private and public investment." Had U.S. military outlays remained at the 1990 level, the peace dividend from the end of the Cold War would have exceeded $400 billion in the next decade and potentially could have been made available for other purposes.

> • **opportunity costs**
> the concept in decision-making theories that when the occasion arises to use resources, what is gained for one purpose is lost for other purposes, so that every choice entails the cost of some lost opportunity.

Finally, critics of realism submit that less-tangible sources of national power now figure more prominently in calculations regarding national defense. Sometimes it is possible for political leaders to get what they want by setting the agenda and determining the framework of a debate, instead of relying upon inducements and threats to coerce people. The ability to get others to embrace your values, to see your objectives as legitimate, tends to be associated with intangible power resources such as the attractiveness of your country's ideals and the seductiveness of its culture. These intangible resources constitute *soft power*, in contrast with the *hard power* usually associated with tangible resources like military and economic strength (Nye 2004). Soft power is "the ability to achieve goals through attraction rather than coercion . . . by convincing others to follow or getting them to agree to norms and institutions that produce the desired behavior" (Keohane and Nye 2001b). If soft power grows in relative importance in today's so-called information age, military force ratios will no longer translate into power potential in the way they once did. Of course, military capability will remain important. While "it could be a mistake to assume that political influence is proportional to military strength, it would be an even bigger mistake to deny any connection between the two" (Majeed 1991).

The Pursuit of Military Capability

How people spend their money reveals their values. Similarly, how governments allocate their revenues reveals their priorities. An examination of national budgets discloses an unmistakable pattern: Although the sources of global political power may be changing, many states continue to seek security by spending substantial portions of their national treasures on arms.

CONTROVERSY

Does High Military Spending Lower Human Security?

Politics requires making hard choices about how public funds should be spent. One such choice is between "guns versus butter"—how much of a country's budget should be allocated to military preparedness as opposed to social welfare programs. The former emphasizes state security; the latter, human security. Neither goal can be pursued without making some sacrifice for the realization of the other.

The guns versus butter trade-off is a significant in every country, and different leaders deal with it in different ways. One way to picture these differences is to group states according to how much of their gross national income (GNI) they devote to the military. As the map below shows, there exist wide variations, with many countries allocating high proportions of their GNI to defense and other countries choosing to

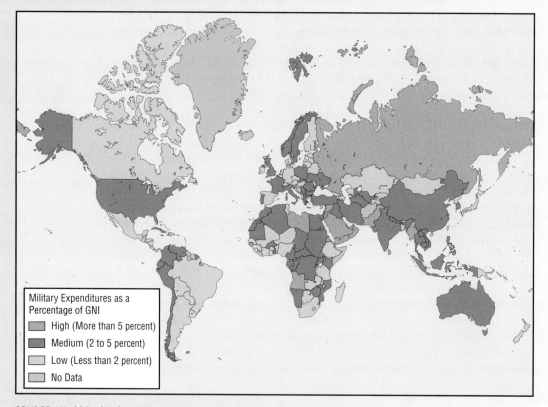

Military Expenditures as a Percentage of GNI

- High (More than 5 percent)
- Medium (2 to 5 percent)
- Low (Less than 2 percent)
- No Data

SOURCE: *World Bank Atlas 2002*, p. 50. Copyright © 2002 by the International Bank for Reconstruction and Development/The World Bank. Reprinted by permission.

spend their wealth on enhancing human security. Indeed, some comparatively wealthy states (Kuwait, Israel, and Brunei) bear a heavy burden, whereas other states that provide a high average income for their citizens (Japan, Austria, and Luxembourg) have a low defense burden. Likewise, the citizens of some very poor countries (Sierra Leone, Mozambique, and Chad) are heavily burdened, whereas those of others (Bhutan and Zaire) are not. Thus, it is difficult to generalize about the precise relationship between a country's defense burden and its citizens' standard of living, human development, or stage of development.

How much should a country spend on national security? To many realists, the price is never too high. However, others argue that high levels of military spending reduce a state's ability to provide for its citizens. This view was expressed by Oscar Arias, the 1987 Nobel Peace laureate and former president of Costa Rica, who wrote in 1999 that "World leaders must stop viewing militaristic investment as a measure of national well-being. The sad fact is that half the world's governments invest more in defense than in health programs. If we channeled just $40 billion each year away from armies and into antipoverty programs, in ten years all of the world's population would enjoy basic social services—education, health care and nutrition, potable water and sanitation. Another $40 billion each year over ten years would provide each person on this planet with an income level above the poverty line for his or her country."

The case of the United States, the world's biggest spender on defense, speaks to Dr. Arias's contention that high military spending reduces social welfare. Consider how the United States ranks on various non-military indicators of human security:

U.S. Rank Compared to 160 Other States

Social Development

Percent population with safe water	1
Percent births attended by trained personnel	2
Female and male literacy rate	4
GNP for each person	5

Economic-Social Standing

Public health expenditures for each person	8
Public education expenditures for each person	9
Public education expenditures for each student	10
Maternal mortality rate	12
Infant mortality rate	13
Life expectancy	14
Percent school-age children in school	18
Under-five mortality rate	18
Contraceptive prevalence	19
Percent infants with low birthweight	29
Number of physicians for each person	39
Number of teachers for each person	39

These rankings (UNDP 2000) raise serious questions about the true costs of national security. Who really pays for defense? If you were a head of state, what budget priorities would you propose for your country's national security and your citizens' human security? How would you reconcile the need for defense with the need to provide for the common welfare? The choices you would make would be difficult, because they entail trade-offs between competing values. For this reason military-spending decisions are highly controversial everywhere. ●

Click on Global Conflict and International Security to access an interactive version of this map and related critical thinking questions.

Trends in Military Spending

The weapons that governments believe they require for national security are costly. World military expenditures in 2000, for example, reached $798 billion, exceeding more than $1.5 million each minute. When measured in constant dollars adjusted for inflation, this level of military spending shows an increase over past levels: 2.7 times that spent in 1960, 1.9 times that of the 1970 total, and 1.2 times the 1980 level. Compared to the mid-1930s, world military spending has increased fifteenfold, a growth rate exceeding that of world population, the rate of expansion of global economic output, and expenditures for public health (SIPRI 2002; U.S. ACDA 1997; Sivard 1991, 1993, 1996).

These aggregate figures do not tell the entire story, because the global total spent for arms conceals widely varying trends for particular groups of countries. Historically, the rich countries have spent the most money on arms acquisitions, a pattern that has continued. In 2000 the Global North spent $539 billion for defense, in contrast with the Global South's $259 billion. Thus the developed countries' share of the world total was 70 percent. However, when measured against other factors, the differences are not so great. Both groups spent 2.6 percent of their GNPs, on average, but the Global North's military spending as a portion of government revenues stood at 9 percent and the Global South's, at 13 percent. While these two groups' military spending levels were quite different, over time they are converging. As Figure 8.1 reveals, the Global South's military expenditure in 1961 was about 7 percent of the world total, but by 2002 it had climbed threefold to approximately one-third. In short, poor states are copying the costly, military budgetary habits of the wealthiest states.

FIGURE 8.1
Changes in the Levels of Military Expenditures since 1960, Global North and Global South

Global military spending has fluctuated since 1960, with total expenditures worldwide peaking in 1987, after which they fell until the terrorist attacks on New York and Washington in 2001. As the trend lines show, the Global North's defense spending declined immediately following the Cold War, but has begun to rise due to increases in American military spending. U.S. president George W. Bush's 2004 federal budget committed more funds to military defense than the amount spent by all other countries combined. The military budgets of the Global South's developing countries have also climbed in recent years, reaching over $259 billion—about one-third of the world's total.

SOURCES: 1961–1995, U.S. ACDA (1971). 1; 1996–2001 SIPRI (1999), 301, and www.SIPRI.com

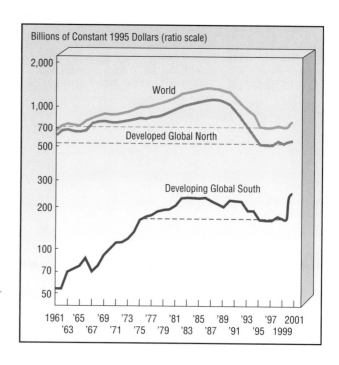

Trends in the Weapons Trade

During the Cold War, many states sought to increase their security by purchasing weapons. The Cold War's end did not slow the arms trade, however. Since 1991, the countries in the Global South have become the leading market for the traffic in arms (see Figure 8.2). The total value of all international arms deliveries between 1991 and 2001 exceeded $325 billion of which 70 percent were exported to developing countries, primarily in Asia and the Middle East (Grimmett 2002, 3).

Besides looking at arms importers, it is also important to observe the activities of arms suppliers. By the end of the Cold War, more than sixty states were selling weapons abroad (Sivard 1991, 11), with the United States dominating the arms export market. Between 1994 and 2001 the United States accounted for a higher proportion of worldwide contracts to sell arms than any other supplier, agreeing to weapons-export contracts exceeding $131 billion, or 44 percent of the $300 billion total worldwide. Economic gain was an important rationale for these sales, as the United States used arms exports to offset its chronic balance-of-trade deficits. In 1998, the United States assigned 6,493 full-time federal employees to handle U.S. arms deals and spent $477 million on promotional activities for U.S. arms dealers (*Harper's*, February 1998, 13). Because the sale of weapons is big business, arms manufacturers constitute a powerful domestic lobby. A highly organized **military-industrial complex** is widely believed to exercise enormous power over defense budgets and arms sales agreements in the United States as well as in many other Global North countries (see Regan 1994).

In addition to reaping economic benefits, states sell weapons for various political reasons, including to support friendly governments and to cultivate new allies. This was illustrated by U.S. arms export policy prior to and in the aftermath of the 1990 Persian Gulf War. The United States delivered 56 percent of the $101 billion in arms sold to the strife-torn Middle East between 1994 and 2001 (Grimmett 2002, 53, 5), allegedly for the purpose of anchoring allies and

• **military-industrial complex** a term coined by U.S. president Eisenhower to describe the coalition among arms manufacturers, military bureaucracies, and top government officials that promotes defense expenditures for its own profit and power.

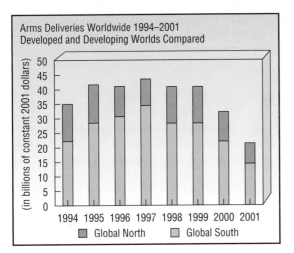

Arms Deliveries Worldwide 1994–2001
Developed and Developing Worlds Compared

(in billions of constant 2001 dollars)

1994 1995 1996 1997 1998 1999 2000 2001
☐ Global North   ☐ Global South

FIGURE 8.2

Arms Deliveries to the Global North and Global South, 1994–2001

The global arms trade has led to the diffusion of military capabilities from the Global North to the Global South. In 2001, the estimated value of all global arms transfers exceeded $21 billion (Grimmett 2002, 3). From 1994 through 2001, arms deliveries to developing countries comprised 69 percent of all arms deliveries worldwide. As a percentage of total national expenditures, some of the world's poorest countries have spent the most on purchasing technologically advanced weapons.
SOURCE: Grimmett (2002), 31.

preserving the military balance of power in that explosive region. Whether arming other countries has accomplished all of its intended political goals is open to question, however. During the Cold War, for example, the United States and the Soviet Union thought they could maintain peace by spreading arms to politically pivotal recipients. Between 1983 and 1987 the United States provided arms to 59 less-developed countries while the Soviet Union supplied 42 (Klare 1990, 12). Yet many of the recipients engaged in war with their neighbors or experienced internal rebellion. Of the top 20 arms importers in 1988, more than half "had governments noted for the frequent use of violence" (Sivard 1991, 17). When seen in this light, it appears to some observers that the U.S. arms export program undermines the current U.S. policy of promoting democracy, because roughly one-third of the recipients of U.S. arms exports in recent years have not been democracies (Blanton and Kegley 1997, 94–95).

The inability of arms suppliers to control the uses to which their military hardware will be put is troubling. "The concern is that friends can become foes, and secrets can be stolen" (J. Brown 1999a). Supplying weapons to other states can backfire, as the United States discovered both when the weapons it sold to Iraq were used against U.S. forces by Saddam Hussein in the Persian Gulf War (Timmerman 1991) and when the Stinger missiles the United States supplied to Taliban forces resisting the Soviet Union's 1979 invasion in Afghanistan fell into the hands of terrorists later opposing the United States. Likewise, in 1982 Great Britain found itself shipping military equipment to Argentina just eight days before Argentina's attack on the British-controlled Falkland Islands (Sivard 1982). Nevertheless, suppliers seem eager to sell to any purchaser, and they continue to sell weapons to both sides of a number of international disputes. Of even greater concern is the possibility of terrorists acquiring weapons of mass destruction on the black market through covert suppliers. It only takes "a few kilograms of plutonium and less than 20 kilograms of highly enriched uranium to make a nuclear bomb [and] about 40 kilograms of weapons-usable uranium and plutonium have been stolen from poorly protected nuclear facilities in the former Soviet Union during the last decade. While most of that material has been retrieved, two kilos of highly enriched uranium taken from a research reactor in Georgia is still missing, and that's just for starters. The real amount of missing weapons-grade material [likely to be part of the illicit trafficking of nuclear material worldwide] could be 10 times higher than is officially known" (*USA Today* 130 [June 2002], 1).

Trends in Weapons Technology

The widespread quest for armaments has created a potentially explosive global environment. This description is especially apt when we consider not only trends in defense expenditures and the arms trade but also the destructiveness of modern weapons.

Nuclear Weapons. Technological research and development has radically expanded the destructiveness of national arsenals. The largest "blockbuster" bombs of World War II delivered a power of ten tons of TNT. The atomic bomb

Hiroshima In an attempt to bring World War II to a speedy close, the United States dropped an atomic bomb on Hiroshima on August 6, 1945. In an instant, the Japanese city lay in ruins.

that leveled Hiroshima had the power of over fifteen thousand tons of TNT. Less than twenty years later, the former Soviet Union built a nuclear bomb with the explosive force of 57 megatons (million tons) of TNT. By 2002, the global stockpile of nuclear warheads exceeded 30,000, with a collective explosive force of over 1.3 million Hiroshima bombs (*Bulletin of the Atomic Scientists,* November/December 2002, 103).

At the start of 2003, there were eight "official" members of the nuclear club—the United States, Russia, Great Britain, France, China, India, Pakistan, and Israel. In addition, North Korea and as many as twenty other states or terrorist organizations were believed seeking nuclear capability. Obstacles to nuclear **proliferation** are weak. First, the expertise necessary for weapons development has spread with the globalization of advanced scientific training. Second, export controls designed to stop technology transfer for military purposes are ineffectual. Finally, the materials needed to make a nuclear weapon are widely available, primarily due to the widespread use of nuclear technology for generating electricity. Today 428 nuclear power and research reactors are in operation in 44 countries throughout the world (*Defense Monitor,* 1 2000, 5). States could reprocess the uranium and plutonium that power plants produce as waste for clandestine nuclear weapons production. Current estimates suggest that commercial reprocessing reactors are producing enough plutonium to make as many as forty thousand nuclear weapons (Map 8.1).

• **proliferation** the spread of weapon capabilities throughout the state system.

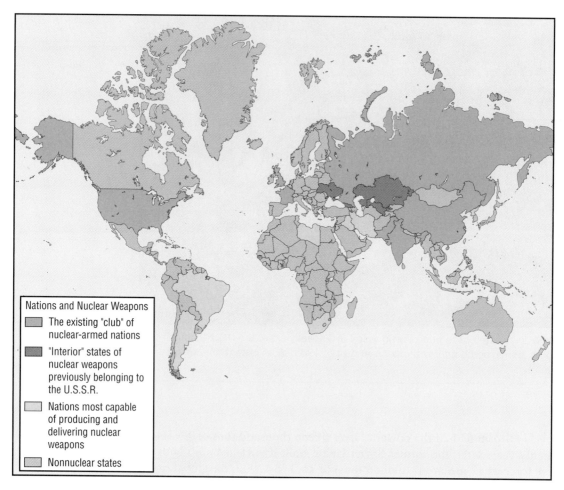

MAP 8.1
Nuclear-Armed Countries, Today and Tomorrow

Despite the end of the Cold War in 1991, nuclear proliferation remains a major global concern. Beyond the United States, Russia, Great Britain, France, China, India, Pakistan, and Israel, four new independent Soviet republics (Ukraine, Kazakhstan, Uzbekistan, and Georgia) still retain the nuclear weapons they acquired from the old Soviet Union. South Africa is believed to already possess the capacity to use nuclear warheads in wartime, and North Korea has pursued a secret uranium-enrichment program in violation of past agreements and in 2003 prepared to restart a nuclear reactor capable of producing weapons-grade plutonium. Five other countries have active nuclear-weapon development programs, which may include the capacity to manufacture and deliver these weapons of mass destruction— Argentina, Brazil, Iran, North Korea, and Taiwan.

SOURCE: Based on data from *Bulletin of the Atomic Scientists* (November–December 2002), 103.

The map legend reads:

Nations and Nuclear Weapons
- The existing "club" of nuclear-armed nations
- "Interior" states of nuclear weapons previously belonging to the U.S.S.R.
- Nations most capable of producing and delivering nuclear weapons
- Nonnuclear states

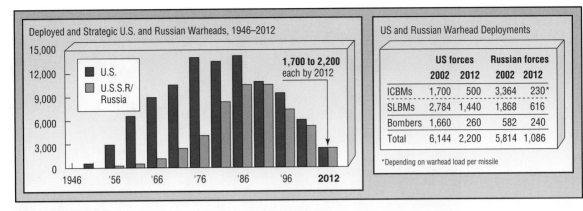

FIGURE 8.3
Caging the Nuclear Threat: The Rise and Fall of U.S. and Russian Nuclear Weapons

In May 2002, presidents George Bush and Valdimir Putin signed the Strategic Offensive Reduction Treaty (SORT), which committed the United States and Russia to reduce their nuclear arsenals by two-thirds within the next 10 years. If enacted, this reduction will greatly reduce the number of nuclear warheads in the world. Whether other nuclear powers will reduce their inventories remains to be seen. Shown here is a comparison of the nuclear arsenals possessed by the United Sates and the Soviet Union/Russia between 1946 and 2002, with the chart on the right breaking down both countries' forces according to their warhead deployments.

SOURCES: Arms Control Association and the Carnegie Endowment for International Peace (left); *The Economist,* May 18, 2002, p. 30 (right). Copyright © 2002 by The Economist Newspaper Ltd. All rights reserved. Reprinted with permission. Further reproduction prohibited. www.economist.com

Nuclear weapons serve as a symbol of status and power. Because of the wide-spread conviction rooted in realism that military might confers political stature, it is understandable why some nonnuclear powers have expressed interest in obtaining these weapons at the very time that the United States and Russia have sought to reduce their arsenals (see Figure 8.3). "There's not a snowball's chance in hell we'll eliminate all nuclear weapons from the face of the earth," explains Matthew Bunn, editor of *Arms Control Today.* "That genie is long since out of the bottle and there's no chance of ever getting him back in (cited in Kegley and Wittkopf 2004, 471)."

Biological and Chemical Weapons. Despite the 1972 Biological Weapons Convention prohibiting the development, production, and stockpiling of biological weapons, many people fear that some states and terrorist organizations are trying to develop such weapons. Similarly, although the 1925 Geneva Protocol banned the use of chemical weapons in warfare, and the Chemical Weapons Convention (CWC), signed by 184 countries by 2002, required the destruction of existing stocks, over twenty states are suspected of producing chemical weapons (Stock and De Geer 1995, 340).

Biological and chemical weapons are sometimes regarded as a "poor man's atomic bomb," because they can be produced at comparatively small cost and cause widespread injury and death. As a result, extremist groups, often operating

Nuclear Testing When informed of the possibility of designing a hydrogen bomb, U.S. president Truman asked, "What the hell are we waiting for?" However, scientists such as Robert Oppenheimer—who headed the Manhattan Project, which produced the atomic bomb—maintained that the hydrogen bomb was inherently immoral because it was so destructive. More than two thousand nuclear-weapons tests have occurred since 1945, and testing has continued. Pictured here is a 1995 French nuclear test in the South Pacific.

beyond the control of weak state governments, may find these weapons of mass destruction to be an effective means of promoting global terror. The proliferation of ballistic missiles among regional rivals in the Middle East, Asia, and elsewhere also raises acute dangers, because they enable such weapons to be delivered at great distances.

Weapons Delivery Systems. Advances in weapons technology have been rapid and extraordinary. Particularly deadly have been the technological refinements that enable states to deliver weapons from as far away as nine thousand miles to within one hundred feet of their targets in less than thirty minutes. During the Cold War, the United States and Soviet Union equipped their ballistic missiles with **multiple independently targetable reentry vehicles (MIRVs),** which enable a single missile to launch several warheads toward different targets simultaneously. One U.S. MX (Peacekeeper) missile equipped with MIRV could carry ten nuclear warheads—enough to wipe out a city and everything else within a 50-mile radius.

Other technological improvements have led to steady increases in the speed, accuracy, range, and effectiveness of weapons. As the recent wars in Kosovo, Afghanistan, and Iraq have shown, **smart bombs** have become a part of the weapons inventory. In addition, a large number of innovative new weapons tech-

• **multiple independently targetable reentry vehicles (MIRVs)** a technological innovation permitting many nuclear warheads to be delivered from a single missile.

• **smart bombs** precision-guided military technology that enables a bomb to search for its target and detonate at the precise time it can do the most damage.

nologies are under development. They include plans to develop energy pulses to take down enemies without necessarily killing them; beamed electromagnetic and sonic wavelengths that can modify human behavior (for example, putting people to sleep through electromagnetic heat and magnetic radiation); the electromagnetic pulse (EMP) bomb, which can be hand delivered in a suitcase and can immobilize an entire city's computer and communications systems; and logic bombs that can confuse and redirect traffic on the target country's air and rail system. Many of these technological advances in warfare are likely to make orthodox ways of classifying weapons systems as well as prior equations for measuring power ratios obsolete.

For decades, a **firebreak** has separated conventional wars from nuclear wars. The term comes from the barriers of cleared land that firefighters use to keep forest fires from racing out of control. In the context of modern weaponry, it is a psychological barrier whose purpose is to prevent even the most intensive forms of conventional combat from escalating into nuclear war. As both nuclear and conventional weapons technologies advance, there is danger that the firebreak is being crossed from both directions—by a new generation of "near-nuclear" conventional weapons capable of levels of violence approximating those of a limited nuclear strike, and by a new generation of "near-conventional" nuclear weapons capable of causing destruction similar to that of the most powerful conventional weapons. Once the firebreak has been crossed, many people fear that a major restraint on the conduct of modern warfare will disappear.

• **firebreak** the psychological barrier between conventional and nuclear war.

In sum, a pervasive sense of insecurity haunts much of the world. The danger of nuclear annihilation has not disappeared with the end of the Cold War. Nor are there effective controls over the proliferation of biological and chemical weapons. The twenty-first century has not become the peaceful and prosperous period many people expected. In response, many national leaders today echo the recommendation of the Roman general, Flavius Vegetius Renatus: "If you want peace, prepare for war." Security, as the Bush administration insisted during the 1990 Persian Gulf War, requires military capability. But since the possession of military capability does not automatically result in its wise use, we turn now to look at how it is employed as an instrument of statecraft. We begin with an examination of nuclear weapons.

Military Strategy in the Nuclear Age

The dropping of the atomic bomb on Japan on August 6, 1945 is the most important event distinguishing pre– from post–World War II international politics. In a blinding flash, the world was transformed from a "balance-of-power" to a "balance-of-terror" system. In the following decades, policymakers in nuclear-armed states had to grapple with two central policy issues: (1) whether they should use nuclear weapons; and (2) how to prevent others from using them. The search for solutions has been critical, for the immediate and delayed effects of a nuclear war are terrifying to contemplate. Simply put, life as we know it would cease. The planet would be uninhabitable, because a **nuclear winter** would result, with devastating consequences: "Fires ignited in such a war could generate enough smoke to obscure the sun and perturb the atmosphere over large

• **nuclear winter** the expected freeze that would occur in the earth's climate from the fallout of smoke and dust in the event nuclear weapons were used, blocking out sunlight and destroying plant and animal life that survived the original blast.

areas . . . [lowering] average planetary temperatures . . . [and darkening] the skies sufficiently to compromise green plant photosynthesis" (Sagan and Turco 1993, 369). It has been estimated that "the missiles on board a single [U.S.] SLBM submarine may be enough to initiate nuclear winter" (Quester 1992)—enough to end human existence.

Although weapons of mass destruction have existed since World War II, the postures of the United States and Soviet Union toward them evolved as technologies, defense needs, capabilities, and global conditions changed. For analytical convenience, we can treat those postures in terms of three periods: compellence, deterrence, and preemption. The first began at the end of World War II and lasted until the Cuban missile crisis. U.S. nuclear superiority was the dominant characteristic of this period. The second began in 1962 and lasted until the breakup of the Soviet Union in 1991. Growing Soviet military capability was the dominant characteristic of this period, which meant that the United States no longer stood alone in its ability to annihilate another country without fear of its own destruction. The third phase began after the end of the Cold War, taking shape as the great powers began revising their strategic doctrines in the light of new global threats.

Compellence

Countries that possess military preeminence often think of weapons as instruments in diplomatic bargaining. The United States, the world's first and, for many years, unchallenged nuclear power, adopted the strategic doctrine of **compellence** (Schelling 1966) when it enjoyed a clear-cut superiority over the Soviet Union. Military capabilities do not have to be used for them to be useful; a state may exercise influence over others simply by "demonstrating the quantity of force and highlighting the capability of, and intention to, use force" (Majeed 1991). The U.S. doctrine of compellence made nuclear weapons tools of political influence, used not for fighting but to convince others to do what they might not otherwise do.

The United States sought to gain bargaining leverage by conveying the impression that it would actually use nuclear weapons. This posture was especially evident during the Eisenhower administration, when Secretary of State John Foster Dulles practiced **brinkmanship,** deliberately threatening U.S. adversaries with nuclear destruction so that, at the brink of war, they would concede to U.S. demands. Brinkmanship was part of the overall U.S. strategic doctrine known as **massive retaliation.** To contain communism and Soviet expansionism, it called for aiming U.S. nuclear weapons at the Soviet Union's population and industrial centers.

Massive retaliation heightened fears in the Kremlin that a nuclear exchange would destroy the Soviet Union but permit the survival of the United States. Thus in addition to augmenting their nuclear capabilities, Soviet leaders accelerated their space program and successfully launched the world's first satellite (*Sputnik*), therein demonstrating Moscow's ability to deliver nuclear weapons beyond the Eurasian landmass. The superpowers' strategic competition now took a new turn, as the United States for the first time faced a nuclear threat to its homeland.

• **compellence** a threat of force aimed at making an adversary grant concessions against its will.

• **brinkmanship** intentionally taking enormous risks in bargaining with an adversary in order to compel submission.

• **massive retaliation** a policy of responding to any act of aggression with the most destructive capabilities available, including nuclear weapons.

Deterrence

As U.S. strategic superiority eroded, American policymakers began to question the usefulness of weapons of mass destruction as tools in political bargaining. They were horrified by the destruction that could result if compellence provoked a nuclear exchange. The nearly suicidal Cuban missile crisis of 1962 brought about a major change in American strategic thought, shifting strategic policy from compellence to **deterrence.**

Whereas compellence contains an offensive coercive threat aimed at persuading an adversary to relinquish something without resistance, deterrence seeks to dissuade an adversary from undertaking some future action. At the heart of deterrence theory is the assumption that the defender has the ability to punish an adversary with unacceptably high costs if an attack is launched. The key elements of deterrence are: (1) *capabilities*—the possession of military resources that can make threats of military retaliation plausible; (2) *credibility*—the belief that the defender will actually follow through on its threats; and (3) *communication*—the facility to send a potential aggressor the clear message that the defender has both the ability and willingness to strike back. Advocates of deterrence argue that it "will succeed if threatened costs can be communicated to the challenger, assessed by the challenger, and believed by the challenger" (Harknett 1994).

Ironically, the shift from compellence to deterrence stimulated rather than inhibited the U.S.-Soviet arms race. A deterrent strategy depends on the unquestionable ability to inflict intolerable damage on an opponent. It requires a **second-strike capability** that enables a country to withstand an adversary's first strike and still retain the ability to retaliate with a devastating counterattack. To ensure a second-strike capability and an adversary's awareness of it, deterrence rationalized an unrestrained search for sophisticated retaliatory capabilities. Any system that could be built was built because, as President Kennedy explained in 1961, "only when arms are sufficient beyond doubt can we be certain without doubt that they will never be employed."

Policymakers coined the phrase **mutual assured destruction (MAD)** to describe the strategic balance that emerged between the United States and the Soviet Union after the Cuban missile crisis. Regardless of who struck first, the other side could destroy the attacker. Under these circumstances, initiating a nuclear war was irrational; the frightening costs outweighed any conceivable benefits. As Soviet leader Nikita Khrushchev put it: "If you reach for the push button, you reach for suicide." Safety, in former British prime minister Winston Churchill's words, was "the sturdy child of terror and survival the twin brother of annihilation."

A new shift in strategic thinking occurred in 1983, when U.S. president Reagan proposed building a space-based defensive shield against ballistic missiles. The **Strategic Defense Initiative (SDI)**, or "Star Wars" as critics labeled it, called for the development of a defense against Soviet ballistic missiles, using orbiting laser-based weapons to destroy missiles launched in fear, anger, or by accident. The goal, as President Reagan defined it, was to make nuclear weapons "impotent and obsolete." Thus SDI sought to shift U.S. nuclear strategy away from mutual assured destruction, which President Reagan deemed "morally unacceptable."

• **deterrence** a strategy designed to dissuade an adversary from doing what it would otherwise do.

• **second-strike capability** a state's capacity to retaliate after absorbing a first-strike attack with weapons of mass destruction.

• **mutual assured destruction (MAD)** a system of deterrence in which both sides possess the ability to survive a first strike and launch a devastating retaliatory attack.

• **Strategic Defense Initiative (SDI)** a plan conceived by the Reagan administration to deploy an antiballistic missile system using space-based lasers that would destroy enemy nuclear missiles.

However, the United States was unable to build a reliable ballistic missile defense during the remaining years of the Cold War.

Preemption

Despite uncertainties about its effectiveness, even with technological advances, the United States has continued to proceed with the development of a ballistic missile defense system. In the first Bush administration, the primary purpose was to protect the United States from a Soviet nuclear attack. However, when the Cold War ended in 1991, the original rationale for such a system faded as Washington and Moscow negotiated a series of historic arms control agreements. Other great powers also reduced the number of nuclear warheads in their arsenals. Worldwide, the total number of nuclear warheads was cut in half in 2002 to less than thirty thousand. As a consequence, the strategic nuclear balance is radically different today than it was during most of the second half of the twentieth century.

The end of the Cold War has not brought strategic planning to a conclusion, however. New nuclear threats are on the horizon. This is why the United States has vigorously pushed forward with plans to develop an antiballistic missile system while simultaneously declaring a willingness to undertake preemptive action against emerging dangers. To justify its new strategy, the administration cites the proliferation of states with nuclear weapons and the challenge of keeping fissile materials out of the hands of terrorists. The challenge is great, because illegal trafficking in the nuclear materials necessary to produce a nuclear bomb is very active, with over four hundred confirmed incidents since 1993 (*Foreign Policy*, January/February 2002, 14).

"We face a threat with no precedent," President George W. Bush insisted during his commencement address at West Point on June 1, 2002. On the one hand, modern technology allows shadowy terrorist networks to launch catastrophic attacks against the United States. On the other hand, these networks cannot be dissuaded by the threat of punishment because they have no fixed territory or populace to protect. "We must take the battle to the enemy," he exhorted, "and confront the worst threats before they emerge."

Bush's call for acting preemptively against terrorists and the states that harbored them was echoed in his September 17, 2002 report, *The National Security Strategy of the United States of America* (NSS). Building on the proposition that "nations need not suffer an attack before they can lawfully take action to defend themselves against forces that present an imminent danger," the report argued that the acquisition of weapons of mass destruction by terrorists and rogue states provided the United States with a compelling case for engaging in anticipatory self-defense. "Traditional concepts of deterrence will not work against a terrorist enemy whose avowed tactics are wanton destruction and the targeting of innocents; whose so-called soldiers seek martyrdom in death and whose most potent protection is statelessness." This requires, it is argued, **preemption** rather than deterrence. As U.S. secretary of defense Donald Rumsfeld put it, "this isn't about punishment. We've got the wrong models in our minds if we're thinking about punishment. We're not. This isn't retaliation or retribution" (cited in Hersh 2002,

• **preemption** a quick first-strike attack that seeks to defeat an adversary before it can organize a retaliatory response.

70). It is striking a menace before it is fully formed, even if the United States must act unilaterally.

The Bush national security strategy has been called the most sweeping reformulation of U.S. strategic thinking in more than half a century (Gaddis 2002). Although under international law states have a legal right to defend themselves against aggression as well as imminent attacks, critics charge that beneath the language of military preemption lies a more radical policy of preventive war. In brief, a *preemptive* military attack entails the use of force to quell or mitigate an impending strike by an adversary. A *preventive* attack entails the use of force to eliminate any possible future strike, even if there is no reason to believe that the capacity to launch an attack is operational. Whereas the grounds for preemption lie in evidence of a credible, imminent threat, the basis for prevention rests on the suspicion of an incipient, contingent threat (Kegley and Raymond 2003).

According to critics of the new Bush strategy, preventive use of military force sets a dangerous precedent. Predicting another state's future behavior is difficult because leadership intentions are hard to discern, information on long-term goals may be shrouded in secrecy, and signals of its policy direction may be distorted by background noise. If suspicions about an adversary become a justifiable cause for military action, then every truculent, self-indulgent leader will have a rough-and-ready pretext for ordering a first strike. In rebuttal, the Bush administration argues that waiting for nuclear threats to fully materialize is waiting far too long.

The strategy of anticipatory self-defense thus raises anew timeless questions about the conditions under which, and the purposes for which, military force is justifiable. What does precaution warrant when nameless, faceless enemies are willing to engage in indiscriminate, suicidal attacks against noncombatants? How can force be used to influence an adversary's decision-making calculus? What are the conditions that affect the success of coercive diplomacy?

The Limits of Coercive Diplomacy

The strategy of **coercive diplomacy** employs threats or limited force to persuade an opponent to stop or undo an action already underway. The goal is to alter the target state's calculation of costs and benefits, so it is convinced that acceding to one's demands will be better than defying them. This may be accomplished by delivering an **ultimatum** that promises an immediate and significant escalation in the conflict, or by issuing a warning and gradually increasing pressure on the target (Craig and George 1990).

Coercive diplomacy's reliance on threats and exemplary uses of force is designed to avoid the bloodshed and expenses associated with traditional military campaigns. It seeks "to resolve without violence, or with only minimal violence, those conflicts that are too severe to be settled by ordinary diplomacy and that in earlier times would have been settled by war" (Snyder and Diesing 1977). Nevertheless, these attempts at intimidation carry some risk of war. Figure 8.4 shows the annual frequency between 1918 and 2001 of 433 international crises involving coercive efforts. Most of these crises were initiated by the great powers, roughly two-thirds occurred in the Global South, and about one of every

• **coercive diplomacy**
the use of threats or limited armed force to persuade an adversary to alter its foreign and/or domestic policies.

• **ultimatum**
a demand that contains a time limit for compliance and a threat of punishment for resistence.

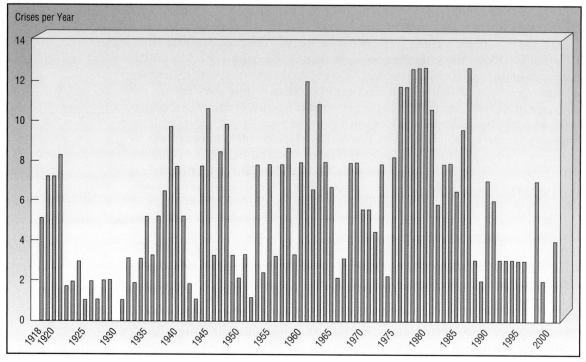

FIGURE 8.4
The Annual Frequency of International Crises, 1918–2001

A crisis in international affairs is a situation that (1) threatens a state's high-priority goals; (2) surprises its political leaders; and (3) restricts the amount of time available for making a response (Hermann 1972). On 433 occasions between 1918 and 2001, crises developed because states confronted each other militarily, in the hopes of forcing concessions. One of the problems with such efforts at coercive diplomacy is that crises can easily escalate to war because of the time pressures, inadequate information, heightened anxieties, and impulsive behavior that normally accompany decision-making procedures during threatening situations.

SOURCE: Based on International Crisis Behavior (ICB) data, provided courtesy of Jonathan Wilkenfeld and Michael Brecher.

• **military intervention** overt or covert use of force by one or more countries that cross the border of another country in order to affect the target country's government and policies.

three lead to war (Brecher 1993, 333, 476). Examples of violence that were preceded by a crisis include World War I (1914), Kashmir (1948 and 2002), Suez (1956), Tibet (1959), the Bay of Pigs (1961), Goa (1961), Kuwait (1990), Yugoslavia (Kosovo, 1999), Macedonia (2001), and Afghanistan (2001).

Orchestrating the mix of threats and armed force can be done in various ways, from traditional "gunboat diplomacy" (intimidating an adversary with a show of naval force) to "tomahawk diplomacy" (striking it with cruise missiles). We will focus first on **military intervention,** the oldest and most common approach to military coercion.

Military Intervention

Intervention can come in many forms. States can intervene physically through direct entry into another country or indirectly with propaganda. They can act alone or in league with other states. Military intervention involves "operations undertaken openly by a state's regular military forces within a specific foreign land in such a manner as to risk immediate combat" (Tillema 1995). Altogether, nearly one thousand individual acts of military intervention were initiated between 1945 and 2001, involving 2.4 million fatalities (Tilleman 2001). Excluded from this estimate are an unknown number of **covert operations.**

Military interventions have often heightened international tension and led to war. Between 1816 and 2001, 41 cases of third-party military intervention into 242 civil wars occurred, with the result that 17 percent were "internationalized" as they were transformed into interstate wars. These statistics raise important questions about the use of military interventions for coercive diplomacy. Do interventions yield positive results, punishing regimes that violate human rights and calming war-torn societies? Or do they make matters worse? Questions along these lines are hotly debated today. In the wake of humanitarian interventions in Kosovo and East Timor in 1999, the great powers struggled unsuccessfully in an effort to reach consensus about whether to intervene in sovereign states when innocent civilians are victimized by tyrants. UN secretary-general Kofi Annan's plea in September 1999 for the permanent members of the Security Council to make "a new commitment to intervention" stirred up an already intense debate about military intervention, even in the name of morality, justice, and human rights.

Few question the necessity to stand up to genocide and intervene to protect the lives of persecuted peoples. However, many great powers remain reluctant to pledge unconditionally their willingness to uphold human rights anywhere they are violated. Instead, they practice selective engagement, picking and choosing when and where they will intervene. Regardless of humanitarian considerations, they generally avoid taking action when their interests appear to be served by non-involvement. On the other hand, they insert themselves when their security appears at stake, as the United States has done recently in attempting to weaken terrorist networks with global reach. Since 1990 the U.S. Army has been deployed abroad three times as often as the number of "major" deployments in the entire period between 1946 and 1989 (*Harper's,* July 1999, 17). But domestic and international criticism stands in the way of its practicing interventionism with abandon. As a result, many of the counterterrorist interventions in the future will likely be conducted in the shadows by covert and clandestine methods.

Policymakers today disagree about the appropriate use of military coercion. Research on coercive diplomacy suggests that its success depends upon the context of each specific situation. The following conditions are thought to favor the effective use of coercive diplomacy (Pape 1996; George 1991):

- *Clarity of user objectives.* The coercing power's demands must be clearly understood by the target state.
- *Asymmetry of motivation favoring the user.* The coercing power must be more highly motivated than the target by what is at stake. Timing is critical.

• **covert operations** secret activities undertaken by a state outside its borders through clandestine means to achieve specific political or military goals.

Military coercion tends to be effective when it occurs prior to the target making a firm commitment on the issue at hand, and when factions exist within the target state's government. It is far more difficult for a coercing power to undo something that has already been accomplished by the target state.

- *Opponent's fear of escalation and belief in the urgency for compliance.* The coercing power must create in the adversary's mind a sense of urgency for compliance with its demand. Two factors are important in affecting an adversary's perceptions: (1) the coercing power's reputation for successfully using armed force in the past, and (2) its capability to increase pressure to a level that the target would find intolerable. Coercion generally fails when the target has the ability to absorb the punishment delivered by the coercing state.

- *Adequate domestic and international support for the user.* In addition to having political support at home, the coercing power is helped when it also can count on support from key states and international organizations.

- *Clarity on the precise terms of settlement.* The coercing power must be able to articulate the specific conditions for ending the crisis, as well as give assurances that it will not formulate new demands for greater concessions once the target capitulates.

While these conditions improve the odds of coercive diplomacy being effective, they do not guarantee success. National leaders who resort to coercive diplomacy start a process over which they have imperfect control.

Given the uncertainties surrounding the use of armed force, states often employ nonmilitary methods to alter an opponent's behavior. Recalling an ambassador and terminating cultural or scientific exchanges are some of the ways states signal their displeasure. Economic sanctions also figure prominently in this regard, being described as "the main tool of coercive diplomacy" (Hoagland 1996) and "the most favored tool of diplomats" (Pound and El-Tahri 1994).

Economic Sanctions

When the Arab members of the Organization of Petroleum Exporting Countries (OPEC) placed an embargo on the shipment of oil to the United States and the Netherlands in 1973, their purpose was to alter these countries' policies toward the Arab-Israeli conflict. When the UN Security Council decided in August 1990 that the world organization should cease trade with Iraq, its purpose was to accomplish the immediate and unconditional withdrawal of Iraqi forces from Kuwait. Both are examples of the use of **economic sanctions**—"deliberate government actions to inflict economic deprivation on a target state or society, through the limitation or cessation of customary economic relations" (Leyton-Brown 1987).

Economic sanctions are an increasingly popular approach to convincing another state to desist from some unacceptable behavior. They include a broad array of instruments: withholding foreign aid, placing tariffs and quotas on imports from a targeted state, boycotting its products, declaring an embargo on the sale of goods to the target, and freezing assets it may have in local banks. Since World War I, there have been 120 observable episodes of economic sanc-

• **economic sanctions** the punitive use of trade or monetary measures, such as an embargo, to harm the economy of an enemy state in order to exercise influence over its policies.

tions, 104 of which have been enacted since World War II (Hufbauer, Schott, and Elliott 1990). The United States has relied heavily on economic sanctions during this period. By 1998, half the world's population lived in countries that had been placed under U.S. sanctions (*Harper's*, February 1998, 13).

The rationale for employing sanctions as instruments of influence stems largely from the fact that they avoid the dangers of using armed force. Military coercion can easily backfire, draining government budgets, producing undue casualties, and provoking widespread criticism at home and abroad. In comparison, economic sanctions appear less risky and far less costly.

Another reason for the rising use of economic sanctions is that today national economies are increasingly integrated through trade, which increases the dependence on others for their own prosperity. This circumstance makes sanctions that threaten targets with the loss of an export market more effective than in the past, when countries could better withstand a foreign embargo on the purchase of their products. Likewise, countries dependent on imports from abroad for their basic needs are highly vulnerable to sanctions, since supply disruptions could bring their economies to a standstill (See Maps 8.2 and 8.3). Economic sanctions are also gaining proponents because more than sixty states are highly vulnerable "single-commodity-dependent economies" which derive at least 40 percent of their export revenues from foreign purchase of a single product (*Handbook of International Economic Statistics* 2001, 72–73).

Five major policy goals are customarily pursued by states when they adopt economic sanctions to pressure a foreign target:

- *Compliance* ("to force the target to alter its behavior to conform with the initiator's preferences"), as in the case of the 1982 U.S. trade embargo on Libya, designed to force it to end its support of terrorism.
- *Subversion* ("to remove the target's leaders . . . or overthrow the regime"), as in the cases of the 1993–1994 U.S. trade embargo on Haiti and the 2002 U.S. efforts to topple Saddam Hussein in Iraq.
- *Deterrence* ("to dissuade the target from repeating the disputed action in the future"), as in the case of the Soviet grain embargo by the United States.
- *International symbolism* ("to send messages to other members of the world community"), as in the case of the British sanctions against Rhodesia after its unilateral declaration of independence in 1965.
- *Domestic symbolism* ("to increase its domestic support or thwart international criticism of its foreign policies by acting decisively"), as in the case of U.S. sanctions against Iran following its seizure of U.S. diplomats in 1979 (Lindsay 1986).

These multiple uses notwithstanding, it is rare for policymakers to advocate the use of economic sanctions without generating criticism. Critics invariably argue that they frequently do not work or fail to accomplish the objectives for which they were initiated (Haass 1997). To be sure, sanctions have a checkered history. At times they have succeeded, such as in the case of Libya, where after a decade of international pressure, Libyan dictator Muammar Qaddafi finally turned over to Western powers for trial two Libyans alleged to have blown up the Pan Am flight 103 over Scotland in 1988 that killed all of its 280 passengers. Despite this

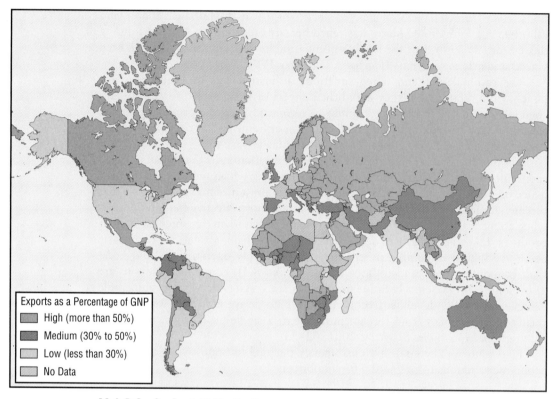

MAPS 8.2 AND 8.3
Vulnerable to Sanctions—Countries Dependent on Trade and Energy Imports

States that are highly dependent on exports for their economic prosperity and/or imports for commercial energy use are vulnerable to manipulation by states that impose sanctions on them. The map on the left shows the number of countries that are dependent on trade. The map on the right shows those that are dependent on foreign suppliers for their energy needs. Note that only a small number of states are net energy exporters.

SOURCES: Exports, World Bank (2002a) 332–334; Energy imports, World Bank (2002b) 158–160; Energy exports, *The Economist* (2002), 52.

and a few other successes, the historical record casts great doubt on the capacity of sanctions to work, even when used by the world's foremost powerful economic power, the United States. Between 1970 and 1990, "just 5 of 39 unilateral U.S. sanctions [achieved] any success at all" (Elliott 1998, 58). Conspicuous in the many cases where U.S. economic coercion failed is the experience with Cuba. The United States placed sanctions on the Castro regime shortly after it came to power in 1959 and forged an alliance with the Soviet Union. In response, Washington banned all trade with Cuba and pressured other countries to do the same, hoping to overthrow the Castro regime. This goal was not realized, as Castro has survived for over forty years.

Cuba is often cited as perhaps the best example of the inherent obstacles to successful sanctions. Other such U.S. failures include the inability of the United

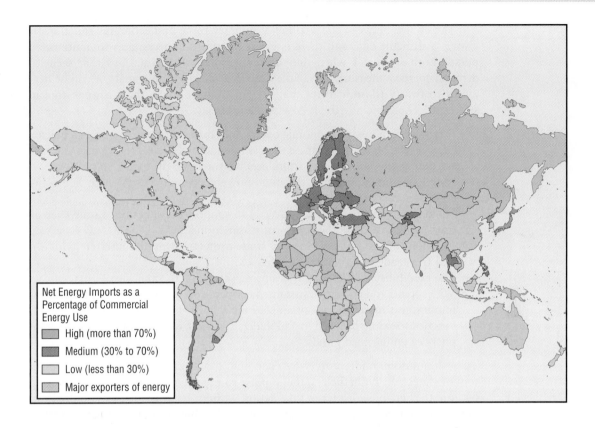

Net Energy Imports as a Percentage of Commercial Energy Use

- High (more than 70%)
- Medium (30% to 70%)
- Low (less than 30%)
- Major exporters of energy

States to impose a partial embargo on the sale of grain to the Soviet Union after its 1979 intervention in Afghanistan as well as the inability of the Reagan administration in 1981 to use sanctions to stop Poland and the Soviet Union from building the trans-Siberian gas pipeline designed to bring Soviet energy into western European markets. These examples suggest that "Sanctions are seldom effective in impairing the military potential of an important power, or in bringing about major changes in the policies of the target country" (Hufbauer, Schott, and Elliott 1990), and "have been absolutely ineffective in bringing about a change of government leadership within a target country" (Cortright and Lopez 1995). Rather than efficiently achieving the foreign policy goals of compliance, subversion, or deterrence, economic sanctions serve an important symbolic function by publicizing unacceptable behavior by other states.

The limitations of economic sanctions as a tool of coercive diplomacy can be seen in the unsuccessful efforts to topple the Iraqi dictator Saddam Hussein after the Persian Gulf War ended in 1991. Despite a UN embargo, Hussein was able to continue exporting oil on the black market through dummy corporations and purchase weapons from foreign manufacturers. Meanwhile, ordinary Iraqis suffered. The death of more than 600,000 Iraqi children as a result of the economic sanctions (*Harper's*, November 2002, 13) led the UN to begin experimenting with so-called "smart" sanctions (Cortright and Lopez 2002), which would target governmental elites, not innocent citizens.

The choice between the options of military force and economic sanctions is always a difficult one, and there is every reason to expect states to continue to pursue both strategies when they are confronted with situations that seem to demand coercive measures. To make sanctions effective, and smart, it will be necessary to rectify those features that previously have made them a weak tool in statecraft. These include the following deficiencies:

- A typical response to economic coercion in the sanctioned society is a heightened sense of nationalism, a *laager* mentality (circle the wagons to face oncoming enemies), which stimulates resistance in the target state.
- Sanctions sometimes hurt the disempowered people they seek to help—the country's average citizens.
- Some governments often act covertly to support the sanctioned state even as they publicly profess their support of sanctions.
- Sanctions are an invisible form of trade protectionism that interfere with liberal free trade and therefore profits.
- The credibility of the state(s) imposing sanctions is often low.
- Widespread and collective sustained cooperation from the international community and international organizations seldom materializes, and unilateral sanctions seldom succeed in a globalized market with many competitive suppliers of embargoed goods.

These limitations underscore why economic sanctions are often criticized as a tool of statecraft. Nonetheless, the impulse to use them is likely to remain strong because they enable a leader to take action without bearing the costs and risks of military coercion. Sanctions appear, therefore, destined to remain a part of states' strategies in the global future.

Building World Security

Since antiquity, preparation for war has often been seen as a prerequisite for security. Calls for a policy of "peace through strength" are understandable in a world where states alone remain responsible for their own self-defense. As former U.S. president Dwight Eisenhower once noted, "until war is eliminated from international relations, unpreparedness for it is well nigh as criminal as war itself."

Fear of national vulnerability in an anarchic, self-help environment induces defense planners to assume the worst about other states' capabilities and intentions. Even if the military capabilities accumulated by a neighbor are defensively motivated, they may trigger a strong reaction. The state "always feels itself weak if there is another that is stronger," observed the eighteenth-century political philosopher Jean-Jacques Rousseau. "Its security and preservation demand that it make itself more powerful than its neighbors. It can increase, nourish, and exercise its power only at their expense. . . . It becomes small or great, weak or strong, according to whether its neighbor expands or contracts, becomes stronger or declines."

State power, Rousseau reminds us, is relative. Efforts to obtain absolute security by one state tend to be perceived as creating absolute insecurity for others, with the result that everyone becomes locked into an upward spiral of countermeasures that diminishes the security of all. Scholars refer to this as a **security dilemma,** a condition that results when each state's increase in military capabilities is matched by the others, and all wind up with no more security than when they began arming (Snyder 1984; Jervis 1976).

Asking whether preparing for war endangers, rather than ensures, national security raises an uncomfortable question that challenges the prevailing approach to national security throughout much of the world's history. Yet many experts believe such questioning is justified. To their way of thinking, security in the twenty-first century must be defined more broadly. First, it should foster international transparency, so states can easily monitor each other's military activities. Second, it should address both military and nonmilitary threats to human survival, including environmental, economic, and epidemiological hazards that can jeopardize the global future. "Defense against military aggression will obviously remain a vital component of security, but it must be joined by defenses against severe environmental degradation, worldwide economic crisis, and massive human suffering. Only by approaching the security dilemma from this multifaceted perspective can we develop the strategies and instruments that will be needed to promote global health and stability." In short, "the concept of 'national security' must be integrated with that of 'world security' " (Klare and Thomas 1991, 3).

At issue is whether this new way of organizing perceptions of national security is an idea whose time has come. As former U.S. assistant secretary of defense Joseph Nye (2001) argues, "Power in the twenty-first century will depend on economic growth and mastering the information revolution, not on the brute nuclear force of the twentieth century." Though the danger of nuclear annihilation continues, it would be foolish to neglect the dangers posed by such emergent threats as global warming, deforestation, the depletion of the earth's finite resources, the continuing impoverishment of the least-developed countries, and the AIDS epidemic. These nonmilitary threats must command attention, as human survival may depend on addressing them.

• **security dilemma** the propensity of armaments undertaken by one state for ostensibly defensive purposes to threaten other states, which arm in reaction, with the result that their national security declines as their arms increase.

Chapter Summary

- In world politics, power refers to the ability of one international actor to control the behavior of another actor, making it continue some course of action, change what it is doing, or refrain from acting.
- Although most scholars agree that states are not equal in their ability to influence one another, there is little consensus on how to best weigh the various factors that contribute to state power. Their impact depends on the circumstances in a bargaining situation between states, and especially on how leaders perceive them.
- National leaders tend to assume that security is a function of power, and power is a function of military capabilities.
- As states spend increasing amounts of national wealth on arms, war-making capabilities have become more widespread than ever. Those countries least

able to afford the broad spectrum of available weapons have made the greatest sacrifices to get them, often reducing the quality of their citizens' lives by retarding social welfare programs and economic development.

- Advances in military technology have increased the destructive capacity of weapons and improved their range and precision.

- Although states ostensibly arm for defensive purposes, neighboring countries frequently perceive their military acquisitions as threatening. When one state's armaments increases are matched by others, everyone winds up paying higher costs with no more security than they had before this vicious cycle began.

- States that enjoy military superiority over their adversaries often think of their weapons as instruments for coercive bargaining. Threats of military force are used for both compellence and deterrence. Deterrence requires three ingredients: (1) capabilities—the possession of military resources to make threats of retaliation plausible; (2) credibility—the belief by others that a state is willing to carry out its threats; and (3) communication—the ability to send an opponent a clear message about one's capabilities and intentions.

- Preemptive military attacks entail the use of force against imminent threats; preventive attacks are aimed at threats that might possibly emerge in the future.

- International interdependence multiplies the opportunities to use economic instruments for coercive purposes, though they often fall short of their objectives. Nonetheless, economic sanctions serve an important symbolic function, providing a policy alternative to the use of military force and a way to publicize unacceptable behavior by other states.

- Although security policies in the twenty-first century will continue to focus on military threats, many nontraditional security threats will demand greater attention, including deforestation, global warming, the depletion of the earth's finite resources, world poverty, as well as AIDS and other diseases.

KEY TERMS

brinkmanship
coercive diplomacy
compellence
covert operations
deterrence
economic sanctions
firebreak
massive retaliation
military-industrial complex

military intervention
multiple independently
   targetable reentry vehicles
   (MIRVs)
mutual assured destruction
   (MAD)
nuclear winter
opportunity costs

power potential
preemption
proliferation
second-strike capability
security dilemma
smart bombs
Strategic Defense Initiative (SDI)
ultimatum

WHERE ON THE WORLD WIDE WEB?

Arms Sales Monitoring Project

http://www.fas.org/asmp/

Concerned with the global production and trade of weapons, the Federation of American Scientists is monitoring arms transfers and making data available to the public through this website. Click on the U.S. Arms Sales Table. Which countries were the biggest recipients of U.S. arms sales? Why? See what was sold to whom and for how much.

Bulletin of the Atomic Scientists

http://www.bullatomsci.org/

After World War II, many of the scientists responsible for the production of the atomic bomb helped form a movement to control nuclear energy. In 1945, they founded the *Bulletin* to advocate international control of the means of nuclear production. Still published today, current and archived issues of the *Bulletin* now appear online. While exploring this site, click on the Doomsday Clock to see how international tensions have brought us alternatively closer to or back from "nuclear midnight."

The Henry L. Stimson Center

http://www.stimson.org/index.html

The Henry L. Stimson Center is a nonprofit, nonpartisan research center that concentrates on the national security policy and technology. It provides information on chemical and biological weapons, nuclear proliferation, and missile defense systems. In addition, it houses important international agreements and searches for ways to eliminate weapons of mass destruction.

SIPRI Military Expenditure Data

http://web.sipri.org/contents/milap/milex/mex_data_index.html

The Stockholm International Peace Research Institute (SIPRI) monitors trends in military expenditures throughout the world. Its website lets you compare military expenditures and evaluate the economic burdens they pose. Choose a country from the Middle East, Far East, and Africa. How does their military spending compare to that of European countries? What conclusions can you draw?

INFOTRAC® COLLEGE EDITION

Search for the following articles in the InfoTrac College Edition database.

Baldwin, David A. "The Sanctions Debate and the Logic of Choice," *International Security* Winter 1999.

Barnett, Roger W. "What Deters? Strength, Not Weakness," *Naval War College Review* Spring 2001.

Mahnken, Thomas G., and Barry D. Watts. "What the Gulf War Can (and Cannot) Tell Us about the Future of Warfare," *International Security* Fall 1997.

Meilinger, Phillip S. "Force Divider: How Military Technology Makes the United States Even More Unilateral," *Foreign Policy* January–February 2002.

van Creveld, Martin. "Some Reflections on the Future of War," *Naval War College Review* Autumn 2000.

For more articles, enter:

"deterrence" in the Subject Guide.

"economic sanctions" in the Subject Guide, and then go to subdivision "analysis."

"international relations" in the Subject Guide, and then go to subdivision "analysis."

"national security" in the Subject Guide, and then go to subdivision "analysis."

"war" in the Subject Guide, and then go to subdivision "analysis."

ADDITIONAL CD-ROM RESOURCES

Click on Global Conflict and International Security to access additional resources related to this chapter.

CHAPTER 9

Realist Paths to Peace
Alliances, Arms Control, and the Balance of Power

As nature abhors a vacuum, so international politics abhors unbalanced power. Faced by unbalanced power, states try to increase their own strength or they ally with others to bring the international distribution of power into balance. The reactions of other states to the drive for dominance of Charles I of Spain, of Louis XIV and Napoleon Bonaparte of France, of Wilhelm II and Adolph Hitler of Germany, illustrate the point.

KENNETH N. WALTZ, political scientist

On March 10, 1661, the 23-year-old Louis XIV became the absolute ruler of France. An ostentatious leader, he selected the sun as his personal emblem, ordered the construction of a magnificent palace at Versailles, and surrounded himself with the pomp and splendor of court life. "The love of glory assuredly takes precedence over all other [passions] in my soul," he once admitted.

Under King Louis XIV, France possessed the largest army in Europe. Professionally trained and amply provisioned, it became the primary instrument in the "Sun King's" quest for glory. His first major use of the army came in 1667 with an attack on the Spanish Netherlands (modern Belgium), a region seen by the Dutch Republic as a buffer against French aggression. Alarmed by the Sun King's move, the Dutch forged the Triple Alliance with England and Sweden, which prompted Louis to negotiate a diplomatic settlement rather than continue fighting.

To prevent another coalition from blocking his next thrust northward, Louis concluded treaties with England and Sweden, and attacked the Netherlands in 1672. French forces quickly overwhelmed the Dutch and marched toward Amsterdam. The city was saved only by opening its dikes to flood the surrounding countryside. With the threat to Amsterdam neutralized, the Dutch pieced together a new anti-French coalition, consisting of Brandenburg, Denmark, and the Austrian and Spanish Hapsburgs. Faced once again with concerted opposition, Louis reverted to negotiation.

With his ambitions in Holland frustrated, the Sun King changed tactics. Over the years, France had acquired many adjacent territories. Louis proposed that France might also hold the title to any lands previously owned by these territories. Suspicious of his aims, the Dutch Republic joined with Austria, Bavaria, the Palatinate, Savoy, Saxony, Spain, Sweden, and ultimately England in the League of Augsburg. After a long, inconclusive war with the League, France lost most of the lands it had claimed.

The last of the armed conflicts comprising the Wars of Louis XIV was fought over Spain's territorial possessions. Since King Carlos II of Spain lacked an heir, he bequeathed his entire inheritance to the grandson of Louis XIV. Shocked by the danger of a Franco-Spanish union, England, the Dutch Republic, and Hapsburg Austria joined together in a Grand Alliance, which later included Brandenburg, Savoy, and Portugal. The so-called War of Spanish Succession began in 1701 and ended 12 years later with the French bid for supremacy defeated. The 1713 Treaty of Utrecht, which spelled out the terms of the peace settlement, confirmed the principles of statecraft inaugurated less than a century earlier by the Peace of Westphalia: Sovereign, territorial states were the primary actors on the world stage, and a balance of power was "the best and most solid foundation of . . . a lasting general concord [among them]." As two scholars of the period have put it, the wars fought by Louis XIV and the counteralliances that blocked his hegemonic ambitions "established the basic patterns that have characterized international relations" ever since (Friedrich and Blitzer 1957).

Realism and the Balancing of Power

Our discussion of conflict and its management in Part III of *The Global Future* has followed a logical progression. Chapter 7 began by exploring why the frequency of war makes preparations for it so necessary. Chapter 8 examined the search for national security through the acquisition of military capabilities. We now take up the question raised by the foreign policy of Louis XIV: How can peace be sustained in a world populated by armed, egoistic states that frequently practice coercive diplomacy?

Political realists and liberals offer different answers to this question. Whereas the former stress the need to uphold a **balance of power** among these wary rivals, the latter advocate building international legal institutions to replace contests of strength. In this chapter, we will concentrate on realist paths to peace: forming alliances with other countries to offset the military might of an adversary, and negotiating arms control agreements to maintain strategic parity.

• balance of power the theory that national survival in an anarchic world is most likely when military power is distributed to prevent a single hegemon or bloc from dominating the state system.

Assumptions of Balance-of-Power Theory

The concept of a balance of power has a long and controversial history. Supporters envision it as a equilibrating process that maintains peace by counterbalancing any state that seeks military preponderance. Critics deny its effectiveness, arguing that it breeds jealousy, intrigue, and antagonism. Part of the difficulty in evaluating these rival claims lies in the different meanings attributed to the concept (Claude 1962; Haas 1953). While "balance of power" may be widely used in everyday discourse, there is confusion over precisely what it entails.

At the core of nearly all of the various meanings of "balance of power" is the idea that national security is enhanced when military capabilities are distributed so that no one state is strong enough to dominate everyone else. If one state gains inordinate power, balance-of-power theory predicts that it will take advantage of its strength and attack weaker neighbors; therefore compelling incentives exist for those threatened to unite in a defensive coalition. According to the theory, their combined military might would deter (or, if need be, defeat) the state harboring expansionist aims. Thus for realists, laissez-faire competition among states striving to maximize their national power yields an international equilibrium, which ensures everyone's survival by checking hegemonic ambitions.

The Balancing Process. Although balancing is occasionally described as an automatic, self-adjusting process, most realists see it as the result of deliberate actions undertaken by national leaders to maintain an equilibrium among contending states. Some actions, like augmenting military capabilities through armaments and alliances, attempt to add weight to the lighter side of the international balance. Others, such as negotiating limits on weaponry and spheres of influence, attempt to decrease the weight of the heavier side. Only by constantly monitoring shifts in relative strength can leaders calibrate their policies to rectify imbalances of power.

Various theorists have attempted to specify a set of rules that must be heeded in order for the balancing process to function effectively. What follows is a brief synthesis of these rules:

1. *Stay vigilant.* Constantly watch foreign developments in order to identify emerging threats and opportunities. Because international anarchy makes each state responsible for its own security, and states can never be sure of one another's intentions, self-interest encourages them to maximize their relative power. As Morton Kaplan (1957) writes: "Act to increase capabilities but negotiate rather than fight . . ." [however] "Fight rather than pass up an opportunity to increase capabilities."

2. *Seek allies whenever you cannot match the armaments of your adversaries.* States align with each other when they adopt a common stance toward some shared security problem. An **alliance** is produced when they formally agree to coordinate their behavior under certain specified circumstances. The degree of coordination may range from a detailed list of military forces that will be furnished by each party in the event of war to the more modest requirement that they will consult with one another should hostilities erupt. According to balance-of-power theory, alliances are the primary means of compensating for an inability to keep up with a rival's arms acquisitions.

   • **alliance** a formal agreement among sovereign states for the purpose of coordinating their behavior to increase mutual security.

3. *Alliances should remain flexible.* Formed and dissolved according to the strategic needs of the moment, alliances must be made without regard to cultural or ideological affinities. Because alliances are instrumental, short-term adjustments aimed at rectifying imbalances in the distribution of military capabilities, past experiences should not predispose states to accept or reject any potential partner. Nowhere is this better seen than in the **balancer** role Great Britain once played in European diplomacy. From the seventeenth through the early twentieth centuries, the British shifted their weight from one side of the Continental balance to the other, arguing that they had no permanent friends and no permanent enemies, just a permanent interest in preventing the balance from tipping either way (Dehio 1962). As described by Winston Churchill, Britain's goal was "to oppose the strongest, most aggressive, most dominating Power on the Continent. . . . [It] joined with the less strong Powers, made a combination among them, and thus defeated and frustrated the Continental military tyrant whoever he was, whatever nation he led."

   • **balancer** an influential global or regional state that throws its support in decisive fashion to the weaker side of the balance of power.

4. *Oppose any state that seeks hegemony.* The purpose of engaging in balance-of-power politics is to survive in a world of potentially dangerous neighbors. If any state achieves absolute mastery over everyone else, it will be able to act with impunity. Under such circumstances, the territorial integrity and political autonomy of other states will be in jeopardy. By joining forces with the weaker side to prevent the stronger side from reaching preponderance, states can preserve their independence. As Joseph Nye (2000) has put it: "Balance of power is a policy of helping the underdog because if you help the top dog, it may eventually turn around and eat you."

5. *Be moderate in victory.* "An equilibrium," argues Edward Gulick (1955), "cannot perpetuate itself unless the major components of that equilibrium

are preserved." In the event of war, the winning side should not eliminate the defeated. Looking forward rather than backward, it should do as little damage as possible to the those it has vanquished because yesterday's enemy may be needed as tomorrow's ally. Victors who couple firmness regarding their own interests with fairness toward the interests of others encourage defeated powers to work within the postwar balance of power. Similarly, states who win at the bargaining table can stabilize the balance of power by granting the other side compensation in return for their concessions.

To sum up, political realists urge states to check the ambitions of anyone who threatens to amass overwhelming power, because aspiring hegemons are a potential threat to everyone. Human beings, they argue, are by nature selfish and short-sighted, but balancing rival interests stabilizes their interactions. Weakness, insist realists, invites aggression. Thus when faced with unbalanced power, national leaders should mobilize their domestic resources or ally with others to bring the international distribution of power back into equilibrium (Vasquez and Elman 2003; Waltz 1979). The response by the Dutch Republic, England, Sweden, and other seventeenth-century states to Louis XIV's drive for dominance exemplifies the balancing process.

Difficulties with Balance-of-Power Systems. Can balancing power further international order, as most realists believe? Critics of balance-of-power theory raise several objections about the proposition that balancing promotes peace. First, some scholars argue that the theory's rules for behavior are contradictory (Riker 1962). On the one hand, states are urged to increase their power. On the other hand, they are told to oppose anyone seeking preponderance. Yet sometimes bandwagoning with (rather than balancing against) the dominant state can increase a weaker country's capabilities by allowing it to share in the spoils of a future victory. Preliminary research on this issue suggests that states that are content with the status quo tend to balance against rising powers more than states that are dissatisfied.

A second objection to balance-of-power theory is that it assumes policymakers possess accurate, timely information about other states. As we have discussed in the previous chapter, "power" is an ambiguous concept. Tangible factors, such as the performance capabilities of the different types of weapons found in an adversary's inventory, are hard to compare. Intangible factors, such as leadership skills and troop morale, are even more difficult to gauge. Without a precise measure of relative strength, how can policymakers know when power is becoming unbalanced? Moreover, in an environment of secret alliances, how can they be sure who is really in league with whom? An ally who is being counted on to balance the power of an opponent may have secretly agreed to remain neutral in the event of a showdown; consequently the actual distribution of power may not resemble the distribution one side or the other imagines (see Controversy: Are Alliances Worth the Costs and Risks?).

Problems in determining the strength of adversaries and the trustworthiness of allies lead to a third objection to balance-of-power theory: The uncertainty of power balances frequently causes defense planners to engage in worst-case

CONTROVERSY ## Are Alliances Worth the Costs and Risks?

States establish alliances when they face common security threats. By acquiring allies, they increase their mutual strength, which enhances their ability to deter an attack and defend themselves if deterrence fails. When danger is acute, many national leaders even make common cause with partners they would otherwise regard as morally repugnant. British prime minister Winston Churchill hinted as much during World War II when he asserted: "If Hitler invaded Hell, I would make at least a favorable reference to the Devil in the House of Commons."

Alliances offer other advantages besides aggregating military capabilities. First, they can help reduce the costs associated with military preparations by spreading them among several states. Second, they furnish a medium for exerting leverage to mobilize or restrain a partner, to neutralize those who might otherwise interfere with some foreign policy undertaking, or to preempt an adversary by bonding with a strategically important country. Finally, alliances may help a state acquire benefits that it could not have attained by acting unilaterally. For instance, a relatively weak state can gain access to additional resources through foreign aid, obtain a steady supply of sophisticated weaponry, or receive instruction on the use of new technology. Even a powerful state can enhance its position through alliance membership by acquiring overseas bases and support facilities from which it may project its power.

These advantages notwithstanding, some foreign policy advisors counsel against joining alliances because they may bind a state to open-ended commitments which later cease to be in its interest. Ever mindful of this risk, national leaders tend to be wary about entrusting their security to the pledges of others. Prudent leaders, the distinguished American statesman George Kennan (1984a) once wrote, "usually shy away from commitments likely to constitute limitations on a government's behavior at unknown dates in the future in the face of unpredictable situations." Alliances, from this perspective, have a short life span. Their usefulness erodes as the threat that brought the allies together declines.

In addition to foreclosing options, military alliances have other drawbacks. First, they might entangle a state in disputes it could otherwise avoid. Second, alliances can provoke the fears of adversaries and thus perpetuate ongoing rivalries. Finally, they may stimulate envy and resentment on the part of friends who are outside the alliance and are therefore not eligible to receive its advantages.

Despite these potential drawbacks, the United States has constructed a welter of military alliances over the past 50 years. Some, like the North Atlantic Treaty Organization (NATO), contained elaborate institutional structures. In building this vast network of alliances, successive American administrations disregarded President George Washington's advice "to steer clear of permanent alliances." Washington felt that whereas a state "may safely trust to temporary alliances for extraordinary emergencies," it is an "illusion . . . to expect or calculate real favors from nation to nation." What do you think? Do the benefits of formal, institutionalized alliances like NATO outweigh their costs and risks? Do the commitments entailed by these kinds of alliances hold U.S. foreign policy hostage to the interests of its partners? Is the United States strong enough today to go it alone in international affairs?

The Granger Collection, NY

• **arms race** an action-reaction process in which rival states rapidly increase their military capabilities in response to one another.

analysis, which can spark an **arms race**. The intense, reciprocal anxiety that shrouds balance-of-power politics fuels exaggerated estimates of an adversary's strength, which prompts one side, and then the other, to expand the quantity and enhance the quality of their weaponry. Critics of realism warn that if a serious dispute occurs between states locked in relentless arms competition, the probability of war increases.

A fourth objection is that balance-of-power theory assumes that decision makers are risk averse. When confronted with countervailing power, they refrain from fighting because the dangers of taking on an equal are too great. Yet national leaders assess risk differently. Some are risk acceptant. Rather than being deterred by equivalent power, they prefer gambling on the chance of winning a victory, even if the odds are long. Marshaling comparable power against adversaries with a high tolerance for risk will not have the same effect as it would on those who avoid risks.

Finally, many people object to the balance-of-power theory because it has not been effective. If the theory's assumptions are correct, historical periods during which its rules were followed should also have been periods in which war was less frequent. Yet a striking feature of those periods is their record of warfare. From Louis XIV through World War II, the great powers participated in a series of increasingly destructive general wars that threatened to engulf and destroy the multistate system. As Inis L. Claude (1989, 78) soberly concludes, it is difficult to consider these wars "as anything other than catastrophic failures, total collapses, of the balance-of-power system. They are hardly to be classed as stabilizing maneuvers or equilibrating processes, and one cannot take seriously any claim of maintaining international stability that does not entail the prevention of such disasters. . . ." Indeed, the historical record has led some theorists to offer **hegemonic stability theory** as an alternative to the balance of power, which postulates that a single, dominant state can guarantee peace better than military parity among contending great powers (Wohlforth 1999; Organski 1968).

• **hegemonic stability theory** the argument that a single dominant state is necessary to enforce international cooperation, maintain international rules and regimes, and keep the peace.

Managing the Balance through a Concert of Great Powers

A significant problem with the balance-of-power system is its haphazard character. To bring order to the system, occasionally the great powers have tried to institutionalize channels of communication. The Concert of Europe that commenced with the Congress of Vienna in 1815 exemplified this strategy. In essence, it was "an exclusive club for the great powers" (Claude 1971).

• **concert** a cooperative agreement among great powers to jointly manage international relations.

The idea behind a **concert** is "rule by a central coalition" of great powers (Rosecrance 1992). It is predicated on the belief that the leading centers of power will see their interests advanced by collaborating to contain conflict from escalating to war in those regions under their mutual jurisdiction. Although it is assumed that the great powers share a common outlook, concerts still allow "for subtle jockeying and competition to take place among them. Power politics is not completely eliminated; members may turn to internal mobilization and coalition formation to pursue divergent interests. But the cooperative framework of a concert, and its members' concern about preserving peace, prevent such balancing from escalating to overt hostility and conflict" (Kupchan and Kupchan 1992).

A common sense of duty is the glue that holds great-power concerts together. When a belief in mutual self-restraint dissipates, concerts unravel. "Friction tends to build as each state believes that it is sacrificing more for unity than are others," notes Robert Jervis (1985). "Each will remember the cases in which it has been restrained, and ignore or interpret differently cases in which others believe they acted for the common good." Overcoming this friction requires continuous consultation in order to reinforce expectations of joint responsibilities. Concert members should not be challenged over their vital interests, nor should they suffer an affront to their prestige and self-esteem (Elrod 1976). A "just" equilibrium among contending great powers bound together in a concert means more than an equal distribution of military capabilities; it includes recognition of honors, national rights, and dignity (Schroeder 1989).

While a concert framework can help manage relations among counterpoised great powers, the normative consensus underpinning this arrangement is fragile and easily eroded. As a result, realists have looked beyond concerts for other ways to steady vacillating power balances. One approach is to limit everyone's arsenals, especially with regard to those weapons that are seen as provocative and thus destabilizing.

Stabilizing Power Balances through Arms Control

Liberal reformers have often questioned the theory that power can be balanced to preserve world order. They have advocated instead the biblical prescription that states should beat their swords into plowshares. The destructiveness of today's weapons have inspired many people once again to take this tenet of liberal theory seriously. But this approach is not solely a liberal preserve. Many realists also see utility in arms limitation, primarily as a way of stabilizing the balance of power. In fact, most policymakers who have negotiated such agreements have been realists who perceived these treaties as a prudent tool to promote their countries' security.

Arms Control versus Disarmament

Although the terms *arms control* and *disarmament* are often used interchangeably, they are not synonymous. **Arms control** refers to agreements designed to regulate arms levels either by limiting their growth or by restricting how they may be used. This is a far more common and less ambitious endeavor than **disarmament,** which is the reduction or elimination of weapons. Controlling war by reducing weapons inventories is hardly a novel idea. Yet until very recently, states have generally failed to negotiate disarmament agreements. True, some countries in the past did reduce their armaments. For example, the Chinese states in 600 BCE formed a disarmament league that produced a peaceful century for the league's members, and Canada and the United States disarmed the Great Lakes through the 1817 Rush-Bagot Agreement. Nonetheless, these kinds of achievements have been relatively rare in history. Most disarmament has been involuntary, the product of reductions imposed by the victors in the immediate aftermath of a war, as when the Allied powers attempted to disarm a defeated Germany after World War I.

• **arms control** bilateral or multilateral agreements to contain arms buildups by setting limits on the number and types of weapons that states are permitted.

• **disarmament** agreements to reduce or eliminate weapons or other means of attack.

In addition to differentiating between arms control and disarmament, we should also distinguish between bilateral and multilateral approaches to limiting weaponry. Because the former involve only two countries, they are often easier to negotiate and to enforce than are the latter, which are agreements among three or more countries. As a result, bilateral arms agreements tend to be more successful than multilateral agreements. By far the most revealing examples are the superpower agreements to control nuclear weapons. Let us briefly look at the record of Soviet-American negotiations before examining the checkered history of multilateral arms control and disarmament.

Bilateral Arms Control and Disarmament

The Cold War between the Soviet Union and the United States never degenerated into open warfare. One of the reasons was the series of more than twenty-five arms control agreements Moscow and Washington negotiated in the wake of the Cuban missile crisis. Beginning with the 1963 Hot Line Agreement, which established a direct radio and telegraph communication system between the two governments, Soviet and American leaders reached a series of modest agreements aimed at stabilizing the military balance and reducing the risk of war. Each of these bilateral treaties lowered tensions and helped build a climate of trust that encouraged efforts to negotiate further agreements.

Perhaps the most important agreements were the Strategic Arms Limitation Talks (SALT) of 1972 and 1979; the Strategic Arms Reduction Treaties (START) of 1991, 1993, and 1997; and the Strategic Offensive Reductions Treaty (SORT) of 2002. The first two agreements stabilized the nuclear arms race, while the remaining ones reduced the weapons in each side's inventory (see Figure 9.1). When the Cold War ended in 1991, the United States had more than 9,500 nuclear warheads and Russia had about 8,000. However, the January 1993 agreement pledged to cut their combined arsenals to about 6,500 by the year 2003. Even more dramatically, this agreement also affected the kinds of weapons each country could possess. Under its terms, Russia and the United States gave up all the multiple independently targetable reentry vehicles (MIRVs) on their land-based intercontinental ballistic missiles (ICBMs) and reduced submarine-launched ballistic missile (SLBM) warheads to no more than 1,750.

The next major step occurred in May 2002 when presidents George W. Bush and Vladimir Putin signed the Strategic Offensive Reductions Treaty (SORT). This brief document calls for the two countries to cut their combined number of strategic nuclear warheads by two-thirds over the next 10 years. Still, both parties were left with enough firepower to retain the deterrent threat of mutual assured destruction (see Chapter 8). In addition, the treaty contained no requirement to destroy warheads taken out of service, and permitted either side to withdraw from the agreement with three months' notice by citing "a supreme national interest." Hence, while this treaty signaled a step toward nuclear disarmament, it was regarded as mostly symbolic in importance (Mendelsohn 2002). That said, the success recently enjoyed by Moscow and Washington inspires hope that negotiations can be expanded to include other states. The history of multilateral arms control and disarmament speaks to this aspiration.

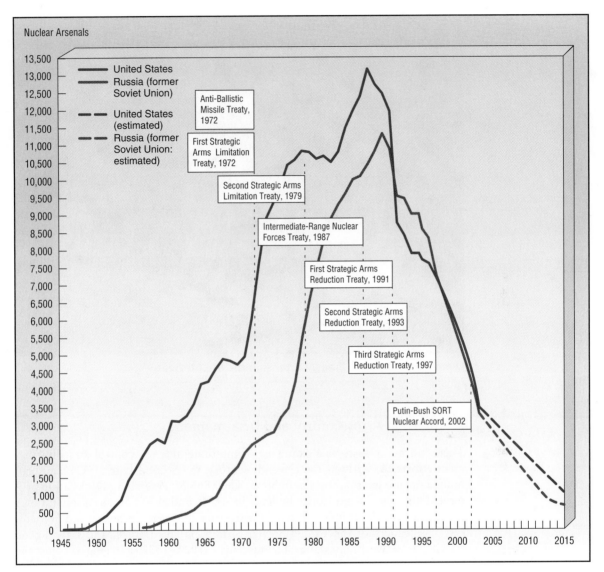

Nuclear Arsenals

- United States
- Russia (former Soviet Union)
- — United States (estimated)
- — Russia (former Soviet Union: estimated)

Anti-Ballistic Missile Treaty, 1972

First Strategic Arms Limitation Treaty, 1972

Second Strategic Arms Limitation Treaty, 1979

Intermediate-Range Nuclear Forces Treaty, 1987

First Strategic Arms Reduction Treaty, 1991

Second Strategic Arms Reduction Treaty, 1993

Third Strategic Arms Reduction Treaty, 1997

Putin-Bush SORT Nuclear Accord, 2002

FIGURE 9.1
Countdown to Strategic Parity: The Negotiated End of the U.S.-Russian Arms Race

After decades of adding weapons to their arsenals, the United States and Russia have, through a series of disarmament agreements, pledged to cut dramatically the number of nuclear warheads in their stockpiles. This has inspired most of the other nuclear powers to also reduce the number of warheads they have deployed. Since its 1986 peak, the size of the global nuclear arsenal has declined by nearly 90 percent. However, fears that the disarmament process will be followed by a new arms race remain, as seen in the 2002 agreement that allows the United States to store rather than destroy its inventory of Cold War warheads and to preserve its missile defense program. The Putin-Bush Strategic Offensive Reductions Treaty (SORT) nonetheless took another sizable step in 2002 toward the goal of eliminating nuclear warheads altogether.

SOURCES: Based on data from Worldwatch data diskette, U.S. Arms Control Association *Fact Files* and *SIPRI Yearbooks*. Worldwatch data Copyright © Worldwatch Institute and the Stockholm International Peace Research Institute.

AP/Wide World Photos

Leonid Brezhnev and Jimmy Carter sign the SALT II Treaty

Multilateral Arms Control and Disarmament

There are many historical examples of multilateral arms control and disarmament efforts. As early as the eleventh century, the Second Lateran Council prohibited the use of crossbows in fighting. The 1868 St. Petersburg Declaration prohibited the use of explosive bullets. In 1899 and 1907, International Peace Conferences at the Hague restricted the use of some weapons and prohibited others. The leaders of the United States, Britain, Japan, France, and Italy signed treaties at the Washington Naval Conferences (1921–1922) agreeing to adjust the relative tonnage of their fleets.

Nearly thirty major multilateral agreements have been signed since the Second World War. Of these, the 1968 Nuclear Nonproliferation Treaty (NPT), which prohibited the transfer of nuclear weapons and production technologies to nonnuclear-weapons states, stands out as the most symbolic multilateral agreement with 187 signatory parties. While adherence to the treaty has been widespread, India and Pakistan have broken the NPT's barriers to become nuclear-weapons states. In addition, Israel is believed to have clandestinely produced nuclear weapons, and countries like Iran and North Korea remain outside the NPT and are seeking to become nuclear-weapon states.

Similar problems plague other multilateral agreements. The 1993 Chemical Weapons Convention (CWC), for example, required all stockpiles of chemical weapons to be destroyed within 10 years. However, the agreement lost some of its authority in 2001 when the Bush administration refused to accept the enforcement measures within the drafted amendment of the packet of chemical and biological germ warfare treaties that included the CWC. This erosion of support for arms control caused UN secretary-general Kofi Annan to warn that "much of the established multilateral disarmament machinery has started to rust."

The Problematic Future of Arms Control and Disarmament

The obstacles to arms control and disarmament treaties are formidable. Critics complain that these agreements frequently regulate obsolete armaments or ones that the parties to the agreement have little incentive for developing in the first place. Even when agreements are reached on modern, sophisticated weapons, the parties often set ceilings higher than the number of weapons currently deployed, so they do not have to slash their inventories.

A second pitfall is the propensity of limits on one type of weapon system to prompt developments in another system. Like a balloon that is squeezed at one end but expands at the other, constraints on certain parts of a country's arsenal can lead to enhancements elsewhere. An example can be seen in the 1972 SALT I agreement, which limited the number of intercontinental ballistic missiles possessed by the United States and the Soviet Union. Although the number of missiles was restricted, no limits were placed on the number of nuclear warheads that could be placed on each missile; consequently both sides began developing multiple independently targetable reentry vehicles (MIRVs). In short, the quantitative freeze on launchers led to qualitative improvements in their warhead delivery systems.

Also reducing faith in the future of meaningful arms control is the slow, weak, and ineffective ability of the international community to ban some of the most dangerous and counterproductive weapons. Consider the case of antipersonnel landmines (APLs). These are weapons that cannot discriminate between soldiers and civilians. Between 100 and 300 million landmines are believed to be scattered on the territory of more than seventy countries (with another 100 million in stockpiles). In the mid-1990s there was about one mine for every fifty humans on earth, and each year they killed or maimed more than twenty-six thousand people—almost all of them civilians. In 1994, not a single state would endorse a prohibition on these deadly weapons. It took a peace activist, Jody Williams, to organize the International Campaign to Ban Landmines that produced the Convention on the Prohibition of the Use, Stockpiling, Production, and Transfer of Antipersonnel Mines and Their Destruction, which was opened for signature in December 1997. For her efforts, she was awarded the Nobel Peace Prize. Still, the challenge of enforcing the ban now signed by 158 states, and the task of removing APLs, remains staggering.

A final problem facing those advocating arms control and disarmament is continuous innovation. By the time limits are negotiated on one type of weapon, a new generation of weapons has emerged. Further complicating matters, modern technology is creating an ever-widening range of novel weapons—increasingly smaller, deadlier, and easier to conceal.

Why do states often make decisions to arm that apparently imprison them in the grip of insecurity? On the surface, the incentives for meaningful arms control seem numerous. Significant controls would save money, reduce tension, reduce the environmental hazards, and diminish the potential destructiveness of war. However, most countries are reluctant to limit their armaments in a self-help system that requires each state to protect itself. Thus states find themselves caught in a vicious cycle summarized by two basic principles: "(1) Don't negotiate when you are behind. Why accept a permanent position of number two?" and (2) "Don't negotiate when you are ahead. Why accept a freeze in an area of military competition when the other side has not kept up with you?" (Barnet 1977).

The tendency of states to make improving their weapons a priority over controlling them is illustrated by the example of nuclear testing (see Map 9.1). The eight known nuclear states conducted a total of 2,052 nuclear explosions in 24 different locations since 1945—an average of one test every 10 days. The partial test ban treaty of 1963, which prohibited atmospheric and underwater testing but not underground explosions, did not slow the pace of testing. Three-fourths of all nuclear tests took place after the ban went into effect in 1963. Today both China and the United States regularly conduct so-called zero-yield nuclear experiments and are suspected of conducting explosive tests so small that they can't be detected.

To sum up, arms control remains a murky policy area, and the past record suggests that we should not exaggerate its potential. As long as aggressive national leaders exist, it would be imprudent to disarm. Limits on weapons may confine the rivalry between states, but they do not remove the underlying source of the conflict. Arms, after all, are less the causes of war than the symptoms of political tension: People "do not fight because they have arms. They have arms because [they are afraid and] they deem it necessary to fight" (Morgenthau 1985).

Balancing Power in the Contemporary International System

The use of alliances and arms control to balance power typically follows one of two distinct patterns (Morgenthau 1985). In the pattern of "direct opposition," one powerful state tries to prevail over another powerful state, which raises arms or seeks allies to offset its adversary's strength. Over time, each increase in military capabilities by one side calls forth an increase by the other. If neither side yields, they may negotiate arms control agreements to stabilize their competition and avoid waging war.

In the more fluid pattern of "competition," encroachments by one state against another also precipitate a quest for arms and allies. But rather than resulting in the formation of rigid, counterbalanced blocs, it triggers shifts in a kaleidoscope of overlapping alliances. The diplomatic checkerboard of eighteenth-century Europe illustrates this second pattern of balance-of-power politics. As described by Michael Doyle (1997, 177), France was sandwiched between its rivals, Britain and Austria (who possessed what today is Belgium); consequently France established ties with Prussia, an enemy of the British and Austrians. Simultaneously, Holland balanced against France with British support, Saxony balanced against Prussia with Austrian support, and Bavaria leaned toward France and Prussia in an effort to balance against Austria. Owing to a desire to

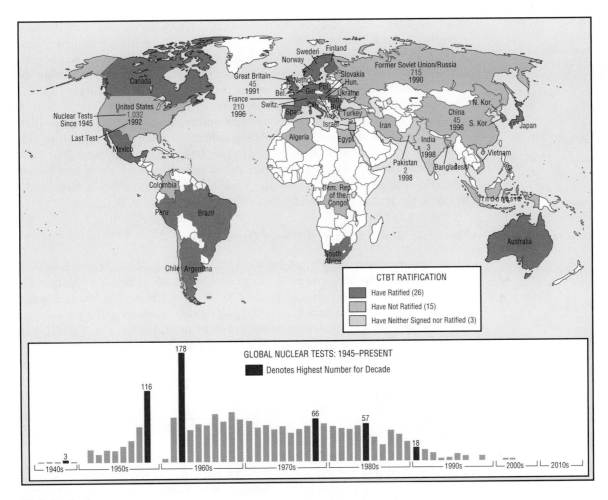

MAP 9.1
Can Arms Control Treaties Arrest the Proliferation of Weapons?

Hope was rising in 1999 that the testing of nuclear weapons, which had been declining since 1945 (see chart at bottom of map of the number of nuclear tests yearly), would stop if the 44 nuclear-capable states ratified the Comprehensive Test Ban Treaty (CTBT). However, the U.S. Senate rejected the test ban, and in so doing opened the way for states like India and Pakistan to resume testing. Headlines compared the U.S. repudiation of this treaty to the same kind of partisan politics that led to the U.S. rejection of the 1919 Treaty of Versailles. The CTBT would have banned all nuclear test explosions worldwide for all time, created a multilateral global monitoring network to detect explosions and verify compliance, and allowed for on-site inspections of areas of clandestine nuclear testing. This map shows that 26 of the 44 nuclear-capable states had ratified the treaty, 15 had not ratified, and 3 had neither signed nor ratified. It also shows the number of nuclear tests conducted by each of the 8 nuclear states through 2002. With the CTBT's collapse, termed by arms-control expert Brent Scowcroft as a "pathetic blow to global arms control," the prospect of continued testing of nuclear weapons is high.
SOURCE: Arms Control Association; Stockholm International Peace Research Institute.

Click on Global Conflict and International Security to access an interactive version of this map and related critical thinking questions.

offset what he saw as an alarming increase in Prussian power ever since it seized the province of Silesia from his country in 1740, Austrian foreign minister Wenzel Kaunitz forged an alliance with France, Austria's longstanding foe and heretofore Prussia's ally. Britain, Austria's former ally, responded by concluding an alliance with Prussia. In what is known as the "Diplomatic Revolution of 1756," the configuration of great-power alliances was completely reversed in response to growing Prussian power. According to the eminent realist Hans J. Morgenthau (1985), if no state possesses overwhelming military superiority, world politics follows either the pattern of direct opposition or the more complex pattern of ever-shifting competition. Having examined the theory of how the balance of power is supposed to operate, let us consider how it actually functioned in world politics since the end of the Second World War.

The Cold War Pattern of Direct Opposition

Most countries were devastated by World War II. The United States, however, was left in a clearly dominant position, its economy accounting for about half the world's combined gross national product (GNP). The United States was also the only country with the atomic bomb, and had demonstrated its willingness to use the new weapon. American hegemony was short lived, however, as the recovery of the Soviet economy and the growth of its military capabilities eroded U.S. supremacy and gave rise to a new distribution of world power. The Soviets broke the U.S. monopoly on atomic weapons in 1949 and exploded a thermonuclear device in 1953, less than a year after the United States. This achievement symbolized the creation of a bipolar system of direct opposition. Military capabilities were now concentrated in the hands of two rival "superpowers," each heading its own bloc of allies.

The formation of the North Atlantic Treaty Organization (NATO), linking the United States to the defense of Western Europe, and the Warsaw Pact, linking the former Soviet Union in an alliance with its Eastern European clients, reinforced this bipolar structure. The opposing blocs formed in part because the superpowers competed for allies and in part because the less-powerful states looked to one superpower or the other for protection. Correspondingly, each superpower's allies gave it forward bases from which to carry on the competition.

By grouping the system's states into two blocs, each led by a superpower, the Cold War's bipolar structure bred insecurity among all. The balance was constantly at stake. Each bloc leader, worrying that its adversary would attain primacy, viewed every move, however defensive, as the first step toward world conquest. Both superpowers attached great importance to recruiting new allies. Fear that an old ally might desert the fold was ever-present. Nonalignment was viewed with suspicion. Bipolarity left little room for compromise or maneuver and worked against the normalization of superpower relations.

The major Cold War coalitions associated with bipolarity began to disintegrate in the 1960s and early 1970s. As their internal cohesion eroded, new centers of power emerged. At the same time, weaker alliance partners were afforded more room for maneuvering. Diverse relationships among the states subordinate to the superpowers developed, such as the friendly relations between the United

States and Romania, and between France and the Soviet Union. The superpowers remained dominant militarily, but this less-rigid system allowed other states to perform more independent foreign policy roles.

Rapid technological innovation in the superpowers' major weapons systems was a catalyst in the dissolving of the Cold War blocs. Intercontinental ballistic missiles (ICBMs), capable of delivering nuclear weapons from one continent to another, lessened the importance of forward bases on allies' territory. Furthermore, the narrowed differences in the superpowers' arsenals loosened the ties that had previously bound allies to one another. The European members of NATO in particular began to question whether the United States would, as it had pledged, protect Paris or Bonn by sacrificing New York. Under what conditions might Washington or Moscow be willing to risk a nuclear holocaust? The uncertainty became pronounced while the pledge to protect allies through **extended deterrence** seemed increasingly insincere.

• **extended deterrence** the use of military threats by a great power to deter an attack on its allies.

The movement toward democracy and market economies by some communist states in the late 1980s further eroded the bonds of ideology that had formerly helped these countries face their security problems from a common posture. The 1989 dismantling of the Berlin Wall tore apart the Cold War architecture of competing blocs. With the end of this division, and without a Soviet threat, the consistency of outlook and singularity of purpose that once bound NATO members together disappeared. Many perceived the need to replace NATO and the defunct Warsaw Pact with a new security arrangement. However, most leaders maintained that some configuration of a European defense architecture was still necessary to cement relationships and stabilize the rush of cascading events.

A Future of Balance-of-Power Competition?

Following the dissolution of the Soviet Union in 1991, most analysts concluded that a new era of unipolarity had arisen, with the United States emerging as the world's only superpower. Columnist Charles Krauthammer proclaimed that "no country has been as dominant culturally, economically, technologically, and militarily in the history of the world since the Roman Empire." For hegemonic stability theorists, this was beneficial. As they see it, a unipolar concentration of power allows the global leader to police chaos and maintain international peace.

Against this optimistic view currently runs a strong suspicion about the future stability of a unipolar world under U.S. management. Warns one critic, "It is virtually universal in history that when countries become hegemons . . . they tend to want everything their own way, and it never works" (Mathews 2000). Others condemn the shortsightedness of U.S. leadership, guided, as they see it, more by self-interests than by ideals, and motivated primarily by a desire to preserve America's position as top dog and less toward multilateral cooperation to promote peace and prosperity.

Regardless of whether the optimists or pessimists are correct, many scholars believe that U.S. preponderance will not last far into the twenty-first century. Other "countries will obstruct American purposes whenever and in whatever way they can, and the pursuit of American interests will have to be undertaken

The Vestiges of Communist Power In 1998, only five countries (China, Cuba, Laos, North Korea, and Vietnam) then remained members of the "communist bloc." Ten years earlier, that coalition consisted of 15 countries. Pictured here is Cuba's Fidel Castro being assisted by Vietnam's general secretary Do Muoi and a Vietnamese soldier at the farewell ceremonies of a 1995 summit in Hanoi. The Cuban leader visited both China and Vietnam to observe how they had adapted Marxism to market economies. The meeting raised the question of whether communist ideology can still unify what remains of the communist bloc in a common coalition. Perhaps national self-interests rather than ideology will cement future alignments, as suggested by the pledge of Russian president Vladimir Putin to strengthen ties with Cuba, its former communist ally.

through coercion rather than consensus. Anti-Americanism will become the global language of political protest—the default ideology of opposition—unifying the world's discontents and malcontents, some of whom, as we have discovered, can be very dangerous" (Zakaria 2002c). Eventually unipolarity will give way to a new configuration of power whose probable consequences are not clear. Some forecast the return of a bipolar pattern of direct opposition, with a new Sino-Russian bloc, European-Russian entente, or Sino-Japanese alliance countering the United States (Brzezinski 1998). Others see the emergence of a more complex pattern of balance-of-power competition, where the United States, China, Japan, Russia, and the European Union would constitute five centers of global power. According to this image of the future, as power becomes more equally distributed, each player will be increasingly assertive, independent, and competitive, leading to confusion about the identity of friends and foes.

Reuters/Archive Photos/CORBIS

Russia and China Seek to Balance U.S. Power In response to NATO's approval of formal enlargement in 1997, both Russia and China agreed to a new "strategic partnership." Russian premier Viktor Chernomyrdin (right) and Chinese president Jiang Zemin met in Moscow in April 1997 to negotiate a joint statement, which called for creation of a new "multipolar" system cemented by a new Sino-Russian axis to counter the threat of global domination by the United States. This friendship treaty was renewed in 2002. The logic of balance-of-power politics rationalizes the formation of these kinds of strategic unions to check the growing influence of a rising great-power rival. The same thinking inspired the 1999 common defense treaty between Japan and the United States to offset the expanding military power of China.

The evolution of the North Atlantic Treaty Organization (NATO) since the end of the Cold War reflects the shifting geopolitical landscape. At first, many observers felt that NATO would disappear along with the rival Warsaw Pact. The purpose for which NATO was first created—containing Soviet expansionism—no longer was relevant, because the threat no longer existed. However, NATO did not dissolve. It reinvented itself, changing its membership and its mission. In January 1994, NATO allowed four formerly communist bloc states (Poland, the Czech Republic, Slovakia, and Hungary) to join the Partnership for Peace (PfP) plan. The PfP did not give them the same guarantee of aid in the event of an attack that the existing full members were promised. But it became a pivotal step in the process of enlargement aimed at creating a peaceful, united, and democratic Europe. As Map 9.2 shows, after admitting the Czech Republic and Poland in 1999, NATO enlarged further in November 2002, when it undertook the biggest expansion in its 53-year history. Bulgaria, Estonia, Latvia, Lithuania, Romania, Slovakia, and Slovenia were admitted as full members along with the 19 existing

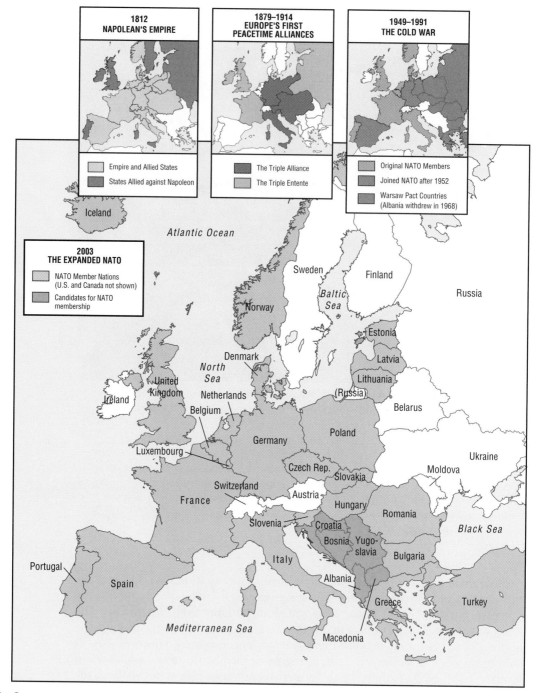

1812
NAPOLEAN'S EMPIRE

Empire and Allied States
States Allied against Napoleon

1879–1914
EUROPE'S FIRST
PEACETIME ALLIANCES

The Triple Alliance
The Triple Entente

1949–1991
THE COLD WAR

Original NATO Members
Joined NATO after 1952
Warsaw Pact Countries
(Albania withdrew in 1968)

2003
THE EXPANDED NATO

NATO Member Nations
(U.S. and Canada not shown)
Candidates for NATO
membership

Iceland

Atlantic Ocean

Sweden
Finland
Russia

Norway
Baltic Sea
Estonia
Latvia
Lithuania
(Russia)
Belarus

Denmark
North Sea
Netherlands
Belgium
United Kingdom
Ireland
Germany
Poland
Ukraine
Moldova
Czech Rep.
Slovakia
Luxembourg
Switzerland
Austria
Hungary
Romania
France
Slovenia
Croatia
Bosnia
Yugo-slavia
Bulgaria
Black Sea
Portugal
Spain
Italy
Albania
Greece
Turkey
Macedonia

Mediterranean Sea

MAP 9.2

The Enlarged NATO in the New Geostrategic Balance of Power

The geostrategic landscape was transformed by NATO's expansion at the start of 2003 to 27 full members. An additional 38 countries work as Partners for Peace in the Euro-Atlantic Partnership Council (EAPC). As shown in this map, NATO now casts its security umbrella across and beyond Europe in its endeavor to create a collective security regime including states that once were its enemies. If NATO succeeds in redefining itself as a coalition of liberal democracies fighting tyranny, terrorism, and a range of other economic and environmental problems, the transformation will defy the tendency for alliances to collapse after the defeat of a common adversary. SOURCE: From *U.S. News and World Report,* July 14, 1997. Copyright © 1997, U.S. News & World Report, L.P. Reprinted with permission.

Andreas Striglios/AFP/Getty Images

Rivalry among Allies Seeking to defuse European allies' anxieties about his plan for the United States to build a missile defense system, President Bush proclaimed his administration's "new receptivity" to the European allies at the June 2001 NATO summit. However, French, German, and other Europeans were not persuaded, and a climate of mistrust among allies prevailed. Shown here is a June 2001 protest demonstration in Europe against the United States.

countries under NATO's security umbrella. In addition, Russia has been invited to formally participate in full decision making on NATO security policies, in order to alleviate any lingering fears that the alliance continues to perceive Moscow as a potential enemy. Thus, NATO, a product of a bygone bipolar world, has become a new security IGO on the global stage, committed to defending its 26 members' borders as though they were their own.

Enlargement of both NATO's membership and its mission opens a new chapter in that organization's history. Revitalized with a larger membership and territorial reach, NATO seeks to orchestrate a cooperative approach to security among liberal democracies. That goal was forcefully expressed by U.S. president George W. Bush in December 2001 at Warsaw University, when he declared that every European democracy—including former parts of the Soviet Union—must be permitted to join an expanded NATO. "The United States is no longer your enemy," Bush declared in urging Russia to be "a partner in peace, a partner in democracy."

Following the 2001 terrorist attacks on the World Trade Center and the Pentagon, NATO invoked its mutual defense principle for the first time, declaring that the attack on the United States was an attack on all members. This helped dispel doubts about NATO's usefulness in addressing twenty-first-century security challenges. "The world has changed," remarked U.S. secretary of state Colin Powell. "Now more than ever, NATO matters." Yet critics assert that the advantages of NATO enlargement are offset by the risk that expansion will reduce the alliance to a mere conference association for discussing security issues. They also complain that enlargement undermines the security of the states it excludes. Not only at times Russia, but also China, Japan, and other powers have complained that the presence of a solidified military alliance in Europe without other strong military alliances to balance it poses a threat to global security. NATO asserts that these charges are unjustified because its new decision rules, giving every full member a veto over decisions regarding military operations, remove the threat of a NATO preemptive strike.

Despite its innovative redesign and new decision rules, NATO cohesion has been affected by the Bush administration's proclaimed war on global terrorism. Friction increased between the United States and its NATO allies after President Bush condemned North Korea, Iran, and Iraq as an "axis of evil," and soon thereafter took military action against Iraq. Illustrating how sensitive alliance politics can be, the German foreign minister, Joschka Fischer, castigated President Bush for treating America's NATO partners as subordinate "satellites," and French President Jacques Chirac criticized what he saw as Washington's disregard of the interests of America's would-be partners in the struggles against terrorism.

Adding to the transatlantic debate over collective defense was the decision by the European Union to create its own rapid deployment force so it could undertake military actions on its own without the approval of the United States. As the European reaction to America's use of its military might demonstrates, the quest for national security in an anarchical world springs from states' uncertainties of the intentions of others. Because the unchecked growth in one country's power makes others insecure, nearly all states continually look for ways to defend themselves. In this sense the realists' military paths to peace discussed in this chapter are intimately related to the widespread quest for armaments described in Chapter 8. Convinced that a more peaceful world is not on the diplomatic horizon, realists insist that the tragic struggle for security among great-powers will continue (Mearsheimer 2001).

The validity of this interpretation of the global future is still at issue, however. In the next chapter we will turn our attention away from the balance-of-power politics of realism and examine proposals by liberal theorists for harnessing international law and organization to create a more peaceful world.

Chapter Summary

- The term *balance of power* is used in many ways. At the core of its many meanings is the idea that state security and survival is most likely when there is a rough military parity among rivals.

- In order to function effectively, balance-of-power theory prescribes that national leaders follow certain rules of statecraft. They should be vigilant, forge alliances when they cannot keep pace with the arms increases of competitors, choose alliance partners on the basis of strategic needs rather than cultural or ideological affinity, always oppose those who seek hegemony, and act with moderation toward those who are defeated in battle.

- Balance-of-power theory is criticized for its logical inconsistencies, the lack of a reliable way for national leaders to gauge accurately the distribution of military capabilities, the propensity to foster rapid arms buildups, the assumption that leaders are risk averse, and its inability to prevent destructive wars.

- Great-power concerts attempt to stabilize power balances by creating regular channels of communication among latent rivals. Concerts are fragile, however. Friction often develops when some members come to believe that they have sacrificed more for the common good than others.

- Some realists argue that military parity can be preserved through arms limitation agreements. Whereas arms control refers to restrictions on the growth of weapons inventories, disarmament pertains to the reduction or elimination of weapons. Arms control agreements have tended to be more effective than disarmament agreements, especially when they involve bilateral negotiations.

- Various obstacles stand in the way of reaching effective arms control agreements. Negotiations are generally slow, they rarely cover new weapons systems, and those agreements that are reached pose difficult verification problems and are hard to enforce.

- Throughout the Cold War, the balance of power between the United States and the Soviet Union followed a pattern of direct bipolar opposition, with two counterbalanced blocs facing off against one another.

- After the collapse of the Soviet Union, the structure of the state system moved toward unipolarity, with the United States standing as the world's sole superpower. Unipolarity has never lasted long in modern history. As described in balance-of-power theory, states eventually combine forces to check the power of the dominate state. Currently, many scholars are debating how long the United States will remain in its dominant position. Some scholars predict that American unipolarity will be followed by a return to the pattern of direct bipolar opposition, with a bloc of states composed of some combination of China, Russia, or Japan counterbalancing the United States. Other scholars disagree. They foresee a return to the classical balance-of-power pattern of fluid competition, involving the United States, China, Russia, Japan, and a united Europe.

KEY TERMS

alliance	balance of power	disarmament
arms control	balancer	extended deterrence
arms race	concert	hegemonic stability theory

WHERE ON THE WORLD WIDE WEB?

Center for Nonproliferation Studies (CNS)

http://cns.miis.edu/index.htm

The Center for Nonproliferation Studies (CNS) at the Monterey Institute of International Relations is the largest nongovernmental organization in the United States devoted exclusively to research and training on nonproliferation issues. At this site you will find articles on featured topics as well as summaries on CNS projects. Its extensive electronic resources are organized according to region of the world, subject, and publication type.

Federation of American Scientists

http://www.fas.org/

Students interested in examining international arms control treaties and related issues should visit the Federation of American Scientists' (FAS) website to find a comprehensive archive of nuclear, chemical, and biological arms control agreements. FAS is a privately funded nonprofit policy organization engaged in analysis and advocacy on science, technology, and public policy issues that con-

cern global security. Topics such as arms sales monitoring, chemical and biological arms, space policy, and nuclear nonproliferation and disarmament are covered extensively.

NATO

http://www.nato.int/

The North Atlantic Treaty Organization's (NATO) website contains information on NATO's enlargement as well as the Partnership for Peace (PfP) initiative. Click on the Partnerships link to get a list of the countries participating in the PfP.

United Nations Conference on Disarmament

http://www.unog.ch/disarm/disarm.htm

The UN Conference on Disarmament web page links to all the major international instruments on disarmament, from the 1949 Geneva Convention through the 1997 antipersonnel landmines convention. Read the texts of some of the most influential international agreements that seek to control or eliminate weapons of mass destruction.

INFOTRAC® COLLEGE EDITION

Search for the following articles in the InfoTrac College Edition database.

Chace, James. "The Balance of Power," *World Policy Journal* Winter 1998.

Collina, Tom Z., and Jon B. Wolfsthal. "Nuclear Terrorism and Warhead Control in Russia," *Arms Control Today* April 2002.

Jervis, Robert. "Arms Control, Stability, and Causes of War," *Political Science Quarterly* Summer 1993.

Ross, Andrew L. "Thinking about the Unthinkable: Unreasonable Exuberance?" *Naval War College Review* Spring 2001.

For more articles, enter:

"balance of power" in the Subject Guide.

"nuclear arms control" in the Subject Guide, and then go to subdivision

"international aspects."

"war" in the Subject Guide, and then go to subdivision "causes of."

ADDITIONAL CD-ROM RESOURCES

Click on Global Conflict and International Security for additional resources related to this chapter.

CHAPTER 10

Liberal Paths to Peace

International Law and Organization

> The road of Beethoven in his Ninth Symphony is also the road followed by the authors of the Preamble of the [United Nations] Charter. It begins with the recognition of the threat under which we all live, speaking as it does of the need to save succeeding generations from the scourge of war which has brought untold sorrow to mankind. It moves on to a reaffirmation of faith in the dignity and worth of the human person, and it ends with the promise to practice tolerance and live together in peace with one another as good neigbours and to unite our strength to maintain peace.
>
> DAG HAMMARSKJÖLD, former UN secretary-general

I n 1979, Nicaraguan dictator Anastasio Somoza was overthrown by a broad-based movement known as the Sandinista National Liberation Front. After ousting Somoza, a Marxist faction within the movement gained power and established ties with Cuba and the Soviet Union. Disturbed by the leftist tilt of the new regime and its support for revolutionary groups elsewhere in Central America, the United States trained antigovernment insurgents, mined three of Nicaragua's harbors, and attacked the country's petroleum facilities in an effort to undermine the Sandinistas. Nicaragua responded by filing suit against the United States on April 9, 1984 in the International Court of Justice (ICJ, or more commonly known as the World Court), the principal judicial organ of the United Nations.

Nicaragua's suit accused the U.S. Central Intelligence Agency of illegally attempting to destabilize and topple the elected Sandinista government. The Reagan administration replied by refusing to recognize the World Court's jurisdiction and withdrawing from further judicial proceedings. Nevertheless, the ICJ heard Nicaragua's arguments, and on June 27, 1986, ruled against the United States. The verdict had little effect on Washington, however. Neither the World Court nor Nicaragua had any means to enforce the judgment.

In denying the ICJ's authority, was the United States acting within its sovereign rights? Or, as others asserted, was it behaving like an outlaw? The decision by the Reagan administration to ignore the World Court in the Nicaragua case raises important questions about the efficacy of international law and organization. Whereas liberal theorists place great stock in these approaches to the control of armed conflict, hard-boiled realists have long scoffed that without compulsory jurisdiction and mechanism to ensure compliance, international judicial procedures will remain a "blind alley" rather than a path to peace (Carr 1939). As one skeptic quipped: "International law is to law as professional wrestling is to wrestling" (*U.S. News & World Report,* September 29, 1993, 8).

The purpose of this chapter is to examine the contributions that international law and organization make to establishing world order. We will begin by analyzing the nature and functions of international law.

International Law and World Order

Throughout recorded history, all autonomous, independent political entities engaged in sustained interaction have developed rules defining appropriate behavior for certain situations. Although the rules of modern international law may not be backed by a formal, unified system of sanctions, both state and non-state actors rely on them to coordinate their behavior and redress grievances. Most of this activity falls within the realm of **private international law**—the regulation of routine transnational activities in such areas as commerce, communications, and travel. This is where the majority of international disputes are regularly settled and where the record of compliance compares favorably with that achieved in domestic legal systems.

• **private international law** law pertaining to routinized transnational intercourse between or among states as well as nonstate actors.

Liberal democracies give citizens the rights of free speech and assembly. Shown here are people exercising those rights in a protest demonstration in October 2002 against U.S. plans to attack Iraq.

In contrast, **public international law** covers relations between governments as well as the interactions of governments with intergovernmental organizations (IGOs) and nongovernmental organizations (NGOs). Most critics of international law focus their attention here rather than on private international law. Their complaints generally emphasize instances where bystanders overlooked the transgressions of aggressive states engaged in illegal activities. As Israeli diplomat Abba Eban once lamented, public international law "is that law which the wicked do not obey and the righteous do not enforce."

Although public international law has deficiencies, that should not lead to the conclusion that it is irrelevant or useless. No legal system can prevent all of its members from breaking laws. There are miscreants who ignore domestic law just as there are states who flagrantly violate international law. In spite of its shortcomings, states themselves find international law useful and expend considerable effort attempting to shape its development. Because this chapter examines the capacity of public international law to control war, our discussion will address only the laws and institutional machinery created to manage armed conflict between states. That is, it will explore that segment of international law popularly regarded as the most deficient.

• **public international law** law pertaining to government-to-government relations.

Sovereignty and the Rules of International Law

Public international law is usually defined as the body of general normative principles and specific legal rules that govern the behavior of states in their relations with one another. Rather than being a static code of conduct, it has evolved significantly over the past four centuries, changing in response to transformations in world politics.

No principle of international law is more critical than state sovereignty. As discussed in previous chapters, sovereignty means that no authority is legally above the state, except that which the state voluntarily confers on the international organizations it joins. Nearly every legal doctrine supports and extends the principle that states are the primary subjects of international law. As outlined in the Montevideo Convention of 1933 on the Rights and Duties of States, a state must possess a permanent population, a well-defined territory, and a government capable of ruling its citizens and of managing formal diplomatic relations with other states. This last criterion is particularly important because the acquisition of statehood ultimately depends on a political entity's acceptance as such by other states, which are entitled to give or withhold **diplomatic recognition**. In short, recognition is a political tool, through which approval of a government can be expressed and certain rights granted.

• **diplomatic recognition** the formal legal acceptance of a state's official status as an independent country. *De facto* recognition acknowledges the factual existence of another state or government short of full recognition. *De jure* recognition gives a government formal, legal recognition.

The Rights of States. Under international law, political entities that meet the criteria of statehood hold certain rights. First, states possess the right of continued national existence, which means the prerogative to use force in self-defense. Second, they have the right of independence, which allows them to manage their domestic affairs without external interference and act as free agents in foreign affairs, negotiating commercial treaties, forming military alliances, and entering into other types of agreements without the supervision of another state. Finally, states also have the right of legal equality. Though unequal in size and strength, states are equal before the law in the sense that they all (1) possess the same privileges and responsibilities, (2) can appeal to the same rules of conduct when defending themselves, and (3) can expect to have these rules applied impartially whenever they consent to a third party help settle their quarrels. The most common third-party procedures used in international dispute resolution include:

- *Good offices:* A third party offers a location for discussions among disputants but does not participate in the actual negotiations.
- *Conciliation:* A third party assists both sides but does not offer any solution.
- *Mediation:* A third party proposes a nonbinding solution to a conflict between states.
- *Arbitration:* A third party gives a binding decision through an ad hoc forum.
- *Adjudication:* A third party gives a binding decision through a standing court.

By defining states' rights in this manner, international law traditionally held that no state could claim jurisdiction over another, nor could it sit in judgment over the validity of the public acts other states initiated under their own laws. Furthermore, heads of state and diplomatic representatives were immune from prosecution in foreign courts.

The Duties of States. Besides recognizing the rights of existence, independence, and equality, international law acknowledges certain corresponding duties. A sovereign state has the right to maintain its corporate personality as a state, but it also possesses a corollary duty of **nonintervention**—not meddling in the internal matters of other states. Another duty is carrying out promissory obligations in good faith. A sovereign state possesses the right to act as a free agent when dealing with others, but it also has a duty to honor agreements not signed under duress. As expressed in the norm *pacta sunt servanda* (treaties are binding), promises made voluntarily by parties to international treaties must be upheld. However, some legal scholars claim that a radical change in the circumstances that existed when a commitment was made can be invoked under the norm *rebus sic stantibus* (as matters stand) as a ground for unilaterally terminating an agreement.

• **nonintervention**
the legal principle prohibiting one state from interfering in another state's internal affairs.

The Limitations of International Law

Sovereignty and the legal principles derived from it provide the foundation upon which the international legal order rests. But because the international legal order is premised upon the voluntary consent of sovereign states, many people question whether international law is *really* law. From their perspective, international law suffers from the following limitations:

- *The international system lacks a legislative body capable of making binding legal rules.* Whereas in most national legal systems a legislature makes domestic laws, there is no global legislature empowered to make international laws. The UN General Assembly makes recommendations, not statutes. According to Article 38 of the Statute of the International Court of Justice, the sources of legal rules are: (1) custom; (2) international treaties and agreements; (3) national and international court decisions; (4) the writings of legal authorities and specialists; and (5) the "general principles" of law recognized since antiquity as part of "natural law" and "right reason." Of these, custom and multilateral treaties signed by a substantial number of states are considered the most important.
- *The international system lacks a judicial body with compulsory jurisdiction that can identify breaches of legal rules and impose remedies for violations.* The International Court of Justice differs from national courts primarily in that its jurisdiction is based on the consent of the disputants. Sovereign states cannot be forced to appear before the ICJ when charged with breaking legal rules, and they are hesitant to give unconditional consent given the risk of receiving an unfavorable verdict on an issue of vital importance.
- *The international system lacks an executive body capable of enforcing legal rules.* Unlike in national legal systems, no centralized mechanism exists to apprehend and punish those who violate legal rules. Although the UN Security Council has the power to act when there is a "threat of breach of international peace and security" (Article 39 of UN Charter), it is often hamstrung by vetoes in cases involving serious militarized disputes, and it is not designed to operate like a municipal police force investigating and bringing to justice those who commit other violations of the law.

• *Without robust global institutions that can make, interpret, and enforce legal rules, international law serves as an instrument of the powerful, justifying the competitive pursuit of national advantage without regard to morality or justice.* By accepting unbridled sovereign autonomy, the international legal system is essentially a "horizontal" normative order composed of laws of coordination, not a "vertical" order based on laws of subordination. Within horizontal orders, the behavior of the powerful has a significant impact in establishing how others should behave. As Stanley Hoffmann (1971) has put it, rules *of* behavior tend to become rules *for* behavior. The legal rules to which the powerful willingly agree are those that serve their interest, legitimizing self-help under the precept that moral considerations must yield to national interest. The outcome of any legal dispute is thus left "to the vicissitudes of the distribution of power between the violator of the law and the victim of the violation." Therefore, Hans J. Morgenthau (1985) concedes, "it makes it easy for the strong both to violate the law and to enforce it, and consequently puts the rights of the weak in jeopardy."

Despite the limitations listed here, most states comply with international law because it communicates the "rules of the game" through which virtually everyone within the international system conducts their relations. By shaping expectations, legal rules reduce uncertainty about the behavior of others and increase predictability in world affairs. Those who consistently play by recognized rules enhance their reputations for trustworthiness; those who opportunistically break them undermine their credibility, which weakens their bargaining positions in future interactions as other states become suspicious about their intentions.

In sum, compliance with law does not necessarily derive from commands backed by punishment from some central authority. States voluntarily observe international legal rules because their long-term self-interests are served by the order that comes from shared expectations. Legal scholar William Slomanson (2003) likens this process to the behavior of motorists at intersections. Most drivers stop when the traffic light is red and go when it turns green, even when no police officer is present to enforce traffic laws. They comply with the law because of a common interest to proceed safely, knowing that collisions would occur if people ignored the signals at intersections. Similarly, "almost all nations observe almost all principles of international law and almost all of their obligations almost all of the time," writes Louis Henkin (1979), because everyone benefits from avoiding the chaos that would otherwise exist.

International Law and the Preservation of Peace

• **just war doctrine** a set of criteria that indicate when it is morally justifiable to wage war and how it should be fought once it begins.

Though rudimentary when compared to national legal systems, international law nonetheless mitigates the most pernicious aspects of an anarchic state system. Among the most important international legal rules prescribing limits on state behavior are those that pertain to the use of armed force. They delineate when it is legitimate for states to employ force, how it should be used, and against whom it may be applied. Because the content of these rules has been heavily influenced by **just war doctrine**, we begin our analysis of the role of international law in preserving peace by examining this ethical tradition.

Erich Lessing/Art Resource, NY/Stedelijk Museum "Het Prinsenhof," Delft, The Netherlands

War and the Birth of Modern International Law
Revolted by the international violence he witnessed during his lifetime, Dutch reformer Hugo Grotius (1583–1645) wrote *On the Law of War and Peace* in the midst of the Thirty Years' War. His treatise called on the great powers to resolve their conflicts by pacific means rather than on the battlefield, and specified the legal principles he felt could encourage cooperation, peace, and more humane treatment of people. Grotius consequently became known as the "father of international law."

Just War Doctrine. The term *just war* originated with Aristotle. Attempts to enumerate criteria for determining whether a particular war was just were subsequently undertaken by the Roman writer Cicero, as well as by early Christian thinkers such as Ambrose, Augustine, and Aquinas. Over the intervening centuries, philosophers and theologians continued to advance contending theories regarding when it would be morally justifiable to use military force as a tool of foreign policy.

The roots of modern just war doctrine lie in the effort of Hugo Grotius to transform these earlier moral theories into a body of international law that would specify those circumstances under which war might be legally initiated and how it should be waged upon its commencement. An eminent Dutch scholar who was outraged by the brutality of the Thirty Years' War (1618–1648), Grotius complained that states "rush to arms" for "trifling pretexts," and then behave "as though by some edict a fury had been let loose to commit every crime." To counteract this deplorable pattern, he drew upon ancient and medieval writers to develop two bodies of rules about warfare, *jus ad bellum* (the justice of a war) and *jus in bello* (justice in a war). The former set the standards by which a political leader could determine whether a war was just. The latter described the military actions that were permissible in fighting a just war.

The rules proposed by Grotius have inspired international lawyers since their publication in 1625 (see Controversy: Was the War in Iraq Just?). Rather than condemning all warfare as intrinsically evil, just-war theorists submit that recourse to war is permissible when the following conditions are met:

1. *Just cause:* The state contemplating the use of military force must have a morally good objective.
2. *Right intention:* War must be waged for the purpose of correcting a wrong and establishing peace and justice, not for revenge or some other malicious reason.

CONTROVERSY ## Was the War in Iraq Just?

On February 5, 2003, U.S. secretary of state Colin Powell delivered a lengthy address to the United Nations Security Council, charging Iraq with a breach of its disarmament obligations under UN Security Council Resolution 1441. American intelligence agencies, Powell asserted, had evidence that Saddam Hussein's regime possessed weapons of mass destruction. After emphasizing the gravity of the threat these weapons posed, Powell reminded his audience of the Iraqi leader's ruthlessness and warned that he would "stop at nothing until something stops him."

Over the next few weeks, U.S. president George W. Bush and other members of his administration reiterated these accusations. On March 17, Bush claimed that Iraq "continued to possess and conceal some of the most lethal weapons ever devised," and threatened military action if Saddam Hussein did not leave the country within 48 hours. When Hussein failed to comply, the United States and its allies launched a series of precision air strikes and swarming ground attacks that quickly overwhelmed Iraqi defenses.

The Bush administration gave three primary justifications for its war against Iraq: (1) Saddam Hussein had weapons of mass destruction; (2) he had close ties with the al Qaeda terrorist network; and (3) his removal from power would provide an opportunity to transform Iraq into a democratic regime, which would change the political atmosphere throughout the entire Middle East.

Yet a year after the president declared victory on May 1 from the flight deck of the USS *Abraham Lincoln,* American and allied troops were locked in fierce fighting with Sunni insurgents in the central Iraqi city of Falluja, and with Shiite militia loyal to the firebrand cleric Muqtada al-Sadr in various southern cities. Though expected to be welcomed with rice and rose petals, the coalition forces came to be seen as occupiers rather than liberators. In a May 2004 poll of Iraqi public opinion sponsored by the U.S. Coalition Provisional Authority, over 80 percent of those interviewed indicated that they had no confidence in the United States after the Abu Ghraib prison abuse scandal, and wanted Washington to withdraw its troops as soon as possible. Meanwhile, the much-touted Iraqi weapons of mass destruction had not been found, and the commission investigating the September 11 terror attacks on the United States indicated that they failed to discover any collaborative relationship between Saddam Hussein and al Qaeda. In response, the Bush administration continued to insist that weapons of mass destruction might still be found, Saddam Hussein had numerous contacts with al Qaeda, and the construction of a democratic regime in Iraq was on track. The war had been just, and the United States would stay the course.

What do you think? Drawing upon the criteria proposed by just war theorists, would you evaluate the 2003 war against Iraq as a just war? Was it initiated for a just cause and with the right intentions? Was it undertaken as a last resort with the appropriate authorization? Did the good toward which the war aimed outweigh the harm caused by the fighting? Do you agree with Vice President Dick Cheney's claim that the "risks of inaction [were] far greater than the risk of action" (Woodward 2004)?

3. *Last resort:* War should not be undertaken until all other reasonable means of resolving the conflict have been exhausted.
4. *Political proportionality:* The harm caused by the fighting must not outweigh the good toward which the war aims.
5. *Declaration by legitimate authority:* Duly constituted rulers must publicly declare a state of war.
6. *Reasonable chance of success:* States must not engage in futile uses of force.

In addition to elucidating *when* it is morally permissible to fight, just war theory also stipulates *how* wars should be fought. While numerous rules have been proposed on the right and wrong ways to conduct war, most revolve around the following two principles:

1. *Discrimination:* Noncombatants must be immune from attack; civilians not engaged in their state's war efforts cannot be targeted.
2. *Military proportionality:* Combatants must cause no more destruction than is required to achieve their military objectives.

These *jus ad bellum* and *jus in bello* standards continue to color thinking about the laws of war. However, the advent of weapons of mass destruction raised new questions about the ethics of war and peace, since their use would violate many of the traditional principles of just war doctrine. A high-yield nuclear device, for example, would not only obliterate the target area, but it would also produce enough radioactive fallout to kill vast numbers of people in countries that had no part in the conflict. Scholars and policymakers alike are now struggling to rethink just war doctrine in the light of the new strategic realities of contemporary warfare.

Problems in the Legal Control of Warfare.   As Figure 10.1 shows, the international community has increasingly rejected the realist contention that states can use military force to achieve their foreign policy objectives. Influenced by many of the standards contained in just war doctrine, the laws of war have sought to prohibit all uses of force by individual states except in self-defense. Traditionally, the right of self-defense has been understood as allowing states recourse to force when repelling actual as well as imminent armed attacks. As articulated by U.S. secretary of state Daniel Webster in 1837, to exercise this right a state must face an "instant, overwhelming necessity . . . leaving no choice of means, and no moment for deliberation." In addition, the defensive reaction must be proportionate to the danger, should not endanger noncombatants to minimize one's own risk, and cannot serve as a **reprisal**. Self-defense is thus restricted to protection, not excessive or punitive measures aimed at redressing injuries.

> • **reprisal** a hostile but legal retaliatory act aimed at punishing another state's prior illegal actions.

Following the promulgation of the UN Charter, appeals to this customary right of self-defense became controversial. The charter addresses self-defense in two places. First, Article 2 (4) declares that "all members shall refrain in their international relations from the threat or use of force against the territorial integrity or political independence of any State, or in any other manner inconsistent with the purposes of the United Nations." Second, Article 51 proclaims that "Nothing in the present Charter shall impair the inherent right of individual or collective self-defense if an armed attack occurs against a Member of the United Nations, until the Security Council has taken the measures necessary to maintain international peace and security." One school of thought about the Charter interprets Articles 2 (4) and 51 as superseding customary international law, and thus limiting forcible self-defense to cases where the Security Council has not yet responded to an armed attack. A second school of thought disagrees. Highlighting the concept of "inherent right" in Article 51, it argues that pre-charter, customary rules of self-defense continue in place. States, in other words, have a right to use military force so long as the traditional criteria of necessity, proportionality, and protection are met.

The difficulty with the second interpretation of self-defense lies in defining what constitutes an "overwhelming necessity." Appeals to the exigencies of

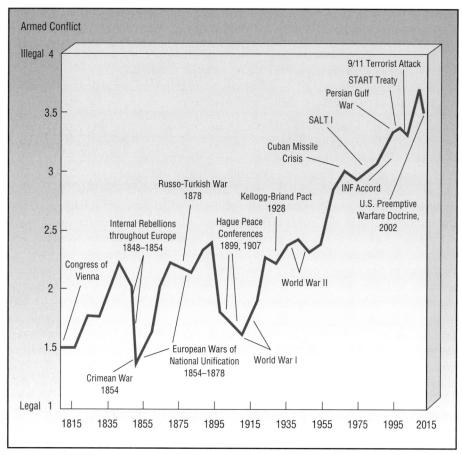

FIGURE 10.1

The Legal Prohibition against Initiating Wars, 1815–2005

Legal restraints on the historic right of states to use war as a tool of foreign policy have grown steadily since World War I. Since the attacks of September 11, 2001, these legal prohibitions have been questioned by U.S. policymakers who favor military preemption against states that support terrorist movements.

SOURCE: Adapted from Transnational Rules Indicators Project, as described in *When Trust Breaks Down: Alliance Norms and World Politics* by Charles W. Kegley, Jr. and Gregory A. Raymond. Copyright © 1990 Charles W. Kegley, Jr. and Gregory A. Raymond. Reprinted with the permission of the University of South Carolina.

• **military necessity**
a legal doctrine asserting that violation of the rules of war may be excused during periods of extreme emergency.

military necessity challenge the wrongfulness of an act on the basis that it was the only means of safeguarding an essential interest against a grave peril (Raymond 1999). According to those who invoke the necessity defense, a state may be absolved from taking military actions that violate the rules of warfare when it faces an absolute strategic imperative that makes it practically impossible to do anything else. Those responsible for national security, they insist, must often make tragic choices among lesser evils. As the former British secretary of state for war Lord Kitchener once put it: "We must make war as we must; not as we should like."

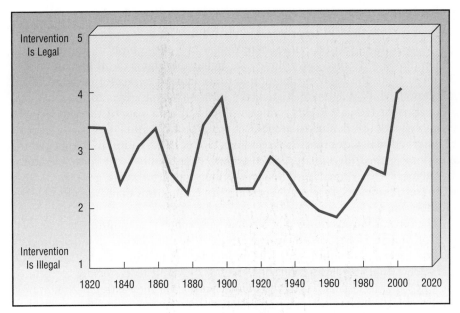

F I G U R E   1 0 . 2
The Changing Status of the Nonintervention Rule in International Law since 1820

Over time, the illegality of intervening into the domestic affairs of sovereign states has changed. Since 1960, international law has adopted an increasingly permissive posture toward this form of coercive diplomacy for a variety of purposes, including preventing genocide, promoting democracy, and combating global terrorism.

SOURCE: From Transnational Rules Indicators Project, as measured in "The Rise and Fall of the Nonintervention Norm: Some Correlates and Potential Consequences" by Charles W. Kegley, Jr., Gregory A. Raymond, and Margaret G. Hermann from the *Fletcher Forum of International Affairs* (Winter 1998).

In addition to the problems that claims of military necessity create for international laws governing the use of force, recent suggestions that the international community has a moral imperative to stop brutal governments from violating the human rights of their citizens raises another set of problems. Allowing the use of coercion by one state to change the political regime in another would significantly change the normative climate of world affairs. As we have seen, the twin principles of sovereignty and nonintervention underpin international law. The only widely accepted exception to the prohibition against interfering in the domestic affairs of other nation-states is military intervention to liberate one's own nationals when they are being held hostage. Yet recently, some powerful states have asserted the right, and even a moral obligation, to use military intervention for humanitarian purposes. As shown in Figure 10.2, the nonintervention principle has begun to erode as a growing proportion of the international community has sought a way to stop human rights abuses in a globalized, interconnected world.

The argument claiming it is legally permissible to intervene with armed force in order to end egregious violations of human rights rests on three propositions.

The first proposition asserts that human rights are an international entitlement. Article 55 (c) of the UN Charter requires member states to promote "universal respect for, and observance of, human rights." Over the past 50 years, the UN has developed a detailed list of inherent, inalienable rights of all human beings. The most important legal formulation of those rights is expressed in the so-called International Bill of Human Rights, the informal name given to the Universal Declaration of Human Rights (which was passed by a vote of the UN General Assembly in 1948), the International Covenant on Civil and Political Rights, and the International Covenant on Economic, Social, and Cultural Rights (which were both opened for signature in 1966 and entered into force a decade later). For advocates of humanitarian intervention, the legal rules governing these rights are regarded as *jus cogens*—peremptory legal norms that override all other considerations.

The second proposition maintains that governments committing grave violations of human rights lose their legitimacy. Although Article 2 (7) of the UN Charter prevents member states from interfering in one another's domestic affairs, the Charter's legal protection does not extend to genocide, torture, or other horrific acts shocking to the conscience of the international community. Those favoring humanitarian intervention argue that governments involved in these abuses forfeit their protection under international law.

The third proposition asserts that the international community has a responsibility to halt human rights violations. According to the International Court of Justice, there are some obligations that a state has "towards the international community as a whole," and all members of that community "have a legal interest in their protection." The entitlement for protection against genocide, slavery, and the like gives legal standing to any member of the international community to impose sanctions if these wrongful acts continue. When massive human rights violations occur, "intervention from the outside is not only legally justified but morally required" (D'Amato 1995).

The advent of these new justifications for military intervention into the domestic affairs of sovereign states reflects a growing sentiment that sovereignty is no longer sacrosanct. Shocked by the carnage in the civil war that broke out in Bosnia during 1992, former British prime minister Margaret Thatcher captured this mood when she lamented, "We cannot just let things go on like this" (*Time*, April 26, 1993, 35). "Something, anything, must be done," implored Nobel laureate Elie Wiesel (*Time*, May 3, 1993, 35). Sovereignty, they and others argued, cannot shield the perpetrators of grievous crimes against humanity from punishment. "There are common norms and standards of conduct and countries must be answerable for failing to observe these" (de Wijk 1998). Heads of state and military commanders who have been involved in **war crimes** must be held accountable.

• **war crimes** acts performed during war that the international community defines as illegal, such as atrocities committed against enemy civilians and prisoners of war.

To deal with the rising concern about serious violations of international humanitarian law, the UN Security Council set up two *ad hoc* criminal tribunals between 1993 and 1994: the International Criminal Tribunal for the former Yugoslavia, and the International Criminal Tribunal for Rwanda. In 1998, 120 countries meeting in Rome voted to establish a *permanent* International Criminal Court (ICC), so future acts of genocide, crimes against humanity, and war crimes would not go unpunished.

UGANDA
Idi Amin

IRAQ
Saddam Hussein

HAITI
Jean-Claude Duvallier

UNITED STATES
George Bush
(Persian Gulf War)

BRITAIN
Margaret Thatcher
(Falklands/Malvinas
War)

YUGOSLAVIA
Slobodan Milosevic
(Convicted)

© Reuters/Rubin Sprich/Archive Photos/CORBIS, © William Campbell, © Vienna Report/Sygma/CORBIS, © Kathy Willens/AP/Wide World Photos, © P. F. Gero, © Matthieu Polak/Sygma/CORBIS

Identifying War Criminals Between 1993 and 1994, the UN Security Council created two special crimes tribunals in The Hague to prosecute war crimes. Swiss criminal lawyer Carla del Ponte (left) was appointed in September 1999 as chief prosecutor for the UN's war crimes tribunals for Yugoslavia and Rwanda, in which 80 prisoners were tried. The principle that national leaders do not hold immunity from prosecution was established after World War II at the Nuremberg and Tokyo war crimes trials, but the norm was not reinforced until the UN responded to the genocide in Bosnia and Rwanda by setting up special-purpose war crimes tribunals. The performance of these tribunals is believed critical to the credibility of the newly created International Criminal Court. The question about precisely what behavior is proscribed for a head of state is creating a new controversy, however. International law still is unclear about the limits. At right are some past heads of state who potentially, according to *Time* (December 14, 1998, 42) could be called before courts to defend their use of arms, either against their own people or during their country's wars. In February 2002, Slobodan Milosevic, the president of the former Yugoslavia, was convicted of criminal charges for starting three wars of ethnic cleansing.

The new International Criminal Court differs from the older International Court of Justice (or "World Court"). Whereas the ICC has criminal jurisdiction to prosecute individuals charged with heinous violations of human rights, the ICJ deals with disputes between sovereign states. Founded in the hope that international adjudication would help resolve disputes before they escalated to war, the ICJ languished through much of the Cold War. As the dispute between Nicaragua and the United States during the mid-1980s demonstrated, powerful countries hesitated to relinquish their military advantage and put issues of importance in the hands of foreign judges that might rule against them. Political realists, depicting the world as a place where states perpetually jockey for relative gains, urge leaders to act in terms of national self-interest, trusting in their own power rather than in international courts. "A statesman who has any other motive," proclaimed one exponent of realism, "would be deserved to be hung" (Johannes Haller cited in Niebuhr 1947).

Despite realist predictions that the World Court would always have more judges than cases, in recent years it has begun to play the kind of role envisioned by its liberal founders. Between 1946 and 1991, the World Court heard only 64 contentious cases between states, rendered judgments on less than half of these, and handed down only 19 advisory opinions. Since then, it has expanded its workload and considered cases dealing with many new issues. Between 1992 and 1995, the ICJ heard 24 cases, and the judicial activity jumped to an average of 16 cases each year between 1996 and 2002. The court also became increasingly active in responding to requests for advisory opinions.

Critics assert that the World Court remains ineffective despite its increased caseload, with many states still refusing to submit their most serious disputes. Supporters, however, point to recent high-profile cases that were successfully resolved. For example, in 1992 Honduras and El Salvador accepted the Court's verdict on a border dispute that had been festering for decades. Unconvinced, the ICJ's critics aver that the Court's successes tend to involve litigants who wish to preserve their overall relationship, not bitter foes locked in high-stakes confrontations.

To sum up, many barriers remain to creating, as John F. Kennedy expressed liberal theory's hope, "a new world of law, where the strong are just and the weak secure and the peace preserved." International judicial institutions remain a far cry from most domestic courts. For some liberal thinkers, one way to dismantle some of the barriers impeding the development of international law is to strengthen international organizations; hence we next consider their role in building and maintaining world peace.

International Organization and World Order

Liberal theorists recommend creating international organizations as a second political path to peace. To understand this recommendation, we must delve into their beliefs about **collective security** as an alternative to balance-of-power politics.

• **collective security** a security regime guided by the principle that an act of aggression by any state will be met with a unified response from the rest.

The League of Nations and Collective Security

The outbreak of World War I, perhaps more than any other event, discredited the argument that peace was a byproduct of international equilibrium. Citing arms races, secret treaties, and competing alliances as sources of acute tension, many liberals viewed power balancing as a *cause* of war instead of an instrument for its prevention. U.S. president Woodrow Wilson voiced the strongest opposition to balance-of-power politics. He hoped to replace it with a League of Nations, based on a system of world order in which aggression by any state would be met by a united international response.

The Logic of Collective Security. Long before Wilson and other liberal reformers called for the establishment of a League of Nations, the idea of collective security had been expressed in various peace plans. Between the eleventh and thirteenth centuries, for example, French ecclesiastic councils held in Poitiers (1000), Limoges (1031), and Toulouse (1210) discussed rudimentary versions of collective security. Similar proposals surfaced in the writings of Pierre Dubois (1306), King George Podebrad of Bohemia (1462), the Duc de Sully (1617–1638), and the Abbé de Saint-Pierre (1713). Underlying these plans was the belief that an organized "community" of power would be more effective in preserving peace than shifting alliances aimed at balancing power.

Collective security is based on the creed voiced by Alexandre Dumas' d'Artagnan and his fellow Musketeers: "One for all and all for one!" In order for collective security to function in the rough-and-tumble environment of international politics, its advocates usually translate the Musketeer creed into the following rules of statecraft:

1. *All threats to peace must be a common concern to everyone.* Peace, collective security theory assumes, is indivisible. If aggression anywhere is ignored, it will eventually spread to other countries and become more difficult to stop; hence an attack on any one state must be regarded as an attack on all states.

2. *Every member of the state system should join the collective security organization.* Instead of maneuvering against one another in rival alliances, states should link up in a single "uniting" alliance. Such a universal collectivity, it is assumed, would possess the international legitimacy and strength to keep the peace.

3. *Members of the organization would pledge to settle their disputes through pacific means.* Collective security is not wedded to the status quo. It assumes that peaceful change is possible when institutions are available to resolve conflicts of interest. In addition to providing a mechanism for mediating disagreements, the collective security organization would also contain a judicial organ authorized to issue binding judgments on contentious disputes.

4. *If a breach of the peace occurs, the organization will apply timely, robust sanctions to punish the aggressor.* A final assumption underpinning the theory holds that members of the collective security organization would be willing and able to give mutual assistance to any state suffering an attack. Sanctions could range from public condemnation to an economic boycott to military retaliation.

In summary, this approach to world order tries to inhibit national self-help by guaranteeing the territorial integrity and political independence of states through "collective self-regulation." The key to its success is universal participation: To deter war, a potential aggressor would need to be faced by the united opposition of the entire international community (Downs 1994; Claude 1962; Thompson, K. 1953).

Difficulties with Collective Security. As discussed in Chapters 2 and 3, the League of Nations was constructed according to the blueprint of collective security. To the disappointment of its advocates, the League was not endorsed by the United States, the very power that had most championed it in the waning months of the First World War. Other problems for the League arose when its members disagreed over how to define "aggression," and how to share the costs and risks of mounting an organized response to aggressors. In the final analysis, collective security theory's central fallacy was that it expected states to be as anxious to see others protected as they were to protect themselves. That assumption did not prove true in the years preceding World War II; consequently the League of Nations never became an effective collective security system.

The United Nations and Peacekeeping

Like the League, the United Nations was established to promote international peace and security after a gruesome world war. Article 1 (1) of its Charter directed the organization to take "effective collective measures for the prevention and removal of threats to the peace." In Article 2, all members were called upon to "refrain in their international relations from the threat or use of force" (paragraph 4) and "settle their international disputes by peaceful means" (paragraph 3).

The architects of the United Nations were painfully aware of the League's disappointing experience with collective security. They hoped a new structure would make the United Nations more effective than the defunct League. Recall from Chapter 6 that the UN Charter established a Security Council of 15 members, a General Assembly composed of representatives from all member states, and an administrative apparatus (or Secretariat) under the leadership of a secretary-general. While the UN's founders voiced support for collective security, the structure they designed was heavily influenced by the idea of a great-power concert. The UN Charter permitted any of the Security Council's five permanent members (the United States, the Soviet Union, Great Britain, France, and China) to veto and thereby block proposed military actions. Because the Security Council could approve military actions only when the permanent members fully agreed, the United Nations was hamstrung by great-power rivalries, especially between the United States and the Soviet Union.

To further enhance the great powers' authority relative to the UN, the Charter severely restricted the capacity of the General Assembly to mount collective action, authorizing it only to initiate studies of conflict situations, bring perceived hostilities to the attention of the Security Council, and make recommendations for initiatives to keep the peace. Moreover, it restricted the role of the secretary-general to that of chief administrative officer. Article 99 confined the secretary-general to alerting the Security Council to peace-threatening situations and to providing administrative support for the operations that the Security Council approved.

Since the UN's structure limited its ability to function as a collective security organization, the United Nations fell short during the Cold War of many of the ideals its more ambitious founders envisioned, principally because its two most powerful members in the Security Council, the United States and the Soviet Union, did not cooperate. Over 230 Security Council vetoes were cast, stopping action of any type on about one-third of the UN's resolutions. Nevertheless, the United Nations found other ways to contribute to world order. Under Secretary-General Dag Hammarskjöld, **preventive diplomacy** replaced collective security as the organization's primary approach to promoting international peace and security. Recognizing that the United Nations had little leverage in areas where the superpowers were heavily engaged, Hammarskjöld sought to involve the UN in other regions and thus prevent Washington and Moscow from intruding into local disputes. His approach was based on the UN experience in the Middle East

• **preventive diplomacy** actions taken in advance of a predictable crisis to prevent superpower involvement and limit violence.

crises of 1956 and 1958, the Laos crisis of 1959, and Congo crisis of 1960. In essence, it involved establishing a cease-fire and inserting UN troops as a buffer to separate the belligerents. Ideally, an impartial UN presence would keep the conflict localized, though it did little to resolve the dispute.

The next major innovation in UN peacekeeping efforts began during the 1980s when the organization moved beyond supervising truces and turned its attention to **peacemaking** and **peace-building.** The former involved the UN in actively working to resolve the underlying dispute between the belligerents; the latter involved it in activities such as monitoring arms control agreements and providing developmental assistance to create the conditions that would make a renewal of the fighting less likely.

The end of the Cold War removed many of the impediments to the UN's ability to return to its primary mission of preserving international security by means that the founders of the UN originally envisioned. The potential to play an active security role was demonstrated in 1990 when Iraq invaded Kuwait. The Security Council promptly passed Resolution 678, authorizing member states "to use all necessary means" to dislodge Iraqi forces from Kuwait. Under the authority of this resolution, on January 17, 1991, a U.S.-led coalition launched military actions against Iraq's armed forces, the fourth largest in the world. Forty-three days later, Iraq agreed to a cease-fire and withdrawal from Kuwait.

Bolstered by this success at collective security, optimism about the UN role in promoting peace started to grow. This optimism was facilitated by the shift of power from the General Assembly back to the Security Council, which authorized the UN to launch twice as many peacekeeping missions between 1988 and 2002 as it had in the previous four decades of its existence. The level of activity has remained high, with the UN managing an average of 15 peacekeeping operations each year since the end of the Cold War (see Map 10.1), and between 1996 at 2001 only six vetoes were cast.

Despite their successes in the aftermath of the Cold War, peacekeeping missions have strained the UN's budget, prompting Secretary-General Kofi Annan to launch a series of organizational reforms aimed at cost containment. Financial restraints have reduced total peacekeeping personnel from 78,000 at the start of 1994 to 46,500 at the start of 2003, with peacekeeping expenditures dropping from $3.4 billion in 1994 to $2.9 billion in 2002. As a result of this downsizing, the UN has increasingly sought to deploy its missions alongside non-UN forces and at other times has requested regional organizations or multiparty state alliances to act as a substitute for the UN. This has raised questions about in whose interest these forces are acting and whether they can be held accountable by the UN.

• **peacemaking**
peaceful settlement processes such as good offices, conciliation, and mediation, designed to resolve the issues that led to armed conflict.

• **peace-building**
post-conflict actions, predominantly diplomatic and economic, that strengthen and rebuild governmental infrastructure and institutions in order to avoid recourse to armed conflict.

Regional Security Organizations and Collective Defense

If the UN remains hampered by a lack of resources, perhaps regional organizations, whose members already share many common interests and cultural traditions, offer better prospects for maintaining peace and security. Indeed, some would argue that the kinds of wars raging today do not lend themselves to control by a worldwide body, because these conflicts are now almost entirely civil wars. The UN was designed to manage interstate wars; it was not conceived as

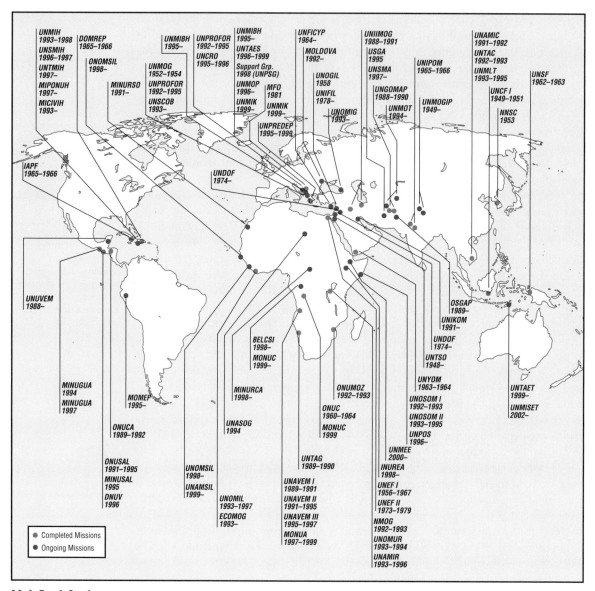

MAP 10.1

UN Peace Missions since 1948

In its first 40 years, only 13 UN peacekeeping missions were undertaken. But between 1986 and 2002 38 major new missions were launched, and as this map shows, UN peacekeepers were sent to flash points in nearly every region of the globe. Since 1989, in each year, on average, more than 15 peacekeeping operations have been active, with 17 underway at the start of 2003 (see figure at top right). As the figure below it on the right shows, since 1993 the number of military and civilian police participating in UN peacekeeping operations each month has averaged over 45,000 personnel from nearly all the UN's 191 members. The cost of keeping UN Blue Helmets in the world's trouble spots has climbed, but so have the budget deficits of members' arrears, compromising the capacity of the UN to carry out the missions the UN members have authorized. Sadly, the need is greatest now when the resources and commitments to global peacekeeping may be declining.

SOURCE: Based on data from the United Nations Department of Public Information.

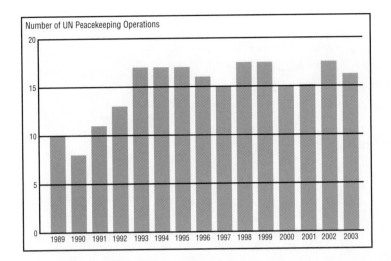

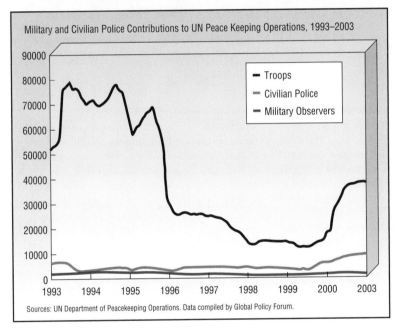

Sources: UN Department of Peacekeeping Operations. Data compiled by Global Policy Forum.

an instrument for dealing with battles inside sovereign borders. This, however, is not the case for regional institutions, who see their security interests vitally affected by armed conflicts within countries in their geographic areas. Hence, regional security organizations can be expected to play an increasingly larger role in the future security affairs of their regions.

The North Atlantic Treaty Organization (NATO) is the best-known regional security organization. Others include the Organization for Security and Cooperation in Europe (OSCE), the ANZUS pact (Australia, New Zealand, and the United States), and the Southeast Asia Treaty Organization (SEATO). Regional

Boris Grdanski/AP/Wide World Photos

The Interventionist Road to Peace? The chaos and killing in failed states provoke widespread concern, but until recently many states and IGOs have been reluctant to intervene militarily to keep the peace in civil wars outside their spheres of influence. NATO's 1999 humanitarian intervention in Kosovo is an exception—the first time that alliance used force "out of area." Here a British tank heading to the Kosovo border in June 1999 is greeted by Albanian Kosovars. The mission was supported by three hundred Eurocorps soldiers provided by the EU, made up largely of French and German officers, in what became the first mission of the EU's newly created Rapid Reaction Force of 60,000 soldiers. At its November 2002 Summit in Prague, NATO created its own rapid-reaction force "to fight anywhere in the world." Humanitarian military interventions could become frequent now that international law has relaxed traditional prohibitions against external interference in the internal affairs of an established state.

organizations with somewhat broader political mandates beyond defense include the Organization of American States (OAS), the League of Arab States, the Organization of African Unity (OAU), the Nordic Council, the Association of Southeast Asian Nations (ASEAN), and the Gulf Cooperation Council.

Although Article 51 of the UN Charter encourages the creation of regional organizations for collective self-defense, it would be misleading to describe NATO and the other regional organizations as a substitute collective security instrument for the UN. They are not. More accurately, regional **collective defense** systems are designed to deter a potential common threat to the region's peace, one typically identified in advance.

Many of today's regional security organizations face the challenge of preserving consensus and solidarity without a clearly identifiable external enemy or

• **collective defense**
a military organization within a specific region created to protect its members from external attack.

common threat. Cohesion is hard to maintain in the absence of a clear sense of mission. Consider NATO, which faces a European security setting marked by ethnopolitical conflicts. NATO's original charter envisioned only one purpose—mutual self-protection from external attack by the Soviet Union; it never defined policing civil wars as a goal. Consequently, until 1995, when NATO took charge of all military operations in Bosnia-Herzegovina from the UN, it was uncertain whether the alliance would survive long beyond the demise of the Soviet Union. Since then, NATO has redefined itself, and in March 1999 it took on a new peacemaking assignment in Kosovo. Today, NATO is an enlarged alliance, with seven new members joining in 2002, and has transformed itself to become both a *military* alliance for enhancing the security of its members and a *political* alliance for encouraging the spread of democracy.

From the philosopher Immanuel Kant onward, liberal theorists have argued that democratization enhances the prospects for peace between states. As discussed in earlier chapters, a growing body of research supports their argument. Constitutionally secure democracies rarely (if ever) make war on one another, and they form the most durable, peaceful leagues (Weart 1994; see also Mandelbaum 2003). This lesson is not lost on the leaders of today's democratic states searching for a principle on which to ground their security policies. NATO and the European Union have insisted on democracy as a condition for membership. Major international organizations from the World Bank to the International Monetary Fund have also made the promotion of democracy a policy priority. Since democratic states have a greater propensity than other types of states to employ amicable, legally binding methods of conflict resolution (Dixon 1994; Raymond 1994), liberals contend that enlarging the community of democracies will exert a pacifying effect on world politics.

Liberal Institutions and the Global Future

Since antiquity, the world has pursued two primary paths to peace. The realist road emphasizes military solutions; the liberal road emphasizes political solutions. This chapter has examined the principal approaches to the control of armed conflict from the liberal theoretical tradition: international law and organization.

Liberals who focus on international law and organization see armed conflict as deriving from deeply rooted institutional deficiencies. They believe weak international institutions make humankind's security subservient to the parochial interests of competing, egoistic states. To change this, they advocate legal and organizational methods to reduce the impact of anarchy on world affairs. For them, the major security problems of our day simultaneously affect many states. Terrorists with global reach, refugees fleeing horrific civil wars, and the proliferation of weapons of mass destruction exemplify these problems. National borders cannot insulate states from security threats lurking over the horizon. Nor can states manage them unilaterally. According to some liberal theorists, the dangers facing humanity are so grave that they require solutions beyond the nation-state.

World Government

If the anarchic state system is a major obstacle to peace, then one possible solution to the problem of war is a world government. The idea is not new. During the early fourteenth century, for example, the Italian poet Dante responded to incessant fighting among the states of his day by proposing that power be centralized in the hands of a universal monarch. While proposals for a world monarchy are rare today, it is not unusual to hear calls for **world federalism;** that is, incorporating previously sovereign states into a single union.

• **world federalism**
a reform movement proposing to combine sovereign states into a single unified federal state.

Federalists reason that if people value humanity's survival in an era of weapons of mass destruction, they will willingly transfer their loyalty to a supranational authority and dismantle the anarchic system of competitive territorial states. Agreeing with Albert Einstein, they argue that "there is no salvation for civilization, or even the human race, other than the creation of a world government." From their point of view, world government is inevitable. Just as city-states were superseded by nation-states, they assume that nation-states will someday be amalgamated into a world-state (Ferencz and Keyes 1991).

It is not surprising that ardent nationalists have vehemently attacked the federalist "top-down" peace plan. Because it seeks to subvert the system of sovereign states, the plan threatens many entrenched interests. Other critics reject the notion that eliminating nation-states will end warfare. Civil wars, such as the one that ravaged the United States between 1861 and 1865, can erupt under a world government. Still other critics fear that such a global political entity would be unresponsive to the local needs of the diverse indigenous cultures that comprise humanity. In sum, aversion to war has not mobilized widespread grassroots enthusiasm for creating a world government. Regional approaches to reforming the world politics have attracted far more adherents.

Regional Integration

• **political integration** the processes and activities by which the populations of two or more states transfer their loyalties to a merged political and economic unit.

While the merging of sovereign states into a world government is unlikely in the foreseeable future, integration is occurring in certain regions of the world. **Political integration** refers to the process of building new political communities that transcend the nation-state. Advocates of political integration seek reform programs that transform international institutions from instruments *of* states to structures *over* them.

• **functionalism** a theory of political integration based on the assumption that technical cooperation among different nationalities in economic and social fields will build communities that transcend sovereign states.

The Functionalist Approach to Integration. In contrast to federalism, **functionalism** is not directed toward creating a world federal government with all its constitutional paraphernalia. Instead, it calls for a "bottom-up," evolutionary strategy based on using specialized technical agencies that solve problems that cross national borders. The Rhine River Commission (1804), the Danube River Commission (1857), the International Telegraphic Union (1865), and the Universal Post Union (1874), were forerunners of these agencies. They were early attempts at crafting administrative units that conformed to the geography of a transnational problem rather than the boundaries of a particular state.

According to functionalists, technical experts, rather than professional diplomats, are the best agents for building collaborative links among people living in separate states. They see diplomats as being overly protective of their country's national interests at the expense of collective human interests. Rather than addressing the immediate sources of national insecurity, the functionalists' peace plan calls for transnational cooperation in technical areas as a first step. Habits of cooperation learned in one technical area (such as transportation), they suggest, will **spill over** into others (such as communication)—especially if the experience is mutually beneficial and demonstrates the potential advantages of further cooperation.

To enhance the probability that cooperative endeavors will prove rewarding, the functionalist plan recommends that less-difficult tasks be tackled first. It assumes that successful mastering of a relatively simple problem will encourage working on other more demanding problems collaboratively. If the process continues unabated, the bonds among people living in different countries will multiply, because no government would oppose a web of functional organizations that provide such clear-cut benefits to its citizens (Mitrany 1966).

Critics charge that as a theory of peace and world order, functionalism does not take into account some important political realities. First, they question its underlying assumption about the causes of war. Functionalism argues that poverty and other socioeconomic woes create frustration, anger, and ultimately war. Critics counter that war may instead cause poverty and other miseries. Addressing issues of poverty may not alleviate war, they also argue, especially if the rapid acquisition of wealth enables dissatisfied states to build armies for war.

Second, functionalism assumes that political differences among countries will be dissolved through the habits of cooperation learned by experts organized transnationally to cope with technical problems such as transportation or telecommunication. The reality, say critics, is that technical cooperation is often more strongly influenced by politics than the other way around. The U.S. withdrawal in the 1980s from the International Labor Organization (ILO) and the UN Educational, Scientific, and Cultural Organization (UNESCO) because Washington felt that those IGOs were too politicized illustrate this charge.

As skeptics conclude, functionalists are naive to argue that technical (functional) undertakings and political affairs can be separated. If technical cooperation becomes as important to state welfare as the functionalists argue, states will assume an active role in technical developments. Welfare and power cannot be separated, because the solution of economic and social problems cannot be divorced from political considerations. The expansion of transnational institutions' authority and competency at the expense of national governments and state sovereignty is, therefore, unlikely.

These criticisms led to the emergence of a second wave of functionalist theorizing, known as **neofunctionalism**. It argues that growing economic interdependence among states requires closer political coordination, which ultimately will lead to greater political integration. In other words, political integration occurs not simply because of pressures to address common technical problems more efficiently; it comes about when the interests of different

• **spill over** the propensity for successful integration across one area of cooperation between states to propel further integration in other areas.

• **neofunctionalism** a revised functionalist theory asserting that the IGOs states create to manage common problems provide benefits that exert pressures for further political integration.

pressure groups, political parties, and government officials converge on a greater role for supranational institutions.

The Neofunctional Approach to Integration. Europe provides the best example of how a group of independent nation-states can become an integrated political community along the lines suggested by neofunctional thinking. In 2004, the European Union (EU) added 10 more countries to its 15-country organization and agreed on a constitution treaty, which must be ratified by all 25 member-country parliaments within two years to take effect. This enlargement created the world's biggest free-trade area, bringing together under a single administrative umbrella over 450 million people (see Chapter 6).

In order to speak with one voice and act in unison on security issues, the EU adopted a Common Foreign and Security Policy (CFSP), which defined as the EU's objectives safeguarding "the common values, fundamental interests, and independence of the Union," strengthening the EU's security, preserving "world peace and international security [as well as promoting] international cooperation to develop and consolidate democracy and the rule of law, and respect for human rights and fundamental freedoms." To fulfill these goals, at the 2001 Nice Summit, the EU established the European Rapid Reaction Force, seen by its founders as a preliminary step toward becoming a military presence on the world stage capable of unilateral action. According to the officials assembled at Nice, this 60,000-strong military force would enable the EU to reduce its dependence on the United States and NATO.

The political unification of Europe represents an enormous achievement, overturning a past of chronic suspicion and warfare. The sovereign state in Europe has lost ground, as "a serious sense of European citizenship, along with the rights that go with it, seems to be laying the basis of a supranational identity" (Cohen, B. 2000), though ratifying the new constitution treaty promises to be a long, difficult process. Britain, Ireland, and Denmark have promised to hold referendums on the document, and several other countries are leaning in the same direction. The outcome of this process remains uncertain. Whereas Irish prime minister Bertie Ahern called the constitution treaty "a great achievement for Europe," Robert Kilroy-Silk, the leader of Britain's Independence Party, called it "the beginning of the end of Britain as a nation-state governing itself" (*International Herald Tribune*, June 21, 2004). High hopes for European integration thus exist alongside fears over the loss of national sovereignty.

European institution building nonetheless has served as a model for integration in other regions, including Africa, Asia, the Caribbean, and South America. However, current evidence suggests that the factors promoting successful integration efforts are many and their mixture complex. It is not enough that two or more countries choose to interact cooperatively. Research indicates that chances of political integration wane without geographical proximity, steady economic growth, similar political systems, supportive public opinion led by enthusiastic leaders, cultural homogeneity, internal political stability, similar experiences in historical and internal social development, compatible economic systems with supportive business interests, a shared perception of a common external threat, bureaucratic compatibilities, and previous collaborative efforts (Cobb and Elder

1970; Deutsch 1957). While not all of these conditions must be present for integration to occur, the absence of more than a few considerably reduces the chances of success. The integration of two or more societies—let alone entire world regions—is, in short, not easily accomplished. Europe's experience indicates that even when conditions are favorable there is no guarantee that integration will proceed automatically.

The substantial difficulty that most regions have experienced in achieving a level of institution building similar to that of the EU suggests the enormity of the obstacles to creating new political communities out of previously divided ones. Even parts of Europe have splintered rather than integrated. In 1991, for example, the Soviet Union shattered into 15 countries. Since then, five additional states have been created from the former Yugoslavia. Between 1990 and 1998, the global rate of new-country creation as a consequence of civil wars was 3.1 new countries each year (Enriquez 1999, 30).

Disintegration of many of the world's 207 currently separate states could multiply the number of independent countries to as many as 500 by the year 2025, according to UN estimates. With fewer than 25 countries ethnically homogeneous and with 3,000–5,000 indigenous peoples interested in securing sovereign homelands, the prospects are high that political disintegration will continue. This division of the globe into more and more smaller states could be slowed if existing states accepted **devolution** (the granting of greater political power to quasi-autonomous regions), as some central governments have done for the purpose of containing separatist revolts. However, in many states where governmental institutions are fragile, the leadership has repressed the minority peoples seeking to share power. About a third of the world's countries contain restless, politically repressed minorities struggling at various levels for human rights and independence (see Allen 2002, 33; Gurr, 2001). Within such countries, uneven growth rates and vast income inequalities between different groups could easily destabilize the political landscape.

In conclusion, contemporary global affairs are being shaped by centripetal and centrifugal pressures. At the same time that unifying forces are pulling some of the planet's inhabitants together, fragmenting forces are pushing others apart. The paradox of twenty-first-century world politics is that political integration and disintegration are occurring simultaneously.

• **devolution** granting political power to ethnopolitical groups within a state under the expectation that greater autonomy for them in particular regions will curtail their quest for independence.

Chapter Summary

- The field of international law is composed of private and public international law. The former pertains to the regulation of transnational activities among individuals and other nongovernmental actors; the latter, to the relations among sovereign states.
- Nearly every legal tenet of public international law supports the principle that sovereign states are the primary actors in world politics. The major rights of states include self-defense, independence and legal equality. The major duties are nonintervention and upholding the commitments that they voluntarily make.

- Although public international law lacks a central authority for punishing violators, states value international law because it performs an important communication function. By communicating the "rules of the game" in world politics, international law helps shape expectations, reduce uncertainty, and enhance predictability.

- For centuries, philosophers, religious leaders, and legal scholars have debated over when it is morally justifiable to go to war and how wars should be conducted. Just war doctrine emphasizes the need for the cause to be just; for the fighting to be undertaken for the right intention, exhausting all other means of resolving the conflict before issuing a public declaration of war; and for using force in a way that discriminates between legitimate and illegitimate targets, causes no more destruction than necessary, and is not undertaken in a futile effort.

- Collective security is often viewed as an alternative to the balance of power as a method for preserving peace. It calls for all states to join a universal organization, pledge to punish aggressors, and resolve their disagreements through pacific means.

- While the architects of the United Nations voiced support for the ideal of collective security, conflict in the Security Council between the United States and the Soviet Union during the Cold War prevented the UN from attaining many of the ideals envisioned by its founders. As a result, the UN has employed a variety of other means to help promote peace, including preventive diplomacy, peacemaking, and peace-building.

- Because the liberal tradition in statecraft sees the anarchic structure of the state system as one of the most important causes of war, many liberal theorists have proposed that the political integration of previously sovereign states might dampen the prospects for war. Whereas some theorists have advocated world federalism as a solution to war, most place greater emphasis on regional integration, though they disagree on how to incorporate independent nation-states into a greater political whole. The European Union is the foremost example of regional integration.

KEY TERMS

collective defense
collective security
devolution
diplomatic recognition
functionalism
just war doctrine
military necessity

neofunctionalism
nonintervention
peace-building
peacemaking
political integration
preventive diplomacy

private international law
public international law
reprisal
spill over
war crimes
world federalism

WHERE ON THE WORLD WIDE WEB?

Carnegie Council on Ethics and International Affairs
http://www.cceia.org/

An excellent inventory of global issues, with Point of View commentary links to other websites dealing with each issue.

The International Court of Justice
http://www.icj-cij.org/

The International Court of Justice (ICJ) is the principal judicial organ of the United Nations. Examine the court's statute to find out who can bring cases before the court. Then, read the biographies of the court's 15 members. Finally, access the Decisions link to examine some of the ICJ's contentious cases.

Multilaterals Project
http://www.tufts.edu/fletcher/multilaterals.html

The Fletcher School of Law and Diplomacy makes available the texts of international multilateral conventions and other instruments. It has a searchable database as well as a list of conventions organized by subject, such as the rules of warfare, the environment, cultural protection, or biodiversity. You can also view the Treaty of Westphalia and the League of Nations covenant. For thorough historical background on a subject, read the documents chronologically.

United Nations Peacekeeping Operations
http://www.un.org/Depts/dpko/dpko/home.shtml

The United Nations has deployed numerous international military and civilian personnel to stop or contain hostilities and supervise the carrying out of peace agreements. Click on an ongoing mission and read about the profile, background, and facts and figures concerning the mission. Do the same thing for an older mission. Are there any similarities or differences?

INFOTRAC® COLLEGE EDITION

Search for the following articles in the InfoTrac College Edition database.

Johnson, James Turner. "The Broken Tradition (Just-War Doctrine)," *The National Interest* Fall 1996.

Schwebel, Stephen M., and Dietmar Prager. "The International Court of Justice: As a Partner in Preventive Diplomacy," *UN Chronicle* Summer 1999.

Tucker, Robert W. "The International Criminal Court Controversy," World Policy Journal Summer 2001.

For more articles, enter:

"just war doctrine" in the Subject Guide.

"International Court of Justice" in the Subject Guide.

"international law" in the Subject Guide, and then go to subdivision " evaluation."

ADDITIONAL CD-ROM RESOURCES

Click on International Law and Organization for additional resources related to this chapter.

The Politics of Global Welfare

What factors most affect the welfare of humanity? World politics may be played out on a large stage, but with the expansion of international communication and commerce, a new era of globalization has arisen, knitting the world into a tight web of interdependence. Money, goods, and people travel across national borders at an accelerating pace. To an increasing extent, what happens in one part of the globe influences what happens elsewhere.

The chapters that follow draw attention to "human security"—the welfare of peoples of the world—and the ways that state-to-state relations and global institutions are transforming humanity's living standards and future prospects. Part IV of *The Global Future* begins by looking at the ways globalization is transforming everyday life (Chapter 11), and then analyzes how changes in international trade and monetary affairs affect world politics (Chapter 12). After exploring the international political economy, the topics of human rights (Chapter 13) and the relationship between population demographics and the earth's ecological system (Chapter 14) are examined.

The Globalization of World Politics

What is globalization? The short answer is that globalization is the integration of everything with everything else. A more complete definition is that globalization is the integration of markets, finance, and technology in a way that shrinks the world from a size medium to a size small. Globalization enables each of us, wherever we live, to reach around the world farther, faster, deeper, and cheaper than ever before and at the same time allows the world to reach into each of us farther, faster, deeper, and cheaper than ever before.

THOMAS FRIEDMAN, journalist

I n the early summer of 2004, Zilog Incorporated closed its manufacturing facilities in southwestern Idaho after a quarter century of operations. Headquartered in San Jose, California, Zilog concentrates on the micro-logic device segment of the semiconductor market, designing and producing devices used in embedded control. Although the firm had design centers in several locations, the Idaho facilities were the firm's only manufacturing plants. With their closure, 150 workers became unemployed. According to company executives, the intention was to convert Zilog into a "fabless" semiconductor company; that is to say, Zilog would continue to design microcontrollers, but would contract with firms in Asia to fabricate them (*Idaho Statesman,* June 20, 2004, B2).

Zilog's decision is an example of offshore outsourcing—subcontracting a business function to a foreign supplier (Drezner 2004). More than 3.3 million U.S. jobs are projected to be lost to outsourcing by 2015, and 14 million (11 percent of the U.S. total) have been identified as at risk of being sent overseas (*Time,* March 1, 2004, 33). In addition to affecting manufacturing, offshore outsourcing also has an impact on jobs in the fields of information technology, document management, customer service, and financial operations. Fearing a growth in unemployment (even in high-tech industries once thought immune to competition from low-cost foreign labor), critics of outsourcing have vehemently condemned corporate executives for "exporting" American jobs.

Yet at the same time that American jobs are moving abroad, new jobs are arriving as foreign firms outsource some of their jobs to the United States. According to the Bureau of Labor Statistics, the number of these jobs increased from 2.5 million in 1983 to 6.5 million in 2000. What in the world is going on? The answer: **globalization.** Money, goods, people, and information are moving across national borders at an accelerating pace, linking societies in ways that are transforming world politics. This interconnectedness creates both possibilities and problems. On the one hand, globalization is generating unprecedented levels of wealth as many firms streamline their operations and discover new overseas markets for their products. On the other hand, it is producing enormous social strain as displaced workers often cannot replace their lost incomes, even when they retrain in a different industry or move to another location. It is understandable, therefore, that the effects of globalization are controversial.

In this chapter we will examine the diverse forces driving the process of globalization. In particular, we will look at the growth of worldwide telecommunication, the increased mobility of capital, labor, goods, and services, and the burgeoning number of new problems that cross national borders. As we consider these issues, it is important to think about the prospects for the continuation of states as sovereign and independent actors. But before inspecting globalization's consequences, we must first examine its causes.

• **globalization** a set of processes that are widening, deepening, and accelerating the interconnectedness among societies.

Saleh RiFai/AP/Wide World Photos

The First McDonald's Franchise Opens in Lebanon

What Is Globalization?

Until the fifteenth century, most civilizations remained relatively isolated from one another. Circumscribed by slow, costly, and often dangerous transportation routes, international intercourse tended to occur within self-contained regions of the world. Except for intermittent trade, occasional waves of migrants, and periodic clashes with invaders, contact with distant peoples was rare.

What distinguishes contemporary world politics from earlier eras is its global scope. Various processes are the widening, deepening, and accelerating worldwide interconnectedness. Rapid, unrestrained communication is perhaps the most significant of these processes. Indeed, many see it as the foundation of an emerging **global village**—a metaphor used by futurologists to portray a world in which borders vanish and people become a single community.

• **global village** a popular image used to describe the growth of awareness that all people share a common fate, stemming from a view that the world is an integrated and interdependent whole.

The Global Information Age

The decline in the importance of geographic distance as a determinant of the cost of communication has been described as perhaps the single most important economic force shaping societies in the first half of the twenty-first century. According to *The Economist* (September 30, 1995, 5–6), "It will alter, in ways that are only dimly imaginable, decisions about where people live and work; concepts of

Sally Wiener Grotta/The Stock Market/CORBIS

The World at One's Fingertips The revolution in telecommunications has contributed to "the death of distance," as virtually instantaneous communications are possible nearly everywhere. Here, in a remote and desolate region of northern Kenya, a Samburu warrior makes a call on his cellular telephone.

national borders; patterns of international trade. Its effects will be as pervasive as those of the discovery of electricity."

The wireless world of cellular phones are becoming available worldwide, enabling many in the world, who have never before made a phone call, to communicate instantly with others. Computers are another potent agent of global communication, with use of the Internet growing from less than 100,000 Internet hosts in 1988 to more than 172 million hosts connecting 689 million people in 2002 (*U.S. News & World Report,* April 22, 2002, 69). Most experts estimate that the Internet will grow by at least 50 percent each year, with the number of web pages increasing nine times faster than world population (Aronson 2001, 545, 547). "Today, one of every twelve people goes online to get news, send e-mail, buy goods, or be entertained" (*Vital Signs 2002,* 82).

Although the entire world is becoming connected, it is happening at different rates: Only one in five Internet users lives in the Global South (*Vital Signs 2002,* 82).

Moreover, the Internet has not liberated most people from their technological dependence on the places in the Global North where the management of most websites is located. Therefore, even if the Internet has made for the worldwide hypermobility of ideas and information, it has contributed to the "soft power" resources of Global North countries. This is especially evident with respect to global e-commerce. "Something like three-quarters of all e-commerce currently takes place in the United States. The country also accounts for 90 percent of commercial websites. Given that the Internet is, by its very nature, global in reach, these two facts raise a vital question about e-commerce for the rest of the world: Is America in general, and are American websites in particular, inevitably going to dominate it?" (*The Economist,* February 26, 2000, 49).

Although some people see the communications revolution as a leveling factor that empowers nongovernmental organizations (NGOs) to organize previously unheard voices into a new lobbying force, critics warn that it is widening the gap between rich and poor. As shown in Figure 11.1, use of the Internet is heavily concentrated in the Global North. Thus its effects remain uneven, benefitting some privileged countries while putting the rest at a great disadvantage. The result is a vast **digital divide**, where one-third of the world's 6 billion people lack access to modern information and communications technology.

• **digital divide** the division between those states that have a high proportion of Internet users and hosts, and those that do not.

Nevertheless, the communications revolution holds great promise for the Global South, since modern information technology may allow poorer countries to "leap frog" technologies in which the Global North invested heavily as it developed economically. Inexpensive wireless phones, for example, enjoy both popularity and promise in many Global South countries, where the cost of stringing line from pole to pole for traditional wired phones is often prohibitive. As programming makes each generation of new software easier to use, the digital divide may gradually close (Samuelson 2002a). But because the social, economic, and geographic factors that created the digital divide are complex, narrowing it will prove difficult. The Global North remains at present the primary beneficiary of the communications revolution. In particular "the United States, where the Internet was developed, continues to dominate this electronic network. About a third of all people online are American" (*Vital Signs 2002,* 82). Consequently, many countries fear that America's technological and information edge will enable it to dominate the global future.

Globalization or Americanization?

Ours is often described as the information age, but a remarkably large portion of the information we receive is controlled by a small number of media sources. In the United States, despite more than 25,000 media outlets, only "twenty-three corporations control most of the business in daily newspapers, magazines, television, books, and motion pictures" (Bagdikian 1992, 4). And as corporate America merges its media sources into ever larger and fewer units—as witnessed in Disney Corporation's buyout of the ABC broadcasting network, as well as Viacom's acquisition of the CBS broadcasting network and the giant spread of Verizon Communications—fewer and fewer corporate executives will control what Americans hear and see about the world around them. Although thousands of

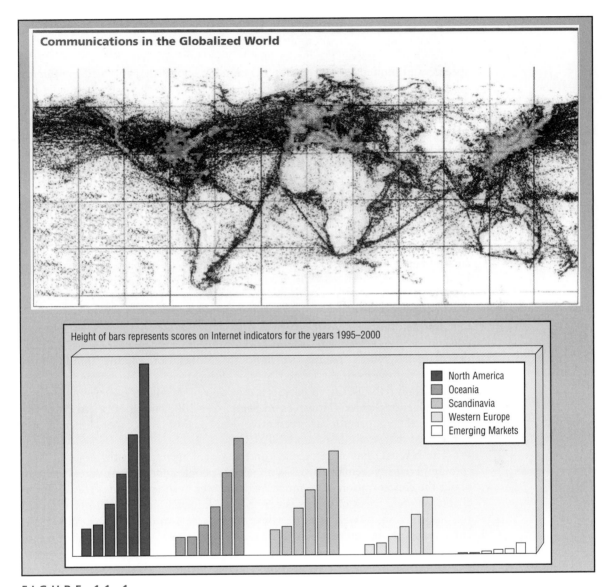

FIGURE 11.1
The Digital Divide

International communications may be creating a global village, but the rate at which information is transferring is uneven in different regions. This figure shows the density with which communications occur in the world and illustrates what is meant by the so-called digital divide, the division of the technological "haves" in the Global North and the technological "have-nots" in the Global South. Note that the highest density of flows is shown in the darker shading across North America, Europe, and Northeast Asia. Bottom: Adapted from *Foreign Policy,* Jan/Feb 2002, p. 50. © 2002 *Foreign Policy,* www.foreignpolicy.com, reprinted with permission.
SOURCE: Flanagan, Frost, and Kugler, 2001, p. 24.

potential sources of information about politics, society, and culture are available, the influence of such media midgets is negligible compared to that of the giants.

The type of power the media wields over international affairs is, in fact, a specific and limited type of power. Scholarship shows that the media influence what people *think about* more than what they *think*. In this way, the media primarily functions to set the agenda of public discussion about current affairs instead of determining public opinion. In the process of **agenda setting** the media shapes international public policy. For example, many national leaders have grumbled about a "CNN-effect," the alleged capacity of round-the-clock news services to highlight certain issues by immediately televising heart-wrenching scenes of famine, atrocities, and other human tragedies to millions of viewers throughout the world. When combined with the use of electronic mail by grassroots activists to mobilize people around the world quickly on a particular issue, governments may find that these issues cannot be ignored.

• **agenda setting** the ability to influence which issues receive attention from governments and international organizations by giving them publicity.

Control of television and other media sources by the United States and a small number of European countries became the focus of a hot dispute with the Global South during the 1980s. Dissatisfied with the media coverage it received from western news agencies, leaders in developing countries demanded a New World Information and Communication Order (NWICO). The flow of images and information from North to South, they insisted, fostered Northern values of consumerism and conspicuous consumption that perpetuated the South's dependence on the North. As the North-South conflict brewed, the United States angrily withdrew from the United Nations Educational, Scientific, and Cultural Organization (UNESCO), in part as a rejection of its role in promoting the new communications order. (However, in September 2002, in an effort to galvanize multilateral support for a preemptive war against Iraq, the United States announced that it would rejoin UNESCO.)

The NWICO has since receded on the global agenda, but the issue of "cultural imperialism" remains alive as numerous people continue to express concern about the concentration of so much media power in so few hands. The ability to shape the preferences of others is easier in an Information Age. Those who control information, as well as those who control access to information, have clear-cut advantages in international bargaining over those whose major source of influence is confined to threatening sanctions. The popularity of the Al Jazeera network in the Middle East illustrates the interest in the Global South for alternatives to the western media, which is often seen as giving a biased, inaccurate portrayal of Southern concerns.

The Economics of Globalization

When the nation-state emerged in seventeenth-century Europe as the primary actor on the world stage, many national leaders sought to increase their power by acquiring territory. Aside from land that held precious metals or offered access to navigable waterways, the most valuable territory in an age without refrigeration contained cereal grains, an easily transported and stored source of food with sufficient nutrition to sustain farmers as well as people not engaged in agriculture.

Opportunity Lost? Globalization has transformed world production and employment patterns, moving both manufacturing and jobs across borders in response to the changing perceptions of investment opportunities held by multinational corporations. Some European companies have moved production to Brazil. Many workers in the Global North fear that manufacturing jobs are moving to Global South countries where production is inexpensive. Globalization often wreaks havoc on local economies and leads to protests against the economic volatility it engenders, as shown here in Brazil.

With the onset of the Industrial Revolution, physical capital (machinery, equipment, buildings, etc.) increased in value as a factor of production, although the demand for coal, iron ore, and later oil continued to underscore the importance of land. Only after World War II did some states shift their emphasis from territorial expansion through military conquest to international commerce. These "trading states" recognized that exporting manufactured goods could fuel economic growth (Rosecrance 1986). Soon they realized that exporting was only one path to prosperity; products could be designed at home but made abroad for both foreign and domestic markets. Rather than goods and services being produced by and for people living within a single territorial state, they are now increasingly produced by people working in different regions of the world for a global marketplace. We are entering an era where traditional territorial distinctions will be less important than the financial and managerial skills to create products, provide services, and control assets globally (Rosecrance 1999).

The Globalization of Trade

After World War II, the victors in that long, debilitating struggle believed that they could stimulate economic growth by removing barriers to international trade. As we have seen in Chapter 6, under the auspices of the General Agreement on Tariffs and Trade (GATT), the so-called "Geneva Round" of negotiations in 1947 reduced **tariffs** by 35 percent. Successive rounds of negotiations in the 1950s, 1960s (the Kennedy Round), 1970s (Tokyo Round), and the 1980s and 1990s (Uruguay Round) virtually eliminated tariffs on manufactured goods.

• **tariff** a tax imposed by governments on imported goods.

• nontariff barrier governmental restrictions not involving a tax or duty that increase the cost of importing goods into a country.

• trade integration economic globalization measured by the extent to which world trade volume grows faster than the world's combined gross domestic product.

The World Trade Organization (WTO), which succeeded GATT in 1994 and enlarged its membership (see Map 11.1), is currently engaged in reducing **nontariff barriers** to international trade (IMF 1997, 113).

The reduction of tariff rates has permitted international trade and world economic output to grow hand in hand. Since the founding of GATT, "the world economy has grown six-fold, in part because trade has expanded sixteen-fold" (Micklethwait and Wooldrige 2001, 22). The impact of the rising volume of goods shipped from one country to another has been enormous, making trade increasingly important to all states.

Trade integration is the measure of the extent to which the growth rate in world trade increases faster than does the growth rate of world gross domestic product. As trade integration grows, so does globalization, because states' interdependence grows when countries' exports account for an increasing percentage of their gross

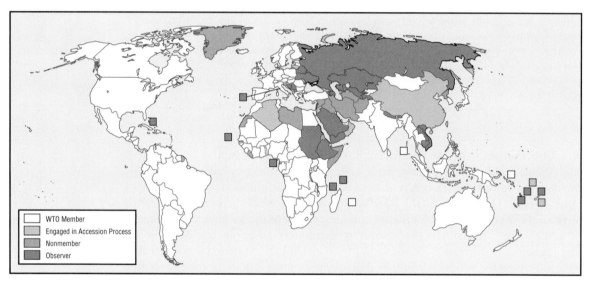

Legend:
- WTO Member
- Engaged in Accession Process
- Nonmember
- Observer

MAP 11.1
The World Trade Organization Goes Global

Click on International Political Economy to access an interactive version of this map and related critical thinking questions.

As of the end of 2002, almost every state has become a member of the World Trade Organization, whose purpose is to promote free trade throughout the globe. 147 countries are now official members; 30 additional countries are "observers" who must begin accession negotiations within five years if they are to gain formal membership. If and when these states join, the volume of international trade will climb, contributing further to the integration of the world marketplace. Why states seek to join the WTO is a puzzle to those who see it as undermining states' sovereign independence. But they overlook the fact that by its rules the WTO is an intergovernmental rather than supranational IGO ruled by consensus. As the WTO is fond of saying, far from being antidemocratic it is "hyperdemocratic," because each and every one of the WTOs has a veto over the rules. The WTO acts as a mere referee when members face trade disputes. In addition, the WTO has few resources. With a staff of only 530 and a budget of $78 million (about one-half of what the World Bank spends on travel), the WTO is a midget in the world of nonstate actors. As WTO Director Mike Moore pointed out in 2001, the World Wildlife Fund has three times the financial budget of the WTO.
SOURCE: World Trade Organization.

domestic product (GDP). As Michael Mazarr (1999) explains, "Measuring global trade as a percentage of GDP is perhaps the simplest and most straightforward measure of globalization. If trade in goods and merchandise is growing faster than the world economy as a whole, then it is becoming more integrated."

Figure 11.2 documents the remarkable speed at which trade integration has progressed between 1971 and 2004. Countries have become more interdependent, and the world increasingly globalized, because international trade has far outpaced growth in the world economy (and in world population as well). Of course, countries differ in the degree to which their economies have become integrated through trade in the global political economy (see Figure 11.3). The pace of trade integration has been higher in the Global South than in the Global North, reflecting the less-developed Global South's rising contribution to world trade and its mounting importance to economic prosperity in the Global North. Not only has the Global South's share of global trade grown (from 23 percent in 1985 to 28 percent in 2002), but its share of global exports in manufactured products has also grown (increasing from 10 percent in 1980 to 27 percent in 2002). In this context the Global South's growth in the share of *new* products for exports is especially impressive, though it is important to bear in mind that South

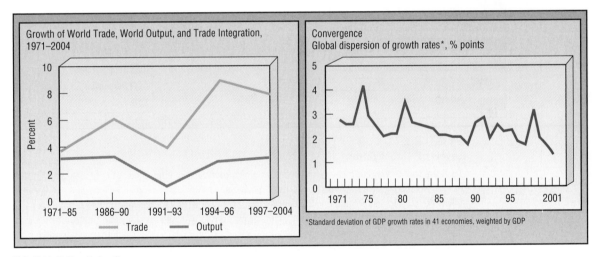

FIGURE 11.2

Trends in Global Trade Integration and the Mutual Interdependence of States' Economies

World economic transactions are more globalized than ever before, and the level of interdependence is growing at an accelerating rate. As the index of trends in world trade integration between 1971 and 2004 on the left shows, global trade has outpaced the rate of world output. The figure on the right measures the "convergence" of countries' economic fortunes, showing the growing extent to which growth rates across countries are tied to one another and can be "hit simultaneously by common global shocks" (*The Economist* September 28, 2002).

SOURCE: Trade integration, from *Global Trends 2005* by Michael J. Mazarr p. 160. Copyright © Michael J. Mazarr. Economic interdependence, from *The Economist,* Sept. 28, 2002. Copyright © 2002 by The Economist Newspaper Ltd. Reprinted with permission. Further reproduction prohibited. www.economist.com.

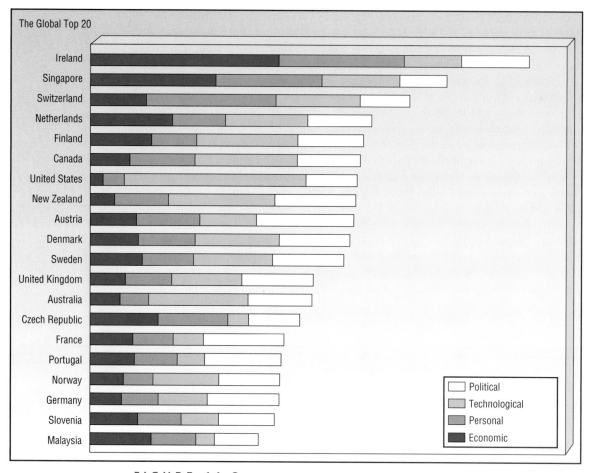

FIGURE 11.3
Levels of Globalization

There are various ways to measure the extent to which countries are integrated in the globalization of the world. This chart scales and ranks the 20 most globalized countries, based on an index that combines the following four factors: political engagement (number of memberships in international organizations, foreign embassies hosted, and UN Security Council missions in which the country participates); technology (number of Internet users, Internet hosts, and secure servers); personal contact (international travel and tourism, international telephone traffic, and cross-border transfers); and economic integration (trade, foreign investment and portfolio capital flows, and income payments and receipts).
SOURCE: A. T. Kearney (2004).

Korea, Singapore, Taiwan, Malaysia, Thailand, and India account for almost two-thirds of this new export trade.

A similar pattern may be emerging with regard to trade in services. Because the United States enjoys comparative advantages in this area, it has been a strong advocate of bringing services under the liberalizing rules of the WTO. Trade in services has already expanded more than threefold since 1980, with the Global North reaping most of the benefits. However, the spread of information technology, the ease with which new business software can be used, and the comparatively lower wage costs in developing economies are among the reasons why the World Bank predicts that developing countries will capture a greater share of world trade in services during the first two decades of the twenty-first century. Global South countries such as India, with significant numbers of educated, English-speaking citizens, are already operating call centers and consumer assistance hotlines for companies based in the Global North.

Selling products to another country often requires companies to establish a presence abroad, where they can produce goods and offer services. Traditionally the overseas operations of multinational corporations (MNCs) were "appendages" of a centralized hub. The pattern nowadays is to dismantle the hub by dispersing production facilities worldwide, which was made economically feasible by the revolutions in communication and transportation (including use of the standardized international shipping container). The sales of most large companies are now geared to the global market and a large proportion of their revenues are generated from sales outside the countries where they are headquartered. This globalization of production is transforming international economics, and MNCs are its primary agents. Some "53,000 multinational corporations and 450,000 foreign subsidiaries sell $9.5 trillion of goods and services across the globe every year. Multinational corporations account for at least 20 percent of world production and 70 percent of world trade" (Held et al., 1999, 135).

By forming **strategic corporate alliances** with companies in the same industry, and by merging with one another, many MNCs now rival nation-states in financial resources. These corporate networks pursue truly global strategies for financial gain, often through long-term supplier agreements and licensing and franchising contracts. Today, "about 70 percent of world trade is intra-industry or inter-firm" (Reinicke 1997). As they funnel large financial flows across national borders, these global corporate conglomerates are integrating national economies into a worldwide market.

• **strategic corporate alliances** cooperation between MNCs and foreign companies in the same industry, driven by the movement of MNC manufacturing overseas.

Among some of the most ardent advocates of globalization, the progressive integration of national economies into a single world marketplace is seen as a panacea for poverty. Such a view is inaccurate, however. Despite evidence that widening and deepening of international trade flows have been associated with economic growth, the distribution of these gains has not been uniform. As the *Human Development Report* of the UN Development Program (1997) observes: "A rising tide of wealth is supposed to lift all boats. But some are more seaworthy than others. The yachts and ocean liners are indeed rising in response to new opportunities, but the rafts and rowboats are taking on water—and some are sinking fast." Trade globalization, in other words, is creating winners and losers, both between and within countries. As a result, a backlash against these inequalities is developing among those groups that see themselves as victims of an integrated trade world (Broad 2002; Aaronson 2002).

The Globalization of Finance

Finance represents another important dimension of economic globalization. It encompasses "all types of cross-border portfolio-type transactions—borrowing and lending, trading of currencies or other monetary claims, and the provision of

Click on International Political Economy for an interactive case study on globalization and the Mexican Peso Crisis.

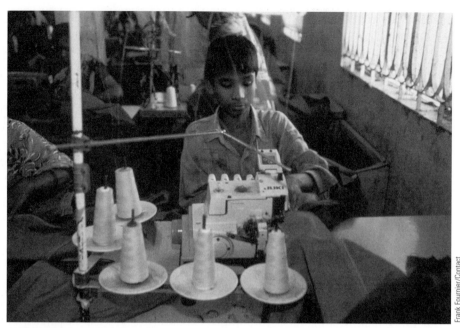

Frank Fournier/Contact

Child Labor in a Global Economy Globalization is sped not only by the rapid expansion of technology but by the availability of extremely low wages in some countries. Here a child labors in Bangladesh, producing goods that cost less than those made where unions protect workers. Such practices have mercantilist nationalists and free-trade critics up in arms, even though open global markets encourage them.

commercial banking or other financial services. It also includes capital flows associated with foreign direct investment—transactions involving significant control of producing enterprises" (Cohen, B. 1996). Evidence of financial globalization abounds. Since World War II, the volume of cross-border capital flows has increased dramatically, and now greatly exceeds the volume of trade. Similarly, cross-border transactions in bonds and equities have increased at an astonishing rate over the past 20 years. In the mid-1990s, "$1,300 billion (roughly the equivalent of the French annual GNP) were being exchanged daily, compared to $18 billion at the beginning of the 1970s" (Pfetsch 1999, 3). "Each day well over a trillion dollars flows around the world, exceeding the volume of trade by 60 times" (Eizenstat 1999, 6).

Further evidence of financial globalization can be seen in recent increases in the daily turnover on the foreign exchange market. On many days, private currency traders may exchange as much as $2 trillion to make profits through **arbitrage** on the basis of minute shifts in the value of states' currencies. "It has become a well-known fact that the daily turnover on the currency markets now often exceeds the global stock of official foreign exchange reserves" (*The Economist,* September 10, 1997). Such interconnected markets require more than ever a reliable system of money to conduct business across borders while coping with an array of fluctuating national currencies.

• **arbitrage** the selling of one currency (or product) and purchase of another to make a profit on the changing exchange rates; traders ("arbitragers") help to keep states' currencies in balance through their speculative efforts to buy large quantities of devalued currencies and sell them in countries where they are valued more highly.

As the market value of stock transactions increased fourfold between 1980 and 2002, the rise or fall in the security market of any one state began to immediately cause similar changes in other countries' stock indexes. "Derivatives" are one tool for managing risk by combining speculation in "options" and "futures" to hedge against volatility in financial markets. They are complex financial contracts whose value is determined from the prices or rates of other securities, but they require no actual purchase of stocks or bonds. Derivatives now account for trillions of dollars in crossborder transactions and are estimated to be the most globalized financial market. Automated online trading for equity sales on the Internet in the emerging digital world economy has lowered the costs and increased the volume of such crossborder exchanges.

The computerization of financial transactions and contracts occurred at the same time that state deregulation of global investments and capital movements gained acceptance. States reduced their authority by relaxing legal control over their economies and by opening their markets to foreign capital. The result has been an upsurge in international financial transactions. According to the **capital mobility hypothesis,** the free or unregulated flow of money across borders has produced the globalization of finance.

• **capital mobility hypothesis** the contention that MNCs' movement of investment capital has led to the globalization of finance.

Because the accelerating mobility of capital means that financial markets are no longer centered within states, the globalized financial system is not subject to regulation by any one state in particular. Most states are losing the capacity to control the flow and level of finance in their national economies. The globalization of finance has expanded the power of private markets and corporations no longer tied to any one country "thereby increasingly undermining state power itself" (Cerny 1994). As the globalization of finance has accelerated, the escalating mobility of capital has undermined the traditional realist assumption that states are autonomous, unitary actors capable of regulating their internal economic affairs.

The lightning speed of capital mobility has made national markets extremely volatile and vulnerable to sudden reversals caused by their dependence on foreign capital, which may flee at the first sign of economic trouble. Capital mobility is at historically high levels, but as Map 11.2 shows, it has some unintended consequences, affecting the developing countries of the Global South negatively, because the flow of capital has declined as the globalization of finance has risen. "Today's capital transactions seem to be 'mostly a rich-rich affair,' a process of 'diversification of finance' rather than 'development finance,' [note economists Maurice Obstfeld and Alan Taylor]. . . . In 1913, the countries at the bottom fifth of income per person received around 25 percent of the world stock of foreign capital. . . . By 1997, the poorest fifth's share was down to under 5 percent, compared with 36 percent for the richest fifth" (*The Economist,* May 18, 2002, 27).

Hence, the globalization of finance and "capital flight" have resulted in mounting inequalities. True, all countries are mutually vulnerable to rapid transfers of capital in an interdependent, globalized financial world. But the Global South is the most dependent and vulnerable. This circumstance suggests why bankers and economists have called for the creation of more reliable multilateral mechanisms for policy coordination to manage the massive crossborder flows of capital.

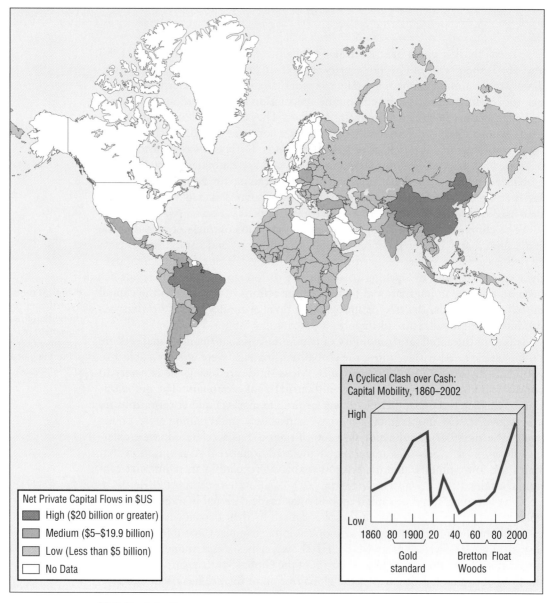

MAP 11.2

The International Flow of Finance Capital

Capital flows internationally through loans by commercial banks and private creditors and through foreign direct investments (FDI) in businesses located in countries different from those of the investors. The movement of capital across borders since the 1950s has expanded as shown in the figure (right) on transformations in capital mobility since 1860. In the globalized political economy the bulk of the money now lands in the rich Global North, and the forty-nine poorest Global South countries receive only 0.5 percent of the total even though their inflows have risen nearly ninefold since 1990 (*Economist,* May 19, 2001, 104). Note that, as we might expect, the wealthy Global North countries exert a disproportionate influence over the global flow of capital.

SOURCE: *Capital mobility figure—From *The Economist,* May 18, 2000, p. 27. Copyright © 2000 by The Economist Newspaper Ltd. All rights reserved. Reprinted with permission. Further reproduction prohibited. www.economist.com

The Challenges of a Borderless World

Thus far we have seen how technological advances in communication and transportation over the past few decades have fueled a series of far-reaching economic changes. The torrent of cross-border trade and financial flows now sweeping across the world raises the question of whether it is still meaningful to think of the nation-state as a basis for organizing economic activities. As globalization has ruptured one national frontier after the next, questions have also been asked as to whether the nation-state is the most effective problem-solving unit for addressing other challenges that face humanity. Three of the most important involve the impact of globalization on the environment, public health, and migration. In each instance, problems in one part of the world have had consequences for people living elsewhere.

Global Ecopolitics

Ever since the rise of the nation-state, political leaders have claimed sovereign rights over their territorial domain, viewing the use of land, water, and airspace as domestic matters. Although some environmental issues are purely local and can be addressed unilaterally, many span national boundaries and require multilateral action. For example, sulfur oxide emissions from industries in one country may fall as acid rain on a neighboring country. Greenhouse gas emissions (carbon dioxide, chlorofluorocarbons, methane, and nitrous oxide) from numerous countries may contribute to global climate warming, which could disrupt weather patterns across the planet and expose coastal lowlands everywhere to the threat of rising seas. The political world may be a checkerboard of sovereign states, but the natural world is a seamless web. Damage to the ecosystem often transcends national jurisdictions. Yet, as we shall see in Chapter 14, many states remain unwilling to relinquish or pool their sovereignty to forge new global institutions that could offer a more effective response to global environmental problems.

Global Health

Humankind and the threat of infectious disease have always coexisted uneasily. Population growth in the Global South has led many people to move into previously uninhabited regions, exposing them to new sources of disease. Moreover, their ability to travel from one continent to another makes it difficult to contain outbreaks to a single locale. Millions of airline travelers, for example, share cabin-sealed environments with passengers who might be infected with potentially fatal diseases. As recent outbreaks of West Nile disease and the illness known as Severe Acute Respiratory Syndrome (SARS) show, a mobile world population has made the spread of disease across borders rapid, frequent, and hard to control.

   The AIDS (acquired immune deficiency syndrome) epidemic has become a symbol for the spread of disease in a shrinking world. It is a global problem, with the number of people infected with HIV—the virus that causes AIDS—climbing to more than an estimated 60 million people. The number is expected to continue to rise even though new public health measures have begun to slow the growth rate in the Global North. AIDS strikes most virulently in the impoverished Global South among youthful wage earners who are the foundation of the labor force, but it undermines economic growth everywhere on the planet. The human toll from AIDS-related disease has been most severe in sub-Saharan Africa, where the disease accounts for three-quarters of the world's HIV infections and is the leading cause of death, cutting life expectancy almost in half. The virus is not confined to any one region, however; it travels throughout the world alongside the more than two million people who cross international borders daily.

Adding to the challenge of preventing infectious diseases is another problem brought on by rising globalization: "As a result of underuse of antibiotics in the developing world and overuse in the developed world, viruses are developing stronger strains that are able to overcome standard antibiotics." The World Health Organization reports that almost all infectious diseases are slowly becoming resistant to existing medicines. "Acute respiratory infections such as pneumonia kill a million more people each year than does AIDS. Diarrheal diseases, tuberculosis, malaria, and measles combined with AIDS and respiratory infections account for 90 percent of total infectious disease deaths worldwide" (Gilman and Gejdenson 2000, 6). And humans are not the only victims of so-called borderless diseases, as was made evident in 2001 when the contagious hoof-and-mouth disease swept through Europe killing livestock. As national leaders desperately tried to seal their frontiers to a virus that spread with frightening speed, many noted that such epidemics in the European Union were increasingly difficult to contain because borders between countries had all but dissolved and it had been years since anybody needed a passport to travel between most European countries.

Another unfortunate byproduct of globalization has been the spread of alien animal, plant, and insect species throughout the globe that are causing massive ecological destruction. As the World Conservation Union (an NGO that includes more than 78 states and over 10,000 scientists) warns, alien species that cross national borders aboard aircraft, ships, or other means of conveyance are doing irreparable damage to thousands of native species and, in the process, creating an enormous problem for the planet's environment and public health. In May 2001 the Union used World Biodiversity Day to heighten awareness of the threat posed by this invasion, which it labeled "among the costliest and least understood aspects of globalization," proclaiming "If this were an invasion from space, governments would be alarmed. But these are not extraterrestrials. They are ordinary animals, plants, and insects that have escaped from their normal environment to wreak havoc someplace else" (James 2001a).

Global Migration

The movement of populations across frontiers has reached unprecedented proportions. Nearly 20 million people in each year from 1998 to 2002 qualified for and received refugee assistance. "The ease of travel and communication, combined with looser borders, gives rise to endless crisscrossing streams of wanderers and guest workers, nomadic adventurers, and international drifters" (Hoffman 2000). Emigration has become routine in the global age, raising a host of political, economic, and social issues. The meaning of citizenship, the composition of the labor force, and the protection of minority rights are just a few of the issues large flows of migrants raise for host countries. Particularly troubling is the moral inconsistency between liberal democracies that simultaneously defend the fundamental right of refugees to emigrate and the absolute right of sovereign states to control their borders.

These environmental, health, and migration problems are representative of the kinds of challenges presented by globalization. Whether nation-states will be able to cope with them remains uncertain. Globalization is eroding state sovereignty, but it is not necessarily creating a global community.

Global Governance or Backlash?

Globalization, driven in large measure by technological revolutions, is likely to continue. Analysts differ over its consequences, depending in part on the political perspectives that inform their worldviews. Some analysts focus on the economic benefits of globalization; others, on its unevenness and the prospects for marginalizing large numbers of people. Some focus on the challenge globalization poses to an international system founded on the sovereign territorial state; others hope cooperation among state and nonstate actors will usher in a new era of global governance (see Controversy: Does Globalization Mean the End of the Age of Nation-States?). We can expect the controversies about globalization's alleged virtues and vices, benefits and costs, to heighten as finance, population, trade, labor, and culture continue to converge globally. While the revolutions in communication and transportation have overcome many of the physical barriers separating the world's people, some have gained and others have lost ground. The global village is not proving to be an equally hospitable home for everyone, and the losers are mounting a backlash.

The key question raised by this chapter concerns the role of the nation-state in the global future. A world of porous borders challenges all territorial states, rich and poor alike. Globalization reduces the capacity of states to exercise political power over the territory in which private-sector actors operate. Although some analysts believe this loss of control probably means that the "nation-state as an externally sovereign actor in the international system will become a thing of the past" (Reinicke 1997), most agree that the nation-state is not about to disappear. Although an erosion of sovereignty is underway, territorial states will still lay claim as the principal source of security and identity in most people's lives. Nevertheless, they will increasingly find themselves sharing the world stage with powerful nonstate actors. In short, we are moving away from a world dominated by a single type of actor and toward one composed of many qualitatively different types of actors.

What does this mean for humanity's ability to address the environmental, health, and other challenges raised by globalization? International regimes such as those that evolved after World War II to promote global governance in trade and monetary affairs may also prove effective in coping with borderless crises. Because "globalization implies that everyone and everything is more closely connected than ever before but on a foundation that is still shaky," a more effective

CONTROVERSY ## Does Globalization Mean the End of the Age of Nation-States?

What does globalization mean for the survival of the state? To some thinkers "it's the end of sovereignty [which] has seen the rise of the European state as the epitome of political organization" (Howell 1998). Still others believe that globalization is simply a new manifestation of old patterns, one that will "in many ways be viewed as a resumption of a trend observed in the world economy a century ago" (IMF 1997). Consider these differing opinions as you read the observations of journalist Neal R. Peirce, who attended the fiftieth Salzburg Seminar of global leaders in 1997 to contemplate the state's future in the face of globalization. Peirce issued this provocative summary of the debate, which provides a good framework for appraising rival ideas about globalization's causes, likely consequences, and probable impact on the survival of the nation-state.

Is the nation-state at the end of its 500-year run? Is it about to succumb to rapid-fire economic globalization, resurgent regions, or to ethnic and tribal rivalries?

Not entirely, say midcareer professionals from some 32 nations who came here in March [1997] to debate the nation-state's future at the elegant eighteenth-century palace that has been the site of the Salzburg Seminar for 50 years.

Whether from advanced or undeveloped, Western or Eastern nations, most participants agreed we'll still need nation-states to give people identity, raise taxes, provide social safety nets, protect the environment, and guarantee internal security.

But for a peek into the deep uncertainties of the twenty-first century and the astounding array of forces now undermining the nation-states, this conference was a remarkable tour de force.

Leading the parade of transformative change are globalization and its accomplices. The computer and telecommunications revolutions enable instant worldwide communications to create new relationships, new economics, whether central governments like them or not.

Multinational corporations now assemble goods from plants across the globe and have moved heavily into services, too—law, accounting, advertising, computer consultation—as if the world were borderless.

Financial markets are also globalized. Where nation-states once sought to set exchange rates, private traders now control currency flows—at a scarcely believable level of $1.3 trillion a day.

The nation-states fatefully shrank their own power by creating supranational institutions such as the United Nations, World Trade Organization and World Bank. Each creates its own cadres of civil servants unaccountable to any single state.

Now comes a rise of influential, globally active nongovernmental organizations—the NGOs—ranging from

architecture for global governance needs to be created (Garten 1999). As Klaus Schwab, president of the World Economic Forum, warned in 2002, multilateral cooperation and coordination are imperative in dealing with the challenges presented by globalization. Because stubborn problems continue to seep through the world's porous borders, many scholars contend that it is time to think seriously about sharing sovereignty. "To agree to share one's sovereignty is difficult," cautions Peter Sutherland, former director-general of the World Trade Organization; consequently "a genuine enhanced institutional sharing, or pooling of sovereignties is today the structural issue which has yet to be settled."

Can states and nonstate actors find a focal point, a norm, around which multilateral cooperation could coalesce? Liberal theorists, who emphasize mutual gains, are optimistic. Realists, who are concerned more with relative gains, remain pessimistic. Regardless of whether the optimists or pessimists are correct,

Greenpeace to Amnesty International to animal rights groups. They got official UN recognition at the Rio Earth Summit in 1992; now they're negotiating to get a voice in official UN deliberations. Yet the NGOs, like multinationals, are mostly based in Europe and North America, feeding off cutting-edge technology, setting new global standards without much accountability to anyone.

Globalization is creating immense wealth. Yet countries unwilling or unequipped to become technologically connected—many in Africa today, for example—face "marginalization," another word for isolation and poverty.

At the Salzburg sessions there was real unease about globalization—a fear that the world order now emerging would be too cruel, too amoral, too exclusive in its power-wielding.

Anil Saldanha, a corporate executive from India, gave voice to these concerns.

"Man is not well," Mr. Saldanha said. "He is going through a process of insularity—insecurity, fright, fear. He doesn't know what's thrust on him, he must cope. So we need to look inward, to express our individuality, spirituality. If we do not put a human face on globalization, bring humanity to the forefront, we may not have far to go."

A global market does not create a global community, another speaker commented.

Yet the conference made it clear that the erosion of the nation-state is not only coming from above, it's creeping up from below.

One force is the rise of subnational regions impatient with the bureaucracy and unresponsiveness of large national governments. Nimble city-states—the "Asian tigers" of Hong Kong, Taiwan, and Singapore, for example—have been recent models of success. In 1970, four U.S. states had trade offices abroad. Now virtually all do and all have official standing in the World Trade Organization.

Ethnic, racial, and religious groups grasping for power are perhaps an even greater pressure from below. The end of the cold war untapped myriad ethnic nationalistic tensions.

Indeed, we may end up with more nation-states. The United Nations had 166 member "states" in 1991. It now has 185 [now 191], and it could one day end up with 400 or more, just because of ethnic divisions. But how many will be viable nations? And what does the developed world do about the collapse of countries worlds removed from its sleek globalization?

New hybrid structures—African, Asian or Latin American emulations of the European Union, for example—may be needed.

Perhaps we'll see forms of community as unknown now as the nation-state was when it burst on the scene in the sixteenth century. ●

SOURCE: Peirce (1997), 9.

technological innovations will continue to facilitate the flow of trade and finance across national boundaries, creating mutual vulnerabilities and blurring the distinction between foreign and domestic economic policy. Globalization presents opportunities as well as risks, and some people are better positioned than others to take advantage of its potential benefits. Moreover, as the earlier example of job loss to overseas outsourcing illustrates, globalization can be a disruptive process.

This chapter began by asking whether globalization will create a global village—one free of conflict and intent only on improving everyone's welfare. Global *pillage* is an alternative description of what can happen. Instead of worldwide prosperity emanating from the free movement of commodities, services, and capital across national borders, will globalization exacerbate existing economic inequities? The next chapter investigates possible answers to this question.

Chapter Summary

- Globalization is a set of processes that are fostering worldwide interconnectedness. Because it is uneven—benefitting some, disadvantaging others—globalization threatens to widen the gulf between the world's rich and poor states.

- Recent advances in telecommunication technology are a major driving force behind globalization. These technologies are changing our conceptions of time and space. With the emergence of a digitized global economy, the boundary between domestic and international transactions is becoming less distinct.

- Technology is reshaping patterns of production, trade, and finance. Markets no longer correspond with national boundaries. Rather than goods and services being produced by and for people living within a particular territorial state, they are now increasingly produced by people from several different states who are aiming at a world market. Similarly, a system of financial arrangements is emerging that is not centered on a single state. As a result, international economic flows are not subject to regulation by any single country.

- Globalization has shrunk geographic distances and linked people together in ways that create new challenges for solving environmental, health, and other problems that do not respect territorial boundaries. Owing to their transnational nature, many of these problems cannot be solved unilaterally. However, states are often hesitant to relinquish or pool their sovereignty in order to strengthen global institutions that can better address borderless crises.

- Globalization is a process unlikely to be forestalled, but the consequences are not easily agreed upon. Regardless of whether globalization is desirable or despicable, state power will retain its relevance in shaping the global future. Nevertheless, the sovereign, territorial state will not be the only important player on the world stage. What the process of globalization has done in recent years is to disaggregate sovereignty, creating multiple layers of authority which are interlaced in ways that blur distinctions between foreign and domestic, and public and private, entities.

KEY TERMS

agenda setting
arbitrage
capital mobility hypothesis
digital divide

globalization
global village
nontariff barriers

strategic corporate alliances
tariffs
trade integration

WHERE ON THE WORLD WIDE WEB?

LaborNet
http://www.labornet.apc.org/

LaborNet provides labor news from around the world. Click on the Strike Page and find out the who, what, where, and why of current strikes anywhere in the world. This website also has extensive links to international labor unions, and also gives the reader a sense of how the Internet has contributed to the globalization of labor.

Migration Dialogue
http://www.migration.ucdavis.edu/

The University of California at Davis has created a website that provides information on issues associated with international migration. Especially useful is "Migration News," which has up-to-date reports on migration issues in various states and regions of the world. Its archive allows you to search news by year and month, so you can track migration issues over time.

The Progress of Nations
http://www.unicef.org/pon99/

As described in this chapter, AIDS is a disease that has spread around the world through the process of globalization. The United Nations Children's Fund (UNICEF) has created a website that details the devastating impact of HIV/AIDS on children. Use this site to analyze the effects of AIDS on children in a variety of countries. Charts present a cross-country comparison of the number of children orphaned by AIDS and the impact it has had on their lives.

Telecom Information Resources on the Internet
http://china.si.umich.edu/telecom/telecom-info.html

The University of Michigan has produced a website that references information sources related to technical, economic, public policy, and social aspects of telecommunications (voice, data, video, wired, wireless, cable television, and satellite). Map 11.1 displays the uneven distribution of Internet connections around the world, and offers evidence to support the concern that the globalization of telecommunications will be concentrated in the Global North. As you visit the Telecom site, see if you can find additional evidence that substantiates this concern. Click on Broadcasters to link to every television and radio broadcaster in the world. Count how many broadcasters are in each country; you will be amazed at the number in the United States.

INFOTRAC® COLLEGE EDITION

Search for the following articles in the InfoTrac College Edition database.

Hoffmann, Stanley. "Clash of Globalizations," *Foreign Affairs* July–August 2002.

James, Harold. "Globalization and Great Depressions," *ORBIS* Winter 2002.

Massing, Michael. "From Protest to Program," *The American Prospect* July 2, 2001.

Taylor, Timothy. "The Truth about Globalization," *Public Interest* Spring 2002.

For more articles, enter:

"anti-globalization movement" in the Subject Guide.

"globalization" in the Subject Guide, and then go to subdivision "analysis."

"globalization" in the Subject Guide, and then go to subdivision "evaluation."

ADDITIONAL CD-ROM RESOURCES

Click on International Political Economy for additional resources related to this chapter.

CHAPTER 12

Markets and Money in a Global Political Economy

The principal challenge of international politics in this era of globalization is to shape innovative forms of international cooperation that can provide an opportunity for citizens of all nations to see their concerns reflected in policy decisions on global issues such as the financial system and international trade.

FERNANDO HENRIQUE CARDOSO, former president of Brazil

On July 26, 1956, Egyptian president Gamal Abdel Nasser announced to a jubilant crowd in Alexandria that he would eradicate the last vestige of Egypt's colonial past by nationalizing the Suez Canal, a vital artery of world commerce linking the Mediterranean to the Red Sea. The canal had been operated by the Universal Suez Canal Company, owned primarily by British and French stockholders. Alarmed that Nasser would now control the waterway through which Britain's oil supply flowed, British prime minister Anthony Eden desperately sought a way to oust the charismatic Egyptian president and regain the canal. Indeed, he was so obsessed with Nasser's actions that his wife allegedly complained that she felt like the canal was running through her drawing room.

Britain's concerns about Nasser were echoed in France and Israel. Political leaders in Paris believed he was helping Algerians resist French colonial rule; those in Tel Aviv grumbled he had closed the Straits of Tiran to Israeli shipping and supported guerrilla attacks against Israel. The United States also found Nasser's behavior deplorable, but insisted on finding a negotiated solution to the dispute. U.S. president Dwight Eisenhower was engaged in a reelection campaign, and the Republican Party had emphasized his contributions to international peace. Unable to secure Washington's backing for a military strike against Nasser, Britain, France, and Israel began planning their next moves in secret.

On October 29, the Israelis attacked the Egyptian army in the Sinai peninsula, and the following day the British and French announced that they would intervene to protect the Suez Canal. British paratroopers landed in Suez and Port Said on November 5, setting off a storm of opposition in the United Nations. Eisenhower was furious with what he saw as British deception on the eve of the American elections. The following day, U.S. secretary of the treasury George Humphrey gave the British an ultimatum: Either agree to a cease-fire or the United States would ruin the pound sterling, Britain's currency. Unless the British withdrew, Humphrey threatened to block their drawing rights on the International Monetary Fund, deny credit from the United States Export-Import Bank, and have the American Federal Reserve sell off large quantities of sterling (Neustadt 1970, 26). Faced with a looming monetary crisis, the British capitulated.

The Suez case illustrates how national security and international economics can impinge on one another. In the complex, interdependent world of the twenty-first century, we can expect the distinction between the "high politics" of security and the "low politics" of economics to become increasingly blurred (Keohane and Nye 1977). Even the security of most militarily powerful states will be affected by trade and monetary issues. The United States currently holds unchallenged might, for example, but its economy depends on foreign capital. According to one analyst, Washington borrows at a rate of more than $500 billion a year, or roughly five percent of its gross domestic product (GDP). This dependence could give foreign countries leverage over the United States. "Simply by dumping U.S. Treasury bills and other dollar-denominated assets, China—which holds more federal U.S. debt than any other country—could cause the value of the dollar to plummet, leading to a major crisis for the U.S. economy" (Schwenninger 2004, 129). Like Great Britain in 1956, the precarious financial position of United States today could undercut its foreign policy.

However, as we saw in the previous chapter, economic globalization creates mutual vulnerabilities. Although China has a large favorable balance of trade with the United States and uses those surplus funds to purchase dollar-denominated assets, a steep decline in the dollar would cause problems within its own economy. Not only would the value of its dollar-denominated assets plummet, but it would jeopardize a major export market. As one analyst notes, "The more China's economy is integrated with the world economy, the more dependent she is on the outside world and the less she can afford to embark on some adventurous course" (James Kynge cited in Grieco and Ikenberry 2003, 13). In short, economic globalization places all states in a delicate position, offering opportunities for growth that promise to improve their welfare while creating new risks that threaten to affect their security.

In view of the importance of international economics in an age of globalization, this chapter will examine how trade and currency exchanges affect human welfare and national security. The quest for wealth is an ageless pursuit. Because it provides the means by which many other values can be realized, the successful management of economics lies at the center of how governments define their national interests. What practices should they embrace to regulate commercial and monetary activities within their borders? What should they do to influence economic exchanges with other states? As former Brazilian president Fernando Henrique Cardoso maintains, these are among the most important issues we face in an era of accelerating globalization. They form the principal concerns within the field of **international political economy.** To introduce this topic, we will first examine the ways in which the world economic system has evolved. This will allow us to then investigate how trade and monetary activities today are creating new issues in the twenty-first century.

• **international political economy** the study of the intersection of politics and economics that illuminates the reasons why changes occur in the distribution of states' wealth and power.

• **international monetary system** the financial procedures governing the exchange and conversion of national currencies so that they can be bought and sold for one another to calculate the value of currencies and credits when capital is transferred across borders through trade, investment, and loans.

Contending Economic Strategies for an Interdependent World

In today's world, politics and economics are merging. The relentless march in the volume of international commerce has made trade increasingly important to countries' economies and is expected to increase at an even faster rate through the year 2015 (*Global Trends 2015*). World trade now accounts for 40 percent of global domestic product, up from 20 percent in 1990 (World Bank 2002a). While trade is the most visible symbol of globalization, the dynamics of the **international monetary system** are equally important. To comprehend the debates that are currently raging over trade and monetary issues, we first need to understand the contending economic philosophies of liberalism and mercantilism, which underpin the strategies different states have adopted in their pursuit of power and wealth.

The Shadow of the Great Depression

In July 1944, 44 states allied in the Second World War against the Axis powers met in the New Hampshire resort community of Bretton Woods. Their purpose was to devise new rules and institutions to govern international trade and monetary relations after the fighting ended. As the world's preeminent economic and military power, the United States played the leading role. Its proposals were shaped by the perception that the Great Depression of the 1930s created the conditions that gave rise to political extremists in Germany, Italy, and Japan. Operating under the philosophy of **commercial liberalism,** the United States sought free trade, open markets, and monetary stability in the hope that they would foster economic growth. Worldwide prosperity, U.S. leaders believed, was the best antidote to political extremism.

The rules established at Bretton Woods, which governed international economic relations for the next 25 years, rested on three political bases (Spero and Hart 1997). First, power was concentrated in the rich Western European and North American countries, which reduced the number of states whose agreement was necessary for effective management of economic relations. Second, the system's operation was facilitated by the dominant states' shared preference for an open international economy with limited government intervention. Third, Bretton Woods worked because the United States assumed the burdens of leadership and others willingly accepted that leadership. The onset of the Cold War helped cement Western unity, because a common external enemy led America's allies to perceive economic cooperation as necessary for both prosperity and military security.

The political bases of the Bretton Woods system crumbled in 1972 when the United States suspended the convertibility of the dollar into gold and abandoned the system of fixed currency exchange rates. Since then, as floating exchange rates and growing capital mobility have made monetary mechanisms unstable, more chaotic processes of international economic relations have materialized. Still, commercial liberalism's preference for market mechanisms over government intervention and the urge to privatize and otherwise reduce government regulation of markets has spread worldwide. Thus it is still useful to characterize the contemporary international economic system as a **Liberal International Economic Order (LIEO)**—one based on such free market principles as openness and nondiscriminatory trade.

Not all states consistently support the liberal tenet that governments should refrain from interfering with trade flows. Commercial liberalism is under attack where political pressure to protect local industries and jobs is growing. States' trade policies are naturally influenced by the desire to increase the domestic benefits of international economic transactions and to lessen their adverse consequences, even if this undermines the expansion of a global capitalist economy propelled by free trade.

The Clash between Liberal and Mercantile Values

How should states behave in the global economy to maximize their gains and minimize their vulnerability? Most controversies in the international political

• **commercial liberalism** an economic theory advocating free markets and the removal of barriers to the flow of trade and capital.

• **Liberal International Economic Order (LIEO)** the set of regimes created after World War II, designed to promote monetary stability and reduce barriers to the free flow of trade and capital.

economy are ultimately reducible to the competing ideologies of liberalism and **mercantilism,** which represent "fundamentally different . . . conceptions of the relationships among society, state, and market" (Gilpin 2001). A comparison of the logic behind the two theoretical traditions can help us to appreciate why different national leaders often pursue disparate policies in their international economic relations, with some advocating free trade and others devising ways to protect their countries from foreign competition.

Commercial Liberalism. As described in Chapter 2, liberalism begins with the presumption that humankind's natural inclination is to cooperate in order to increase prosperity and enlarge individual liberty under law. Commercial liberal theory has many variations, but all liberal thinkers agree that everyone benefits from unfettered exchanges. Open markets and free trade are seen as engines of progress, capable of lifting the poor from poverty and expanding political liberties (see Bhagwati 1999).

Adam Smith, the eighteenth-century political economist who helped define the precepts of classical liberalism, used the metaphor of the unregulated market's "invisible hand" to show how the collective or public interest can be served by humans' natural tendency to "truck, barter, and exchange" in pursuit of private gain. David Ricardo, a nineteenth-century British political economist, added an important corollary to liberal thought by demonstrating that when all states specialize in the production of those goods in which they enjoy a **comparative advantage** and trade them for goods in which others enjoy an advantage, a net gain in welfare for both states, in the form of higher living standards, will result. The principle of comparative advantage underpins commercial liberalism's advocacy of free trade as a method for capital accumulation. Material progress is realized and mutual gains are achieved, according to this principle, when countries specialize in the production of what they can produce least expensively; are willing to purchase, from other countries, goods that are costly for them to produce; and, in addition, do not restrict the flow of trade across borders.

Liberals such as Smith and Ricardo believed that economic processes governing the production, distribution, and consumption of goods and services operate according to certain natural laws; consequently markets work best when free of government interference. Transferring the logic of **laissez-faire economics** to the international level, commercial liberals suggest that removing trade restrictions among nations promotes more equal access to scarce resources, attracts foreign capital and expertise, and fosters competition—which generates pressure for increasing efficiency to lower production costs (Todaro 2000). These economic benefits are thought to have positive political consequences. Because war reduces profits by interrupting commerce, high levels of international trade create a material incentive for states to resolve their disputes peacefully. Besides encouraging states to find amicable solutions to their disagreements, trade also makes conflict resolution easier by increasing international communication and eroding parochialism. In the words of Richard Cobden, a prominent nineteenth-century British liberal: "Free Trade! What is it? Why, breaking down the barriers that separate nations; those barriers behind which nestle the feelings of pride, revenge,

• mercantilism the seventeenth-century theory preaching that trading states should increase their wealth and power by expanding exports and protecting their domestic economy from imports.

• comparative advantage the concept in liberal economic theory that a state will benefit if it specializes in those goods it can produce comparatively cheaply and acquires through trade goods that it can only produce at a higher cost.

• laissez-faire economics from a French phrase (meaning literally "let do") that Adam Smith and other commercial liberals in the eighteenth century used to describe the advantages of free-wheeling capitalism without government interference in economic affairs.

hatred, and jealousy, which every now and then burst their bounds, and deluge whole countries with blood (cited in Wolfers and Martin 1956, 193)."

There is a fly in this liberal ointment, however. Although commercial liberal theory promises that the "invisible hand" will maximize efficiency so that everyone will gain, it does not promise that everyone will gain equally. Productivity varies among individuals. "Under free exchange, society as a whole will be more wealthy, but individuals will be rewarded in terms of their marginal productivity and relative contribution to the overall social product" (Gilpin 2001). This applies at the global level as well: The gains from international trade may be distributed quite unequally, even if the principle of comparative advantage governs. Commercial liberal theory ignores these differences, as it is concerned with *absolute* rather than relative gains. Other theorists, however, are more concerned with the relative distribution of economic rewards.

Mercantilism.   In contrast to liberalism, mercantilism advocates government regulation of economic life to increase state power and security. It emerged in Europe as the leading political economy philosophy after the decline of feudalism and helped to stimulate the first wave of Europe's imperialist expansion, which began in the fifteenth century. Accumulating gold and silver was seen by early mercantilists as the route to state power and wealth. Later mercantilists focused on building strong, self-sufficient economies by curbing imports, subsidizing strategically targeted enterprises, and protecting domestic companies from foreign competition.

Today's so-called **neomercantilists** support trade policies "whereby a state seeks to maintain a balance-of-trade surplus and to promote domestic production and employment by reducing imports, stimulating home production, and promoting exports" (Walters and Blake 1992). These "new" mercantilists are sometimes called "economic nationalists." In their view, states must compete for position and power, and economic resources are the source of state power. From this it follows that "economic activities are and should be subordinate to the goal of state building and the interests of the state." (Gilpin 2001).

Mercantilism shares much in common with political realism: Realists and mercantilists both see the state as the principal world actor; both view the international system as anarchical; and both dwell on the aggressively competitive drive of people and states for advantage. While commercial liberals emphasize the mutual benefits of cooperative trade agreements, mercantilists are more concerned that the gains realized by one side of the bargain will come at the expense of the other. For mercantilists, relative gains are more important than both parties' absolute gains. An American economic nationalist, for instance, would complain about a trade agreement that promised the United States a 5 percent growth in income and the Chinese 6 percent. Although the bargain would ensure an eventual increase in U.S. living standards, its position compared with China's would slip. Calculations such as these explain why trade agreements that promise mutual gains often encounter stiff resistance. It also explains why those who fear the loss of domestic manufacturing and high-skilled service jobs to foreign competitors also lobby for mercantilist measures, and why they sometimes succeed against the unorganized interests of consumers who benefit from free trade.

• **neomercantilism** a contemporary version of classical mercantilism which advocates promoting domestic production and a balance-of-payment surplus by subsidizing exports and using tariffs and nontarriff barriers to reduce imports.

• **protectionism** a policy of creating barriers to foreign trade, such as tariffs and quotas, that protect local industries from competition.

• **import quotas** limits on the quantity of particular products that can be imported.

• **export quotas** barriers to commerce agreed to by two trading states to protect their domestic producers.

• **orderly market arrangements (OMAs)** voluntary export restrictions that involve a government-to-government agreement and often specific rules of management.

• **voluntary export restrictions (VERs)** a protectionist measure popular in the 1980s and early 1990s, in which exporting countries agree to restrict shipments of a particular product to a country to deter it from imposing an even more onerous import quota.

• **countervailing duties** tariffs imposed by a government to offset suspected subsidies provided by foreign governments to their producers.

• **antidumping duties** tariffs imposed to offset another state's alleged selling of a product at below the cost to produce it.

• **infant industry** a newly established industry that is not yet strong enough to compete effectively in the global marketplace.

Protectionism is the generic term used to describe a number of mercantilist policies designed to keep foreign goods out of a country and to support the export of domestically produced goods to other countries. These policies include:

- *Quotas.* Two types of quotas are common. **Import quotas** unilaterally specify the quantity of a particular product that can be imported from abroad. **Export quotas** result from negotiated agreements between producers and consumers and restrict the flow of products (e.g., shoes or sugar) from the former to the latter. An **orderly market arrangement (OMA)** is a formal agreement in which a country agrees to limit the export of products that might impair workers in the importing country, often under specific rules designed to monitor and manage trade flows. Exporting countries are willing to accept such restrictions in exchange for concessions on other fronts from the importing countries. The Multi-Fiber Arrangement (MFA) is an example of an elaborate OMA that restricts exports of textiles and apparel. It originated in the early 1960s, when the United States formalized earlier, informal **voluntary export restrictions (VERs)** negotiated with Japan and Hong Kong to protect domestic producers from cheap cotton imports. The quota system was later extended to other importing and exporting countries and then, in the 1970s, to other fibers, when it became the MFA. Under both import and export quotas, governments rather than the marketplace regulate the flow of goods between countries.

- *Tariffs.* Instead of using quotas, governments can limit imports by placing a tax on foreign goods. The tax may be a fixed amount imposed on each unit of an item being imported, or it may be based on some percentage of the value of each unit. Under what is known as "strategic trade policy," governments sometimes provide subsidies to a particular industry in order to make its goods more competitive abroad. Two protectionist responses to this practice are **countervailing duties,** the imposition of tariffs to offset alleged subsidies by foreign producers, and **antidumping duties** imposed to counter the alleged sale of products at below the cost of production.

- *Nontariff barriers.* Governments may limit imports without resorting to direct tax levies. Nontariff barriers cover a wide range of creative government regulations designed to shelter particular domestic industries from foreign competition, including health and safety regulations, as well as arcane government purchasing procedures.

Realist theory helps to account for states' impulse to engage in protectionism. Recall that realism argues that states in an anarchic, self-help environment often shun cooperation because they are suspicious of one another's motives. Uncertainty encourages each state to spend "a portion of its effort, not forwarding its own good, but in providing the means of protecting itself against others" (Waltz 1979). Among developing countries whose domestic industrialization goals may be hindered by the absence of protection from the Global North's more efficient firms, the **infant industry** argument is often used to justify mercantilist trade policies. According to this argument, tariffs or other forms of protection are necessary to nurture young industries until they eventually mature and lower production costs to compete effectively in the global marketplace.

In sum, the insecurity that breeds political competition frequently occurs in international economic relations. Those who see states' power and wealth as inextricably linked conclude that "even if nation-states do not fear for their physical survival, they worry that a decrease in their power capabilities relative to those of other states will compromise their political autonomy, expose them to the influence attempts of others, or lessen their ability to prevail in political disputes with allies and adversaries" (Mastanduno 1991). Thus many states are "defensively positional actors" that seek not only to promote their domestic well-being but also to defend their rank (position) in comparison with others (Grieco 1995).

Hegemony and the Management of the Global Economy

The relative gains issue speaks to the difficulties of achieving international cooperation under anarchical conditions and explains why some domestic producers vigorously oppose liberal (open) international economies despite the evidence that free trade promotes economic growth. Thus while some people see an unregulated market as the best method for providing the greatest good for the greatest number, others prefer protectionism over the liberalization of trade. According to many scholars, the key to bringing order to this competitive environment lies in the emergence of an all-powerful hegemon.

Hegemony is the ability to "dictate, or at least dominate, the rules and arrangements by which international relations, political and economic, are conducted" (Goldstein 1988). In the world economy it occurs when a single great power garners a sufficient amount of material resources to channel the international flow of raw materials, capital, and trade.

Charles Kindleberger (1973), an international economist, first theorized about the need for a liberal hegemon to open and manage the global economy. In his explanation of the 1930s Great Depression, Kindleberger concluded that "the international economic and monetary system needs leadership, a country which is prepared, consciously or unconsciously, . . . to set standards of conduct for other countries; and to seek to get others to follow them, to take on an undue share of the burdens of the system, and in particular to take on its support in adversity." Britain played this role from 1815 until the outbreak of World War I in 1914, and the United States assumed the British mantle in the decades immediately following World War II. In the interwar years, however, Britain was unable to play its previous leadership role, and the United States, although capable of leadership, was unwilling to exercise it. The void, Kindleberger concluded, was a principal cause of the "width and depth" of the Great Depression throughout the world in the 1930s.

According to what has become known as **hegemonic stability theory,** a preponderant state is able to design and promote rules for the whole global system that protect its own long-term interests. Hegemons such as the United States (and Britain before it), whose domestic economies are based on capitalist principles, have championed liberal international economic systems, because their comparatively greater control of technology, capital, and raw materials has given them

• **hegemonic stability theory** a school of thought that argues free trade and economic order depend on the existence of an overwhelmingly powerful state willing and able to use its strength to open and organize world markets.

more opportunities to profit from a system free of protectionist restraints. When they have enforced such free-trade rules, the hegemon's economies typically have served as "engines of growth" for others in the "liberal train."

Hegemons have also had special responsibilities. They have had to manage the international monetary system to enable one state's money to be exchanged for other states' money, make sure that countries facing balance-of-payments deficits (imbalances in their financial inflows and outflows) could find the credits necessary to finance their deficits, and serve as lenders of last resort during financial crises. When the most powerful liberal states could not perform these tasks, they have often backtracked toward more closed (protected or regulated) domestic economies, and in doing so have undermined the open international system that was previously advantageous to them. This kind of departure historically has made quotas, tariffs, and nontariff barriers to trade more widespread. In short, hegemonic states not only have had the greatest capacity to make a free-trade regime succeed but in the past they also have had the greatest responsibility for its effective operation and preservation. To interpret whether hegemonic stability theory is likely to hold in the future, a closer look at the theory's logic is useful.

The Hegemonic Pillars of Open Markets and Free Trade

• collective goods goods from which everyone benefits regardless of their individual contributions.

Much of the discussion about the free movement of commodities across national borders centers on the concept of public or **collective goods**—benefits that everyone shares and from which no one can be excluded selectively. National security is one such collective good that governments try to provide for all of their citizens, regardless of the resources that individuals contribute through taxation. In the realm of economic analysis, an open international economy permitting the relatively free movement of commodities is similarly seen as a desirable collective good, inasmuch as it permits economic benefits for all states that would not be available if the global economy were closed to free trade.

According to hegemonic stability theory, the collective good of an open global economy needs a single, dominant power—a hegemon—to remain open and liberal. A major way in which the hegemon can exercise leadership is to open its own market to less-expensive imported goods even if other countries **free ride** by not opening their own markets. However, if too many states refuse to forego the short-term gains of free riding and capitulate to domestic protectionist pressures, the entire liberal international economy may collapse.

• free riders those who enjoy the benefits of collective goods but pay little or nothing for them.

The analogy of a public park helps us to illustrate this dilemma. If there were no central government to provide for the maintenance of the park, individuals themselves would have to cooperate to keep the park in order (the trees trimmed, the lawn mowed, and so on). But some may try to come and enjoy the benefits of the park without pitching in. If enough people realize that they can get away with this—that they can enjoy a beautiful park without helping with its upkeep—it will not be long before the once beautiful park looks shabby. Cooperation to provide a public good is thus difficult. This is also the case with the collective good of a liberal international economy, because many states that enjoy the collective good of an orderly, open, free-market economy pay little or nothing for it. A hegemon typically tolerates some free riders, partly because the benefits that the hegemon provides, such as a stable global currency, encourage other states to accept its rules. But if the costs of leadership multiply and everyone's benefits seem to come at the expense of the hegemon, it will become less tolerant of free riding and may gravitate toward more coercive policies. In such a situation, the open global economy could crumble amidst a competitive race for individual gain at others' expense.

A Liberal Economic Order without Hegemonic Leadership?

Although hegemonic powers benefit from the liberal economic systems that their power promotes, the very success of liberalism eventually erodes the pillars that support it.

Competition fostered by open markets and free trade encourages productive efficiency and economic growth, which affects the international distribution of industrial power. As economic strength shifts from the hegemon to other states, the capacity of the hegemon to maintain the system decreases (Gilpin 1987). The leading economic power's ability to adapt is critical to maintaining its dominant position. Britain was unable to adapt and fell from its top-ranked position. Many wonder if the United States is destined to suffer the same fate, not because of economic failure but because of the lack of political will to exercise leadership through concerted multilateral action (Nye 2002b). At the twenty-first century's dawn, the United States stood as an economic superpower; however the circumstances confronting the United States today may be eroding its capacity to continue exercising hegemonic leadership.

At present, the United States has the world's largest economy, but few predict that position of dominance will remain indefinitely. The U.S. share of world output has fallen steadily since World War II. In 1947, the United States accounted for nearly 50 percent of the combined gross world product (largely because the war ravaged the territory of its industrial competitors). By 1960, its share had slipped to 28 percent, by 1970 to 25 percent, and by the 1990s to 20 percent—less than what it had been during the Spanish-American War, when the country first emerged as a world power (D. White 1998, 42). Another symptom of economic strain is that the U.S. share of world financial reserves has declined. The United States went from being the globe's greatest creditor country in 1980 to the world's largest debtor by 1990. A third symptom is the fact that the U.S. trade deficit reached the highest level ever by 2004. Finally, alongside these debt burdens and trade imbalances, U.S. investment in public infrastructure to stimulate future growth is lower than that of all the other G-7 industrialized powerhouses, a problem that will ultimately reduce the United States' "ability to compete with other economies because of its low savings rate and insufficient investment in education" (Thurow 1998). These trends suggest that U.S. advantages in the global marketplace will not continue. The United States possesses the world's strongest economy, but strains are appearing as the cost of the U.S. war against Iraq continues to mount.

What will happen if the willingness of the United States to lead declines? Have the institutions and rules put into place to govern the liberal economic order in the post–World War II era now taken on a life of their own? Commercial liberals think so, arguing that trade liberalization may be too deeply entrenched for it to collapse. "Built-in restraints on imposing new trade barriers have never been greater" (Stokes 2000). "By providing more information, establishing mechanisms for monitoring and generating shared expectations, institutions can create an environment in which interstate cooperation is possible even without a single dominant leader" (Krasner 1993). The free-trade regime may no longer depend on the existence of an all-powerful hegemon.

To better evaluate this argument and probe the likely future of global economics, let us now inspect how those international trade and monetary rules have evolved since the Second World War.

The Changing Free-Trade Regime

In the period immediately following World War II, when the United States became the world's dominant political power, it simultaneously became the pre-eminent voice in international trade affairs. The liberal trading system the United States chose to promote rejected the **beggar-thy-neighbor policies** widely seen as a major cause of the economic depression of the 1930s. Removing barriers to trade became a priority and led to the recurrent rounds of trade negotiations that produced remarkable reductions in tariff rates. As the large U.S. market was opened to foreign producers, other countries' economies grew, and rising trade contributed to a climate that encouraged others to open their markets as well.

The General Agreement on Tariffs and Trade (GATT) became the principal international organization designed to promote and protect free trade in the aftermath of World War II. GATT was never intended to be a formal institution with enforcement powers. Instead, a premium was placed on negotiations and reaching consensus to settle disputes among parties to the agreement, which was first and foremost a commercial treaty. As trade disputes multiplied, GATT increasingly became involved in legalistic wrangling. In 1995, GATT was superseded by the World Trade Organization (WTO), a new free-trade IGO with "teeth" (see Table 12.1 and Figure 12.1). The WTO represents a breathtaking step in free-trade management, although it has also provoked violent disagreements over the nature of global capitalism (see Controversy: Are World Trade Organization Economic Policies Consistent with Social and Environmental Protection?). The WTO extended GATT's coverage to products, sectors, and conditions of trade not previously covered adequately. It also enhanced previous dispute-settlement procedures by making the findings of its arbitration panels binding on the domestic laws of participating states (GATT's findings were not binding). Finally, the WTO deals with the problem of free riding by being available only to states that belong to GATT, subscribe to all of the Uruguay Round agreements, and make market access commitments (under the old GATT system, free riding was possible when some small states were permitted to benefit from trade liberalization without having to make contributions of their own).

The creation of the WTO signaled a victory for multilateralism, because it "reduced the powers of all governments to regulate behavior and set independent economic policies" (Thurow 1998). Trade squabbles will nonetheless

• **beggar-thy-neighbor policies** the attempt to promote trade surpluses through policies that cause other states to suffer trade deficits.

TABLE 12.1 AND FIGURE 12.1

A GATT-WTO Chronology

Date	Summary
1947	Birth of the GATT, signed by 23 countries on October 30 at the Palais des Nations in Geneva.
1948	The GATT comes into force. First meeting of its members in Havana, Cuba.
1949	Second round of talks at Annecy, France. Some 5,000 tariff cuts agreed to; 10 new countries admitted.
1950–51	Third round at Torquay, England. Members exchange 8,700 trade concessions and welcome four new countries.
1956	Fourth round at Geneva. Tariff cuts worth $1.3 trillion at today's prices.
1960–62	The Dillon Round, named after U.S. undersecretary of state Douglas Dillon, who proposed the talks. A further 4,400 tariff cuts.
1964–67	The Kennedy Round. Many industrial tariffs halved. Signed by 50 countries. Code on dumping agreed to separately.
1973–79	The Tokyo Round, involving 99 countries. First serious discussion of nontariff trade barriers, such as subsidies and licensing requirements. Average tariff on manufactured goods in the nine biggest markets cut from 7 percent to 4.7 percent.
1986–93	The Uruguay Round. Further cuts in industrial tariffs, export subsidies, licensing, and customs valuation. First agreements on trade in services and intellectual property.
1995	Formation of WTO with power to settle disputes between members.
1997	Agreements concluded on telecommunications services, information technology, and financial services.
1999	The "Millennium Round" convenes in Seattle in November to organize for a new round of multilateral trade negotiations. Thousands demonstrate against globalization and trade liberalization, including numerous NGOs pressuring the WTO to advance their agendas.
2000	The WTO grows to 135 members, and more than 30 other states are applicants for membership. WTO opens new negotiations to revamp rules of trade on agricultural goods and services.
2001	WTO resumes discussions in Doha, Qatar, in hope that the remote setting will prevent protest disruptions from antiglobalization protestors. One hundred forty-two states unsuccessfully chart a path for the world's biggest economies to deal cooperatively with regionalism between competitive trade blocs and to raise hopes for recovery.
2002	WTO convenes in New York. Later admits China and Taiwan to its membership, which grows to 145 members.
2003	Trade negotiations at the WTO meeting in Cancun, Mexico collapse due to disagreements over trade-related aspects of intellectual property rights and agricultural issues. With the addition of Armenia and the Former Yugoslav Republic of Macedonia, membership in the WTO increases to 147 members.

The liberalization of the international trading system is the product of cooperative efforts within the framework of the General Agreement on Tariffs and Trade, as shown in this summary (top) and the growth of trade among the WTO's members since 1985 (bottom). The free-trade regime has greatly aided the expansion of global trade. One indicator of the growing magnitude of trade interdependence is the fact that world trade now accounts for 25 percent of all countries' GDP—twice its share in 1970 (*The Economist,* September 28, 2002, 22).

SOURCE: Adapted from *The Economist,* May 16, 1998, p. 22 (top) and Aug. 28, 1998, p. 52 (bottom). Copyright © 1998 by The Economist Newspaper Ltd. All rights reserved. Reprinted with permission. Further reproduction prohibited. www.economist.com

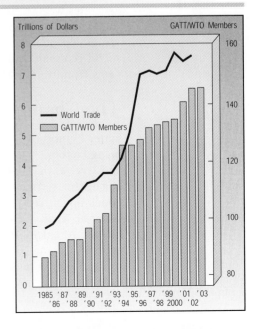

CONTROVERSY

Are World Trade Organization Economic Policies Consistent with Social and Environmental Protection?

In late November 1999, the then 135-member countries of the World Trade Organization (WTO) and 30 additional observer states made final preparations to stage in Seattle what was billed as the Millennium Round on trade negotiations—the follow-up to the Uruguay Round of trade talks completed in 1993. At the time the mood was optimistic. The meeting promised to celebrate the free-trade regime for the global marketplace and the contributions that lower trade barriers arguably had made to the growth of international exports and, for many members (particularly the United States), their longest and largest peacetime economic expansion in the twentieth century. There appeared to be widespread recognition that a world without walls promotes prosperity and welfare.

A half-century of generally rising prosperity had generated a climate of enthusiasm for the power of free trade. Fears of imports tend to recede in good economic times, and, with the best decade ever, most leaders in the twilight of the twentieth century emphasized the sunnier side of free trade. The delegates to the Seattle meetings shared the liberal conviction that countries, companies, and consumers had much to gain by a globalized economy freed from restraints on the exchange of goods across borders. They expected added benefits from a new trade round that could slash tariffs and other trade barriers in agriculture, manufactured goods, and services.

That mood and the seeming consensus on which it was based was shattered when the Seattle trade talks opened. An estimated fifty thousand to one hundred thousand protesters and grassroots anti-WTO activists, who differed widely in their special interests (the poor, environment, labor, women, indigenous people), joined hands to shout their common opposition to the general idea of globalization and free trade. A plane trailed a banner proclaiming "People Over Profits: Stop WTO" as part of what became known as "The Battle in Seattle." A tirade against open trade ensued, fueled by citizen backlash (Broad 2002; Aaronson 2002).

The Seattle conference will be remembered as the moment when the debate over the benefits and costs

continue despite overwhelming profits from trade liberalization. Free trade generates wealth, but it also brings risks. As Joseph Grieco and John Ikenberry (2003) explain: Open markets stimulate economic growth, but they can also create dependencies. "So a state contemplating expanding its exposure to the world economy must calculate the trade-offs between the absolute economic gains from trade and the losses it produces in terms of autonomy.

The Changing International Monetary Regime

States cannot always trade as they wish. Their exports and imports depend on many factors, especially on changes in global demand and prices for the goods and services that countries' producers sell in the global marketplace. The mechanisms for setting the currency exchange rates by which the value of traded goods are priced heavily influence international trade. Indeed, the monetary system is crucial for international trade, for without a stable and predictable method of calculating the value of sales and foreign investments, those transactions become too risky, causing trade and investment activities to fall. In short, the success of international trade depends on the health of the monetary system.

of the globalized economy rose to the pinnacle of the global agenda. The immediate target of the demonstrations was the WTO; however, the organization itself was simply a convenient symbol of a much larger sea of discontent. The WTO protests—and the failure of the WTO conference attendees to compromise on tightly held positions and agree on even a minimal accord—exposed the deep divisions about the best ways to open global commerce and adopt new rules at a time of rapid change.

Controversies about globalization, free trade, and global governance are multiple. At the core is the question of whether a globalized economy is inevitable and, if so, is it an antidote to human suffering or a source of new inequities. The debates are explosive, because everyone is affected, but in quite different ways. Many are enjoying the boom years under liberalized trade engineered by the WTO's trade agreements. But the celebration is confined largely to the privileged, powerful, and prosperous. Many others see themselves as clear victims of an open global economy, as when a factory closes and workers lose their jobs. Those discontented with globalized free trade include a diverse coalition of protestors, many of whom harbor very specific concerns about wages, the environ-

ment, and human rights issues. Labor leaders contend that the WTO is sacrificing worker rights; environmental groups complain that when green values collide with world commerce, environmental standards are left out of trade negotiations; and human rights activists accuse the WTO of serving the preferences of multinational corporations for erasing trade barriers in ways that fail to protect human rights. In addition, enraged trade ministers from the Global South's developing countries see a Global North conspiracy in the WTO's efforts to adopt core labor standards, because the less-developed Global South views such high-sounding rules as a method to take away the comparative advantages Global South developing nations enjoy with lower wage scales.

These, and other issues, are certain to continue as major controversies. What do you think? Is the WTO a valuable tool for improving global governance or a threat to human welfare? Is the WTO and the free trade practices it promotes too strong or too weak? Does the WTO put corporate profits above human rights and environmental protection, as critics charge? Or do you agree with WTO director general Mike Moore's claim that "Trade is the ally of working people, not their enemy." ●

The Elements of Monetary Policy

Monetary and financial policies are woven into a complex set of relationships between states and the international system, and, because monetary and currency issues have their own specialized technical terminology, they are difficult to understand. However, the essentials are rather basic. "Monetary policy works on two principal economic variables: the aggregate supply of money in circulation and the level of interest rates." Monetarist economic theory assumes that the **money supply** (currency plus commercial bank demand deposits) is related to economic activity. Increases in the supply facilitate economic growth by enabling people to purchase more goods and services, but a supply that grows too fast may lead to inflation. Through controlling the level of the money supply, some monetarists contend, "governments can regulate their nations' economic activity and control inflation" (Todaro 2000, 657), though others worry that its effects are too unpredictable in the short run to guide policy.

To understand the importance of monetary policies as a determinant of states' trade, growth rates, and wealth consider both why **exchange rates** fluctuate and the impact of these currency fluctuations. Money works in several ways and serves different purposes. First, money must be widely accepted, so that

• **money supply** the total amount of currency in circulation in a state, calculated to include demand deposits—such as checking accounts—in commercial banks and time deposits—such as savings accounts and bonds—in savings banks.

• **exchange rate** the rate at which one state's currency is exchanged for another state's currency in the global marketplace.

people earning it can use it to buy goods and services from others. Second, money must serve to store value, so that people will be willing to keep some of their wealth in the form of money. Third, money must act as a standard of deferred payment, so that people will be willing to lend money knowing that when the money is repaid in the future, it will still have purchasing power.

Governments attempt to manage their currencies to prevent inflation. Inflation occurs when the government creates too much money in relation to the goods and services produced in the economy. As money becomes more plentiful and thus less acceptable, it cannot serve effectively to store value or to satisfy debts or as a medium of exchange.

Movements in a state's exchange rate occur in part when changes develop in peoples' assessment of the national currency's underlying economic strength or the ability of its government to maintain the value of its money. A deficit in a country's **balance of payments,** for example, would likely cause a decline in the value of its currency relative to that of others. This happens when the supply of the currency is greater than the demand for it. Similarly, when those engaged in international economic transactions change their expectations about a currency's future value, they might reschedule their lending and borrowing. Fluctuations in the exchange rate could follow.

Speculators—those who buy and sell money in an effort to make a profit—may also affect the international stability of a country's currency. Speculators make money by guessing the future. If, for instance, they believe that the Japanese yen will be worth more in three months than it is now, they can buy yen today and sell them for a profit three months later. Conversely, if they believe that the yen will be worth less in three months, they can sell yen today for a certain number of dollars and then buy back the same yen in three months for fewer dollars, making a profit. The globalization of finance now also encourages managers of investment portfolios to move funds from one currency to another in order to realize gains from differences in states' interest rates.

In the same way that governments try to protect the value of their currencies at home, they try to protect them internationally by intervening in currency markets. Their willingness to do so is important to importers and exporters, who depend on orderliness and predictability in the value of the currencies they deal in to carry out transnational exchanges. Governments intervene when countries' central banks buy or sell currencies to change the value of their own currencies in relation to those of others. Unlike speculators, however, governments are pledged not to manipulate exchange rates so as to gain unfair advantages, for states' reputations as custodians of monetary stability are valuable. Whether governments can affect their currencies' values in the face of large transnational movements of capital is, however, increasingly questionable. So is the value of any country's currency in relation to any other's.

The Bretton Woods Monetary System

When the leaders of the capitalist West met in Bretton Woods, New Hampshire in 1944, they were acutely aware of the need to create a reliable mechanism for determining the value of countries' currencies in relation to one another, and

> • **balance of payments** a calculation summarizing a country's financial transactions with the external world, determined by the level of credits (export earnings, profits from foreign investment, receipts of foreign aid) minus the country's total international debts (imports, interest payments on international debts, foreign direct investments, and the like).

agreed to a set of concepts to define monetary and currency policy for conducting international trade and finance. Recognizing that a shared system and vocabulary was a necessary precondition for trade, and from it post–World War II economic recovery and prosperity, the negotiating parties agreed that the postwar monetary regime should be based on **fixed exchange rates** and assigned governments primary responsibility for enforcing its rules. In addition, they foresaw the need to create what later became the International Monetary Fund (IMF), to help states maintain equilibrium in their balance of payments and stability in their exchange rates with one another. The International Bank for Reconstruction and Development, known as the World Bank, was also created to aid recovery from the war.

Today the IMF and World Bank are important, if controversial, players in the global monetary and financial systems. Their primary mission is to serve as "lenders of last resort" when its member states face financial crises, providing those seeking assistance meet the often painful conditions requiring domestic adjustments to strengthen their economies. In the period immediately after World War II, these institutions commanded little authority and too few resources to cope with the enormous devastation of the war. The United States stepped into the breach.

The U.S. dollar became the key to the hegemonic role that the United States eagerly assumed as manager of the international monetary system. Backed by a vigorous and healthy economy, a fixed relationship between gold and the dollar (pegged at $35 per ounce of gold), and the U.S. commitment to exchange gold for dollars at any time (known as "dollar convertibility"), the dollar became universally recognized as a "parallel currency," accepted in exchange markets as the reserve used by monetary authorities in most countries and by private banks, corporations, and individuals for international trade and capital transactions.

To maintain the value of their currencies, central banks in other countries either bought or sold their own currencies, using the dollar to raise or depress their value. Thus the Bretton Woods monetary regime was based on fixed exchange rates and ultimately required a measure of government intervention for its preservation.

To get U.S. dollars into the hands of those who needed them most, the Marshall Plan provided Western European states billions of dollars in aid to buy the U.S. goods necessary for rebuilding their war-torn economies. The United States also encouraged deficits in its own balance of payments as a way of providing **international liquidity** in the form of dollars.

In addition to providing liquidity, the United States assumed a disproportionate share of the burden of rejuvenating Western Europe and Japan. It supported European and Japanese trade competitiveness, permitted certain forms of protectionism (such as Japanese restrictions on importing U.S. products), and condoned discrimination against the dollar (as in the European Payments Union, which promoted trade within Europe at the expense of trade with the United States). The United States willingly incurred these leadership costs and others' free riding because subsidizing economic growth in Europe and Japan would widen the U.S. export markets and strengthen the West against communism's possible popular appeal.

Although this system initially worked well with the United States operating as the world's banker, the costs grew as the enormous number of dollars held by

> • **fixed exchange rates** a system under which states establish the parity of their currencies and commit to keeping fluctuations in their exchange rates within narrow limits.

> • **international liquidity** reserve assets used to settle international accounts.

others made the U.S. economy increasingly vulnerable to financial shocks from abroad. U.S. leaders found it difficult to devalue the dollar without hurting America's allies; nor could inflationary or deflationary pressures at home be managed without hurting allies abroad. This reduced the United States' ability to use the normal methods available to other states for dealing with the disruption caused by deficits in a country's **balance of trade,** such as adjusting interest and currency exchange rates.

• **balance of trade** a calculation based on the value of merchandise goods and services imported and exported. A deficit occurs when a country buys more from abroad than it sells.

The End of Bretton Woods

As early as 1960 it was clear that the dollar's top currency status could not be sustained. After 1971, U.S. president Nixon abruptly announced—without consulting with allies—that the United States would no longer exchange dollars for gold. With the price of gold no longer fixed and dollar convertibility no longer guaranteed, the Bretton Woods system gave way to a substitute system based on **floating exchange rates.** Market forces, rather than government intervention, were expected to determine currency values. A country experiencing adverse economic conditions now saw the value of its currency fall in response to the choices of traders, bankers, and businesspeople. This was expected to make its exports cheaper and its imports more expensive, which in turn would pull its currency's value back toward equilibrium—all without the need for central bankers to support their currencies. In this way, it was hoped that the politically humiliating devaluations of the past could be avoided.

• **floating exchange rates** an unmanaged process whereby market forces rather than governments influence the relative rate of exchange for currencies between countries.

Those expectations were not met. Beginning in the late 1970s, escalating in the 1980s, and persisting through the 1990s, a rising wave of financial crises, both in currency and banking, occurred (see World Bank 2002a). These have been compounded by massive defaults by countries unable to service their debts. Thirty-seven countries currently have foreign debts in excess of $10 billion—a staggering sum of indebtedness that leaves many countries exposed to external economic and political influence (*The Economist* 2002, 38; see also Allen 2002).

Financial crises have become increasingly frequent around the world as a result of the inability of states to manage income, debt, and inflation in a monetary system fraught with wild currency exchange rate gyrations. In the past 35 years, more than one hundred major episodes of banking insolvency occurred in 90 developing and emerging countries. The financial cost of these crises, in terms of the percentage of GDP lost, has been huge. The disastrous debts generated by banking and currency disruptions forced governments to suffer, on average between 1970 and 1997, direct loses of nearly 15 percent of their GDP for each crisis and more than a 5 percent decline in output growth after each crisis (World Bank 1999a, 126).

In response to the growing awareness of the extent to which the health of others' economies depended on the value of the U.S. dollar internationally (which in turn depended on the underlying strength of the U.S. economy), since 1985 the **Group of Five** has adhered to the landmark agreement reached secretly at the Plaza Hotel in New York City, in which they pledged to collectively coordinate their economic policies through management of exchange rates internationally and interest rates domestically.

• **Group of Five (G-5)** a group of advanced industrialized democracies composed of the United States, Britain, France, Japan, and Germany.

Money Makes the World Go Round Currency moves throughout the world according to rules governing exchange rates. Monetary policies create currency dilemmas which sometimes unleash hostile feelings. For example, when finance ministers lower interest rates in ways that benefit a country with high unemployment, that shift breeds inflation in other countries with low unemployment. Some people opposed to the integration of international finance see monetary adjustments as a conspiracy designed to enrich the wealthy few at the expense of others. Shown here, Czech police pass under a protest banner reading, "Money makes the world go round—but in which direction?" at the September 2000 annual economic summit of the IMF and the World Bank in Prague.

The **Group of Seven** (the **G-7,**) and the **Group of Eight** (the **G-8** with the inclusion of Russia in 1997) have sought to carry out the pledge to coordinate global monetary policy. However, at the G-8 summit in Genoa in July 2001, it was clear that the leading industrial powers were unable to reach consensus about the best way to manage exchange rates, monetary and fiscal policies, and trade relations in order to sustain global economic growth.

In the absence of true collective management of global monetary conditions, it appears likely that the volume of world trade and the activities of currency speculators (who use sophisticated global electronic technologies and rely on about two thousand "hedge funds" to make profits in currency trading) will increasingly determine national currency values. An average of over $1.5 trillion in currency trading occurs each day—a transfer of capital greater than one-fourth of the world's average *weekly* level of international trade. International sales of stocks and bonds have mushroomed as well and promise to rise through increased investor trading on the Internet. In the volatile world of mobile capital, wide fluctuations in national currencies' exchange rates have become common.

• **Group of Seven (G-7)/Group of Eight (G-8)** the G-5 plus Canada and Italy; since 1997, known as the G-8 with the addition of Russia.

The Domino Effect in Global Finance When a country's economy collapses, foreign capital flees in panic. No worldwide central bank exists to cushion such crashes. Money problems in one country lead to money problems in others, provoking currency depreciations and plunges in stock prices at home and abroad. Here stunned brokers react to the January 1998 plummet of Hong Kong stocks that caused the key indexes elsewhere in Asia, London, Frankfurt, New York, and Paris to fall. Described as "the worst international financial crisis in fifty years," it took "global finance to the edge of collapse" (Altman and Cutter 1999).

© Eric Feferberg/AFP/Getty Images

The globalization of finance and the removal of barriers to capital flows across borders expose national economies to shocks, with little hope that such volatility will vanish.

Plans for Reforming the International Financial Architecture

No institution currently has global responsibility for the arrangement of capital flows, although there does exist a set of principles and rules of relatively universal scope (Berthelot 2001). Hardly anyone is happy with the prevailing weak and somewhat haphazard global financial architecture, but it appears that only when severe financial crises occur that threaten a global recession that sufficient pressure mounts to engineer new reforms.

Many proposals have been advanced for reforming the international monetary system to help cushion the aftershocks of the rapid movement of investment funds among countries that creates booms and busts, such as the 1980s Latin American debt crisis and the global crisis that followed on the heels of the 1997–1998 flight of capital from Asia. Some see reversion to the pre–World War I gold standard as preferable to the exchange rates with highly fluctuating currencies. Others recommend something like the Bretton Woods system of fixed but adjustable rates.

What these and other proposals seek is a mechanism for creating the currency stability and flexibility on which prosperity through trade depends and which the current system has failed to achieve. However, there is little agreement on how to bring about reforms. With global democratization, most governments face domestic pressures to sacrifice such goals as exchange rate stability for unemployment reduction, so it seems likely that floating exchange rates, with all their costs and uncertainties, are here to stay.

As one observer notes, "The reality is that the leading powers in the world economy have too much of a stake in existing arrangements to show much appetite for reinventing the IMF or for charting a new Bretton Woods" (Blustein 1999, 6). Thus despite a proliferation of schemes for rebuilding the international financial architecture, "the prospects are for incremental tinkering rather than wholesale restructuring" (Babai 2001, 418).

Global Economic Concerns in the Twenty-First Century

Since 1950 world trade has grown sixteenfold, exceeding $7.4 trillion. In the same period, gross world product has grown sevenfold, reaching $48 trillion by the early twenty-first century (*Vital Signs 2002*, 45). The exponential growth of trade has contributed measurably to the unprecedented rise in global economic prosperity. Reductions in barriers to free trade are expected to accelerate these trends if world trade continues to expand faster than real world output (see Figure 12.2). The expected consequence is that countries will be bound ever more tightly in interdependent economic relationships. Indeed, one estimate predicts that by the year 2015 world trade will comprise 40 percent of world GDP (*Global Trends 2015*).

Many states see advantages in accepting the **most-favored-nation (MFN) principle** (which holds that the tariff preferences granted to one state must be granted to all others exporting the same product) and the **nondiscrimination** rule (goods produced at home and abroad are to be treated the same). However, free trade is attractive only if everyone, developed Global North and developing Global South countries alike, can benefit. Today numerous states remain tempted to enhance their domestic well-being by protectionist means. As shown in Figure 12.3, many of them have retained nontariff barriers to free trade even as tariff walls have come down. According to one observer, this kind of economic nationalism "could propel the preeminent economic powers—and the rest of the world with them—into an era of 'real-economik,' in which parochial economic interests drive governments to pursue marginal advantage in an international system marked by growing interdependencies" (Peterson, E. 1998). "Trade may be global," warn Ramesh Thakur and Steve Lee (2000), but "politics is still local." If neomercantilism spreads, the preservation of the free-trade regime is unlikely throughout the twenty-first century.

• **most-favored-nation (MFN) principle** unconditional nondiscriminatory treatment in trade between contracting parties guaranteed by GATT; in 1997, U.S. senator Daniel Patrick Moynihan introduced legislation to replace the term with "normal trade relations" (NTR) to better reflect its true meaning.

• **nondiscrimination** a principle for trade that proclaims that goods produced at home and abroad are to be treated the same for import and export agreements.

The Fate of Free Trade

Protectionist pressure is rising in the United States and elsewhere. In a recent public opinion poll conducted by the University of Maryland's Program on International Policy Attitudes, American support for free trade fell in most every income group between 1999 and 2004 (*Idaho Statesman*, February 24, 2004, 2). Job losses, attributed by many people to corporate offshore outsourcing, has fueled calls for protectionism. Throughout modern history, recession has been "the midwife of protectionism. In good times, peoples and nations are happy to enjoy the benefits of open trade. Come bad times, they are tempted to minimize short-run pain through protection" (*The Economist*, January 2, 1999). Unfortunately for the fate of the liberal international regime, the threats to global prosperity are multiplying at the same time that the dependency of countries on volatile foreign

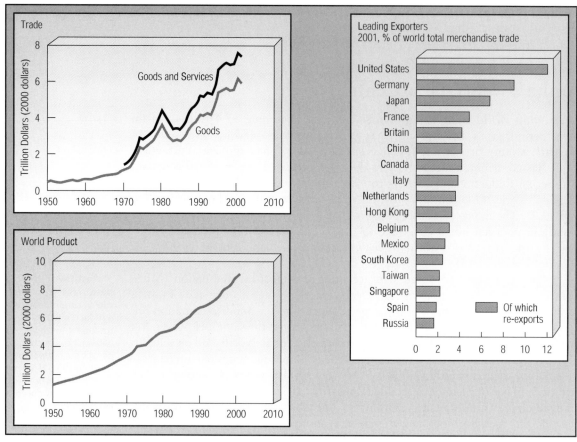

FIGURE 12.2
The Growth of Global Trade and Wealth

Since 1970, the volume of world trade has increased on average nearly 4 percent each year. When global trade has risen, almost always so has world wealth. Trade liberalization and market reforms within many countries have spurred both these trends steadily upward. The top figure on the left captures the rising volume of world exports since 1950, and the bottom figure displays the increasing level of gross world product for the same 1950–2001 period. Although trade integration is deepening, the benefits of trade and of a booming global economy are not evenly distributed, as some countries are not participating at the same levels as others. The chart on the right rank orders the top exporting countries according to the percent of total world merchandise trade they control; these 17 leaders in trade in 2002 captured most of the nearly $6 trillion in global merchandise exports.

Note: Annual growth rates beyond 2003 are projections.

SOURCES: Global trade and economic growth from *Vital Signs* 2002, p. 59, 61. Copyright © 2002 Worldwatch Institute. www.worldwatch.org; leading exporters from *The Economist,* May 18, 2002, p. 25. Copyright © 2002 by The Economist Newspaper Ltd. All rights reserved. Reprinted with permission. Further reproduction prohibited. www.economist.com.

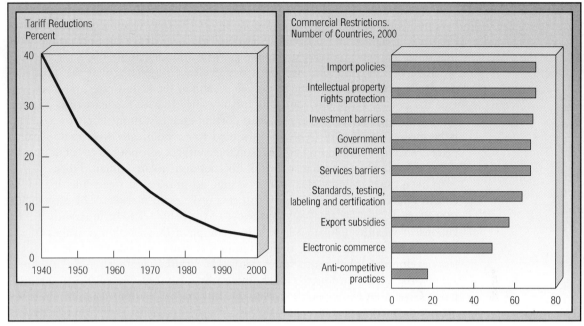

FIGURE 12.3
The Persistence of Nontariff Barriers to World Trade

All states want other countries to purchase their exports and most try to protect domestic producers from foreign imports. To promote trade, the industrialized countries have greatly reduced tariffs, as shown in the figure on the left. The reduction of tariffs has fostered the growth of trade. However, as the table on the right shows, the temptation to restrict trade has been difficult to resist, and many countries have imposed various nontariff barriers to protect their domestic economies from external imports. According to the Office of U.S. Trade Representative, in 2002 roughly sixty countries had established mechanisms for restricting trade with the rest of the world (not including America's own elaborate restrictions and anticompetitive policies and practices). Thus, the struggle between the liberal value of free trade and the mercantilist value of protectionism is far from over.

SOURCES: Office of the U.S. Trade Representative, with information on commercial restrictions on imports summarized by *The Economist,* April 7, 2001, p. 121. Copyright © 2001 by The Economist Newspaper Ltd. All rights reserved. Reprinted with permission. Further reproduction prohibited. www.economist.com

capital is creating an inherently unstable situation. If global trade experiences anemic growth or worse, declines, this slump will cause the demand for exports to drop, and the world's consumers are likely to respond to the slowdown by turning away from the free-trade regime that engineered their previous period of unprecedented growth.

Domestic economic policies also tend to shape many countries' foreign trade policies. Observe in this context how countries differ in the extent to which they regulate their national economies and the degree to which the level of economic freedom within states predicts the level of growth they experience. Overwhelming evidence shows that economic freedom makes for prosperity; those countries that do not interfere with trade at home tend to have the highest average economic growth rates. Liberalism in domestic economic policy pays many financial, political and security dividends. Compare the rankings of countries according to their economic freedom, and we see much evidence supporting the view that open markets stimulate economic growth (Mandelbaum 2003).

Referring to Map 12.1, we see strong evidence suggesting that the most economically free states not only grow their wealth at the fastest rates, but also provide the best or safest environments for investments with the least risk. In addition, these open economies are the least corrupt and least prone to civil wars. This is because economically free countries tend to be politically free; that is, ruled democratically with legal ways for resolving conflicts, as opposed to economically repressed countries, which also curtail liberties and violate human rights.

Given the seemingly clear-cut economic advantages of free trade, it is difficult to understand why many governments resist open markets. The answer lies in the fact that trade can appear in the eye of the beholder to be inherently unfair. Unions in wealthy Global North states complain that the lower wages of the Global South countries give them "unfair" advantages and, for their part, the less-developed Global South states complain that they cannot "fairly" compete against their more productive, technologically advanced Global North counterparts. Given that many people in both wealthy and poor countries think that they are not competing on a level playing field, the age-old debate between free traders and mercantilists is likely to persist as a global issue.

Emerging Regional Trade Policies

For some time, analysts have worried about the possibility that regional trading arrangements will push the open-trading regime, which is central to the Liberal International Economic Order, toward closure. The United States first experimented with creating trade partnerships within particular regions in 1984, with the Caribbean Basin Initiative to reduce tariffs and provide tax incentives to promote industrialization and trade in Central America and the Caribbean. This was soon followed in 1987 with free-trade agreements with Israel and Canada, and in 1989 with the North American Free Trade Agreement (NAFTA, signed by Canada, Mexico, and the United States in 1993). In addition, at their April 2001 Quebec Summit, the United States and thirty-three Western Hemispheric democracies took a bolder step when they pledged to build a Free Trade Area of the Americas (FTAA), creating the world's largest barrier-free trade zone, from the Arctic to Argentina, linking markets to 800 million people.

• **regional currency union** the pooling of sovereignty to create a common currency (such as the EU's euro) and single monetary system for members in a region, regulated by a regional central bank within the currency bloc to reduce the likelihood of large-scale liquidity crises.

Efforts to link the countries of the Western Hemisphere in an economic partnership are seen by many as a response to European integration. Since the 1950s, European leaders have tried methodically to build a continent-wide economic union. By 2002, they had established a **regional currency union,** with a single currency (the euro) designed to facilitate economic flows among EU members. Although some EU states (Britain, Denmark, and Sweden) have thus far not adopted the euro, its supporters insist that the euro will strengthen European economic consciousness and transform the continent into a single market for business (Samuelson 2002b).

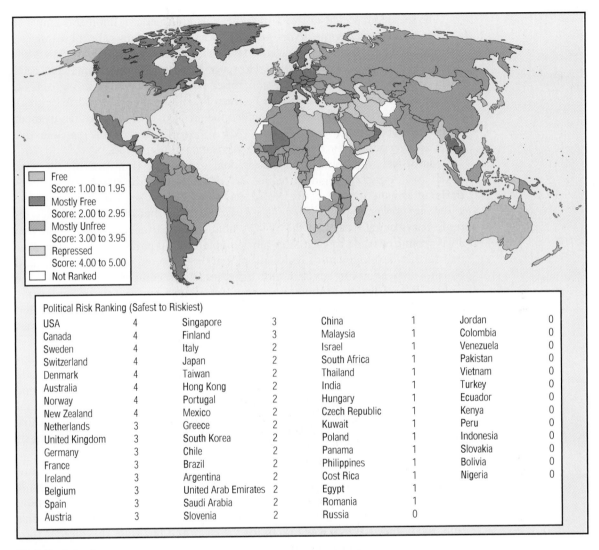

Political Risk Ranking (Safest to Riskiest)

USA	4	Singapore	3	China	1	Jordan	0
Canada	4	Finland	3	Malaysia	1	Colombia	0
Sweden	4	Italy	2	Israel	1	Venezuela	0
Switzerland	4	Japan	2	South Africa	1	Pakistan	0
Denmark	4	Taiwan	2	Thailand	1	Vietnam	0
Australia	4	Hong Kong	2	India	1	Turkey	0
Norway	4	Portugal	2	Hungary	1	Ecuador	0
New Zealand	4	Mexico	2	Czech Republic	1	Kenya	0
Netherlands	3	Greece	2	Kuwait	1	Peru	0
United Kingdom	3	South Korea	2	Poland	1	Indonesia	0
Germany	3	Chile	2	Panama	1	Slovakia	0
France	3	Brazil	2	Philippines	1	Bolivia	0
Ireland	3	Argentina	2	Cost Rica	1	Nigeria	0
Belgium	3	United Arab Emirates	2	Egypt	1		
Spain	3	Saudi Arabia	2	Romania	1		
Austria	3	Slovenia	2	Russia	0		

M A P   1 2 . 1
Ranking Countries by Their Economic Freedom and Political Risk

Much evidence points to the conclusion that states with the most economic freedom have the highest rates of long-term economic growth. According to a widely used index of market openness, at the start of 2003, 71 of 156 countries were either economically "free" or "mostly free" while 85 were "mostly unfree" or "repressed." The political risk ranking in the chart above suggests that the most economically free countries are also the most stable and, as a consequence, the safest environments for corporations and private investors to make investments. Note: Map based rankings through the year 2002, followed by political risk rankings.

SOURCE: Map from Heritage Foundation website at www.heritage.org; political risk from *World Trade* 14, June 2001, p. 36.

The successful Mercosur free-trade zone in South America is another example of a regional economic regime. Its six member countries—Argentina, Brazil, Paraguay, Uruguay, and later Chile and Bolivia—expanded trade sixfold in 1998 to $18.2 billion (from only $3.6 billion in 1991). However, Mercosur's progress stalled in 2002 when Argentina, facing a deep recession, raised tariffs in violation of the agreement, and the barriers posed by differences between Brazil's floating *real* and Argentina's *peso* pegged to the U.S. dollar compounded the problem. The enlarged ten-member Association of Southeast Asian Nations (ASEAN) free-trade region is representative of yet another among the many multilateral regional trading blocs.

Many feel that these types of regional arrangements are consistent with GATT's rules and see regional regimes as vital pieces in the step toward a free-trade agreement for the entire global economy. Others see the division of the globe into competing trade blocs as a danger, fretting that existing regional free-trade zones actually violate the WTO's nondiscrimination principle by moving away from free trade toward inter-bloc competition. In particular, the critics fear that further development of regionalized markets centered on Asia, Europe, and North America has already split globalized trade into competing trade blocs (see Figure 12.4). Currently, almost three-quarters of exports in Asia go within the APEC region to other Asian countries, two-thirds of European exports go within the European Union, and more than half of exports by North American countries stay within the NAFTA bloc (World Bank 2002a, 345).

The ultimate impact of the trend toward regionalization of the world political economy remains uncertain. Some analysts believe the formation of trade blocs will undermine global free trade and thereby plague world economic growth in the years ahead. Others are concerned with the possibility that regional economic centers will undermine security relationships. If trade-bloc rivalry intensifies, still others warn of a cutthroat mercantile rivalry in which the fear of one another may be the only force binding the regional members together.

Those outside the world's major trading blocs have ample reason to be concerned about the prospect of a world divided into separate regional centers. It leaves them outside the system altogether. Therefore, even though developing Global South countries in the past have regarded the GATT/WTO as a rich man's club, today they see it as a guardian for the clear and fair rules they need if they are to successfully enter the global arena.

The Future of Global Economic Governance

International trade and finance can be likened to a global game of dominoes. If the world's biggest economy (the United States) falters, how, in an integrated global system fraught with competition, can other countries' economies stay upright? In a global recession, how can any one country prosper when its fate depends on the economic growth of everyone else? These concerns were underscored in 2001 when the World Bank warned that the global economy could not fly forever on a single engine—the U.S. economy.

The architecture of the Liberal International Economic Order constructed at Bretton Woods a half-century ago appeared to depend not only on a consensus about the appropriate shape of the world political economy but also on U.S. lead-

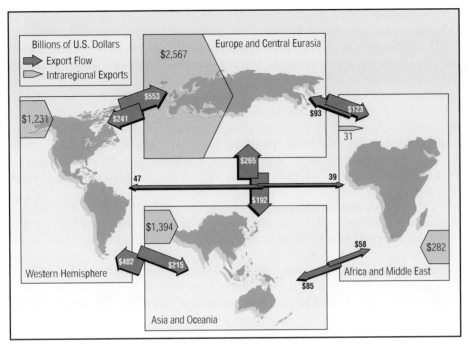

FIGURE 12.4
Trade Blocs and the Regionalization of Global Trade

A trend shaping the global political economy has been the propensity of trade flows to concentrate *within* regions instead of *between* them. The economist Paul Krugman calls this "the localization of the world economy" to describe the tendency to trade with neighbors rather than with distant countries. This trend has resulted in the formation of four major trade blocs all promoting the removal of state barriers to free trade but more so inside each bloc than among all countries. The above map shows the shape of exports within and between the four major trade blocs. Note that trade flows are far from equal—the dollar value of exports varies in directional balance across the major trade regions, showing that the liberal goal of a single global marketplace remains just that, an ideal or aspiration yet to be realized.
SOURCE: World Trade Organization, 2002.

ership. The United States is still the dominant state in the world political economy and continues to perform many hegemonic functions: It tries to maintain a comparatively open market for others' goods, manage the international monetary system, provide capital to would-be borrowers facing financial stress, and coordinate economic policies among the world's leading economies. Today, however, U.S. willingness to absorb the costs of leadership has waned. More worrisome still, the United States has increasingly shown a strong preference for taking a unilateral approach toward international problems. This "go-it-alone" posture is especially evident with respect to free trade. In March 2002, for example, President George W. Bush placed significant restrictions on imported steel. Shortly thereafter, a major trade battle ensued as European and Asian officials issued an immediate warning that they would challenge the U.S. violation of its commitment to free trade in the World Trade Organization.

Washington's trade policy reflects two instincts: (1) open foreign markets to U.S. exports and (2) cushion the impact of imports on the U.S. economy. Of course, the United States is not alone in this regard. Other states also have placed national interests above international ideals. For instance, the European Union discourages beef imports with a tariff of 213 percent, while Japan limits wheat with a 353 percent charge, and Canada restricts butter with a 360 percent tax. Many of the agricultural commodities produced in Global North countries and protected by tariff and nontariff barriers can be grown cheaply in the Global South. "This kind of protectionism as practiced by the wealthiest industrialized countries is simply indefensible," says Nicholas Stern, chief economist of the World Bank. "The cost to developing countries is much greater in lost export opportunities than the amount of official aid they receive each year." (Drozdiak 2001, 17).

Clearly, the liberal trading agreements so slowly built up over the past five decades remain fragile. The combination of a global slowdown, financial market volatility, a deepening of U.S. trade imbalances, and worldwide excess of manufacturing capacity could easily bring about a global upsurge in protectionism. Yet, as U.S. Federal Reserve chairman Alan Greenspan (2004) warns, "the protectionist cures advanced to address these hardships will make matters worse rather than better." Protectionism, he concluded, will "do little to create jobs and if foreigners retaliate, we will surely lose jobs."

A new wave of mercantilism and trade wars is not preordained. A number of other important developments are also likely to influence the future direction of the world political economy, and these, in combination, are likely to sustain and strengthen the liberal free-trade regime that has contributed to global economic growth. World commerce has become globalized; global financial flows outstrip trade transactions within countries; and market forces almost everywhere are now being given a freer rein to determine economic outcomes. With trade growing rapidly in the absence of barriers, and with the expansion of free-trade areas, pressure to preserve the liberal trade regime has increased. Multinational corporations are playing a larger role in the continuing growth of commercial liberalism worldwide, and they are supported in this aspiration by the powerful WTO, the conversion of eastern Europe and China to acceptance of freer trade, and the opening up of restrictive markets to exports. All these developments suggest that the prospects for commercial liberalism to gain strength are promising.

Some theorists believe that the spread of liberal market philosophies will eliminate the need for new institutions to cope with the changing world political economy. Others caution that the unregulated market should not be considered the ideal, because coordinating institutions are needed to manage sustained growth. The task of reaching agreement about what economic policies countries should adopt is difficult due to the absence of a true consensus about what the world political economy should look like, as the continuing contest between liberalism and mercantilism (as well as the conflict between rich and poor countries) illustrates. Furthermore, the globalization of commerce and finance increasingly seems to shape, rather than be shaped by, states' policies—thus challenging the sovereign prerogatives of states themselves.

The face of the future thus remains uncertain. If liberals are correct, the process of globalization will hasten the trend toward interdependence and integration and, with that, the prospects for economic prosperity and political harmony. If mercantilists are right, however, an emerging era of geoeconomic rivalry will increase states' vulnerability and thus the likelihood of political conflict. Meanwhile, national leaders are struggling with how to reconcile domestic political pressures to protect jobs from overseas outsourcing with external economic forces over which they have little control. In the tug-of-war between the competing values of trade liberalization and protectionism, leaders will constantly face trade-offs as they balance policy initiatives seeking to promote growth with those designed to protect autonomy. How they manage these trade-offs will have profound effects on the global future.

Chapter Summary

- World politics and economics are inextricably linked. Whether a state's economic system is open or closed, events in the global political economy have domestic consequences. As a result, policymakers play two-level games. The moves they make on the international level affect what they can do on the domestic level, and vice versa.
- Most debates today in the field of international political economy are ultimately reducible to the competing theories of commercial liberalism and mercantilism. Whereas liberals advocate open markets and free trade, mercantilists call for government regulation of economic endeavors to increase state power and security. Although free trade contributes to economic growth, its benefits are not distributed equally.
- Rules governing international commerce evolve according to the wishes of the powerful. The Bretton Woods agreements of 1944 established a Liberal International Economic Order (LIEO), which rested on three political bases: the concentration of power in the hands of a small number of states, the existence of a cluster of interests shared by those states, and the presence of a hegemonic power (the United States) willing to exercise a leadership role.
- The postwar Liberal International Economic Order led to a dramatic upswing in the exchange of goods and services among states, which brought about an increasingly integrated and prosperous global economy.
- The immediate postwar economic system was a dollar-based system, with the United States operating, in effect, as the world's banker. By the early 1970s, however, U.S. leadership was no longer readily accepted by others or willingly exercised by Washington. Power had become more widely dispersed among states. Where hegemony once reigned, various groups of industrialized nations now participated in a series of quasi-official negotiating forums to deal with monetary issues.
- The simultaneous pursuit of liberalism and mercantilism today shows states' determination to reap the benefits of interdependence while minimizing its costs. It also reveals the tension between the promise that everyone will benefit and the fear that the benefits will not be equally distributed. The absence of world government encourages each state to be more concerned with how it fares competitively in relation to other states—its relative gains—than

collectively with its absolute gains. These simple yet powerful ideas shed light on the reasons why the United States, the principal advocate of free trade in the post–World War II era, has increasingly engaged in protectionism.

• Economic nationalism and a retreat from multilateral economic cooperation threaten to undermine the overall prospects for world economic growth. Given the growing regionalization of trade and the formation of competitive trade blocs, the rise of regional neomercantilism is a possibility. However, economic globalization is likely to accelerate, and, as competition expands wealth and reduces the costs of both products and labor, the economic fate of the world's six billion people will be tied closer together, making the welfare of any one important to the welfare of all.

KEY TERMS

antidumping duties
balance of payments
balance of trade
beggar-thy-neighbor policies
collective goods
commercial liberalism
comparative advantage
countervailing duties
exchange rate
export quotas
fixed exchange rates
floating exchange rates
free riders

Group of Five (G-5)
Group of Seven (G-7)/Group
    of Eight (G-8)
hegemonic stability theory
import quotas
infant industry
international liquidity
international monetary system
international political economy
laissez-faire economics
Liberal International Economic
    Order (LIEO)

mercantilism
money supply
most-favored-nation (MFN)
    principle
neomercantilism
nondiscrimination
orderly market arrangements
    (OMAs)
protectionism
regional currency union
voluntary export restrictions
    (VERs)

 ## WHERE ON THE WORLD WIDE WEB?

Organization for Economic Co-operation and Development

http://www.oecd.org/

The Organization for Economic Co-operation and Development (OECD) began with the purpose of rebuilding war-ravaged economies after World War II and administering the distribution of the Marshall Plan's aid to Europe. Today, the OECD promotes policies that contribute to the expansion of world trade on a nondiscriminatory basis. It provides a forum in which the governments of the 30 member states can compare their experiences and

further the principles of a market economy. From the OECD's home page, you can access the largest source of comparative statistical data on the industrialized countries.

Trade Resources

http://www.usitc.gov/tr/tr.htm

The United States International Trade Commission (USITC) has created an information referral service for those seeking information related to international trade and investment. Considering investments in Canada? Want to export tractors to Russia? This website provides Internet resources to help those interested in international trade and investment to obtain information on their client country, research various products, access trade assistance, understand patent law, or view international law.

World Bank

http://www.worldbank.org/

The World Bank is the largest source of development assistance, providing nearly $30 billion in loans annually. The Bank was first created to aid European countries in their recovery from World War II. Today the Bank's mission is to help developing countries achieve stable, sustainable, and equitable growth. Its main focus is to help the poorest people and the poorest countries to grow economically.

World Trade Organization

http://www.wto.org/

The World Trade Organization (WTO) is a multilateral, global intergovernmental organization (IGO). Its main purposes are to administer trade agreements between countries, monitor trade policies, and provide technical assistance and training for developing countries. Unlike many international organizations, the WTO has a mechanism for settling international disputes with limited enforcement abilities. Click on the Dispute Settlement link on the home page to review the status of current WTO disputes.

INFOTRAC® COLLEGE EDITION

Search for the following articles in the InfoTrac College Edition database.

Heginbotham, Eric, and Richard J. Samuels. "Mercantile Realism and Japanese Foreign Policy," *International Security* Spring 1998.

Litan, Robert E. "The 'Globalization' Challenge," *Brookings Review* Spring 2000.

Sampson, Gary P. "The Environmentalist Paradox: The World Trade Organization's Challenges," *Harvard International Review* Winter 2002.

Taylor, Chantell. "NAFTA, GATT, and the Current Free Trade System: A Dangerous Double Standard for Workers' Rights," *Denver Journal of International Law and Policy* Fall 2000.

For more articles, enter:

"International Monetary Fund" in the Subject Guide, and then go to subdivision "economic policy."

"mercantilism" in the Subject Guide.

"World Trade Organization" in the Subject Guide, and then go to subdivision "powers and duties."

ADDITIONAL CD-ROM RESOURCES

Click on International Political Economy to access additional resources related to this chapter.

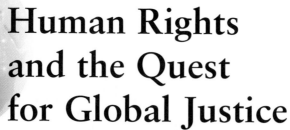

Human Rights and the Quest for Global Justice

Recognition of the inherent dignity and of the equal and inalienable rights of all members of the human family is the foundation of freedom, justice and peace in the world.

UNIVERSAL DECLARATION OF HUMAN RIGHTS, 1948

At 1:00 AM on December 20, 1989, U.S. troops supported by stealth aircraft invaded Panama in what President George Bush called Operation Just Cause. The purpose of the operation was to capture General Manuel Noriega, a military dictator who had gained control over Panama six years earlier. During his time in power, Noriega repressed opposition movements, manipulated elections, and ordered the murder of dissident political leaders. Up to this point, his ruthless behavior had been overlooked because he had previously assisted the United States in its fight against communism in Central America. By 1987, however, Noriega's human rights abuses as well as his involvement in narcotics trafficking and money laundering led Bush's predecessor, Ronald Reagan, to impose economic sanctions on Panama.

Sanctions did little to weaken Noriega's dictatorship. On December 16, 1989, following the murder of an unarmed U.S. marine lieutenant by members of the Panama Defense Forces, the wounding of another American serviceman, and the arrest and brutal interrogation of a U.S. naval officer and his wife, Bush decided to remove Noriega by force. When justifying his decision in an address to the nation on December 20, the president insisted that Noriega's behavior created an imminent danger to U.S. citizens in Panama. While Bush spoke of protecting Americans abroad, speeches delivered by U.S. diplomats Thomas R. Pickering to the United Nations Security Council on December 20 and by Luigi R. Einaudi to the Organization of American States (OAS) on December 22 emphasized the humanitarian duty to protect foreign nationals. Noriega, argued Pickering, "repeatedly obstructed the will of the Panamanian people." Panamanians, he added, "have a right to be free." For the Bush administration, the issue was not merely guarding U.S. national security interests; the "will of the Panamanian people is what we are here defending." Pointing to a series of conditions that made the use of force lawful, he concluded by stressing that the invasion occurred "only after exhausting the full range of alternatives (*Panama: A Just Cause* 1989, 1)."

With the intervention framed by Pickering in terms of a *legally permissible* response by the United States to egregious human rights violations, Einaudi proceeded to explain why the president faced a *moral necessity* that obliged him to act. He began by proclaiming that there are times when "history appears to incarnate some great and irresistible principle." The world community, he continued, was "once again living in historic times, a time when a great principle . . . [was] spreading across the world like wild fire." The principle was "the revolutionary idea that the people, not governments, are sovereign." Panamanians were "sick of stolen elections, sick of military dictatorships, sick of narco-strongmen, and sick of the likes of Manuel Noriega." Would the OAS, he asked, be willing to forfeit the "moral authority which it enjoys throughout the hemisphere by challenging the just verdict that history had decreed upon Manuel Noriega?" By supporting the United States, Einaudi proclaimed that the OAS would "put itself on the right side of history (*Panama: A Just Cause.* 1989, 2–3)."

The 1989 U.S. intervention into Panama raises several questions about the role of **human rights** in world politics. What are human rights? How well are they

• **human rights** the political and social entitlements recognized by international law as inalienable and valid for individuals in all countries by virtue of their humanity.

observed around the world? When a sovereign state violates them, is it legally permissible for others to intervene on behalf of the victims? Do other states have a moral responsibility to intervene? If a humanitarian intervention occurs, how should it be conducted? Are appeals to universal human rights merely a cover for actions that the intervening state takes out of its own narrow political interests?

Until relatively recently, the theoretical study of world politics neglected human rights. It pictured the plight of the ordinary people as a matter of domestic politics, shielded from outside scrutiny by a state's sovereignty. This neglect today seems strange, because social scientists can use their humanity as a means of understanding. As the anthropologist Robert Redfield (1962) argued, "The physicist need not sympathize with his atoms, nor the biologist with his fruit flies, but the student of people and institutions must employ [one's] natural sympathies in order to discover what people think or feel." Moreover, understanding how people think and feel has grown in importance as the world community increasingly recognizes the inherent moral status of humans and the concomitant obligation of states to protect that status. Ordinary people are becoming empowered, and should not be seen as "simply hapless victims of fate, devoid of any historical agency" (Saurin 2000).

The purpose of this chapter is to examine the human condition and assess its prospects for the global future. There are now more than six billion people on the face of the earth, and the world population is growing. Between two and four billion more people will be added to the planet's population between now and the last quarter of the twenty-first century. With these numbers comes a concern over how humanity will fare in the decades ahead. To what extent will people around the world have a voice in shaping their destiny?

Evaluating the Human Condition

"Man is born free, and everywhere he is in chains," the eighteenth-century political philosopher Jean Jacques Rousseau bemoaned in his famous 1762 book, *Social Contract*. Times have since changed, but for some parts of the world Rousseau's characterization of the human condition remains valid. Despite some people enjoying unprecedented standards of living, a daunting scale of poverty is evident throughout the world (see Map 13.1). Even more troubling, the gap between rich and poor is increasing: "In the past 15 years, per capita income has declined in more than 100 countries . . . [but] the number of poor people will increase sharply . . . to more than 100 million from 40 million, if current trends continue, according to World Bank estimates" (Speth 1999a, 6).

Consumption patterns show other discrepancies. One-fifth of the world's wealthiest people have "90 percent of all Internet accounts, 74 percent of all phone lines, [and] 82 percent of all export markets" (McGurn 2002, 23). "The poorest 20 percent of the world's population receives only 0.2 percent of global commercial bank lending, 1.3 percent of global investment, 1 percent of global trade and 1.4 percent of global income" (Saurin 2000, 208). The "world's three

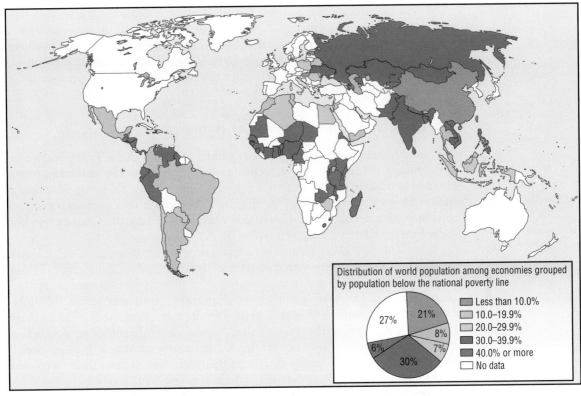

Distribution of world population among economies grouped by population below the national poverty line

27%   21%

8%

6%   7%

30%

- Less than 10.0%
- 10.0–19.9%
- 20.0–29.9%
- 30.0–39.9%
- 40.0% or more
- No data

M A P   1 3 . 1

The Percentage of People Living Below the Poverty Line, 1984–2000

As this map shows, if measured according to the World Bank's standard of $1.08 dollars or less a day in purchasing power parity (PPP) terms, huge proportions of the world's population live in extreme poverty. The purchasing power parity adjusts for different relative prices among countries. It is a method of calculating exchange rates that attempts to value different currencies at rates such that each currency can purchase an equal basket of goods (Colander 2001, 383). *The Economist* has formulated a PPP index based on the price of a Big Mac sold by McDonald's in more than 120 countries.

SOURCE: *World Bank Atlas,* 2002, p. 24. Copyright © 2002 by the International Bank for Reconstruction and Development/The World Bank.

richest individuals are now worth more than the forty-eight poorest nations" (Easterbrook 2002, 17).

Another indicator of the state of humanity is the deplorable conditions in which many people live. Life expectancy in the Global South has been increasing over the past few decades, but still averages less than sixty years; in the Global North it exceeds eighty years. In the Global South, infant mortality rates are among the highest in the world and less than half of the adult population is literate (a proportion even lower among women). "Among the 4.4 billion people in developing countries around the world, three-fifths live in communities lacking basic sanitation; one third go without safe drinking water; one quarter lack adequate housing; [and] one fifth are undernourished" (Speth 1999a, 6).

Given the serious deprivations facing so many people, there are ample reasons for humanitarian concern. Crushing poverty and lack of opportunity is a recipe for hopelessness, desperation, and violence. Recognizing this problem, scholars and governmental officials have debated the complex relationship between human rights and development ever since the UN Commission on Human Rights first wrestled with the issue in 1977.

The Democratic Underpinnings of Human Development

The human dimension of development gained attention in the 1970s when analysts realized the importance of focusing on aspects of human welfare not measured by economic indicators that describe a country's wealth. Beyond looking at indicators such as the average income for each person in a particular country, analysts began devoting attention to different levels of education and factors that contributed to living a long, rewarding life.

Many factors affect human development. Among them, political freedom stands out. The degree to which countries rule themselves democratically and protect civil liberties is a potent determinant of human development. Map 13.2 shows the various levels of human development in countries across the globe. One conclusion that the United Nations Development Program has drawn from the data displayed in the map is that human development flourishes where democracy flourishes. "Politics matter for human development because people everywhere want to be free to determine their destinies, express their views, and participate in the decisions that shape their lives" (UNDP 2002).

Alongside democracy, national economic growth also contributes to human development. For human development goals to be met, prosperity clearly helps. Strong evidence supports the proposition that "as peoples' basic security needs are met in richer countries, they turn their attention to important secondary concerns—such as liberty, a desire for which seems to be inherent in human nature but can only emerge reliably when more fundamental issues of personal safety, food, shelter, and other basic needs are met" (Mazarr 1999). Thus, when countries are grouped and ranked according to their human development performance, as we might expect, the level of human development is highest in the Global North, where economic prosperity is also highest on average; conversely, it is generally lower in the Global South where per capita economic output is substantially lower. Nevertheless, the link between economic well-being and human development is not automatic. Two countries with similar per capita incomes can have very different levels of human development, because some governments are more effective in converting national wealth into better lives for their people (UNDP 1999, 129). Equatorial Guinea and the Czech Republic, for example, ranked 38 and 39 out of 173 countries, respectively, on per capita gross domestic product (GDP) in 2002, adjusted for purchasing power parity. When compared on the UN Development Program's human development index (a measure based on life expectancy, literacy, education, and income), Equatorial Guinea ranked 111 and the Czech Republic 33 (*The Economist*, August 3, 2002, 82). In short, income alone is not a good predictor of human development. How countries politically organize themselves to promote the human welfare of their citizens makes a crucial difference.

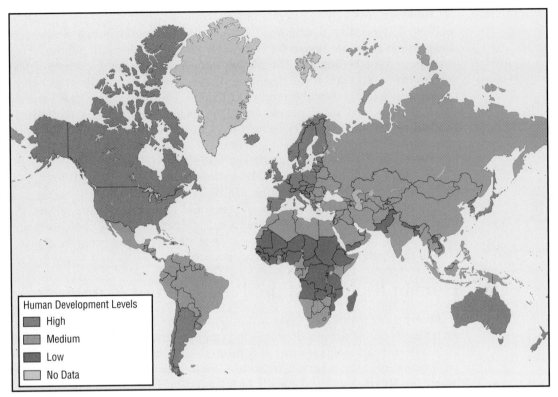

M A P   1 3 . 2
The Map of Human Development

This map shows the level of human development in the countries of the world, based on an index that uses life expectancy, literacy, average number of years of schooling, and income to assess a country's performance in providing for its people's welfare and security. Note the wide variation. Although poorer Global South countries have made big gains in the past quarter century (following political reforms leading to greater democracy and economic reforms leading to free markets), a gap in levels of human development is apparent, and parallels to some degree the gap between the Global North and the Global South.
SOURCE: United Nations Human Development Report, 2002; United Nations Development Programme 2002, pp. 38–41.

Human Development in an Age of Globalization

The rapid transfer of capital and investment across borders that is integrating the world's economies has led to widespread speculation that globalization will provide a cure for the chronic poverty facing the majority of humanity. Impressive gains have been made in Global South countries over the past three decades, notes a recent United Nations study: "A child born today can expect to live eight years longer than one born 30 years ago. Many more people can read and write, with the adult literacy rate having increased from an estimated 47 percent in 1970 to 73 percent in 1999. [And the] share of rural families with access to safe water has grown more than five-fold" (UNDP 2001, 10). According to global optimists, these gains suggest that poverty can be eradicated.

However, critics complain that globalization is part of the problem, not the solution. Capital may flow more freely around the world, but it flows most slowly to places where human suffering is the greatest. A skeptical political economist from Mexico cautions: "Developing countries today are a much more heterogeneous group than at the beginning of the postwar period, [but] globalization is not helping them become more equal. The poorest are not catching up. . . . More and more people across the planet have become increasingly exposed to the amenities of the global marketplace, although mostly as permanent window shoppers and silent spectators. The large majority of humankind, however, is rapidly being left outside and far behind" (Heredia 1999).

Although progress in human development has occurred and will likely persist, so will trends that can erode human welfare, making the early twenty-first century appear to be both the best of times and the worst of times. Thus, the future of world politics will be not only a struggle between the Global North and Global South but also a contest between those who see global progress as possible and those who see global regress as inevitable.

Human Rights and the Protection of People

Rights are entitlements that a person has to something. By acknowledging a right, we set limits on the actions of others and empower the right-holder to have nullified any encroachments into what is protected. As stated earlier, human rights are entitlements that a person possesses simply because he or she is a human being. As such, they are held equally by all and cannot be lost or forfeited (Donnelly 1993).

Unfortunately, not everyone enjoys all of the human rights recognized by international law. Three areas that remain problematic are the rights of women, indigenous peoples, and refugees.

The Subordinate Status of Women and Its Consequences

Over the past three decades, the status of women has become a major human rights concern (see Table 13.1). Increasingly people have realized that women have an important influence on human development, and that their treatment is an issue that affects everyone.

Women throughout the world continue to be disadvantaged relative to men in various ways. They have less access to primary education and to advanced training in professional fields, such as science, engineering, law, and business. In addition, within occupational groups, they are almost always in less-prestigious jobs, where they receive less pay than men in comparable positions and they face formidable barriers to advancement. Although these and other gender differences have narrowed in recent years, particularly in Global North countries, gender inequalities remain widespread. Women's share of earned income in developing countries is less than a third of men's. Furthermore, their share of administrative and managerial jobs is minuscule. Much the same holds true in politics: Females hold 14 percent of the seats in parliaments worldwide and only 6 percent of national government posts (*State of the World* 2002, 145; UNDP 2001, 210–229).

TABLE 13.1

Important Steps on the Path Toward Human Rights and Gender Empowerment

Year	Conference	Key Issue
1968	United Nations International Conference on Human Rights (Teheran)	"Parents have a basic human right to decide freely and responsibly on the number and spacing of their children."
1974	World Population Conference (Bucharest)	"The responsibility of couples and individuals [should take] into account the needs of their living and future children, and their responsibilities toward the community."
1975	International Women's Year Conference (Mexico City)	"The human body, whether that of a woman or man, is inviolable, and respect for it is a fundamental element of human dignity and freedom."
1979	Convention on the Elimination of All Forms of Discrimination Against Women (New York)	Article 12 calls on countries to "take all appropriate measures to eliminate discrimination against women in the field of health care in order to ensure, on a basis of equality of men and women, access to health care services, including those related to family planning."
1984	World Population Conference (Mexico City)	"Governments can do more to assist people in making their reproductive decisions in a responsible way. [Family planning is] a matter of urgency."
1992	United Nations Conference on Environment and Development (Rio de Janeiro)	Agenda 21 calls for "women-centered, women-managed, safe and accessible, responsible planning of family size and service."
1993	United Nations World Conference on Human Rights (Vienna)	The Vienna Declaration includes nine paragraphs on "The Equal Status and Human Rights of Women," and, for the first time recognizes that "violence against women is a human-rights abuse."
1994	International Conference on Population and Development (Cairo)	Program of Action "reaffirms the basic human rights of all couples and individuals to decide freely and responsibly the number and spacing of children and to have the information, education, and means to do so."
1995	United Nations Fourth World Conference on Women (Beijing)	Sets a wide-ranging, ambitious agenda for promoting human development by addressing gender inequality and women's rights.
1999	United Nations Conference on World Population (The Hague)	Drafts recommendations on humane assistance for international family planning programs in the light of the possibility that the global population could start to decline in the late twenty-first century.
2002	World Summit on Sustainable Development (Johannesburg)	Drafts resolutions to combat abject and dehumanizing poverty, stressing the importance of reform to encourage gender equality and the rights of women in order to stimulate sustainable economic growth.

The need to extend women equal rights is now widely recognized. "The river of thought on human rights and development runs inexorably toward the emancipation of women everywhere and the equality of men and women," notes one report (*State of the World* 2002), which also warns, "eddies and rivulets carry the water backwards every day—as when pregnant girls are expelled from school, or when the genitals of young women are cut in a ritual destruction of their capacity for sexual pleasure."

Addressing women's rights is difficult because the issues touch deeply entrenched as well as widely divergent religious and cultural beliefs. In certain Islamic countries, for example, women must hide their faces with veils in public, and women and men are often completely separated in social and religious activities. For many in liberal Western countries, these traditions are difficult to

Graeme Ewens/Panos Pictures

Human Courage in the Face of Urbanization

understand. On the other hand, various Western ideas about gender roles can be perplexing to people elsewhere (Crossette 1995). These religious and cultural differences notwithstanding, international progress on securing women's human rights has been slow, despite the fact that "only when the potential of all human beings is fully realized can we talk of true human development" (UNDP 1995).

The Precarious Life of Indigenous Peoples

• **indigenous peoples** the native ethnic and cultural inhabitant populations within countries ruled by a government controlled by others, often referred to as the "Fourth World."

As noted in Chapter 6, where we first addressed the topic of nonstate actors (NGOs), **indigenous peoples** are members of ethnic groups native to a geographic location now controlled by another state or political group. The planet is populated by an estimated six thousand separate indigenous "nations," each of which has a unique language, culture, and strong, often spiritual, ties to an ancestral homeland. There are today at least 300 million indigenous peoples comprising more than 5 percent of the world's population living in roughly seventy countries (*The State of Indigenous People* 2002). Recall that this segment of global society is conventionally referred to as the "Fourth World" to heighten awareness of their poverty and lack of self-rule (Wilmer 1993).

Many indigenous peoples feel persecuted because their livelihoods, lands, and cultures are threatened. In part, these fears are inspired by the 130 million indigenous peoples who were slaughtered between 1900 and 1987 by state-sponsored violence in their own countries (Rummel 1994). The mass killing of Armenians by Turks, of Jews (and other groups) by Hitler, of Cambodians by the Khmer Rouge, and of the Tutsi of Rwanda by the Hutu exemplify the atrocities committed during the past century. Responding to the tragedy of the Nazi holocaust, Polish jurist Raphael Lemkin coined the word **genocide** from the Greek word *genos* (race, people) and the Latin *caedere* (to kill), and called for it to be singled out as the gravest violation of human rights, a heinous crime the international community would be morally responsible for punishing (Turk 2001).

Various native peoples are now fighting back across the globe against the injustice they perceive states to have perpetrated against them (see Gurr, et al. 2001). This is not to suggest that all indigenous minority groups are bent on using violence to attain power. The members of many such nonstate nations are divided about objectives, and militants who are prepared to fight for independence are usually in a minority. In fact, most Fourth World indigenous movements only seek a greater voice in redirecting the policies and allocation of resources within existing states and are eliciting the support of NGOs and IGOs to pressure states to recognize their claims and protect their rights.

A substantial number of indigenous movements in the last decade have successfully negotiated settlements resulting in devolution—the granting of political power to increase local self-governance. Examples include the Miskitos in Nicaragua, the Gagauz in Moldova, and most regional separatists in Ethiopia and in India's Assam region. Yet, as suggested by the continuing hostilities between the Chechens and the Russian Federation, resolving clashes between aspiring peoples and established states can be extremely difficult.

The goal expressed in the UN Charter of promoting "universal respect for, and observance of, human rights and fundamental freedoms" for everyone is a challenge for many nationally diverse countries, because protecting the human rights and civil liberties of minority populations is inherently difficult. The division of these states along ethnic and cultural lines makes them inherently fragile. Consider the degree to which minority groups compose many states: for example, the share of indigenous populations in Bolivia is 70 percent and Peru, 40 percent. Or consider the number of distinct languages spoken in some countries, with Indonesia's 670 languages, Nigeria's 410, India's 380, Australia's 250, and Brazil's 210 being conspicuous examples (Durning 1993, 83, 86).

Racism and intolerance are hothouses for fanaticism and violence. The belief that one's nationality is superior to all others undermines the concept of human rights (Clapham 2001). Although interethnic competition is a phenomenon that dates back to biblical times, it remains a contemporary plague. According to *The Minorities at Risk Project* (see Gurr 1993, 2001), over 450 ethnopolitical minority groups have been involved in serious, often violent, struggles since 1945, and there exist many risks of new ethnonationalist wars. A few analysts have gone so far as to predict that conflict within and between ethnically divided states could become a major axis on which twenty-first-century world politics revolves.

Click on **Global Conflict and International Relations** for an interactive Case Study on Genocide in Rwanda.

• **genocide** the deliberate extermination of an ethnic or minority group.

Click on **International Law and Organization** for an interactive map of the indigenous peoples of the world and related critical thinking questions.

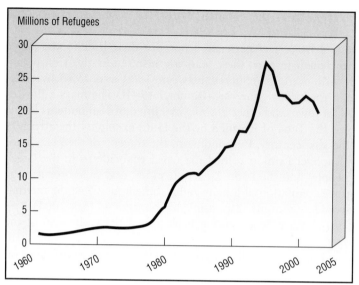

FIGURE 13.1
The World Refugee Crisis

The number of refugees receiving assistance from the UN has risen exponentially in the last four decades. More than 400 million people are estimated to have fled their home countries to avoid persecution or starvation, and at least 11.3 million are today refugees who have found asylum in another country (UNDP 2002, 219).

SOURCE: Adapted from *World Population Prospects.* The United Nations is the author of the original material. Reprinted by permission of United Nations Publications.

The Global Refugee Crisis

• **human security** a concept that refers to the degree to which the welfare of individuals is protected and advanced, in contrast to national security which puts the interests of states first.

• **refugees** people who flee for safety to another country because of a well-founded fear of persecution.

• **displaced people** people involuntarily uprooted from their homes but still living in their own countries.

Nowhere are the problems of **human security** more evident than in the refugee crisis that now prevails. **Refugees** are individuals whose religion, ethnicity, political opinions, or membership in a particular social group make them targets of persecution in their homelands and who migrate from their country of origin. According to the UN High Commissioner for Refugees (UNHCR), the world's refugee population by 2003 was approximately 20 million, or one out of each 300 persons throughout the world (see Figure 13.1). This estimate does not count numerous **displaced people** living in situations similar to those of refugees but held hostage in their own countries and prevented from crossing borders to freedom (*Foreign Policy*, March/April 2002, 31).

Refugees and displaced persons are often the victims of war. For example, the Persian Gulf War in 1991 created a refugee population of 5 million; genocide in Rwanda in 1994 drove more than 1.7 million refugees from their homelands; and the armed conflict between 1991 and 1999 that accompanied the breakup of the former Yugoslavia uprooted nearly 3 million people. More recently, the UN estimates that 3.6 million people have been displaced during the war against al Qaeda and the Taliban in Afghanistan.

Refugees on Desperate Roads Leading Nowhere Most refugees are homeless people in search of sanctuary. Pictured here in 2001 is the makeshift tent housing for 80,000 Afghan refugees at Jalozal in Pakistan. The UN budgeted to help 800,000 Afghan refugees return to their homeland in January 2002 following the war against the Taliban, but since then 1.5 million returned (*Harper's,* October 2002, 11).

A large proportion of the world's refugees and displaced people flee their homelands when ethnic and religious conflicts weaken the capacity of governments to maintain domestic law and order. As public authority dissolves amid rising civil strife, some people move because "they cannot expect, at home, the protection of the police, access to a fair trial, redress of grievances through the courts, prosecution of those who violate their rights, or public assistance in the face of disaster" (Newland 1994).

People also leave home in search of economic opportunity. Legal migrants—particularly young people in the Global South without productive employment—are among those leaving at record rates, mostly to Global North countries, though migration also is occurring *between* developing Global South countries.

Some leaving their home states are the best educated and most talented, causing a serious **brain drain,** but most are not. The majority of migrants take low-wage jobs shunned by local inhabitants. Typically this means migrants earn less than the citizens of those states but more than they would earn in their homelands when performing the same tasks. Host countries may admit migrants (as Europe did during the 1970s guest worker era) not only because they accept low wages for undesirable jobs, but also because in many places the host pays little if anything for migrants' health, education, and welfare needs. On the other hand, the home (sending) countries sometimes encourage people to emigrate as a way of exporting unwanted elements of the population, reducing unemployment, or in the expectation that the emigrants will send much of their income back to their needy families in their homeland.

• **brain drain** the exodus of the most educated people from their homeland to a more prosperous foreign country where the opportunities for high incomes are better, which deprives their homeland of their ability to contribute to its economic development.

CONTROVERSY

What Is Security?

How should *security* be defined? Policymakers disagree. Some see it primarily in military terms; others in human welfare terms. Underlying the disagreement lies a different conception of what is most important on the global agenda. One tradition gives states first priority and assumes that protecting their territorial integrity must be foremost in the minds of national leaders. Others challenge this conception and give primacy to the security of individual people, arguing that social and environmental protection must therefore be seen as a global priority, because all people depend on a clean, healthy environment for survival.

What do you think? To what extent should social and environmental protection be considered security issues? In considering this question, take into consideration the following interpretation.

The traditional concept of national security that evolved during the Cold War viewed security as a function of the successful pursuit of interstate power competition. . . . Environmental security represents a significant departure from this approach to national security. It addresses two distinct issues: the environmental factors behind potentially violent conflicts, and the impact of global environmental degradation on the well-being of societies and economies. The idea that environmental degradation is a security issue when it is a cause of violent conflict appears to be consistent with the traditional definition of national security. However, . . . [the] focus on threats that do not involve an enemy state or political entity disturbs many theorists and practitioners of national security,

for whom the only issues that should be viewed as "security" issues are those that revolve around conflict itself. . . .

The case for environmental security rests primarily on evidence that there has been serious degradation of natural resources (fresh water, soils, forests, fishery resources, and biological diversity) and vital life-support systems (the ozone layer, climate system, oceans, and atmosphere) as a result of the recent acceleration of global economic activities. These global physical changes could have far-reaching effects in the long run. Each of these environmental threats to global well-being is subject to significant empirical and scientific uncertainty. . . . The uncertainties . . . are comparable, however, to those associated with most military threats that national security establishments prepare for. Military planning is based on "worst-case" contingencies that are considered relatively unlikely to occur, yet military preparations for such contingencies are justified as a necessary insurance policy or "hedge" against uncertainty. . . .

The relationship between scarce natural resources and international conflict is not a new issue. But unlike traditional national security thinking about such conflict, which focuses on nonrenewable resources like minerals and petroleum, the environmental security approach addresses renewable resources—those that need not be depleted if managed sustainably. (Porter 1995, 218–220) ●

SOURCE: Excerpt reprinted with permission from *Current History* magazine (May, 1995), p. 218–222. Copyright © 1995 Current History, Inc.

• asylum the provision of sanctuary to safeguard refugees escaping from the threat of persecution in the country where they hold citizenship.

In sum, a combination of push and pull factors has propelled migration to the forefront of the global humanitarian agenda. War, ethnic and religious conflict, human rights violations, and famine all *push* millions beyond their homelands; but migrants also are *pulled* abroad by the promise of economic opportunity and political freedom elsewhere. However, many refugees are finding the doors to safe havens closing. Only a fraction of the 450,000 applying for political **asylum** in 2001 in 25 European countries received sanctuary (*The Economist*, March 31, 2001, 15). Security concerns stimulated by terrorist fears are some-

times at work, as in the United States, where many believe the catastrophic terrorist attacks of September 11, 2001, would not have occurred had immigration
controls been tighter. Economic concerns may also play a role, as unemployed
low and semi-skilled citizens express resentment about increased competition for
scarce jobs.

Efforts to toughen domestic refugee legislation and criteria for granting asylum raise important ethical issues. Where will the homeless, the desperate, the
weak and the poor find sanctuary—a safe place to live where human rights are
safeguarded? Will the rich countries act with compassion or respond with indif-
ference? And more broadly, what is the best way to view human security and reconcile it with national security? These questions may involve irreconcilable values, and will thus make the global refugee crisis a topic of intense debate for years
to come (see Controversy: What Is Security?)

Responding to Human Rights Abuses

The idea of human rights has advanced over the past few decades from a mere
slogan to a program of action. As the examples of the status of women, indigenous peoples, and refugees illustrate, much work remains to be done on implementing the human rights program. Nevertheless, as UN secretary-general Kofi
Annan pointed out in 1999, "States are now widely understood to be instruments
at the service of their people, and not *vice versa*. At the same time . . . the fundamental freedom of each individual, enshrined in the Charter of the UN and
subsequent international treaties—[has] been enhanced by a renewed and spreading consciousness of individual [human] rights. When we read the Charter today,
we are more than ever conscious that its aim is to protect individual human
beings, not to protect those who abuse them."

Internationally Recognized Human Rights

The body of legal rules and norms designed to protect individual human beings
is anchored in the ethical requirement that every person should be treated with
equal concern and respect (Donnelly 1993). The Universal Declaration of Human
Rights, unanimously adopted by the UN General Assembly on December 10,
1948, is the most authoritative statement of these norms. It "establishes a broad
range of civil and political rights, including freedom of assembly, freedom of
thought and expression, and the right to participate in government. The declaration also proclaims that social and economic rights are indispensable, including
the right to education, the right to work, and the right to participate in the cultural life of the community. In addition, the preamble boldly asserts that 'it is
essential, if man is not to be compelled to have recourse, as a last resort, to rebellion against tyranny and oppression, that human rights should be protected by
the rule of law' " (Clapham 2001). These rights have since been codified and
extended in a series of treaties, most notably in the International Covenant on
Civil and Political Rights, and the International Covenant on Economic, Social,
and Cultural Rights (which were both open for signature in 1966 and entered
into force a decade later).

There are many ways to classify the rights listed in these treaties. Charles Beitz (2001, 271), an authority on international ethics, groups them into five categories.

1. *Rights of the person:* "Life, liberty, and security of the person; privacy and freedom of movement; ownership of property; freedom of thought, conscience, and religion, including freedom of religious teaching and practice 'in public and private'; and prohibition of slavery, torture, and cruel or degrading punishment."

2. *Rights associated with the rule of law:* "Equal recognition before the law and equal protection of the law; effective legal remedy for violation of legal rights; impartial hearing and trial; presumption of innocence; and prohibition of arbitrary arrest."

3. *Political rights:* "Freedom of expression, assembly, and association; the right to take part in government; and periodic and genuine elections by universal and equal suffrage."

4. *Economic and social rights:* "An adequate standard of living; free choice of employment; protection against unemployment; 'just and favorable remuneration'; the right to join trade unions; 'reasonable limitation of working hours'; free elementary education; social security; and the 'highest attainable standard of physical and mental health.' "

5. *Rights of communities:* "Self-determination and protection of minority cultures."

Although the multilateral treaties enumerating these rights are legally binding on the states ratifying them, many have either not ratified them or done so with significant reservations. When states specify reservations, they are expressing agreement with the broad declarations of principle contained in these treaties while indicating that they object to certain specific provisions and elect not to be bound by them. The United States, for example, ratified the International Covenant on Civil and Political Rights with reservations in 1992, but has not ratified the International Covenant on Economic, Social, and Cultural Rights. As this example illustrates, countries who agree with the general principle that all human beings possess certain rights that cannot be withheld may still disagree on the scope of these rights. Thus some emphasize rights associated with the rule of law and political rights; while others stress the importance of economic and social rights.

The Challenge of Enforcement

Once the content of human rights obligations was enumerated in multilateral treaties, international attention shifted to monitoring their implementation and addressing violations. The policy question now facing the world is what steps can and should be taken to safeguard these rights. Agreement has yet to be reached on the extent to which the international community has a responsibility to intervene in order to enforce human rights. As the International Commission on Intervention and State Sovereignty noted in its December 2001 report, *The Responsibility to Protect,* "If intervention for human protection purposes is to be

Human Rights versus States' Rights How a state treats its own citizens was, until very recently, its own business under the nonintervention rule in international law. Now the international community has defined the humane treatment of people as a fundamental human right, and the UN Security Council has stretched the traditional definition of threats to international peace in order to authorize various kinds of intervention to protect the universal human rights of people within states. Shown here is an example of the kind of state behavior at the center of the debate: To deter crime, China's leaders have ordered the execution of hundreds of alleged criminals, but some other states have complained that capital punishment is a violation of human rights.

accepted, including the possibility of military action, it remains imperative that the international community develop consistent, credible, and enforceable standards to guide state and intergovernmental practice."

Agreement about the principles that should guide **humanitarian intervention** has proven elusive. The issue is not whether there exists a compelling need and moral obligation to express concerns about populations at risk of slaughter, starvation, or persecution; the issue is about how to craft a just response, when any response will comprise an interference in the domestic affairs of a sovereign state. The rationale for intervening into the internal affairs of other states has been expressed by William Schulz, the executive director of the NGO Amnesty International. Political realists, he argues, "regard the pursuit of rights as an unnecessary, sometimes even a dangerous extravagance, often at odds with our national interest. What they seem rarely to garner is that in far more cases than they will allow, defending human rights is a prerequisite to *protecting* that interest."

• **humanitarian intervention** the use of peacekeeping forces by foreign states or international organizations to protect endangered people from gross violations of their human rights.

Children and Human Rights Violations Sadly, children are often victims of human rights abuses. The UN Children's Fund estimates that some "200,000 children a year are trafficked in West and Central Africa. Girls are affected worst; most end up as domestic workers or prostitutes. Boys are forced to work on coffee or cocoa plantations or as fishermen" (*Time,* April 30, 2001, 39). Shown here is one tragic case: A starving farmer in Afghanistan, Akhtar Mohammed, watching his 10-year-old son, Sher, whom he traded to a wealthy farmer in exchange for a monthly supply of wheat. "What else could I do?" he asked. "I will miss my son, but there was nothing to eat."

Human rights buttress political and economic freedom "which in turn tends to bring international trade and prosperity. And governments that treat their own people with tolerance and respect tend to treat their neighbors in the same way" (Schulz 2001, 13, 14).

Humanitarian intervention refers to actions taken by the international community to assist the population of a state experiencing unacceptable, persistent levels of human suffering caused by natural disaster, political collapse, or deliberate government policy (Malaquias 2001). The decision to engage in humanitarian intervention is controversial, because it pits the legal principle of territorial sovereignty against what some see as a moral duty to protect vulnerable populations

TABLE 13.2

Major Conventions in the Development of International Human Rights

1948	Universal Declaration of Human Rights
1949	Convention on the Prevention and the Punishment of the Crime of Genocide
1950	Convention for the Suppression of the Traffic of Persons and the Exploitation of the Prostitution of Others
1951	Convention Relating to the Status of Refugees
1953	Convention on the Political Rights of Women
1959	Declaration of the Rights of the Child
1965	International Convention on the Elimination of All Forms of Racial Discrimination
1966	International Covenant on Civil and Political Rights
1966	International Covenant on Economic, Social, and Cultural Rights
1966	Optional Protocol to the International Covenant on Civil and Political Rights
1967	Declaration of Territorial Asylum
1969	Inter-American Convention on Human Rights
1973	Principles of International Co-Operation in the Punishment of War Crimes and Crimes against Humanity
1977	Protocols on Humanitarian Law for International Armed Conflicts and Noninternational Armed Conflicts
1979	Convention on the Elimination of All Forms of Discrimination Against Women
1981	Declaration on the Elimination of All Forms of Intolerance and of Discrimination Based on Religion or Belief
1984	Convention against Torture and Other Cruel, Inhuman, or Degrading Treatment or Punishment
1989	Second Optional Protocol to the International Covenant on Civil and Political Rights, Aiming at the Abolition of the Death Penalty
1989	Convention on the Rights of the Child
1991	Convention on the Prevention and Suppression of Genocide
1992	Declaration of Principles of International Law on Compensation to Refugees
1993	Vienna Convention on Human Rights
1993	Declaration on the Rights of Persons Belonging to National or Ethnic, Religious, or Linguistic Minorities
1993	Declaration on the Elimination of Violence against Women
1994	African Convention on Human and Peoples' Rights
2000	Convention Prohibiting Trafficking of Women and Children for Prostitution
2000	International Convention for the Suppression of the Financing of Terrorism

Note: The International Covenant on Civil and Political Rights, the International Covenant on Economic, Social, and Cultural Rights, and the Optional Protocol were all adopted in 1966 and entered into force in 1976.

from egregious violations of human rights. Because concerns for human rights have gained stature under international law and are being monitored more closely by IGOs and NGOs than ever before, we can expect human rights to receive continuing attention, as long as people continue to be in need of help when they are caught in emergency situations such as the threat of famine or genocide.

The global community has expanded its legal protection of human rights significantly over the past 50 years. As Table 13.2 shows, a large number of conventions have been enacted that have steadily endowed individuals with rights—asserting that people must be treated as worthy of the freedom and dignity traditionally granted by international law to states and rulers. "The old assumption that national sovereignty trumps all other principles in international relations is under attack as never before" (Rieff 1999, 67). Nevertheless, the persistence of human suffering undermines the standards for a just global society called for by the Universal Declaration of Human Rights. "As with most declarations of faith, their adherents—first and foremost governments—have frequently failed to live up to them [even though] practically all governments say they accept the basic code of conduct these declarations expound. The continuing effort to achieve and maintain those standards is the frontier between civilization and barbarism" (Urquhart 2001).

Promoting the rights and dignity of ordinary people around the world is a formidable challenge. Although some individuals believe that everyone, by virtue of being human, has certain inherent and inalienable rights that warrant international protection, others remain skeptical of claims that we all have transcendent moral obligations to humanity as a whole. The idea of a humanitarian imperative—a conviction that human suffering obliges others to respond—has ancient roots. From Zeno (335–263 BCE) and Chrysippus (250–207 BCE) through Seneca (4 BCE–65 CE) and Marcus Aurelius (121–180 CE), Greek and Roman Stoics believed in the equality and unity of humankind. Eleanor Roosevelt was a modern champion of this cosmopolitan ideal, and the energetic leadership she displayed was largely responsible for global acceptance in 1948 of the Universal Declaration of Human Rights. Her noble pursuit shows that one person can make a difference in transforming world politics. When thinking about the human condition in the early twenty-first century, we can profit by the inspiration of her nightly prayer: "Save us from ourselves and show us a vision of a world made new."

Chapter Summary

- Although some of humanity enjoys an unprecedented standard of living, a daunting amount of poverty and misery is evident throughout the world.
- Women throughout the world continue to be disadvantaged relative to men in various ways.
- Roughly 5 percent of the world's population is composed of indigenous peoples. Many of them feel persecuted because their livelihoods and cultures are threatened by the governments of those states in which they reside; consequently some have joined separatist movements to pursue self-determination, while others have tried to negotiate a measure of local self-governance.
- A combination of push and pull forces have propelled migration to the forefront of population dynamics. Migrants are pushed out of their homelands by war, famine, and human rights violations. They are pulled abroad by the hope of freedom and economic opportunity.
- Over the past 50 years, the United Nations has developed a detailed list of inherent, inalienable rights of all human beings. They can be grouped into five general categories: rights of the person, rights associated with the rule of law, political rights, economic and social rights, and rights of communities.
- Various international treaties and conventions have sought to protect human rights. However, agreement on the principles that should guide states on when humanitarian intervention is justifiable has proven elusive.

KEY TERMS

asylum
brain drain
displaced people

genocide
human rights
human security

humanitarian intervention
indigenous peoples
refugees

WHERE ON THE WORLD WIDE WEB?

Amnesty International

http://www.amnesty.org/

Amnesty International is an international non-governmental organization (NGO) with a global reach and a specific purpose. Its activities are concentrated on prisoners around the world who are detained solely for their ethnicity, gender, religion, or political beliefs. Amnesty International advocates the release of all prisoners of conscience, the availability of a fair and prompt trial for political prisoners, and the abolishment of the death penalty, torture, and the cruel and inhuman treatment of prisoners.

NetAid

http://www.netaid.org

NetAid is an effort to use the unique networking capabilities of the Internet to promote development and alleviate extreme poverty across the world. NetAid issues periodic calls to action on items of urgency and focuses attention on what works. Read about efforts aimed at ending hunger, helping refugees, saving the environment, securing human rights, and relieving debt. This site also suggests actions you can take to address some of these issues.

The United Nations and the Status of Women: Setting the Global Gender Agenda

http://www.un.org/Conferences/Women/PubInfo/
Status/Home.htm

The United Nations and its programs have provided the most important international forums on women's rights. This website explains the major UN programs that advance women's rights, including the Committee on the Elimination of Discrimination against Women, UN Actions for Women, Commission on the Status of Women, Women in Development, and the Convention on the Elimination of All Forms of Discrimination against Women.

United Nations High Commissioner for Refugees

http://www.unhcr.ch/

Any study of population dynamics requires that one consider migration. The UN High Commissioner for Refugees leads and coordinates international action for the worldwide protection of refugees and the resolution of refugee problems. This website offers a wealth of information on refugees, and is a good place to start examining the issues involved. The "Protecting Refugees" link describes one of the fundamental aspects of the UNHCR. The "Statistic" link gives you current numbers on refugees, worldwide as well as by country.

INFOTRAC® COLLEGE EDITION

Search for the following articles in the InfoTrac College Edition database.

Ballard-Reisch, Deborah S., Paaige K. Turner, and Marcia Sarratea. "The Paradox of Women in Zimbabwe: Emancipation, Liberation, and Traditional African Values," *Women and Language* Fall 2001.

Chi-Ying Chung, Rita. "Psychosocial Adjustment of Cambodian Refugee Women: Implications for Mental Health Counseling," *Journal of Mental Health Counseling* April 2001.

Patrinos, Harry Anthony. "The Cost of Discrimination in Latin America," *Studies in Comparative International Development* Summer 2000.

Schulz, William, Robin Fox, and Francis Fukuyama. "The Ground and Nature of Human Rights: Another Round," *The National Interest* Summer 2002.

For more articles, enter:

"human rights" in the Subject Guide, and then go to subdivision "analysis."

"indigenous peoples" in the Subject Guide, and then go to subdivision "economic aspects."

"refugees" in the Subject Guide, and then go to subdivision "care and treatment."

ADDITIONAL CD-ROM RESOURCES

Click on International Law and Organization and Global Conflict and International Security for additional resources related to this chapter.

CHAPTER 14

Population Growth, Resource Scarcity, and the Preservation of the Global Environment

Chances are that you will never meet any of the estimated 247 human beings who were born in the past minute. In a population of six billion, 247 is a demographic hiccup. In the minute before last, however, there were another 247. In the minutes to come, there will be another, then another, then another. By next year at this time, all those minutes will have produced nearly 130 million newcomers in the great human mosh pit. That kind of crowd is very hard to miss.

JEFFREY KLUGER, demographer

According to the folk tales of Central Asia, centuries ago an advisor to a powerful king invented an intriguing game. It was played by moving pieces on a board containing eight columns and eight rows of squares. The king was so delighted with the game that he offered to reward his advisor with gold and jewels. The advisor declined, protesting that he was a humble man with simple tastes. Rather than accept such a lavish reward, he asked that he be given a single grain of rice for the first square of his board game, twice for the second square, twice that for the third, and so on, until each of the 64 squares had their complement of rice. The king quickly agreed to the what he believed was a modest request. When the Master of the Royal Granary counted out the grains, the numbers began small enough (1, 2, 4, 8, 16, 32, 64, . . .), but before long, he realized the staggering numbers that would soon be involved. For the 64th square alone, 9,223,372,036,854,775,808 grains would be needed to meet the advisor's request. That would amount to roughly 153 billion tons of rice, enough to fill 31 million cargo ships full if each ship held approximately 5,000 tons (Dörner 1996, 111). Of course, that would be merely the amount of rice on the last square of the board game. The next-to-the-last square would take half as much, only 4,611,686,018,427,387,904 grains, the square before it, 2,305,843,009,213,693,952 grains, and so on.

The story of the king's advisor is a fable that reminds us of the consequences of exponential growth. Under certain conditions, amazing configurations can develop over time. Ever since the Reverend Thomas Malthus proposed in 1798 that when unchecked, population increases in a geometric ratio (e.g., 1 to 2, 2 to 4, 4 to 8) while subsistence increases in only an arithmetic ratio (1 to 2, 2 to 3, 3 to 4), demographers have speculated about the long-term consequences of rapid population growth. Earth's population at the beginning of the twentieth century totaled 1.7 billion people; today it exceeds 6 billion. Every three years, it grows roughly by the size of the United States, with some 230,000 people added to the world total every day (Reid 1998, 58). Will these kinds of increases in the world's population continue in the decades ahead? If so, what impact would they have on the planet's **carrying capacity**—the earth's ability to support and sustain life? Will population growth outstrip natural resources? Can enough food be produced to feed the billions who will be born in the future? These concerns have attracted the attention of various scholars and policy makers who are studying how current demographic and environmental trends may affect the global future.

• **carrying capacity** the maximum biomass that can be supported by a given territory.

The **tragedy of the commons** is a metaphor that highlights the potential impact of human behavior on the planet's resources and its delicately balanced ecological systems. First articulated in 1833 by English political economist William Foster Lloyd and later by contemporary human ecologist Garrett Hardin, the commons metaphor depicts a medieval English village, where the "green" was common property on which all villagers could graze their cattle. Freedom of access to the commons was a cherished village value. Sharing the common grazing area worked well as long as usage by individuals (and their cattle) didn't reduce the land's usefulness to everyone else. Assuming the villagers were driven by the profit motive and no laws existed to restrain their greed, herders had an incentive to increase their

• **tragedy of the commons** a metaphor, widely used to explain the impact of human behavior on ecological systems, that explains how rational self-interested behavior by individuals may have a destructive collective impact.

The UN has estimated that India's population reached 1 billion in August 1999 and predicts that India will be the world's most populous country by 2050. Shown here is a railway station in Bombay, India, on the day world population reached 6 billion, October 12, 1999.

stock as much as possible. In the short run, the addition of one more animal would produce a personal gain whose feeding costs would be borne by everyone. But if everyone increased their stock of cattle, in the long run the village green would be destroyed by overgrazing. The lesson? "Ruin is the destination toward which all men rush," Hardin (1968) concluded, "each pursuing his own best interest."

This chapter uses the tragedy of the commons metaphor to explore how demography, resources, and the environment influence the global future. More specifically, we will examine how changes in world population affect the prospects for preserving for future generations the planet's ecology on which life itself depends.

Population Growth as a Global Political Challenge

How many people can the earth support? What are the implications of population growth for the quality of life on this planet? "The most important aspect of necessity that we must now recognize," Hardin (1968) wrote in explaining the tragedy of the commons, is that the "Freedom to breed will bring ruin to

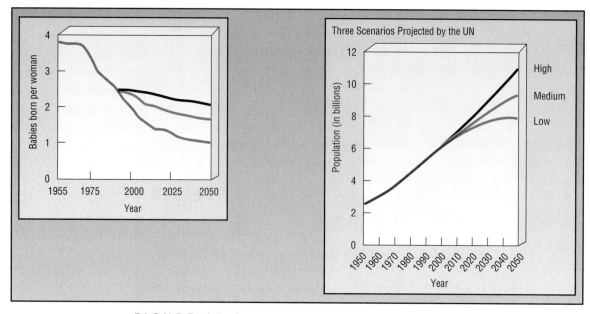

FIGURE 14.1
World Population Growth Projections to the Year 2050

In the twentieth century world population grew from less than 2 billion people to more than 6 billion, with each billion added in less time than the previous billion. World population is growing at 1.3 percent, each year. Between 1.2 and 2.2 billion additional people will be living on the earth by the middle of the twenty-first century, depending on how fast fertility rates (the number of babies born for each woman) fall (see figure on left) and life spans increase. The figure on the right sketches three potential scenarios for the future, showing that "by 2050 world population is expected to be between 7.9 billion (low variant) and 10.9 billion (high variant), with the medium variant producing 9.3 billion" (UNPD 2001). SOURCE: United Nations Population Division (UNPD 2001).

all. . . . The only way we can preserve and nurture other and more precious freedoms is by relinquishing the freedom to breed." Of course, not everyone agrees with Hardin's demographic projections and his call for strict controls over human reproduction. To dissect his argument, it is helpful to trace the global trends in population growth, giving particular attention to changes in fertility and mortality rates (see Figure 14.1).

The story of population growth is told in its statistics: The annual rate of population growth in the twentieth century increased from less than 1 percent in 1900 to a peak of 2.2 percent in 1964. It has since dropped to about 1.3 percent. Despite the recent drop in rate, however, the absolute number of people *added* each year has been significant, growing from 16 million in 1900 to an additional 77 million new people in 2001. Earth is certain to have many more people by the mid-twenty-first century, well beyond the 6.2 billion already roaming the planet. Yet the feared "population explosion" once believed certain is now expected to be far less dramatic than previously predicted (*Vital Signs 2002*, 88).

If a catastrophic population explosion is unlikely, why then do population issues remain so controversial in world politics? We can begin to answer that question by exploring how population dynamics are affecting countries in the Global North and South in different ways.

The Demographic Divide between the Global North and South

Population growth rates are not the same throughout the world. They are much higher in the developing Global South countries than in the wealthy countries in the Global North, a trend that is expected to continue. This "demographic divide," as projected in Figure 14.2, suggests why population dynamics have important political and economic ramifications.

Because population growth is occurring in precisely those countries least able economically to support more people, global population cannot be expected to stabilize until it falls below replacement-level fertility in the developing countries. In 2002, the worldwide average number of children born to a woman during her lifetime—the total **fertility rate**—was around 2.8. However, these projections for the entire globe overlook the different rates for the rich and the poor. Although the world's population grew by 77 million people in 2001, 95 percent of the continuing global population surge were added in the developing Global South (*Vital Signs 2002*, 88), already home to 5 billion people, or more than 80 percent of the world's population (UNPD 2001). Hence, global population growth is the result of new births in the developing Global South, where the fertility rate averaged 3.1 children for each mother (and 5.8 for the least-developed countries). In contrast, the wealthy, developed Global North's fertility rate has actually declined to 1.6 children for each woman, which is below **replacement-level fertility.** Fertility rates around the world must fall to an average of 2.1 children for each woman in order to fall to replacement level. Yet, throughout much of the Global South, the preferred family size remains far in excess of the replacement level, especially in the poorest countries (UNDP 2001).

The developing countries' high fertility rates have important economic consequences. Almost all the problems in the North-South dispute can be traced to disparities in income and economic growth that are directly linked to the differentials in population growth rates. A brief look at these dynamics completes the picture of ongoing political conflict between the haves and the have-nots.

Population Momentum. The surge in the Global South's population in the twentieth century is easily explained as a combination of high birthrates and rapidly falling death rates. But to understand the population surge projected throughout the twenty-first century—when birthrates throughout the world will decline—we have to understand the force of population momentum, the continued growth of population for decades into the future because of the large number of women now entering their childbearing years. Like the inertia of a descending airliner when it first touches down on the runway, population growth simply cannot be halted even with an immediate, full application of the brakes. Instead, many years of high fertility mean that more women will be entering their reproductive years than in the past. Not until the size of the generation giving

• **fertility rate** the average number of children born to women during their reproductive years.

• **replacement-level fertility** one couple replacing themselves with two children, so that a country's population will remain stable if this rate prevails.

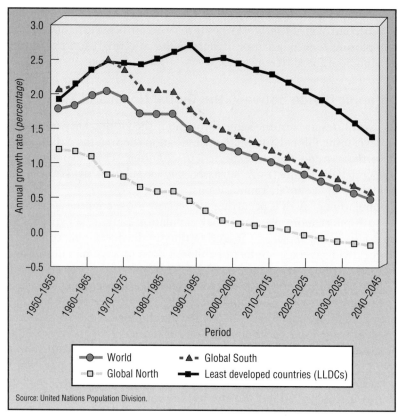

FIGURE 14.2
The Global North—Global South Population Divide

Overpopulation is much feared, but the UN estimates that we can expect a "slowing of population growth rates" followed by "slow reductions in the size of world population" (Wattenberg 2002). Nearly all the population growth in the twenty-first century will occur in the Global South. Assuming continuing declines in fertility, Global South population is expected to rise to 8.2 billion in 2050 (in the absence of such declining birth rates, the less-developed countries will reach 11.9 billion by 2050) (UNPD 2001). The map that accompanies this figure shows that life expectancy is increasing, as people everywhere are living longer, and this growth in the number of elderly people will affect the size of each country's expected population by the year 2050. When interpreting these projections, also take into account the number of people within each country as controlled by geographical size, known as "population density." Some countries are very crowded and others are not. For example, Singapore is the most congested country in the world, with 6,587 for each square kilometer, while people in Australia are the least likely to bump into each other, with only two people for each square kilometer.

SOURCES: Adapted from the United Nations Population Division (left); *The Economist,* Nov. 3, 2001, p. 3 (right). Copyright © 2001 by The Economist Newspaper Ltd. All rights reserved. Further reproduction prohibited.

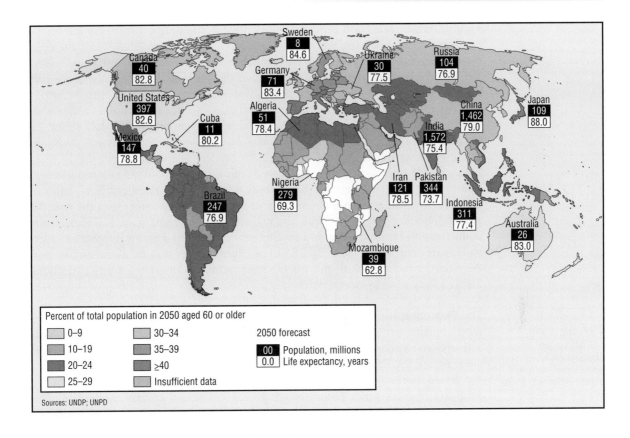

Percent of total population in 2050 aged 60 or older

- 0–9
- 10–19
- 20–24
- 25–29
- 30–34
- 35–39
- ≥40
- Insufficient data

2050 forecast

| 00 | Population, millions |
| 0.0 | Life expectancy, years |

Sources: UNDP; UNPD

birth to children is no larger than the generation among which deaths are occurring will the population growth come to a halt.

Sub-Saharan Africa and Western Europe illustrate the force of population momentum. Africa's demographic profile is one of rapid population growth, as each new age group (cohort) contains more people than the one before it. Thus, even if individual African couples choose to have fewer children than their parents, Africa's population will continue to grow because there are now more men and women of childbearing age than ever before. In contrast, Europe's population profile is one of slow growth, as recent cohorts have been smaller than preceding ones. In fact, Europe has moved beyond replacement-level fertility to become a "declining" population, described by low birthrates and a growing number of people who survive middle age. A product of an extended period of low birthrates, low death rates, and increased longevity, Europe is best described as an aging society, where the low birthrates and aging populations have caused alarms that the number of European newborns will not be sufficient to renew populations.

As the Global North generally ages, much of the Global South continues to mirror the sub-Saharan African profile: Because each cohort is typically larger than the one before it, the number of young men and women entering their reproductive years will also continue to grow. The resulting differences in these demographic momentums will produce quite different population profiles in the developed and the developing worlds. The example of Germany illuminates the contrast. Germany has at present a low birthrate of 1.3 per woman and a large number of people who survive middle age; in the year 2030, people over 65 will account for almost half the adult population (compared with one-fifth in 2001). The net result will be that Germany's total population of 82 million will shrink to about 70 million, and the number of working-age people will fall about 25 percent (from 40 million to 30 million). "The figures are pretty much the same for most other developed countries—Italy, France, Spain, Portugal, the Netherlands, Sweden. . . . The only developed country that has so far avoided this fate is America. But even there the birthrate is well below replacement level, and the proportion of older people in the adult population will rise steeply in the next 30 years" (Drucker 2001, 5). Thus, the population divide will grow; Global North countries will become older and smaller while the United States is "getting older, to be sure, but also bigger. By 2050 the United States will be alone as the only developed country among the world's twenty most-populous countries" (Srodes 2001, 13).

The Demographic Transition.   High rates of population growth place an enormous burden on a country's economy. The theory of **demographic transition** attempts to explain when population growth in the Global South countries will slow, easing the economic strain on developing countries.

Based on the historical experience of Europe and North America, the theory proposes that countries pass through a series of stages as they modernize. The first stage, traditional society, is characterized by a combination of high birth and death rates, which produce relatively stable populations. Birth rates are high because children provide labor that contributes to family income; death rates, because disease is unchecked by effective, widespread health programs. As societies modernize, they enter a second stage: Birth rates remain high, but improvements in nutrition, medical techniques, and public health facilities reduce death rates, which lead to increased population growth. Once people begin to live longer lives, couples "realize that more of their children will live to adulthood, and therefore, . . . feel secure that they can have fewer births and still achieve their desired number of surviving children" (Lutz 1994). In this third stage, birth rates decline along with death rates, yielding little or no population growth.

Demographic transition is now under way virtually everywhere in the world, but at much different rates in different countries and regions. Whereas in the Global North, birth and death rates have converged at a low level, in most of the Global South, birth rates have remained high but death rates have declined rapidly due, in part, to more effective public health programs. If these trends continue, Global North countries will possess an increasingly aged world population. According to a 2001 U.S. Census Bureau report, the world's senior population over the age of 60 had tripled over the past 50 years, and, at the present rate, in 50 years the number of people older than 60 will again triple. Thus by the middle of the century, the elderly would comprise a third of humanity, outnumbering the world's youths, with two older persons for every child. Further-

• **demographic transition** an explanation of population changes that highlights the role of birth and death rates in moving countries from stable to rapidly increasing and finally to declining populations.

more, those 80 years or over are expected to increase even faster, more than five-fold by 2050 (UNPD 2001).

This unprecedented aging of the world could create economic problems of crisis proportions. With the percentage of taxpaying workers shrinking, the budgets of state governments could be overwhelmed by attempts to provide retirement and health benefits for the elderly. In addition, dwindling birthrates, lengthening life spans, and early retirements could spell trouble for a worker-hungry Global North in need of immigrants to supply labor. The graying of world population does not leave the developing countries immune from the challenge faced by the Global North, because in developing countries the pace of aging is even faster, with the proportion of the population over 60 rising from 8 percent in 2002 to 20 percent in 2050. This gives the poorest societies less time to cope as they continue to simultaneously try to confront the scourges of poverty and disease.

International Responses to Population Growth

The international community convened its first World Population Conference in Bucharest during 1974 to address policy issues raised by the world's growing population. Many Global South delegates concluded from Europe's and North America's demographic transitions that declining fertility rates flowed more or less automatically from economic growth and proposed policies that focused on economic development rather than population control. They called on the Global North for economic development assistance, reasoning that the population problem would then take care of itself. The slogan "development is the best contraceptive" reflected the prevailing view.

A decade later, a second World Population Conference was held in Mexico City. By then, a new consensus had converged around the critical importance of family planning. However, the United States, previously a major advocate of this viewpoint, argued that free-market principles ought to take precedence over government intervention in population matters. Rejecting pessimistic, "limits-to-growth" analyses, the U.S. delegation argued that markets effectively maintain a balance among population, resources, and the environment.

The debate over population policies did not end after Mexico City. In 1994 the UN-convened International Conference on Population and Development in Cairo concluded that population stabilization could be achieved only in conjunction with efforts to promote sustainable economic growth, supported by increases in foreign aid. This conclusion was reaffirmed at the August 2002 Johannesburg World Conference on Sustainable Development. Specific goals were set at both conferences, which included improving access to family-planning services, health care, and primary education, as well as lowering the rates of infant, child, and maternal mortality. However, the proposals emanating from these conferences were only recommendations, not binding on governments. Indeed, few countries could be expected to act on all of them, particularly given the enormous resources their realization demands. As a result, governments in the Global North are being asked to contribute more to family planning, education, and health care programs in the Global South. Since domestic political support for foreign aid among donor countries has greatly declined, large subsidies are unlikely.

Prospects for a Global Population Implosion

The discussions at Cairo and Johannesburg assumed that population growth would continue in the Global South. We have seen why this is likely, but it is worth bearing in mind that population projections can be misleading, because natural or human-made events may overturn the conditions that produced today's trends. For example, current projections could be invalidated overnight by a nuclear war or a terrorist act of mass destruction with biological weapons, rendering obsolete today's life expectancy of nearly 80 years in the Global North. Other threats, such as the outbreak of a widespread, deadly contagious disease, also could produce a **population implosion**—a severe reduction in world population. We take a brief look at two possible sources of implosion: **pandemics** and famine.

The Threat of Contagious Diseases

On a global level, life expectancy at birth has increased each year since 1950, climbing at the start of 2003 to 66 years. However, this trend could be reversed if globally transmittable diseases cut into the extension of life spans made possible by improvements in health care, nutrition, water quality, and public sanitation. For example, drug-resistant strains of tuberculosis (TB) have developed recently, and they can be passed from one country to the next by a sneeze on an international flight. Preventing the outbreak of a highly contagious disease within any region of the world is virtually impossible in an age of globalization.

The grim possibility that virulent disease will reduce the world's population is evident from the spread of the human immunodeficiency virus (HIV) that causes AIDS (acquired immune deficiency syndrome). On the eve of World AIDS Day in November 2001, UN secretary-general Kofi Annan reminded his audience that the facts about AIDS are frightening: "Every day more than 8,000 people die of AIDS. Every hour almost 600 people become infected. Every minute a child dies of the virus." Most health experts agree with Annan's warning that "in the ruthless world of AIDS there is no us and them." At the current pace, some countries "could lose 20 percent of their gross domestic product due to the effects of AIDS on their work force and productivity" (*Vital Signs 2002*, 90). The 2002 *UNAIDS* report warned that AIDS could kill nearly 30 million people worldwide over the next two decades. More than 90 percent of new infections occur in the Global South, but the contagion respects no borders.

The Threat of Famine

At the same time that medical experts worry that death rates due to tuberculosis, AIDS, Ebola, and other diseases could take a horrific toll on humanity, agricultural specialists shudder at the possibility of food shortages. If Earth's population grows to 9 billion, will food production keep pace? Whereas pessimists warn of

---

• **population implosion** a rapid reduction of population that reverses a previous trend toward progressively larger populations.

• **pandemic** a disease that spreads throughout one or more continents.

mass starvation, optimists claim these fears are unwarranted (see Controversy: How Many People Can the Earth Support?), arguing that technological break-throughs in the field of genetic engineering will revolutionize farming and feed future generations.

Genetically engineered crops are created to develop a desired trait, such as herbicide tolerance or increased oil content. Unlike crop varieties developed through traditional plant breeding, **transgenetic crops** often contain genes from unrelated species—of plant, animal, bacteria, or other origin—with which the crop could not reproduce naturally. Despite lingering consumer unease, geneti-cally engineered crops "are gaining ground. In 2001, 53 million hectares were planted with transgenetic crops, a 19 percent rise over the previous year. Thirteen countries now grow genetically modified soybeans, maize, corn, cotton, or canola. America accounts for two-thirds of global production but China, South Africa, and Australia are rapidly increasing their share" (*The Economist*, Janu-ary 19, 2002, 90). Moreover, as the risk of plant and animal extinction escalates, scientists have turned to the desperate strategy of seeking to replicate them in sur-rogate forms through cloning. Needless to say, this approach has met with con-siderable opposition from groups who feel that tampering with life is immoral.

Geneticists could revolutionize agriculture and transform the capability of the planet to feed the world's growing population. However, the increasing avail-ability of commercially produced and globally marketed genetically engineered agricultural products is a growing controversy. Should scientists manipulate nature for human needs? Are gene-spliced plants and hormone-treated meat safe? Do crops created through genetic engineering contain allergens that may cause serious allergic reactions and endanger public health?

In summary, mounting a sustained effort to address the consequences of world population growth remains a formidable challenge. An interdependent and rapidly globalizing world promises that none will be immune to population trends, especially those that strain the natural environment on which we depend. Population politics are linked directly to the issue of protecting the planet's ecol-ogy, which we now examine.

• transgenetic crops
new crops with improved characteristics created artificially through genetic engineering, which combines genes from species that would not naturally interbreed.

Environmental Security and Sustainable Development

When U.S. astronauts first viewed Earth from the Apollo spacecraft, they described how the clouds and continents flowed into one another without regard to the political boundaries humans had drawn across the planet. Improvement in space technology since the 1960s has enabled the world to see a different set of images—of atmospheric pollution that encircles the globe; of violent winter and summer storms pounding islands with relentless fury; of massive holes in the ozone shield that protects humans from dangerous ultraviolet rays; and of van-ishing forests and widening deserts.

To explore the linkage between population pressures and global environ-mental challenges, we need to examine *ecopolitics*—how political actors influ-ence perceptions of, and policy responses to, managing the impact of human

CONTROVERSY # How Many People Can the Earth Support?

Are there limits to the size of world population beyond which humanity will perish? Two thousand years ago, when the earth had about the same number of people as the United States does today, few would have pondered that question. They do now, because with 8 to 10 billion people expected to live on the planet in the twenty-first century, the possibility has arisen that food scarcities will lead to famine and armed conflict over agriculture products.

It is unclear whether this grim outcome will materialize, however. Demographic and environmental scientists are divided in their evaluations about the planet's future carrying capacity—the limits on its ability to supply the resources to sustain a growing human population. Two major broadly defined groups of analysts approach these issues quite differently. Taking their name and orientation from Thomas Malthus and his classic 1798 *Essay on the Principle of Population,* the first group, neo-Malthusians, believes that world population is pushing against the earth's resources, straining its ability to meet the needs of this generation and the next. Sometimes called "growth pessimists," many neo-Malthusian ecologists point to a host of disconcerting facts about the present global condition: "Since Malthus wrote, the human population has grown by a factor of six, and total human energy use by a factor of one hundred or so. . . . The forest cover of the earth has been cut by a third and the area of undisturbed wetlands by half. The composition of the atmosphere has been altered by human-generated pollution. Hundreds of millions of people have starved to death; thousands of species have gone extinct" (Meadows 1993).

In contrast with the pessimism of neo-Malthusians, the second group, the cornucopians (known as "growth optimists"), emphasizes quite different global trends. Observing that global life expectancy has more than doubled since 1950 to 66 years, they conclude

Genetic Engineering in Agriculture A Chinese farmer harnesses a transgenetic cow to produce milk and power.

that rapid population growth has occurred not because human beings suddenly started breeding like rabbits but because they finally stopped dropping like flies. Despite the growth of global population from 1.6 billion in 1900 to more than 6.3 billion in 2003, cornucopians argue that "global health and productivity have exploded. Today human beings eat better, produce more, and consume more than ever. . . . Overpopulation [they argue] is a problem that has been misidentified and misdefined. The term has no scientific definition or clear meaning. The problems typi-

Isabelle Rouvillois/AFP/Getty Images

Freak Food or Unfair Foreign Trade? A Greenpeace activist in France protests the import of genetically modified corn, which the United States produces for export around the globe.

cally associated with overpopulation (hungry families, squalid and overcrowded living conditions) are more properly understood as issues of poverty," which is directly traceable to the policies of presiding governments (Eberstadt 1995).

What do you think? Is population growth a serious problem? Or, will technological advances be sufficient for the earth to provide enough resources for its people? Among the advances some people tout are genetically modified or transgenetic livestock and crops. Shown here is one example on which these "cornucopian" enthusiasts pin their hopes: A farmer in

China, cultivates a field using a new breed of cow developed by researchers in Africa that is strong enough to work in the field without reducing its capacity to produce milk or to breed. Critics of genetically modified crops, like the Greenpeace activist shown in the photo on the right vandalizing a field of transgenetic corn in 1998, complain that genetic engineering is harmful to public health. "Far from being a solution to the world's hunger problem," complain some experts (Rosset 1999), "the rapid introduction of genetically engineered crops may actually threaten agriculture and food security." ●

behavior on their environments. By taking an ecopolitical perspective, we can broaden our conception of security, pushing it to include processes that may imperil our ecological niche on the planet.

One of the key concepts embraced by those who look at security from ecopolitical perspectives is **sustainable development.** The movement for sustainable development began in earnest in 1972, when the United Nations convened the first UN Conference of the Human Environment in Stockholm. Conferences have since been held on a wide range of environmental topics, with scores of treaties negotiated and new international agencies put into place to promote cooperation and monitor environmental developments. The concept of sustainable development enjoys widespread support among governments and a broad range of NGOs that are particularly active in shaping the global environmental agenda. According to the 1987 report of the World Commission on Environment and Development—popularly known as the "Brundtland Commission" after the Norwegian prime minister who chaired it—a "sustainable society" is one that "meets the needs of the present without compromising the ability of future generations to meet their own needs."

Another milestone in the movement to foster sustainable development was the Earth Summit, which took place in Rio de Janeiro in 1992. Formally known as the UN Conference on Environment and Development, the meeting brought together more than 150 states, 1,400 nongovernmental organizations, and 8,000 journalists. Prior to the Earth Summit, environment and economic development had been treated separately—and often regarded as being in conflict with each other. In Rio, the concept of sustainability galvanized a simultaneous treatment of environmental and development issues, and paved the way for the UN World Summit on Sustainable Development that concluded in early September 2002 in Johannesburg. These and other international conferences have stressed that what happens anywhere ultimately affects conditions everywhere, and therefore protecting the global environment is a security issue.

Sustainability cannot be realized without dramatic changes in the social, economic, and political practices of an increasingly interconnected world. But is that possible? The metaphor of the tragedy of the commons provides little basis for optimism, whether applied to individuals or states. When rational, self-interested actors strive for relative gains in the absence of strong international regulation, everyone's well-being may plummet.

To better understand the multiple tensions that global environmental problems pose in an anarchical world, we turn next to consider three interrelated clusters of issues on the global ecopolitical agenda: (1) oil and energy, (2) climate change and ozone depletion, and (3) biodiversity and deforestation. The clusters illustrate the problems and pitfalls that states and nonstate actors (IGOs and NGOs) face as they seek environmental security and sustainable development.

The Ecopolitics of Energy

In April 1990, the average price for a barrel of internationally traded crude oil was less than $15. Five months later—stimulated by Iraq's invasion of the tiny oil sheikdom of Kuwait—it rose to more than $40. For the third time in less than

• **sustainable development**
economic growth that does not deplete the resources needed to maintain growth.

two decades, the world suffered an oil shock when the price paid for the most widely used commercial energy source skyrocketed.

The 1990 Persian Gulf War was precipitated by Iraq's attempt to subjugate Kuwait and acquire its oil. Some critics of U.S. president George W. Bush maintain that his decision to go to war against Iraq in 2003 was also influenced by economic considerations involving oil. While the president's supporters vigorously deny this charge, ensuring access to the region's oil is nonetheless critical to the economic fortunes of the Global North, because almost all the oil that is inexpensive to extract lies within the borders of a handful of countries around the Persian Gulf.

Global Patterns of Oil Consumption.   The importance of oil to the Global North generally and the United States in particular is evident from their disproportionate share of energy consumption. The average person living in Europe uses more than twice as much energy as people in the Global South, while Canada and the United States use more than six times as much.

Oil consumption has been spiraling upward for decades, reaching 3.5 billion tons per day by the beginning of the twenty-first century, when oil supplied about 87 percent of the world's commercial energy (*Vital Signs 2002*, 38). The industrialization of many emerging Global South economies has contributed to the growing demand, and the global shift to oil has been propelled by the aggressive production and promotion of a small group of multinational corporations (MNCs). Their operations encompass every aspect of the business, from exploration to the retail sale of products at their gas stations. For decades, their search for, production of, and marketing of low-cost oil was largely unhindered. Concessions from the oil-rich Middle East were easy to obtain, which reduced incentives for developing technologies for alternative energy sources. Eventually, many of the world's major oil-producing states were able to wrest control from the oil companies, and they formed a **cartel** known as the Organization of Petroleum Exporting Countries (OPEC) in an effort to maximize profits. Because the resources OPEC controls cannot be easily replaced, it has been able to use oil as an instrument of coercive diplomacy. By cutting production to limit world supplies, OPEC can trigger sharp price increases to exert pressure on countries that rely on oil as their primary source of energy.

• **cartel** an organization of the producers of a commodity that seeks to regulate the pricing and production of that commodity to increase revenue.

Is Energy Security an Elusive Goal?   The question of oil supplies has great importance to world politics, because oil is not being discovered at the same rate it is being used: "For every two barrels pumped out of the ground, the [oil companies] find less than one barrel to add to reserves. Production in the United States peaked thirty years ago. Russia peaked in 1987. North Sea production appears to be peaking now. [About] 70 percent of the oil consumed today was found twenty-five years ago or longer. . . . Meanwhile, demand for oil keeps moving up [and] the era of cheap and abundant oil is drawing to a close" (Quinn 2002, 43).

To properly characterize the present problem, the world does not now face the immediate threat of running out of oil; it faces instead the problem that oil reserves are concentrated in a small number of countries. Because OPEC

Yanin Arthus Bertrand/CORBIS

The Unforgiving Cost of Nuclear Power Failure Using nuclear power to generate energy appears inexpensive and cost-efficient, but involves risks, not only increasing the probability of nuclear weapons proliferation but also the potential of producing toxic byproducts that could have a devastating effect on the environment. Shown here is the town of Pripyat, Ukraine, that was abandoned after the Chernobyl accident, in which thousands died; hundreds of thousands were forced to evacuate their homes; and the radioactive fallout—the equivalent of 10 Hiroshima bombs—permanently poisoned agricultural land the size of the Netherlands. Despite strong opposition from the public, in 2001, Russia prepared to open its borders to become the largest international repository for radioactive nuclear wastes, in the hope of earning $21 billion over the next two decades (Tyler 2001).

members, who control approximately half of the world's oil reserves, are drawing down their reserves at half the average global rate, it seems almost inevitable that OPEC's share of the world oil market will grow. This means that OPEC is critical to global oil supply, the Middle East is critical to OPEC, and countries that depend on oil imports from this volatile, unstable source are highly vulnerable to disruptions—such as the United States (the percentage of whose oil from foreign suppliers exceeds 60 percent [*Harper's*, November 2001, 92] and whose oil inventories hit a 23-year low in 2002).

OPEC's future role could change significantly since its finances and political clout depend heavily on factors largely outside its control—changes in international demand (consumption) and supply. Moreover, we now may be witnessing the advent of a potentially historic juncture that could overturn the place of oil in the twenty-first-century's global political economy, largely because "World energy needs are projected to double in the next several decades, but no credible geologist foresees a doubling of world oil production, which is expected to peak within the next few decades" (Brown and Flavin 1999, 6). This places oil-producing countries in a powerful bargaining position. Unless "new reserves are discovered outside the Middle East, global dependence on Persian Gulf oil will grow [and] this is a long-term problem [especially] for the United States . . . because for three decades Americans have only haphazardly tried to fortify themselves against a catastrophic cutoff of oil from the Middle East, which accounts for about a third of world production and two-thirds of known reserves" (Samuelson 2001a, A17).

Owing to the vulnerability of the United States and other wealthy Global North countries to economic pressure from oil-producing states, efforts are underway to transform the global energy system. According to one projection, the primary energy resources in the years ahead "may be the most abundant ones on Earth: the sun, the wind, and other renewable sources of energy [such as] hydrogen, the lightest and most abundant element in the universe." Humans only became dependent on nonrenewable finite stocks of fossilized fuel when Europeans began mining coal in the seventeenth century. "From a millennial perspective, today's hydrocarbon-based civilization is but a brief interlude in human history" (Flavin and Dunn 1999, 23).

The impact of such a global transformation would be huge, overturning the past 125-year pattern in world energy development and consumption. A number of energy analysts and industry officials suggest we can expect a gradual shift from oil to unconventional (such as tar sands and shale) and renewable sources of energy. In a speech delivered in 1999, Mike Bowlin, chairman and CEO of the ARCO Oil Company, asserted that the world is moving "along the spectrum away from carbon and headed toward hydrogen and other forms of energy" (*Vital Signs 1999*, 48). As Figure 14.3 shows, advocates of environmentally friendly, renewable energy supplies picture a radically different twenty-first century. They urge immediate planning for a new global "eco-economy, one that satisfies today's need without jeopardizing the prospects of future generations to meet theirs by altering how we light our homes, what we eat, where we live, how we use our leisure time, and how many children we have" (Brown 2002). Many people remain skeptical of their vision, but if alternatives to oil become technologically and economically viable, their development would reduce dependence on oil from the volatile Middle East.

In a world in which population growth means an increasing demand for energy, scarcities of vital resources can easily lead to armed conflict. Common property resources and their preservation will be a core security concern in the twenty-first century. In an ecologically interdependent world without strong global governing institutions, where actions anywhere have external costs almost everywhere, managing airsheds and other common-pool resources will become a major challenge.

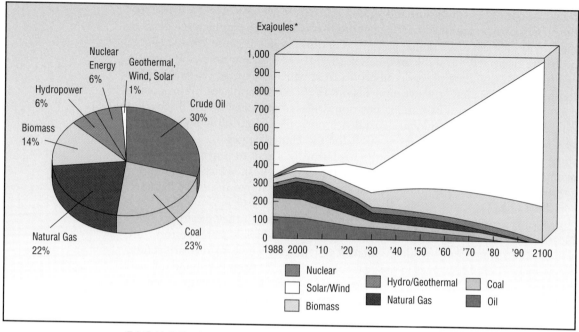

FIGURE 14.3

Phasing Out Fossil Fuels? The Potential for Renewable Energy to Supply the World's Energy Needs by the Year 2100

The global economy's need for energy continues to increase, requiring more energy than is ultimately available from nonrenewable resources. Thus rising demand is likely to change the current distribution of sources on which the world relies to meet its energy needs (left). As the Fossil Free Energy Scenario prediction (right) suggests, it would be possible to tap renewable sources to meet the world's entire energy needs by the end of the twenty-first century. For example, it is estimated that more than fifty Global South countries could produce as much energy from the biomass residues generated by sugar production as they presently obtain from oil; that less than 5 percent of the globe's small-scale hydropower has been exploited; and that land-based wind turbines could provide 20 million megawatt-hours of electricity each year—twice as much as the world consumed in 1987 (Crump 1998, 223). Renewable energy from replaceable sources also has the advantage of doing relatively little damage to the environment. Whether these sources of energy will actually be harnessed remains to be seen, because the relatively low financial cost of using the planet's nonrenewable resources (like oil, which takes millions of years to form) makes them economically attractive.

*A joule is a unit of work or energy, equivalent to 0.239 calories (1 exajoule equals 10^{18} joules).

Note: Percentages do not equal 100 due to rounding errors.

SOURCE: Adapted from Crump (1998), 193 (left) and 223 (right).

The Ecopolitics of the Atmosphere

For years, scientists have warned that global warming—the gradual rise in world temperature—would cause destructive changes in climatological patterns, resulting in rising sea levels, melting glaciers, and powerful storms. The consensus today is that the extent of climate change is greater than once believed, and human activities have played a role in increasing the temperature on the surface

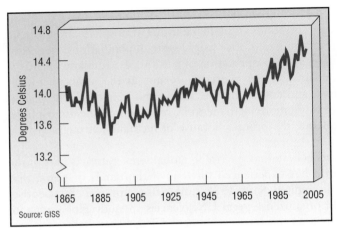

FIGURE 14.4
Rising Average Global Temperatures at the Earth's Surface since 1867

The World Meteorological Organization (WMO) monitors average global surface temperatures at thousands of sites around the world, and its records show that global warming is not a myth. For nearly 140 years, the world's temperature has seesawed up and down, usually by tiny fractions of degrees. But since the mid-1970s, the mercury has largely been on the rise, and the WMO predicts that the average global surface temperature could jump 3.6 degrees Celsius by the end of the twenty-first century—more than triple the rise of the past one hundred years.

Note: Five-year averages of global temperatures.

SOURCE: *Vital Signs 2002*, p. 51. Copyright © 2002 Worldwatch Institute. www.worldwatch.org.

of the planet. In response, many scientists have called upon the international community to reduce emissions of carbon dioxide and other gases, which they blame for global warming.

Climate Change.   Major gaps in our knowledge of climate change remain, but few climate scientists think the world can afford to wait for answers. The changes are substantial and threatening. Most scientists believe that the gradual rise in the earth's temperature—especially evident since the late eighteenth century when the invention of power-driven machinery produced the Industrial Revolution—is caused by an increase in human-made gases that alter the atmosphere's insulating effects. The gas molecules, primarily carbon dioxide (CO_2) and chlorofluorocarbons (CFCs), trap heat emitted from Earth that would otherwise escape into outer space. As these gases are released into the atmosphere they create a **greenhouse effect** that has caused the global temperature to rise. As shown in Figure 14.4, the temperature on the earth's surface has increased nearly a half degree since 1950. According to the U.S. National Climatic Data Center, 13 of the hottest years since record-keeping began over a century ago have occurred since 1987, with the five hottest occurring since 1997, and 2003 registering as the second hottest year on record.

The earth's temperature is now between 0.3 and 0.6 degrees Celsius higher than it was in 1880 and is projected to further increase by 3.6 degrees Celsius by

• **greenhouse effect**
the phenomenon producing planetary warming when gases released by burning fossil fuels act as a blanket in the atmosphere, thereby increasing temperatures.

2100 if preventive action is not taken (Soroos 2001). Although CO_2 is the principal greenhouse gas, concentrations of methane in the atmosphere are growing more rapidly. Methane gas emissions arise from livestock populations, rice cultivation, and the production and transportation of natural gas. To many scientists' alarm, the largest concentrations of methane are not in the atmosphere but locked in ice, permafrost, and coastal marine sediments. This raises the probability that warming will cause more methane to be released into the atmosphere, which would then accelerate the process because of methane's strong warming potential.

While some scientists believe that the rise in global temperature is part of the cyclical change the world has experienced for tens of thousands of years, that view has been steadily discredited. Since 1988, hundreds of atmospheric scientists from around the world organized several UN agencies to study global climate change. The team, known as the Intergovernmental Panel on Climate Change (IPCC), stated in 1995 its belief that global climate trends are "unlikely to be entirely due to natural causes," that humans are to blame for at least part of the problem, and that the consequences are likely to be very harmful and costly. Without significant efforts to reduce the emission of greenhouse gases, they estimated that the increase in global temperatures by the year 2100 would be faster than any experienced in recorded human history.

Thus, the world has already entered a period of climatic instability likely to cause widespread economic, social, and environmental dislocation over the twenty-first century. The effects of continued temperature rises could be both dramatic and devastating:

- Sea levels could rise up to three feet, mostly because of melting glaciers and the expansion of water as it warms up. That will flood vast areas of low-lying coastal land, including major river deltas; most of the beaches on the U.S. Atlantic coast; part of China; and the Maldive Islands, the Seychelles, and the Cook and Marshall Islands. More than 1 million people could be displaced, and 30 million would be put at risk of at least one flood per year.
- Winters would get warmer and warm-weather hot spells (such as the 1995 summer heat wave that killed 500 people in Chicago) would become more frequent and more severe.
- Rainfall would increase globally, but only the areas already prone to flooding would flood more often and more severely, with freak storms such as the 1997 El Niño surge of storms in the Pacific and the flooding in the Dakotas becoming more common. Since water evaporates more easily in a warmer world, drought-prone regions would become even dryer. As oceans heat, hurricanes, which draw their energy from warm oceans, would become even stronger.
- Entire ecosystems would vanish from the planet, and a hotter earth would drive some plants to higher latitudes and altitudes and require farmers to irrigate and change their crops and agriculture practices.
- The combination of flooding and droughts would cause tropical diseases such as malaria and dengue fever to flourish in previously temperate regions that were formerly too cold for their insect carriers.

© Greenpeace/Daniel Beltra

Cold Comfort for Global Warming Global emissions of carbon dioxide and other greenhouse gases are rising and may contribute to global warming. If the earth continues to heat, oceans will rise and land will be submerged. Pictured here is the Bering Glacier at the edge of Vitus Lake in Alaska, which according to Greenpeace has shrunk about 40 feet in length during the past century due to global warming. An even more dramatic indicator of the effect of global warming began on January 31, 2002, when the Larsen B patch of floating ice shelf in Antarctica—30 to 40 miles across (the size of Rhode Island), 700 feet thick, and weighing 500 billion tons—collapsed from warming temperatures in less than a month (Stott 2002). The U.S.-based National Snow and Ice Data Center described it as "the largest single event in a series of retreats by ice shelves in the peninsula over the last 30 years."

CO_2 emissions from the burning of fossil fuels have climbed steadily, rising fourfold since 1950. The industrial Global North states are the principal sources, accounting for three-fourths of global CO_2 emissions (see Map 14.1). The United States emits more CO_2 into the atmosphere that any other state. Due to its big buildings, millions of cars, and relatively inefficient industries, the U.S. CO_2 emissions for each person are five times the world average. Elsewhere, China is a major and growing source of concern because coal emits more atmospheric pollutants than other fossil fuels, and three-fourths of China's energy for its fast-growing economy comes from coal. China now accounts for about 10 percent of all greenhouse gas emissions, making it the fastest-growing major contributor to global warming.

Coal is a major source of atmospheric sulfur and nitrogen oxides. These pollutants return to Earth, typically after traveling long distances, in the form of **acid rain,** which adds to the acidification of lakes, the corrosion of materials and

Click on Global Challenges and Issues for an interactive version of this map and related critical thinking questions.

• **acid rain** precipitation that has been made acidic through contact with sulfur dioxide and nitrogen oxides.

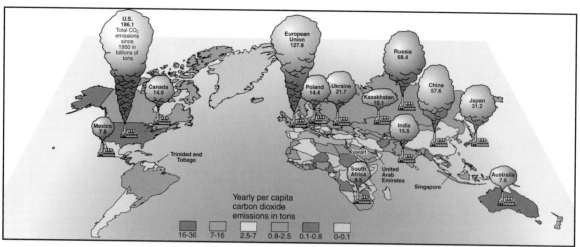

MAP 14.1

Who's to Blame for Global Warming?

This map shows the yearly carbon dioxide emissions in tons for each person in each country. The Kyoto Protocol of 2001 needed the support of countries accounting for 55 percent of greenhouse-gas emissions to come into force, and it received it even though the United States, which is responsible for most greenhouse gases, did not ratify the treaty.

SOURCE: From *TIME*, April 9, 2001, p. 30–31. Copyright © 2001 TIME, Inc. Reprinted by permission.

structures, and the impairment of ecosystems. Acid rain is a serious problem in much of China. Because the oxides that cause it are also transboundary pollutants, China's domestic energy policies have become a major irritant in its relations with its neighbors, particularly South Korea and Japan. Nonetheless, China plans to increase the amount of coal it burns by nearly 900 million tons a year by 2010. Other Asian states are following in its path, including India which, like China, has sizable coal deposits. Already China and India account for 15 percent of global greenhouse emissions, and their combined share of CO_2 emissions is expected to grow.

To combat the danger of accelerating global warming, 179 countries reached a new climate-control treaty in Kyoto during 2001 that for the first time formally required industrialized countries to cut emissions of gases linked to global warming. However, the United States refused to go along with the agreement and became the only country opposing the treaty, arguing that the emission reduction targets placed an unfair burden on Global North countries while not devoting sufficient attention to emissions from countries like China and India.

Ozone Depletion. The story of climate change is similar to states' efforts to cope with depletion of the atmosphere's protective **ozone layer.** In this case, however, an international regime has emerged, progressively strengthened by mounting scientific evidence that environmental damage was directly caused by human activity.

• **ozone layer** the protective layer of the upper atmosphere over the earth's surface that shields the planet from the sun's harmful impact on living organisms on the planet.

Ozone is a pollutant in the lower atmosphere, but in the upper atmosphere it provides the earth with a critical layer of protection against the sun's harmful ultraviolet radiation. Scientists have discovered a marked depletion of the ozone layer—most notably an "ozone hole" over Antarctica that has grown larger than the continental United States, and they have linked the thinning of the layer to chlorofluorocarbons (CFCs)—a related family of compounds known as halons, hydrochlorofluorocarbons (HCFCs), methyl bromide, and other chemicals (Benedick 1998). Depletion of the ozone layer exposes humans to health hazards of various sorts, particularly skin cancer, and threatens other forms of marine and terrestrial life.

Scientists began to link halons and CFCs to ozone depletion in the early 1970s. Even before their hypotheses were confirmed, the United Nations Environment Program (UNEP) sought some form of regulatory action. Despite scientific uncertainty and policy differences, the 1987 landmark Montreal Protocol on Substances That Deplete the Ozone Layer treaty was signed and "initiated dramatic declines in CFC output, which is many times below peak production years, the late 1980s." World CFC production between 1989 and 1999 declined 86 percent (*Vital Signs 2002*, 55). However, in spite of reductions in CFCs over the past decade, the ozone hole over Antarctica continues to expand and is expected to accelerate before it begins to regenerate itself. One reason is that while the production of CFCs in the Global North declined sharply in the 1990s, production in the Global South surged, and increased demand for refrigerators, air conditioners, and other products using CFCs is offsetting the gains realized by stopping production in the Global North. Developed countries agreed to provide aid to help the developing countries adopt CFC alternatives, but have failed to provide all of the resources promised. Without this support, many in the Global South may not be able to keep their end of the global bargain. Meanwhile, a significant illegal trade in both virgin and recycled CFCs has emerged, threatening to further undermine the positive effects of the ozone regime.

Having scientific evidence, many believe, is what made the ozone initiative successful. Other factors contributing to its success included precise targets and timetables, verification mechanisms, and a mechanism for financial and technology transfers to assist Global South countries in assuming specific obligations (Simonis and Brühl 2002). Can the ozone regime serve as a model for breakthroughs on other global environmental issues? To explore this question, we turn finally to the problems facing the world's biological heritage.

The Ecopolitics of Biodiversity

Forests are critical in preserving the earth's biodiversity and to protecting the atmosphere and land resources. For these reasons they have been a rising ecological issue on the global agenda. Some rules have emerged to guide international behavior in the preservation of **biodiversity**, but issues concerning forests have proven much more difficult to address.

• **biodiversity** the variety of life on earth.

Deforestation.   Each minute, on average, 52 acres of the world's forests are lost (*Time*, April 13, 1998, 199). Destruction of tropical rain forests in such places as

Brazil, Indonesia, and Malaysia is a matter of special concern, since much of the world's genetic heritage is found there.

The representatives sent to the 1992 Earth Summit hoped to secure an easy victory on a statement of principle for global forest conservation. But opposition quickly developed to the principle that the global interest makes all countries responsible for protecting national forests. The Global South—led by Malaysia, a principal exporter of tropical wood products—objected especially vigorously to the view that the world's forests were a common property resource. These developing countries feared that accepting this view would enable the Global North to interfere with the local management of their tropical forest resources. In the end, the Earth Summit backed away from the goal of establishing international guidelines for trade in "sustainably managed" forest products. The situation today remains largely unchanged.

• **desertification** the creation of deserts due to soil erosion, over-farming, and deforestation, which converts cropland to nonproductive, arid sand.

Meanwhile, high population growth rates, industrialization, and urbanization increase pressure on farm forests and marginal land poorly suited to cultivation. This has led to **desertification,** which makes an increasing portion of the earth's landmass useless for agricultural productivity or wildlife habitats. In addition, freshwater supplies are being depleted. "There's water everywhere, of course, but less than three percent of it is fresh, and most of that is locked up in polar ice caps and glaciers, unrecoverable for practical purposes. Lakes, rivers, marshes, aquifers, and atmospheric vapor make up less than one percent of the earth's total water, and people are already using more than half of the accessible runoff. Water demand, on the other hand, has been growing rapidly—it tripled worldwide between 1950 and 1990—and water use in many areas already exceeds nature's ability to recharge supplies. By 2025, the demand for water around the world is expected to exceed supply by 56 percent" (Finnegan 2002, 44).

Click on Global Challenges and Issues for an interactive version of this map and related critical thinking questions.

Soil degradation has stripped billions of acres of the earth's surface from productive farming; almost 4 billion acres of top soil are estimated to erode worldwide each year (*Harper's,* June 2000, 23). Soil erosion and pollution are problems both in densely populated developing countries and in the more highly developed regions of mechanized industrial agriculture. "Since 1950, 11 percent of the planet's vegetation (approximately [2.9 billion acres]), has suffered land degradation" (Crump 1998, 78). Map 14.2 shows the regions of the globe where desertification is occurring most rapidly. Based on previous trends, it has been estimated that an area of one-fourth to one-half of an American football field is deforested each time another person is added to the world population (J. Cohen 1995, 338). This means that the addition of another billion people will require as much as 2.5 million square kilometers of additional land for food production and other uses.

In the Global North, reforestation has alleviated some of the danger. This is not the case in many cash-starved Global South countries, however, which eagerly sell timber for income and to make room for their growing populations.

Endangered Species. Biodiversity is an umbrella term that refers to the earth's variety of life. Technically it encompasses three basic levels of organization in living systems: genetic diversity, species diversity, and ecosystem diversity. Until

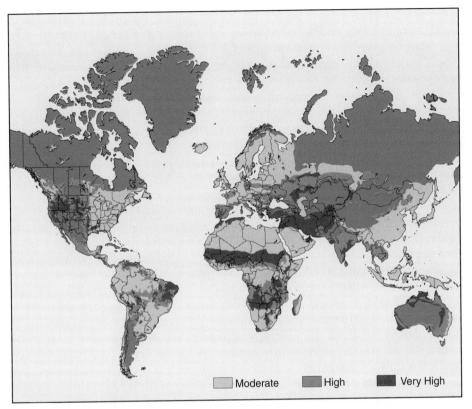

Moderate   High   Very High

M A P   1 4 . 2
Loss of Forest and Ground to Deserts

Deforestation and desertification are global phenomena. "This map shows the degree to which certain regions of the world are at risk of desertification—formation or expansion of degraded dry lands as the result of climate change and human activity. Primary causes include adverse agricultural and industrial practices, deforestation and overgrazing" (James 2002c). "Worldwide, more than 10 million acres of farmland are becoming unproductive deserts each year" (Seck 1999, 9), and tropical forests in Central and South America, Africa, and Southeast Asia are being cleared at an alarming rate. The 1999 UN Convention to Combat Desertification (CCD) seeks to stop the spread of deserts, which now cover 2 million square miles inhabited by one-third of the world's population" (Hottelet 1999, 8).
SOURCE: Originally developed from map located on U.S. Department of Agriculture website at www.nrcs.usda.gov.

recently, public attention has been focused almost exclusively on preserving species diversity, including old growth forests, tall grass prairies, wetlands, coastal habitats, and coral reefs.

Forests, especially tropical forests, are important to preserving biodiversity because they are home to countless species of animals and plants, many of them still unknown. Scientists believe that the global habitat contains between 8 and 10 million species. Of these, only about 1.5 million have been named, and most of them are in the temperate regions of North America, Europe, Russia, and Australia (Edwards 1995, 215). Destruction of tropical forests, where two-thirds to

Click on Global Challenges and Issues for an interactive map showing biodiversity levels worldwide and for related critical thinking questions.

three-fourths of all species are believed to live, thus threatens the destruction of much of the world's undiscovered biological diversity and genetic heritage.

Many experts worry that the planet is heading toward major species extinction. Of the 242,000 plant species surveyed by the World Conservation Union in 1997, some 33,000, or 14 percent, are threatened with extinction, mainly as a result of clearing land for housing, roads, and industries. Even more troubling is the fact that clearing of tropical rain forests to make room for farms and ranches is doubly destructive. From the viewpoint of climate change, green plants remove CO_2 from the atmosphere during photosynthesis. That is, the natural processes that remove greenhouse gases are destroyed when forests are cut down, and, as the forests decay or are burned, the amount of CO_2 discharged into the atmosphere increases.

Although threats to biodiversity have implications for all species—thus resembling threats to other common property resources—biodiversity's distributional characteristics also make it unique. Because so much of the earth's biological heritage is concentrated in the tropics, the Global South has a growing concern about protecting its interest in the face of the recent claims that the genetic character of the many species of plants and animals should be considered a part of the global commons and therefore available for commercial use by all, for their medical benefit. Pharmaceutical companies in particular have laid claim to Global South resources. They actively explore plants, microbes, and other living organisms in tropical forests for possible use in prescription drugs. In fact, approximately 25 percent of the prescription drugs used in the United States have active ingredients extracted or derived from plants (Miller 1995, 110). In view of UN estimates that about 50,000 plant and animal species become extinct each year, global environmental issues will remain controversial as the international community wrestles with the ethics of biodiversity preservation.

Future Environmental Policy Choices

We began our exploration of world politics in Chapter 1 by focusing our attention on the interaction of autonomous, territorial states that have no higher authority governing their behavior. Since the birth of the modern state system some three and a half centuries ago, world population has increased eightfold, fossil fuel consumption has risen from nearly nothing to more than 7 billion metric tons of coal equivalent annually, and the use of nonfuel minerals has skyrocketed. Demographic pressures combined with resource-intensive industrialization have placed enormous stress on the global environment. Earth's atmosphere and oceans are becoming polluted; its natural resources, depleted. When the Johannesburg World Summit on Sustainable Development concluded in September 2002, "Threats [were] higher than ever to natural resources such as forests, fish, and clean water and air. The richest one-fifth of mankind . . . [were consuming] energy and resources at such a high rate that providing a comparable lifestyle to the rest of the world's population would require the resources of four planets the size of the earth" (James 2002b, 1).

Some of the world's environmental problems are localized and can be addressed through unilateral action. Yet, as we have seen in this chapter, many others span the boundaries between territorial states and require multilateral solutions. The political world may be a checkerboard of sovereign states, but the natural world is a seamless web.

Recognizing that Earth's ecosystem transcends national jurisdictions, the international community has taken various steps to address many environmental threats. International environmental treaties have grown exponentially over the past 80 years; however many ecologists fear that still not enough is being done to save the global commons for future generations. Because damage caused by environmental degradation accumulates slowly, is unequally distributed, and remedies remain expensive, many states hesitate to join environmental-preservation efforts unless they are sure that others will act as well. Earth's atmosphere and oceans are common-pool resources: They do not belong to any single state, and everyone can benefit from their use regardless of whether they help pay for the costs of their preservation. As a result, many states are tempted to be free riders, negotiating treaties that "reflect the lowest common denominator of perceived interests" that "maximize the responsibilities of other nations while minimizing their own obligations" (Soroos 1999). Many environmentalists express misgiving about the United States. Of the UN's 31 major global environmental agreements, the United States has only ratified 10 (*Harper's*, August 2001, 16). They worry that if the world's most powerful state refuses to lead, the prospects for forging new rules and institutions for protecting Earth's ecosystem are dim.

Under the auspices of the United Nations, concern has been repeatedly voiced about the need to protect the environment. However, pledges about safeguarding the planet's ecology in the face of rising world population have *not* significantly improved the global environment. Despite expressing concern about the global future, national leaders have failed to make firm commitments to sustainable development that might reconcile the conflicts between economic growth and environmental protection.

Differences between the rich Global North and the developing Global South will continue to spark controversy about such issues as the transfer of resources and technology needed to deal with climate change, biodiversity, and a host of other specific problem areas. However, one encouraging trend is that, as Global North countries move into the information age and their economies shift away from "smokestack" industries toward cleaner service-oriented activities, it is likely that the adverse environmental consequences of these advanced countries' economic activities will decline. Trade with other states, nevertheless, will ensure continuing pressures on global resources and the environmental burdens they pose. Wealthy countries that have depleted their resources or passed strict laws to protect them can easily look overseas for desired commodities, in ways that shift the environmental stress of high consumption to someone else's backyard. In 1999, these concerns provoked Leon Brittan, the European Union commissioner for external trade, to argue that "the economic case for pursuing the process of trade liberalization is an overwhelming one. But it is impossible to ignore the fact that . . . there are widespread fears of the social and environmental consequences of the combination of liberalization and globalization."

"The ability of states to regulate usage of the global common spaces in the twenty-first century has far-reaching consequences for the environment and for humankind" (Joyner 2001). We stand at a critical juncture. According to Paul Crutzen, a Nobel Prize-winning atmospheric chemist, we are witnessing the beginning of a new era, a time when human influences on the planet will trump natural climate swings (*U.S. News & World Report,* special edition, 2004). The path humanity takes will affect global welfare far into the future. Yet many people remain complacent; ominous predictions have been made before and have been proven wrong. Moreover, numerous environmental risks are only visible in the long term, while countermeasures are costly in the short term. But evidence of serious ecological problems is getting harder to ignore, and because the stakes are so high, all the pieces in the puzzle—population, natural resources, technology, and preferences in lifestyles—must be worked on simultaneously, through coordinated, multilateral efforts. "All things are connected," Chief Seattle of the Suquamish tribe once told the U.S. government. "Man did not weave the web of life; he is merely a strand in it. Whatever he does to the web, he does to himself."

Chapter Summary

- The global environment is a system of delicately and tightly integrated components that together impose limits on the planet's carrying capacity. If population growth exceeds that carrying capacity, it could result in lost economic opportunities, environmental degradation, and domestic strife.
- The planet has become a demographically divided world, with Global North countries experiencing low or declining growth and Global South countries experiencing high levels of growth. Population growth in the Global South will create pressures toward outward movement, and the aging of the industrial societies of the Global North will encourage them to search for new sources of labor. These forces will place migration at the center of national political agendas.
- As trends in births, deaths, and migration unfold worldwide, they will promote significant change in world politics, aggravating some existing problems as valuable resources become increasingly scarce, and creating new challenges as the natural environment experiences greater strain.
- Rapid increases in the rate of energy usage in general and petroleum in particular are primarily post–World War II phenomena. The impact of oil price and production policies on the international political economy derives from the uneven distribution of the demand and supply of oil.
- International efforts to address the problems of global warming and the depletion of the atmosphere's protective ozone layer have yielded mixed results. Attempts to deal with climate change remain confined to voluntary restraints. In contrast, an international regime has emerged to restrict the use of ozone-depleting chemicals.
- Deforestation is a global phenomenon, but its rate is much higher in the Global South than in the Global North. While some norms have emerged to guide states in preserving biodiversity, the world's forests remain at risk of destruction through commercial exploitation and agricultural expansion.

- Differences between the countries of the Global North and South over world-wide ecopolitical issues will continue to spark controversy in the global future. The controversy arises in part from clashing views over the responsibility for causing and solving the environmental problems facing the world today.

KEY TERMS

acid rain
biodiversity
carrying capacity
cartel
demographic transition

desertification
fertility rate
greenhouse effect
ozone layer
pandemic

population implosion
replacement-level fertility
sustainable development
tragedy of the commons
transgenetic crops

WHERE ON THE WORLD WIDE WEB?

International Data Base

http://www.census.gov/ipc/www/idbnew.html

The U.S. Census Bureau offers you the chance to use their computerized bank of demographic data. From their home page you can look at the Summary Demographic Data to see totals in population and rates of growth for every country in the world. Click on "Population Pyramids" to compare countries according to their age distributions. First, choose the United States. What age groups had the largest concentration of people in 1997? Does this change in the year 2025? What about in the year 2050 (when you will probably be retired)? Is there a big difference between male and female populations? Now, choose a country in Africa. How is the pyramid for this country different from the one for the United States? How does it change across time? What conclusions can you draw about the problems each of the countries may face given the number of citizens in different age categories in different time periods?

Earth Times

http://www.earthtimes.org/

Earth Times is an independent international electronic newspaper devoted to reporting global and national issues relating to the environment, sustainable development, population, human rights,

and current affairs. This award-winning site will give you up-to-date reports on and analyses of ecological issues.

IISDnet

http://www.iisd.org/default.asp

The International Institute for Sustainable Development (IISD) has produced a website to help users learn about sustainable development, provide information on controversial topics, explore issues in environmental management, and show how businesses can turn sustainability into a competitive advantage. The site also includes a Sustainable Development Timeline, where you can follow how our society has tried to integrate protection of the environment with the establishment of healthy societies and economies.

Climate Change

http://www.nationalgeographic.com/

The National Geographic Society has an extensive website that covers many aspects of the interactions of humans with the environment. Enter the search terms "global warming" and "climate change" in the site's search engine. What are examples of climate change affecting a single animal or plant species? How is climate change affecting humans?

INFOTRAC® COLLEGE EDITION

Search for the following articles in the InfoTrac College Edition database.

Catley-Carlson, Margaret, and Judith A. M. Outlaw. "Poverty and Population Issues: Clarifying the Connections," *Journal of International Affairs* Fall 1998.

Lee, Kai N. "Searching for Sustainability in the New Century," *Ecology Law Quarterly* February 2001.

Postel, Sandra L., and Aaron T. Wolf. "Dehydrating Conflict," *Foreign Policy* September 2001.

Rowland, F. Sherwood. "Climate Change and Its Consequences: Issues for the New U.S. Administration," *Environment* March 2001.

For more articles, enter:

"global warming" in the Subject Guide, and then go to subdivision "analysis."

"population" in the Subject Guide, and then go to subdivision "economic aspects."

"population policy" in the Subject Guide.

ADDITIONAL CD-ROM RESOURCES

Click on Global Challenges and Issues for additional resources related to this chapter.

Glossary

A

acid rain precipitation that has been made acidic through contact with sulfur dioxide and nitrogen oxide.

agenda setting the ability to influence which issues receive attention from governments and international organizations by giving them publicity.

alliance a formal agreement among sovereign states for the purpose of coordinating their behavior to increase mutual security.

antidumping duties tariffs imposed to offset another state's alleged selling of a product at below the cost to produce it.

appeasement a strategy of making concessions to another state in the hope that, satisfied, it will not make additional claims.

arbitrage the selling of one currency (or product) and purchase of another to make a profit on the changing exchange rates; traders ("arbitragers") help to keep states' currencies in balance through their speculative efforts to buy large quantities of devalued currencies and sell them in countries where they are valued more highly.

arms control bilateral or multilateral agreements to contain arms buildups by setting limits on the number and types of weapons that states are permitted.

arms race an action-reaction process in which rival states rapidly increase their military capabilities in response to one another.

asylum the provision of sanctuary to safeguard refugees escaping from the threat of persecution in the country where they hold citizenship.

asymmetric war an armed conflict between belligerents of vastly unequal military strength, in which the weaker side is often a nonstate actor that relies on unconventional tactics.

autocratic rule a governmental system where unlimited power is concentrated in the hands of a single person.

B

balance of payments a calculation summarizing a country's financial transactions with the external world, determined by the level of credits (export earnings, profits from foreign investment, receipts of foreign aid) minus the country's total international debts (imports, interest payments on international debts, foreign direct investments, and the like).

balance of power the theory that national survival in an anarchic world is most likely when military power is distributed to prevent a single hegemon or bloc from dominating the state system.

balance of trade a calculation based on the value of merchandise goods and services imported and exported. A deficit occurs when a country buys more from abroad than it sells.

balancer an influential global or regional state that throws its support in decisive fashion to the weaker side of the balance of power.

bandwagon the tendency for weak states to seek alliance with the strongest power, irrespective of that power's ideology or form of government, in order to increase security.

barter the exchange of one good for another rather than the use of currency to buy and sell items.

beggar-thy-neighbor politics the attempt to promote trade surpluses through policies that cause other states to suffer trade deficits.

bilateral relationships or agreements between two states.

biodiversity the variety of life on Earth.

bipolar an international system with two dominant power centers.

brain drain the exodus of the most educated people from their homeland to a more prosperous foreign country where the opportunities for high incomes are better, which deprives their homeland of their ability to contribute to its economic development.

brinkmanship intentionally taking enormous risks in bargaining with an adversary in order to compel submission.

bureaucratic politics model a description of decision making that sees foreign policy choices as based on bargaining and compromises among government agencies.

Bush Doctrine a policy that singles out states that support terrorist groups and advocates military strikes against them to prevent a future attack on the United States.

C

capital mobility hypothesis the contention that MNCs' movement of investment capital has led to the globalization of finance.

carrying capacity the maximum biomass that can be supported by a given territory.

cartel an organization of the producers of a commodity that seeks to regulate the pricing and production of that commodity to increase revenue.

coercive diplomacy the use of threats or limited armed force to persuade an adversary to alter its foreign and/or domestic policies.

cognitive dissonance the psychological tendency to deny or rationalize away discrepancies between one's preexisting beliefs and new information.

collective defense a military organization within a specific region created to protect its members from external attack.

collective goods goods from which everyone benefits regardless of their individual contributions.

collective security a security regime based on the principle that an act of aggression by any state will be met by a collective response from the rest.

colonialism the rule of a region by an external sovereign power.

commercial liberalism an economic theory advocating free markets and the removal of barriers to the flow of trade and capital.

comparative advantage the concept in liberal economic theory that a state will benefit if it specializes in those goods it can produce comparatively cheaply and acquires through trade goods that it can only produce at a higher cost.

compellence a threat of force aimed at making an adversary grant concessions against its will.

complex interdependence a model of world politics based on the assumptions that states are not the only important actors, security is not the dominant national goal, and military force is not the only significant instrument of foreign policy.

concert a cooperative agreement among great powers to jointly manage international relations.

consequentialism an approach to evaluating moral choices on the basis of the results of the action taken.

constitutional democracy a governmental system in which political leaders' power is limited by a body of fundamental principles, and leaders are held accountable to citizens through regular, fair, and competitive elections.

containment a term coined by U.S. policymaker George Kennan for deterring expansion by the Soviet Union, which has since been used to describe a strategy aimed at preventing a state from using force to increase its territory or sphere of influence.

countervailing duties tariffs imposed by a government to offset suspected subsidies provided by foreign governments to their producers.

covert operations secret activities undertaken by a state outside its borders through clandestine means to achieve specific political or military goals with respect to another.

crosscutting cleavages a situation where politically relevant divisions between international actors are contradictory, with their interests pulling them together on some issues and separating them on others.

D

decolonization the achievement of independence by countries that were once colonies of other states.

democratic peace the theory that although democratic states sometimes wage wars against other states, they do not fight each other.

demographic transition an explanation of population changes that highlights the role of birth and death rates in moving countries from stable to rapidly increasing and finally to declining populations.

dependency theory a view of development asserting that the leading capitalist states dominate and exploit the poorer countries on the periphery of the world economy.

dependent development the industrialization of areas outside of the leading capitalist states within the confines set by the dominant capitalist states, which enables the poor to become wealthier without ever catching up to the core Global North countries.

desertification the creation of deserts due to soil erosion, overfarming, and deforestation, which converts cropland to nonproductive, arid sand.

détente a strategy of relaxing tensions between adversaries to reduce the possibility of war.

deterrence a strategy designed to dissuade an adversary from doing what it would otherwise do.

development the processes through which a country increases its capacity to meet its citizens' basic human needs and raise their standard of living.

devolution granting political power to ethnopolitical groups within a state under the expectation that greater autonomy for them in particular regions will curtail their quest for independence.

digital divide the division between those states that have a high proportion of Internet users and hosts, and those that do not.

diplomatic recognition the formal legal acceptance of a state's official status as an independent country. *De facto* recognition acknowledges the factual existence of another state or government short of full recognition. *De jure* recognition gives a government formal, legal recognition.

disarmament agreements to reduce or eliminate weapons or other means of attack.

displaced people people involuntarily uprooted from their homes but still living in their own countries.

diversionary theory of war the contention that leaders initiate conflict abroad as a way of steering public opinion at home away from controversial domestic issues.

domino theory a metaphor popular during the Cold War which predicted that if one state fell to communism, its neighbors would also fall in a chain reaction, like a row of falling dominoes.

dualism the existence of a rural, impoverished, and neglected sector of society alongside an urban, developing, or modernizing sector, with little interaction between the two.

E

economic sanctions the punitive use of trade or monetary measures, such as an embargo, to harm the economy of an enemy state in order to exercise influence over its policies.

ethnopolitical group people whose identity is primarily defined by their sense of sharing a common ancestral nationality, language, cultural heritage, and kinship ties.

exchange rate the rate at which one state's currency is exchanged for another state's currency in the global marketplace.

export quotas barriers to commerce agreed to by two trading states to protect their domestic producers.

export-led industrialization a growth strategy that concentrates on developing domestic export industries capable of competing in overseas markets.

extended deterrence the use of military threats by a great power to deter an attack on its allies.

F

failed states countries whose governments have little or no control over their territory and population.

failing states states in danger of political collapse due to overwhelming internal strife.

fertility rate the average number of children born to a woman during her lifetime.

firebreak the psychological barrier between conventional and nuclear war.

First World the relatively wealthy industrialized countries that share a commitment to varying forms of democratic political institutions and developed market economies.

fixed exchange rates a system under which states establish the parity of their currencies and commit to keeping fluctuations in their exchange rates within narrow limits.

floating exchange rates an unmanaged process where by market forces rather than governments influence the relative rate of exchange for currencies between countries.

foreign direct investment (FDI) an investment in a country involving a long-term relationship and control of an enterprise by nonresidents and including equity capital, reinvestment of earnings, other long-term capital, and short-term capital as shown in balance of payments.

free riders those who enjoy the benefits of collective goods but pay little or nothing for them.

functionalism a theory of political integration based on the assumption that technical cooperation among different nationalities in economic and social fields will build communities that transcend sovereign states.

G

genocide the deliberate extermination of an ethnic or minority group.

geopolitics a school of thought claiming that states' foreign policies are determined by their location, natural resources, and physical environment.

Global North a term used to refer to the world's wealthy, industrialized countries located primarily in the Northern Hemisphere.

Global South a term used to designate the less-developed countries located primarily in the Southern Hemisphere.

global village a popular image used to describe the growth of awareness that all people share a common fate, stemming from a view that the world is an integrated and interdependent whole.

globalization a set of processes that are widening, deepening, and accelerating the interconnectedness among societies.

greenhouse effect the phenomenon producing planetary warming when gases released by burning fossil fuels act as a blanket in the atmosphere, thereby increasing temperatures.

Group of 77 (G-77) the coalition of Third World countries that sponsored the 1963 Joint Declaration of Developing Countries calling for reforms to allow greater equity in North-South trade.

Group of Seven (G-7)/Group of Eight (G-8) a group of advanced industrialized democracies composed of the United States, Britain, France, Japan, Germany, Canada, and Italy that meets in regular economic summit conferences; since 1997, known as the G-8 with the addition of Russia.

groupthink the propensity for members of small, cohesive groups to accept the group's prevailing attitudes in the interest of group harmony, rather than speak out for what they believe.

H

Heavily Indebted Poor Countries (HIPCs) the subset of countries identified by the World Bank's Debtor Reporting System whose ratios of government debt to gross national product are so substantial that they cannot meet their payment obligations without experiencing political instability and economic collapse.

hegemon a single, overwhelmingly powerful state that exercises predominate influence over the global system.

hegemonic stability theory a school of thought that argues free trade and economic order depend on the existence of an overwhelmingly powerful state willing and able to use its strength to open and organize world markets.

high politics the category of global issues related to military and security aspects of relations between governments and peoples.

human rights the political and social entitlements recognized by international law as inalienable and valid for individuals in all countries by virtue of their humanity.

human security a concept that refers to the degree to which the welfare of individuals is protected and advanced, in contrast to national security which puts the interests of states first.

humanitarian intervention the use of peacekeeping forces by foreign states or international organizations to protect endangered people from gross violations of their human rights.

I

import quotas limits on the quantity of particular products that can be imported.

import-substitution industrialization a strategy for economic development that involves encouraging domestic entrepreneurs to manufacture products traditionally imported from abroad.

indigenous peoples the native ethnic and cultural inhabitant populations within countries ruled by a government controlled by others, often referred to as the "Fourth World."

individual level of analysis an analytical approach to the study of world politics that emphasizes the psychological factors motivating people who make foreign policy decisions on behalf of states and other global actors.

infant industry a newly established industry that is not yet strong enough to compete effectively in the global marketplace.

information warfare attacks on an adversary's telecommunications and computer networks to degrade the technological systems vital to its defense and economic well-being.

intergovernmental organizations (IGOs) institutions created and joined by states' governments, which give them authority to make collective decisions to manage particular problem(s) on the global agenda.

international liquidity reserve assets used to settle international accounts.

international monetary system the financial procedures governing the exchange and conversion of national currencies so that they can be bought and sold for one another to calculate the value of currencies and credits when capital is transferred across borders through trade, investment, and loans.

international political economy the study of the intersection of politics and economics that illuminates the reasons why changes occur in the distribution of states' wealth and power.

international regimes sets of principles, norms, rules, and decision-making procedures agreed to by a group of states to guide their behavior in particular issue areas.

irredentism efforts by an ethnonational or religious group to regain control of territory by force so that existing state boundaries will no longer separate the group.

isolationism a policy of withdrawing from active participation with other actors in world affairs and instead concentrating state efforts on managing internal affairs.

J

just war doctrine a set of criteria that indicate when it is morally justifiable to wage war and how it should be fought once it begins.

L

laissez-faire economics from a French phrase (meaning literally "let do") that Adam Smith and other commercial liberals in the eighteenth century used to describe the advantages of free-wheeling capitalism without government interference in economic affairs.

least developed of the less-developed countries (LLDCs) the most impoverished states in the Global South.

Liberal International Economic Order (LIEO) the set of regimes created after World War II, designed to promote monetary stability and reduce barriers to the free flow of trade and capital.

long-cycle theory a theory that focuses on the rise and fall of the leading global power as the central political process of the modern world system.

low politics the category of global issues related to the economic, social, and environmental aspects of relations between governments and people.

M

massive retaliation a policy of responding to any act of aggression with the most destructive capabilities available, including nuclear weapons.

mercantilism the seventeenth-century theory preaching that trading states should increase their wealth and power by expanding exports and protecting their domestic economy from imports.

military intervention overt or covert use of force by one or more countries that cross the border of another country in order to affect the target country's government and policies.

military necessity a legal doctrine asserting that violation of the rules of war may be excused during periods of extreme emergency.

military-industrial complex a term coined by U.S. president Eisenhower to describe the coalition among arms manufacturers, military bureaucracies, and top government officials that promotes defense expenditures for its own profit and power.

mirror images the tendency of people in competitive interaction to perceive each other similarly—to see an adversary the same way as an adversary sees them.

modernization a view of development that argues that self-sustaining economic growth is created through technological innovation, efficient production, and investments from capital accumulation.

money supply the total amount of currency in circulation in a state, calculated to include demand deposits—such as checking accounts—in commercial banks and time deposits—such as savings accounts and bonds—in savings banks.

most-favored-nation (MFN) principle unconditional nondiscriminatory treatment in trade between contracting parties guaranteed by GATT; in 1997, U.S. senator Daniel Patrick Moynihan introduced legislation to replace the term with "normal trade relations" (NTR) to better reflect its true meaning.

multinational corporations (MNCs) business enterprises headquartered in one state that invest and operate extensively in other states.

multiple independently targetable reentry vehicles (MIRVs) a technological innovation permitting many nuclear warheads to be delivered from a single missile.

multipolar an international system with more than two dominant power centers.

mutual assured destruction (MAD) a system of deterrence in which both sides possess the ability to survive a first strike and launch a devastating retaliatory attack.

N

nationalism the belief that political loyalty lies with a body of people who share ethnicity, linguistics, or cultural affinity, and perceive themselves to be members of the same group.

neofunctionalism a revised functionalist theory asserting that the IGOs states create to manage common problems provide benefits that exert pressures for further political integration.

neomercantilism a contemporary version of classical mercantilism which advocates promoting domestic production and a balance-of-payment surplus by subsidizing exports and using tariffs and nontariff barriers to reduce imports.

New International Economic Order (NIEO) the 1974 policy resolution in the UN that called for a North-South dialogue to open the way for the less-developed countries of the Global South to participate more fully in the making of international economic policy.

newly industrialized countries (NICs) prosperous members of the Global South, which have become important exporters of manufactured goods.

nonalignment a foreign policy posture that rejects participating in military alliances with rival blocs for fear that formal alignment will entangle the state in an unnecessary war.

nondiscrimination a principle for trade that proclaims that goods produced at home and abroad are to be treated the same for import and export agreements.

nongovernmental organizations (NGOs) transnational organizations of private citizens that include foundations, professional associations, multinational corporations, or groups in different countries joined together to work toward common interests.

nonintervention the legal principle prohibiting one state from interfering in another state's internal affairs.

nonstate actors all transnationally active groups other than states, such as international organizations whose members are states (IGOs) and nongovernmental organizations (NGOs) whose members are individuals and private groups from more than one state.

nontariff barrier governmental restrictions not involving a tax or duty that increase the cost of importing goods into a country.

nuclear winter the expected freeze that would occur in the earth's climate from the fallout of smoke and dust in the event nuclear weapons were used, blocking out sunlight and destroying plant and animal life that survived the original blast.

O

official development assistance (ODA) grants or loans to countries from other countries, usually channeled through multilateral aid organizations, for the primary purpose of promoting economic development and welfare.

opportunity costs the concept in decision-making theories that when the occasion arises to use resources, what is gained for one purpose is lost for other purposes, so that every choice entails the cost of some lost opportunity.

orderly market arrangements (OMAs) voluntary export restrictions that involve a government-to-government agreement and often specific rules of management.

overlapping cleavages a situation where politically relevant divisions between international actors are complementary; interests pulling them apart on one issue are reinforced by interests that also separate them on other issues.

ozone layer the protective layer of the upper atmosphere over the earth's surface that shields the planet from the sun's harmful impact on living organisms on the planet.

P

pandemic a disease that spreads throughout one or more continents.

peace-building post-conflict actions, predominantly diplomatic and economic, that strengthen and rebuild governmental infrastructure and institutions in order to avoid recourse to armed conflict.

peaceful coexistence Soviet leader Nikita Khrushchev's 1956 doctrine that war between capitalist and communist states is not inevitable and that interbloc competition could be peaceful.

peacemaking peaceful settlement processes such as good offices, conciliation, and mediation, designed to resolve the issues that led to armed conflict.

polarity the degree to which military and economic capabilities are concentrated among the major powers in the state system.

polarization the degree to which states cluster in alliances around the most powerful members of the state system.

political efficacy the extent to which a policymaker believes in his or her ability to control events politically.

political integration the processes and activities by which the populations of two or more states transfer their loyalties to a merged political and economic unit.

politics the exercise of influence to affect the distribution of values, such as power, prestige, and wealth; to Harold Lasswell, the process that determines "who gets what, when, how, and why."

pooled sovereignty legal authority granted to an IGO by its members to make collective decisions regarding specified aspects of public policy heretofore made exclusively by each sovereign government.

population implosion a rapid reduction of population that reverses a previous trend toward progressively larger populations.

power the ability to make someone continue a course of action, change what he or she is doing, or refrain from acting.

power cycle theory the contention that armed conflict is probable when a state passes through certain critical points along a generalized curve of relative power, and wars of enormous magnitude are likely when several great powers pass through critical points at approximately the same time.

power potential the relative capabilities or resources held by a state that are considered necessary to its asserting influence over others.

power transition theory the contention that war is likely when a dominant great power is threatened by the rapid growth of a rival's capabilities, which reduces the difference in their relative power.

preemption a quick first-strike attack that seeks to defeat an adversary before it can organize a retaliatory response.

preventive diplomacy actions taken in advance of a predictable crisis to prevent superpower involvement and limit violence.

private international law law pertaining to routinized transnational intercourse between or among states as well as nonstate actors.

procedural rationality a method of decision making based on having perfect information with which all possible courses of action are carefully evaluated.

proliferation the spread of weapon capabilities throughout the state system.

protectionism a policy of creating barriers to foreign trade, such as tariffs and quotas, that protects local industries from competition.

public international law law pertaining to government-to-government relations.

R

rapprochement in diplomacy, a policy seeking to reestablish normal relations between enemies.

rational choice decision-making procedures guided by careful definition of problems, specification of goals, weighing the costs, risks, and benefits of all alternatives, and selection of the optimal alternative.

Reagan Doctrine a pledge of U.S. backing for anticommunist insurgents who sought to overthrow Soviet-supported governments.

refugees people who flee for safety to another country because of a well-founded fear of persecution.

regional currency union the pooling of sovereignty to create a common currency (such as the EU's euro) and single monetary system for members in a region, regulated by a regional central bank within the currency bloc to reduce the likelihood of large-scale liquidity crises.

relative deprivation people's perception that they are unfairly deprived of the wealth and status in comparison to others who are advantaged but not more deserving.

relative gains a measure of how much one side in an agreement benefits in comparison to the other's side.

replacement-level fertility one couple replacing themselves with two children, so that a country's population will remain stable if this rate prevails.

reprisal a hostile but legal retaliatory act aimed at punishing another state's prior illegal actions.

S

satisficing the tendency for decision makers to choose the first available alternative that meets minimally acceptable standards.

schematic reasoning the process by which new information is interpreted by comparing it to generic concepts stored in memory about certain stereotypical situations, sequences of events, and characters.

secession the attempt by a religious or ethnic minority to break away from an internationally recognized state.

Second World during the Cold War, the group of countries, including the Soviet Union and its then-Eastern European allies, that shared a commitment to centrally planned economies.

second-strike capability a state's capacity to retaliate after absorbing a first-strike attack with weapons of mass destruction.

security community a group of states whose high level of noninstitutionalized collaboration results in the settlement of disputes by compromise rather than by force.

security dilemma the propensity of armaments undertaken by one state for ostensibly defensive purposes to threaten other states, which arm in reaction, with the result that their national security declines as their arms increase.

self-determination the doctrine that people should be able to determine the government that will manage their affairs.

self-fulfilling prophecy the tendency for one's expectations to evoke behavior that helps to make the expectations become true.

self-help the principle that in anarchy actors must rely on themselves.

smart bombs precision-guided military technology that enables a bomb to search for its target and detonate at the precise time it can do the most damage.

socialization the processes by which people learn the beliefs, values, and behaviors that are acceptable in a given society.

sovereignty under international law, the principle that no higher authority is above the state.

sphere of influence the area dominated by a great power.

spill over the propensity for successful integration across one area of cooperation between states to propel further integration in other areas.

standard operating procedures (SOPs) rules for reaching decisions about particular types of situations.

state an organized political entity with a permanent population, a well-defined territory, and a government.

state level of analysis an analytical approach to the study of world politics that emphasizes how the internal attributes of states influence their foreign policy behavior.

state-sponsored terrorism formal assistance, training, and arming of foreign terrorists by a state in order to achieve foreign policy goals.

strategic corporate alliances cooperation between multinational corporations and foreign companies in the same industry, driven by the movement of MNC manufacturing overseas.

Strategic Defense Initiative (SDI) a plan conceived by the Reagan administration to deploy an antiballistic missile system using space-based lasers that would destroy enemy nuclear missiles.

sustainable development economic growth that does not deplete the resources needed to maintain growth.

system a set of interconnected parts that function as a unitary whole. In world politics, the parts consist primarily of states, corporations, and other organizations that interact in the global arena.

systemic level of analysis an analytical approach to the study of world politics that emphasizes the impact of international structures and processes on the behavior of global actors.

T

tariff a tax imposed by governments on imported goods.

terrorism the premeditated use or threat of violence perpetrated against noncombatants, usually intended to induce fear in a wider audience.

theory a set of interrelated propositions that explains an observed regularity.

Third World a Cold War term to describe the developing countries of Africa, Asia, and Latin America.

trade integration economic globalization measured by the extent to which world trade volume grows faster than the world's combined gross domestic product.

tragedy of the commons a metaphor, widely used to explain the impact of human behavior on ecological systems, that explains how rational self-interested behavior by individuals may have a destructive collective impact.

transgenetic crops new crops with improved characteristics created artificially through genetic engineering, which combines genes from species that would not naturally interbreed.

transnational banks (TNBs) the world's top banking firms, whose financial activities are concentrated in transactions that cross state borders.

transnational relations interactions across state boundaries that involves at least one actor that is not the agent of a government or intergovernmental organization.

Truman Doctrine the declaration by President Harry S. Truman that U.S. foreign policy would use intervention to support peoples who allied with the United States against external subjugation.

two-level games a concept that refers to the interaction between international bargaining and domestic politics.

U

ultimatum a demand that contains a time limit for compliance and a threat of punishment for resistance.

unilateral a strategy that relies on independent, self-help behavior in foreign policy.

unipolar an international system with one dominant power center.

unitary actor an agent in world politics (usually a sovereign state) assumed to be internally united, so that changes in its internal circumstances do not influence its foreign policy as much as do the decisions that actor's leaders make to cope with changes in its global environment.

V

voluntary export restrictions (VERs) a protectionist measure popular in the 1980s and early 1990s, in which exporting countries agree to restrict shipments of a particular product to a country to deter it from imposing an even more onerous import quota.

W

war crimes acts performed during war that the international community defines as illegal, such as atrocities committed against enemy civilians and prisoners of war.

world federalism a reform movement proposing to combine sovereign states into a single unified federal state.

X

xenophobia a fear of foreigners.

Z

zero-sum game a situation in which what one side wins, the other side loses.

References

Aaronson, Susan Ariel. (2002) *Taking Trade to the Streets: The Lost History of Public Efforts to Shape Globalization.* Ann Arbor: University of Michigan Press.

Allen, John L. (2002) *Student Atlas of World Politics,* 5th ed. New York: Dushkin/McGraw-Hill.

Allison, Graham, and Philip Zelikow. (1999) *Essence of Decision: Explaining the Cuban Missile Crisis,* 2nd ed. New York: Longman.

Altman, Roger C., and C. Bowman Cutter. (1999) "Global Economy Needs Better Shock Absorbers," *International Herald Tribune* (June 16): 7.

Angell, Norman. (1910) *The Great Illusion: A Study of the Relationship of Military Power in Nations to Their Economic and Social Advantage.* London: Weidenfeld & Nicholson.

Ardrey, Robert. (1966) *The Territorial Imperative: A Personal Inquiry into the Animal Origins of Property and Nations.* New York: Atheneum.

Aronson, Jonathan D. (2002) "The Communications and Internet Revolution," pp. 540–551 in John Baylis and Steve Smith (eds.), *The Globalization of World Politics,* 2nd ed. Oxford: Oxford University Press.

Ayoob, Mohammed. (1995) *The Third World Security Predicament.* Boulder, Colo.: Lynne Rienner.

Babai, Don. (2001) "International Monetary Fund," pp. 412–418 in Joel Krieger (ed.), *The Oxford Companion to Politics of the World,* 2nd ed. New York: Oxford University Press.

Bagdikian, Ben H. (1992) *The Media Monopoly.* Boston: Beacon Press.

Baldwin, David A. (1989) *Paradoxes of Power.* New York: Basil Blackwell.

Barber, Benjamin R. (1995) *Jihad vs. McWorld.* New York: Random House.

Barnet, Richard J. (1977) *The Giants: Russia and America.* New York: Simon & Schuster.

Barnet, Richard J., and John Cavanagh. (1994) *Global Dreams: Imperial Corporations and the New World Order.* New York: Simon & Schuster.

Baron, Samuel H., and Carl Pletsch (eds.). (1985) *Introspection in Biography: The Biographer's Quest for Self-Awareness.* Hillsdale, N.J.: Analytic Press.

Beckman, Peter R., and Francine D'Amico (eds.). (1994) *Women, Gender, and World Politics.* Westport, Conn.: Bergin & Garvey.

Beitz, Charles R. (2001) "Human Rights as a Common Concern," *American Political Science Review* 95 (June): 269–282.

Benedick, Richard E. (1998) *Ozone Diplomacy.* Cambridge: Harvard University Press.

Bennett, A. Leroy. (1988) *International Organizations,* 4th ed. Englewood Cliffs, N.J.: Prentice Hall.

Bergesen, Albert, and Ronald Schoenberg. (1980) "Long Waves of Colonial Expansion and Contraction, 1415–1969," pp. 231–277 in Albert Bergesen (ed.), *Studies of the Modern World-System.* New York: Academic Press.

Berthelot, Yves. (2001) "The International Financial Architecture—Plans for Reform," *International Social Science Journal* 170 (December): 586–596.

Bhagwati, Jagdish. (1999) *A Stream of Windows: Trade, Immigration, and Democracy.* Cambridge, Mass.: MIT Press.

Bienefeld, Manfred. (1994) "The New World Order: Echoes of a New Imperialism," *Third World Quarterly* 15 (March): 31–48.

Blanton, Shannon Lindsey, and Charles W. Kegley, Jr. (1997) "Reconciling U.S. Arms Sales with America's Interests and Ideals," *Futures Research Quarterly* 13 (Spring): 85–101.

Blustein, Paul (1999) "Currencies in Crisis," *Washington Post National Weekly Edition* (March 1): 6–7.

Brecher, Michael. (1993) *Crises in World Politics.* Oxford, Eng.: Pergamon.

Brecke, Peter. (1999) "The Characteristics of Violent Conflict since 1400 A.D.," paper presented at the annual meeting of the International Studies Association, Washington, D.C., February 17–20.

Bremer, Stuart A. (1992) "Dangerous Dyads: Conditions Affecting the Likelihood of Interstate War, 1816–1965," *Journal of Conflict Resolution* 36 (June): 309–341.

Broad, Robin (ed.). (2002) *Global Backlash: Citizen Initiatives for a Just World Economy.* Lanham, Md.: Rowman and Littlefield.

Broder, David. (2002) "Senator Brings Vietnam Experiences to Bear on Iraq," (Columbia, S.C.) *The State* (September 18): A15.

Bronfenbrenner, Urie. (1971) "The Mirror Image in Soviet-American Relations," *Journal of Social Issues* 27 (No. 1): 46–51.

Brown, Justin. (1999) "Arms Sales: Exporting U.S. Military Edge?" *Christian Science Monitor* (December 2): 2.

Brown, Lester R. (2002) "Planning for the Eco-economy," *USA Today* (March): 31–35.

Brown, Lester R., and Christopher Flavin. (1999) "A New Economy for a New Century," pp. 3–21 in

Lester R. Brown, et al., *State of the World 1999*. New York: Norton.

Brown, Lester R., et al. (1999) *State of the World 1999*. New York: Norton.

Brzezinski, Zbigniew. (1998) "The Grand Chessboard," *Harvard International Review* 20 (Winter): 48–53.

Bueno de Mesquita, Bruce. (1981) "Risk, Power Distributions, and the Likelihood of War," *International Studies Quarterly* 25 (December): 541–568.

Bull, Hedley. (1977) *The Anarchical Society: A Study of Order in World Politics*. New York: Columbia University Press.

Bullock, Alan. (1962) *Hitler: A Study in Tyranny*. New York: Harper & Row.

Caldwell, Dan. (1977) "Bureaucratic Foreign Policy Making," *American Behavioral Scientist* 21 (September–October): 87–110.

Caporaso, James A. (1993) "Global Political Economy," pp. 451–481 in Ada W. Finifter (ed.), *Political Science: The State of the Discipline II*. Washington, D.C.: American Political Science Association.

Caporaso, James A., and David P. Levine. (1992). *Theories of Political Economy*. New York: Cambridge University Press.

Cardoso, Fernando Henrique and Enzo Faletto. (1979) *Dependency and Development in Latin America*. Berkeley: University of California Press.

Carr, E. H. (1939) *The Twenty-Years' Crisis, 1919–1939*. London: Macmillan.

Cashman, Greg. (2000) *What Causes War?* 2nd ed. Boston: Lexington Books.

Cerny, Philip G. (1994) "The Dynamics of Financial Globalization," *Policy Sciences* 287 (No. 4): 319–342.

Chaliand, Gerard, and Jean-Pierre Rageau. (1993) *Strategic Atlas*, 3rd ed. New York: Harper Perennial.

Chase-Dunn, Christopher. (1989) *Global Formation: Structures of the World-Economy*. Oxford: Basil Blackwell.

Checkel, Jeffrey T. (1998) "The Constructivist Turn in International Relations Theory," *World Politics* 50 (January 1998): 324–348.

Christensen, Thomas J., and Jack Snyder. (1990) "Chain Gangs and Passed Bucks: Predicting Alliance Patterns in Multipolarity," *International Organization* 44 (Spring): 137–168.

Clapham, Andrew. (2001) "Human Rights," pp. 368–370 in Joel Krieger (ed.), *The Oxford Companion to Politics of the World*, 2nd ed. New York: Oxford University Press.

Claude, Inis L., Jr. (1989) "The Balance of Power Revisited," *Review of International Studies* 15 (January): 77–85.

———. (1971) *Swords into Plowshares*, 4th ed. New York: Random House.

———. (1967) *The Changing United Nations*. New York: Random House.

———. (1962) *Power and International Relations*. New York: Random House.

Cobb, Roger, and Charles Elder. (1970) *International Community*. New York: Harcourt, Brace & World.

Cohen, Benjamin J. (2000) *The Geography of Money*. Ithaca, N.Y.: Cornell University Press.

———. (1996) "Phoenix Risen: The Resurrection of Global Finance," *World Politics* 48 (January): 268–296.

———. (1973) *The Question of Imperialism*. New York: Basic Books.

Cohen, Eliot A. (1998) "A Revolution in Warfare," pp. 34–46 in Charles W. Kegley, Jr. and Eugene R. Wittkopf (eds.), *The Global Agenda*, 4th ed. New York: McGraw-Hill.

Cohen, Joel E. (1998) "How Many People Can the Earth Support?" *New York Review of Books* 45 (October 8): 29–31.

———. (1995) *How Many People Can the Earth Support?* New York: Norton.

Colander, David C. (2001) *Macroeconomics*, 4th ed. New York: McGraw-Hill.

Cortwright, David, and George A. Lopez (eds.). (2002) *Smart Sanctions: Targeting Economic Statecraft*. Landham, Md.: Rowman and Littlefield.

———. (1995) "The Sanctions Era: An Alternative to Military Intervention," *Fletcher Forum of World Affairs* 19 (May): 65–85.

Craig, Gordon A., and Alexander L. George. (1990) *Force and Statecraft*, 2nd ed. New York: Oxford University Press.

Crossette, Barbara. (1995) "The Second Sex in the Third World," *New York Times* (September 10): E1, E3.

Crump, Andy. (1998) *The A to Z of World Development*. Oxford, Eng.: New Internationalist Publications.

D'Amato, Anthony. (1995) *International Law: Process and Prospect*. Irvington, N.Y.: Transnational Publishers.

Davis, Wade. (1999) "Vanishing Cultures," *National Geographic* (August): 62–89.

Dehio, Ludwig. (1962) *The Precarious Balance*. New York: Knopf.

DeRivera, Joseph H. (1968) *The Psychological Dimension of Foreign Policy*. Columbus, Ohio: Merrill.

de Tocqueville, Alexis. (1969 [1835]) *Democracy in America*. New York: Doubleday.

Deutsch, Karl W. (1978) *The Analysis of International Relations*, 2nd ed. Englewood Cliffs, N.J.: Prentice-Hall.

———. (1974) *Politics and Government*. Boston: Houghton Mifflin.

———. (1957) *Political Community and the North Atlantic Area*. Princeton, N.J.: Princeton University Press.

Deutsch, Karl W., and J. David Singer. (1964) "Multipolar Power Systems and International Stability," *World Politics* 16 (April): 390–406.

DeVecchi, Robert, and Arthur C. Helton. (1999) "The United Nations Requires an Upgrade," *International Herald Tribune* (September 20): 16.

de Wijk, Rob. (1998) "Towards a New Political Strategy for NATO," *NATO Review* 46: 14–18.

Dickinson, G. Lowes. (1926) *The International Anarchy, 1904–1914.* New York: Century.

Diehl, Paul F. (1985) "Contiguity and Military Escalation in Major Power Rivalries. 1816–1980," *Journal of Politics* 47 (4): 1203–1211.

DiRenzo, Gordon J. (ed.). (1974) *Personality and Politics.* Garden City, N.Y.: Doubleday-Anchor.

Dixon, William J. (1994) "Democracy and the Peaceful Settlement of International Conflict," *American Political Science Review* 88 (March): 14–32.

Donnelly, Jack. (1993) *International Human Rights.* Boulder, Colo.: Westview.

Doran, Charles F. (2000) "Confronting the Principles of the Power Cycle: Changing Systems Structure, Expectations, and War," pp. 332–368 in Manus I. Midlarsky (ed.), *Handbook of War Studies II.* Ann Arbor: University of Michigan Press.

———. (1989) "Power Cycle Theory of Systems Structure and Stability: Commonalities and Complementarities," pp. 83–110 in Manus I. Midlarsky (ed.), *Handbook of War Studies.* New York: Unwin Hyman.

Doran, Charles F., and Wes Parsons. (1980) "War and the Cycle of Relative Power," *American Political Science Review* 74: 947–965.

Dörner, Dietrich. (1996) *The Logic of Failure.* Reading, Mass.: Addison-Wesley.

Dorraj, Manochehr. (1995) "Introduction: The Changing Context of Third World Political Economy," pp. 1–13 in Manochehr Dorraj (ed.), *The Changing Political Economy of the Third World.* Boulder, Colo.: Lynne Rienner.

Dos Santos, Theotonio. (1970) "The Structure of Dependence," *American Economic Review* 60 (May): 231–236.

Dougherty, James E., and Robert L. Pfaltzgraff, Jr. (2001) *Contending Theories of International Relations,* 5th ed. New York: Longman.

Downs, George W. (ed.). (1994) *Collective Security beyond the Cold War.* Ann Arbor: University of Michigan Press.

Doyle, Michael W. (1997) *Ways of War and Peace.* New York: Norton.

Drezner, Daniel W. (2004) "The Outsourcing Bogeyman," *Foreign Affairs* 83 (May/June): 22–34.

Drozdiak, William. (2001) "Protectionism in the Global Age," *Washington Post National Weekly* (May 21–27): 17.

Drucker, Peter. (2001) "A Survey of the Near Future," *The Economist* (November 3): 3–19.

Durant, Will. (1954) *Our Oriental Heritage.* New York: Simon and Schuster.

Durning, Alan Thein. (1993) "Supporting Indigenous Peoples," pp. 80–100 in Lester R. Brown, et al. (eds.), *State of the World 1993.* New York: Norton.

East, Maurice A. (1978) "The International System Perspective and Foreign Policy," pp. 143–160 in Maurice A. East, Stephen A. Salmore, and Charles F. Hermann (eds.), *Why Nations Act: Theoretical Perspectives for Comparative Foreign Policy Studies.* Beverly Hills: Sage.

Easterbrook, Gregg. (2002) "Safe Deposit: The Case for Foreign Aid," *New Republic.* (July 29): 16–20.

Easton, Stewart C. (1964) *The Rise and Fall of Western Colonialism.* New York: Praeger.

Eberstadt, Nicholas. (1995) "Population, Food, and Income: Global Trends in the Twentieth Century," pp. 7–47 in Ronald Bailey (ed.), *The True State of the Planet.* New York: Free Press.

The Economist. (2002) *Pocket World in Figures.* London: Profile Books.

Edwards, Stephen R. (1995) "Conserving Biodiversity: Resources for Our Future," pp. 212–265 in Ronald Bailey (ed.), *The True State of the Planet.* New York: Free Press.

Eizenstat, Stuart. (1999) "Learning to Steer the Forces of Globalization," *International Herald Tribune* (January 22): 6.

Elliott, Kimberly Ann. (1998) "The Sanctions Glass: Half Full or Completely Empty?" *International Security* 23 (Summer): 50–65.

Elrod, Richard. (1976) "The Concert of Europe: A Fresh Look at an International System," *World Politics* 28 (January): 159–174.

Emmanuel, Arghiri. (1972) *Unequal Exchange: An Essay on the Imperialism of Trade.* New York: Monthly Review Press.

Emmott, Bill. (2002) "Present at the Creation: A Survey of America's World Role," *The Economist* (June 29): 1–34.

Enloe, Cynthia H. (2001) "Gender and Politics," pp. 311–315 in Joel Krieger (ed.), *The Oxford Companion to Politics of the World,* 2nd ed. New York: Oxford University Press.

———. (2000) *Maneuvers: The International Politics of Militarizing Women's Lives.* Berkeley: University of California Press.

Enriquez, Juan. (1999) "Too Many Flags?" *Foreign Policy* 116 (Fall): 30–50.

Escobar, Arturo. (2000) "The Invention of Development," pp. 93–96 in Robert M. Jackson (ed.), *Global Issues 00/01,* 16th ed. Guilford, Conn.: Dushkin/McGraw-Hill.

———. (2001b) "Sovereignty," pp. 789–791 in Joel Krieger (ed.), *The Oxford Companion to Politics of the World.* New York: Oxford University Press.

Falk, Richard. (1998) *Law in an Emerging Global Village: A Post-Westphalian Perspective.* Ardsley, N.Y.: Transnational Publishers.

Falk, Richard, and Andrew Strauss. (2001) "Toward Global Parliament," *Foreign Affairs* 80 (January/February): 212–218.

Ferencz, Benjamin B., and Ken Keyes, Jr. (1991) *Planet-Hood*. Coos Bay, Ore.: Love Line Books.

Festinger, Leon. (1957) *A Theory of Cognitive Dissonance*. Evanston, Ill.: Row, Peterson.

Fieldhouse, D. K. (1973) *Economics and Empire, 1830–1914*. Ithaca, N.Y.: Cornell University Press.

Fields, Lanny B., Russell J. Barber, and Cheryl A. Riggs. (1998) *The Global Past*. Boston: Bedford.

Finnegan, William. (2002) "Leasing the Rain," *The New Yorker* (April 18): 43–53.

Flanagan, Stephen J., Ellen L. Frost, and Richard Kugler. (2001) *Challenges of the Global Century*. Washington, D.C.: Institute for National Strategic Studies, National Defense University.

Flavin, Christopher, and Seth Dunn. (1999) "Reinventing the Energy System," pp. 23–40 in Lester R. Brown, et al., *State of the World 1999*. New York: Norton.

Frank, André Gunder. (1969) *Latin America: Underdevelopment or Revolution*. New York: Monthly Review Press.

Freud, Sigmund. (1968) "Why War," pp. 71–80 in Leon Bramson and George W. Goethals (eds.), *War*. New York: Basic Books.

Friedman, Thomas L. (2000) "Corporations on Steroids," (Columbia, S.C.) *The State* (February 8): A9.

———. (1999) *The Lexus and the Olive Tree: Understanding Globalization*. New York: Farrar, Straus, Giroux.

Friedrich, Carl J., and Charles Blitzer. (1957) *The Age of Power*. Ithaca, NY: Cornell University Press.

Fukuyama, Francis. (1999) *The Great Disruption: Human Nature and the Reconstitution of Social Order*. New York: Free Press.

———. (1989) "The End of History?" *National Interest* 16 (Summer): 3–16.

Gaddis, John Lewis. (2002) "A Grand Strategy," *Foreign Policy* 133 (November/December): 50–57.

———. (1997) *We Now Know: Rethinking Cold War History*. New York: Oxford University Press.

Garten, Jeffrey A. (1999). "Beware the Weak Links in Our Globalization Chain," *International Herald Tribune* (August 19): 8.

Geller, Daniel S. (2000) "Power and International Conflict," pp. 259–277 in John A. Vasquez (ed.), *What Do We Know About War?* Lanham, Md.: Rowman & Littlefield.

Geller, Daniel S., and J. David Singer. (1998) *Nations at War: A Scientific Study of International Conflict*. Cambridge: Cambridge University Press.

George, Alexander L. (1991) *Forceful Persuasion: Coercive Diplomacy as an Alternative to War*. Washington, D.C.: United States Institute of Peace.

Gilman, Benjamin A., and Sam Gejdenson. (2000) "Preventing Disease: We're All in This Together," *International Herald Tribune* (July 4): 6.

Gilpin, Robert. (2001) "Three Ideologies of Political Economy," pp. 269–286 in Charles W. Kegley, Jr. and Eugene R. Wittkopf (eds.), *The Global Agenda*, 6th ed. Boston: McGraw-Hill.

———. (1987) *The Political Economy of International Relations*. Princeton, N.J: Princeton University Press.

Gleditsch, Nils Petter, Peter Wallensteen, Mikael Eriksson, Margareta Sollenberg, and Havard Strand. (2002) "Armed Conflict 1946–2001: A New Dataset," *Journal of Peace Research* 39 (September): 615–637.

Global Trends 2015. (2002) Washington, D.C.: Central Intelligence Agency.

Glynn, Patrick. (1993) "Letter to the Editor," *Foreign Policy* 90 (Spring): 171–174.

Goldstein, Joshua. (2002) *War and Gender*. Cambridge: Cambridge University Press.

———. (1988) *Long Cycles: Prosperity and War in the Modern Age*. New Haven, Conn.: Yale University Press.

Grant, Rebecca, and Kathleen Newland (eds.). (1991) *Gender and International Relations*. Bloomington: Indiana University Press.

Greenspan, Alan. (2004) "The Critical Role of Education in the Nation's Economy." Speech delivered at the Greater Omaha Chamber of Commerce (February 20). Retrieved at www.federalreserve.gov/boarddocs/speeches/2004/200402202/default.htm.

Greenstein, Fred I. (1987) *Personality and Politics*. Princeton, N.J.: Princeton University Press.

Gregor, Thomas, and Clayton A. Robarchek. (1996) "Two Paths to Peace: Semai and Mehinaku Nonviolence," pp. 159–188 in Thomas Gregor (ed.), *A Natural History of Peace*. Nashville: Vanderbilt University Press.

Grieco, Joseph M. (1995) "Anarchy and the Limits of Cooperation," pp. 151–171 in Charles W. Kegley, Jr. (ed.), *Controversies in International Relations Theory*. New York: St. Martin's.

Grieco, Joseph M., and John I. Ikenberry. (2003) *State Power and World Markets*. New York: Norton.

Grimmett, Richard F. (2002) *Conventional Arms Transfers to Developing Nations, 1994–2001*. Washington, D.C.: Congressional Research Service.

Gulick, Edward V. (1955) *Europe's Classical Balance of Power*. Ithaca, N.Y.: Cornell University Press.

Gurr, Ted Robert. (2001) "Managing Conflict in Ethnically Divided Societies," pp. 173–186 in Charles W. Kegley, Jr. and Eugene R. Wittkopf (eds.), *The Global Agenda*, 6th ed. Boston: McGraw-Hill.

———. (2000) *Peoples versus States: Minorities at Risk in the New Century*. Washington, D.C.: United States Institute of Peace Press.

———. (1993) *Minorities at Risk: A Global View of Ethnopolitical Conflicts.* Washington, D.C.: United States Institute of Peace Press.

———. (1970) *Why Men Rebel.* Princeton, N.J.: Princeton University Press.

Gurr, Ted Robert, Monty G. Marshall, and Deepa Khosla. (2001) *Peace and Conflict 2001.* College Park, Md.: Integrated Network for Societal Conflict Research, University of Maryland.

Haas, Ernst B. (1953) "The Balance of Power: Prescription, Concept, or Propaganda?" *World Politics* 5 (July): 442–477.

Haass, Richard N. (1997) "Sanctioning Madness," *Foreign Affairs* 76 (December): 74–85.

Handbook of International Economic Statistics (2001) Langley, Va.: U.S. Central Intelligence Agency.

Hansenclever, Andreas, Peter Mayer, and Volker Rittberger (1996) "Interests, Power, and Knowledge," *Mershon International Studies Review* 40 (October): 177–228.

Hardin, Garrett. (1968) "The Tragedy of the Commons," *Science* 162 (December): 1243–1248.

Harknett, Richard J. (1994) "The Logic of Conventional Deterrence and the End of the Cold War," *Security Studies* 4 (Autumn): 86–114.

Harman, Willis. (1976) *An Incomplete Guide to the Future.* Stanford, Calif.: Stanford Alumni Association.

Held, David, and Anthony McGrew, with David Goldblatt, and Jonathan Perraton. (2001) "Managing the Challenge of Globalization and Institutionalizing Cooperation through Global Governance," pp. 136–148 in Charles W. Kegley, Jr. and Eugene R. Wittkopf (eds.), *The Global Agenda,* 6th ed. Boston: McGraw-Hill.

———. (1999) *Global Transformations: Politics, Economics and Culture.* Stanford, Calif.: Stanford University Press.

Henkin, Louis. (1979) *How Nations Behave: Law and Foreign Policy.* New York: Columbia University Press.

Hensel, Paul R. (2000) "Theory and Evidence on Geography and Conflict," pp. 57–84 in John A. Vasquez (ed.), *What Do We Know About War?* Lanham, Md.: Rowman & Littlefield.

Heredia, Blanca. (1999) "Prosper or Perish? Development in the Age of Global Capital," pp. 93–97 in Robert M. Jackson (ed.), *Global Issues 1999/00,* 15th ed. Guilford, Conn.: Dushkin/McGraw-Hill.

Hermann, Charles F. (1972) "Some Issues in the Study of International Crisis," pp. 3–17 in Charles F. Hermann (ed.), *International Crises.* New York: Free Press.

Hermann, Margaret G. (1976) "When Leader Personality Will Affect Foreign Policy: Some Propositions," pp. 326–333 in James N. Rosenau (ed.), *In Search of Global Patterns.* New York: Free Press.

Hersh, Seymour M. (2002) "Manhunt: The Bush Administration's New Strategy in the War Against Terrorism," *New Yorker* (December 23 & 30): 66–74.

Herz, John H. (1951) *Political Realism and Political Idealism.* Chicago: University of Chicago Press.

Hilsman, Roger. (1967) *To Move a Nation.* New York: Doubleday.

Hoagland, Jim. (1996) "Yes, Sanctions Can Be Effective, but You Have to Work at It," *International Herald Tribune* (February 8): 8.

Hoffman, Eva. (2000) "Wanderers by Choice," *Utne Reader* (July/August): 46–48.

Hoffmann, Stanley. (1971) "International Law and the Control of Force," pp. 34–66 in Karl W. Deutsch and Stanley Hoffmann (eds.), *The Relevance of International Law.* Garden City, N.Y.: Doubleday-Anchor.

———. (1961) "International Systems and International Law," pp. 205–237 in Klaus Knorr and Sidney Verba (eds.), *The International System.* Princeton, N.J.: Princeton University Press.

Hopf, Ted. (1998) "The Promise of Constructivism in International Relations Theory," *International Security* 23 (Summer): 171–200.

Hopkins, Terence K., and Immanuel Wallerstein, (eds.). (1996) *The Age of Transitions: Trajectory of World Systems 1945–2025.* London: Zed Books.

Hottelet, Richard C. (1999) "Desertification: Forgotten Threat," *Christian Science Monitor* (December 15): 8.

Howard, Michael E. (1978) *War and the Liberal Conscience.* New York: Oxford University Press.

Howell, Llewelyn D. (1998) "The Age of Sovereignty Has Come to an End," *USA Today* 127 (September): 23.

Hufbauer, Gary Clyde, Jeffrey J. Schott, and Kimberly Ann Elliott. (1990) *Economic Sanctions Reconsidered,* 2nd ed. Washington, D.C.: Institute for International Economics.

Hume, David. (1817) *Philosophical Essays on Morals, Literature, and Politics,* vol. 1. Washington, D.C.: Duffy.

Huntington, Samuel P. (1996) *The Clash of Civilizations and the Remaking of World Order.* New York: Simon & Schuster.

———. (1991) *The Third Wave: Democratization in the Late Twentieth Century.* Norman: University of Oklahoma Press.

International Monetary Fund (IMF). (1997) *World Economic Outlook.* Washington, D.C.: International Monetary Fund.

Jaggers, Keith, and Ted Robert Gurr. (1995) "Transitions to Democracy: Tracking Democracy's Third Wave," *Journal of Peace Research* 32 (November): 469–482.

Jain, Subhash, and Piotz, Chelminski. (1999) "Beyond Buzzwords—Defining 'Globalization,' " *International Herald Tribune* (April 25): 9.

James, Barry. (2002a). "Talks to Tackle Threat to Biodiversity," *International Herald Tribune* (August 23): 1, 9.

———. (2002b) "World Loses Ground to Deserts," *International Herald Tribune* (April 4): 1, 10.

———. (2001) "Mischievous Species Capitalize on Globalization," *International Herald Tribune* (May 21): 1, 9.

Janis, Irving. (1982) *Groupthink: Psychological Studies of Policy Decisions and Fiascoes,* 2nd ed. Boston: Houghton Mifflin.

Jensen, Lloyd. (1982) *Explaining Foreign Policy.* Englewood Cliffs, N.J.: Prentice Hall.

Jervis, Robert. (1992) "A Usable Past for the Future," pp. 257–268 in Michael J. Hogan (ed.), *The End of the Cold War.* New York: Cambridge University Press.

———. (1985) "From Balance to Concert: A Study of International Cooperation," *World Politics* 38 (October): 58–79.

———. (1976) *Perception and Misperception in World Politics.* Princeton, N.J.: Princeton University Press.

Joyner, Christopher C. (2002) "The United Nations: Strengthening an International Norm," pp. 147–172 in Peter J. Schraeder (ed.), *Exporting Democracy.* Boulder, Colo.: Lynne Rienner.

———. (2001) "Global Commons: The Oceans, Antarctica, the Atmosphere, and Outer Space," pp. 354–389 in P. J. Simmons and Chantal de Jonge Oudraat (eds.), *Managing Global Issues.* Washington, D.C.: Carnegie Endowment for International Peace.

Juergensmeyer, Mark. (2003) "The Religious Roots of Contemporary Terrorism," pp. 185–193 in Charles W. Kegley, Jr. (ed.), *The New Global Terrorism.* Upper Saddle River, N.J.: Prentice Hall.

Kaplan, Morton A. (1957) *System and Process in International Politics.* New York: Wiley.

Kapstein, Ethan Barnaby. (1991–1992) "We Are Us: The Myth of the Multinational," *National Interest* 26 (Winter): 55–62.

Kearney, A. T. (2004) "Measuring Globalization" *Foreign Policy* (March/April): 54–69.

Keegan, John. (1999) *The First World War.* New York: Knopf.

———. (1993) *A History of Warfare.* New York: Vintage.

Kegley, Charles W., Jr. (1994) "How Did the Cold War Die? Principles for an Autopsy," *Mershon International Studies Review* 38 (April): 11–41.

Kegley, Charles W., Jr., and Eugene R. Wittkopf. (2004) *World Politics: Trend and Transformation,* 9th ed. Belmont, Calif.: Wadsworth.

Kegley, Charles W., Jr., and Margaret G. Hermann. (2002) "In Pursuit of a Peaceful International System," pp. 15–29 in Peter J. Schraeder (ed.), *Exporting Democracy.* Boulder, Colo.: Lynne Rienner.

Kegley, Charles W., Jr., and Gregory A. Raymond. (2003) "Preventive War and Permissive Normative Order," *International Studies Perspectives* 4 (November): 385–394.

———. (2002a) *Exorcising the Ghost of Westphalia: Building World Order in the New Millennium.* Upper Saddle River, N.J.: Prentice Hall.

———. (2002b) *From War to Peace: Fateful Decisions in World Politics.* Boston: Bedford/St. Martin's, and Belmont, Calif.: Wadsworth.

———. (1999) *How Nations Make Peace.* Boston: Bedford/St. Martin's.

———. (1994) *A Multipolar Peace? Great-Power Politics in the Twenty-First Century.* New York: St. Martin's.

———. (1990) *When Trust Breaks Down: Alliance Norms and World Politics.* Columbia: University of South Carolina Press.

———. (1982) "Alliance Norms and War: A New Piece in an Old Puzzle," *International Studies Quarterly* 26 (December): 572–595.

Kegley, Charles W., Jr., Gregory A. Raymond, and Margaret G. Hermann. (1998) "The Rise and Fall of the Nonintervention Norm," *Fletcher Forum of World Affairs* 22 (Winter/Spring): 81–101.

Kelman, Herbert C. (1965) *International Behavior.* New York: Holt, Rinehart & Winston.

Kennan, George F. (1985) "Morality and Foreign Policy," *Foreign Affairs* 64 (Winter): 205–218.

———. (1984) *The Fateful Alliance.* New York: Pantheon.

———. (1967) *Memoirs.* Boston: Little, Brown.

———["X"]. (1947) "The Sources of Soviet Conduct," *Foreign Affairs* 25 (July): 566–582.

Kennedy, Paul. (1987) *The Rise and Fall of the Great Powers.* New York: Random House.

Keohane, Robert O., and Joseph S. Nye. (2001a) *Power and Interdependence,* 3rd ed. New York: Addison Wesley-Longman.

———. (2001b) "Power and Interdependence in the Information Age," pp. 26–36 in Charles W. Kegley, Jr. and Eugene R. Wittkopf (eds.), *The Global Agenda,* 6th ed. Boston: McGraw-Hill.

———. (1977) *Power and Interdependence.* Boston: Little, Brown.

———, (eds.). (1971) *Transnational Relations and World Politics.* Cambridge: Harvard University Press.

Khripunov, Igor. (1997) "Have Guns Will Travel," *Bulletin of the Atomic Scientists* 53 (May/June): 47–51.

Kilborn, Michael. (1997) "Liberty's Ebb and Flow," *The Christian Science Monitor* (May 9): 18–19.

Kim, Dae Jung, and James D. Wolfensohn. (1999) "Economic Growth Requires Good Governance," *International Herald Tribune* (February 26): 6.

Kim, Woosang. (1989) "Power, Alliance, and Major Wars, 1816–1975," *Journal of Conflict Resolution* 32 (3): 255–273.

Kindleberger, Charles P. (1973) *The World in Depression, 1929–1939.* Berkeley: University of California Press.

Kissinger, Henry A. (2001) *Does America Need a Foreign Policy?* New York: Simon and Schuster.

———. (1992) "Balance of Power Sustained," pp. 238–248 in Graham Allison and Gregory F. Treverton (eds.), *Rethinking America's Security*. New York: Norton.

Klare, Michael T. (2001) "The New Geography of Conflict," *Foreign Affairs* 80 (May/June): 49–61.

———. (1999) "The New Arms Race," pp. 139–143 in Robert M. Jackson (ed.), *Global Issues 1999/00*, 15th ed. New Guilford, Conn.: Dushkin/McGraw-Hill.

———. (1990) "Wars in the 1990s: Growing Firepower in the Third World," *Bulletin of the Atomic Scientists* 46 (May): 9–13.

Klare, Michael T., and Daniel C. Thomas (eds.). (1991) *World Security: Trends and Challenges at Century's End*. New York: St. Martin's.

Kluger, Jeffrey. (2001) "A Climate of Despair," *Time* (April 9): 30–35.

Korany, Bahgat. (1986) *How Foreign Policy Decisions Are Made in the Third World*. Boulder, Colo.: Westview Press.

Krasner, Stephen P. (1993) "International Political Economy," pp. 453–455 in Joel Krieger (ed.), *The Oxford Companion to Politics of the World*. New York: Oxford University Press.

Krauthammer, Charles. (1993) "How Doves Become Hawks," *Time* (May 17): 74.

Kugler, Jacek. (1993) "War," pp. 962–966 in Joel Krieger (ed.), *The Oxford Companion to Politics of the World*. New York: Oxford University Press.

Kupchan, Charles H., and Clifford A. Kupchan. (1992) "A New Concert for Europe," pp. 249–266 in Graham Allison and Gregory F. Treverton, (eds.), *Rethinking America's Security: Beyond the Cold War to a New World Order*. New York: Norton.

Landes, David S. (1998) *The Wealth and Poverty of Nations: Why Are Some So Rich and Some So Poor?* New York: Norton.

Laqueur, Walter. (2001) "Terror's New Face," pp. 82–89 in Charles W. Kegley, Jr. and Eugene R. Wittkopf (eds.), *The Global Agenda*, 6th ed. Boston: McGraw-Hill.

Larson, Deborah Welch. (1994) "The Role of Belief Systems and Schemas in Foreign Policy Decision-Making," *Political Psychology* 15 (March): 17–33.

Lave, Charles A., and James G. March. (1975) *An Introduction to Models in the Social Sciences*. New York: Harper & Row.

Lebow, Richard Ned. (1981) *Between Peace and War*. Baltimore: Johns Hopkins University Press.

Levy, Jack S. (2001) "War and Its Causes," pp. 47–56 in Charles W. Kegley, Jr. and Eugene Wittkopf (eds.), *The Global Agenda*, 6th edition. Boston: McGraw-Hill.

———. (1998) "The Causes of War and the Conditions of Peace," *American Review of Political Science* 1: 139–165.

———. (1989a) "The Causes of War: A Review of Theories and Evidence," pp. 209–333 in Philip E. Tetlock, Jo L. Husbands, Robert Jervis, Paul C. Stern, and Charles Tilly (eds.), *Behavior, Society, and Nuclear War*. New York: Oxford University Press.

———. (1989b) "The Diversionary Theory of War: A Critique," pp. 259–288 in Manus I. Midlarsky (ed.), *Handbook of War Studies*. Boston: Unwin Hyman.

———. (1985) "The Polarity of the System and International Stability: An Empirical Analysis," pp. 41–66 in Alan Ned Sabrosky (ed.), *Polarity and War*. Boulder, Colo.: Westview.

Leyton-Brown, David. (1987) "Introduction." pp. 1–4 in David Leyton-Brown (ed.), *The Utility of International Economic Sanctions*. New York: St. Martin's Press.

Lind, Michael. (1993) "Of Arms and the Woman," *New Republic* (November 15): 36–38.

Lindblom, Charles E. (1979) "Still Muddling, Not Yet Through," *Public Administration Review* 39 (November/December): 517–526.

Lindsay, James M. (1986) "Trade Sanctions as Policy Instruments," *International Studies Quarterly* 30 (June): 153–173.

Lipson, Charles. (1984) "International Cooperation in Economic and Security Affairs," *World Politics* 37 (October): 1–23.

Lorenz, Konrad. (1963) *On Aggression*. New York: Harcourt, Brace & World.

Lutz, Wolfgang. (1994) "The Future of World Population," *Population Bulletin* 49 (June): 1–47.

Mackinder, Sir Halford. (1919) *Democratic Ideals and Reality*. New York: Holt.

Mahan, Alfred Thayer. (1890) *The Influence of Sea Power in History*. Boston: Little, Brown.

Majeed, Akhtar. (1991) "Has the War System Really Become Obsolete?" *Bulletin of Peace Proposals* 22 (December): 419–425.

Malaquias, Assis V. (2001) "Humanitarian Intervention," pp. 370–374 in Joel Krieger (ed.), *The Oxford Companion to Politics of the World,* 2nd ed. New York: Oxford University Press.

Mandelbaum, Michael. (2002) *The Ideas That Conquered the World*. New York: Public Affairs/Perseus.

Mansfield, Edward D., and Jack Snyder (1996) "The Effects of Democratization on War," *International Security* 20 (Summer): 196–207.

Mastanduno, Michael. (1991) "Do Relative Gains Matter?" *International Security* 16 (Summer): 73–113.

Mathews, Jessica T. (2000) "National Security for the 21st Century," pp. 9–11 in Gary Bertsch and Scott James (eds.), *Russell Symposium Proceedings*. Athens: University of Georgia.

———. (1998) "Are Networks Better than Nations?" pp. 8–11 in James M. Lindsay (ed.), *Perspectives: Global Issues*. Boulder, Colo.: Coursewise Publishing.

Mazarr, Michael J. (1999) *Global Trends 2005*. London: Palgrave.

McGranahan, Donald. (1995) "Measurement of Development," *International Social Science Journal* 143 (March): 39–59.

McGurn, William. (2002) "Pulpit Economics," *First Things* 122 (April): 21–25.

Meadows, Donella H. (1993) "Seeing the Population Issue Whole," *The World & I* 8 (June): 396–409.

Mearsheimer, John J. (2001) *The Tragedy of Great Power Politics.* New York: Norton.

———. (1995) "A Realist Reply," *International Security* 20 (Summer): 82–93.

———. (1994/95) "The False Promise of International Institutions," *International Security* 19 (Winter): 5–49.

Melloan, George. (2002) "Bush's Toughest Struggle Is with His Own Bureaucracy," *Wall Street Journal* (June 25): A19.

Mendelsohn, Jack. (2002) "America and Russia: Make-Believe Arms Control," *Current History* 101 (October): 325–329.

Micklethwait, John, and Adrian Wooldridge. (2001) "The Globalization Backlash," *Foreign Policy* (September/October): 16–26.

Midlarsky, Manus I. (ed.). (2000) *Handbook of War Studies II.* Ann Arbor: University of Michigan Press.

———. (1988) *The Onset of World War.* Boston: Unwin Hyman.

Miller, Marian A. L. (1995) *The Third World in Global Environmental Politics.* Boulder, Colo.: Lynne Rienner.

Mitrany, David. (1966) *A Working Peace System.* Chicago: Quadrangle.

Modelski, George, and William R. Thompson. (1999) "The Long and the Short of Global Politics in the Twenty-First Century: An Evolutionary Approach," *International Studies Review,* special issue, edited by Davis B. Bobrow: 109–140.

———. (1996) *Leading Sectors and World Powers.* Columbia: University of South Carolina Press.

Morgenthau, Hans J. (1985) *Politics among Nations,* 6th ed. Revised by Kenneth W. Thompson. New York: Knopf.

Morris, Desmond. (1969) *The Human Zoo.* New York: Dell.

Murray, Williamson, and Allan R. Millett. (2000) *A War to Be Won.* Cambridge, Mass.: Harvard University Press.

National Commission on Terrorist Attacks Upon the United States. (2004) *The 9/11 Commission Report.* New York: Norton.

Neustadt, Richard E. (1970) *Alliance Politics.* New York: Columbia University Press.

Newland, Kathleen. (1994) "Refugees: The Rising Flood," *World Watch* 7 (May/June): 10–20.

Niebuhr, Reinhold. (1947) *Moral Man and Immoral Society.* New York: Scribner's.

Nye, Joseph S., Jr. (2004) *Soft Power: The Means to Success in World Politics.* New York: Public Affairs Press.

———. (2002a) "The Dependent Colossus," *Foreign Policy* (March/April): 74–76.

———. (2002b) *The Paradox of American Power.* New York: Oxford University Press.

———. (2001) "The Changing Nature of World Power," pp. 95–107 in Charles W. Kegley, Jr. and Eugene R. Wittkopf (eds.), *The Global Agenda,* 6th ed. Boston: McGraw-Hill.

———. (2000) *Understanding International Conflict,* 3rd ed. New York: Longman.

———. (1990) *Bound to Lead: The Changing Nature of American Power.* New York Basic Books.

Onuf, Nicholas. (1989) *World of Our Making: Rules and Rule in Social Theory and International Relations.* Columbia: University of South Carolina Press.

Organski, A. F. K. (1968) *World Politics.* New York: Knopf.

Organski, A. F. K., and Jacek Kugler. (1980) *The War Ledger.* Chicago: University of Chicago Press.

Ostrom, Charles W., Jr., and John H. Aldrich. (1978) "The Relationship Between Size and Stability in the Major Power International System," *American Journal of Political Science* 22 (November): 743–771.

Packenham, Robert. (1992) *The Dependency Movement.* Cambridge, Mass.: Harvard University Press.

Panama: A Just Cause. (1989) Washington, D.C.: United States Department of State, Bureau of Public Affairs, Current Policy No. 1240.

Pape, Robert A. (1996) *Bombing to Win: Air Power and Coercion in War.* Ithaca: Cornell University Press.

Peterson, Erik. (1998) "Looming Collision of Capitalisms?" pp. 296–307 in Charles W. Kegley, Jr. and Eugene R. Wittkopf (eds.), *The Global Agenda,* 5th ed. New York: McGraw-Hill.

Peterson, V. Spike, and Anne Sisson Runyan. (1993) *Global Gender Issues.* Boulder, Colo.: Westview Press.

Pfetsch, Frank L. (1999) "Globalization: A Threat and a Challenge for the State," paper presented at the European Standing Conference on International Studies, Vienna, September 11–13.

Peirce, Neal R. (1997) "Does the Nation-State Have a Future?" *International Herald Tribune* (April 4): 9.

Porter, Gareth. (1995) "Environmental Security as a National Security Issue," *Current History* 94 (May): 218–222.

Pound, Edward T., and Jihan El-Tahri. (1994) "Sanctions: The Pluses and Minuses," *U.S. News & World Report* (October 31): 58–71.

Puchala, Donald J. (1994) "Some World Order Options for Our Time," *Peace Forum* 11 (November): 17–30.

Putnam, Robert D. (1988) "Diplomacy and Domestic Politics: The Logic of Two-Level Games," *International Organization* 42 (Summer): 427–460.

Quester, George. (1992) "Conventional Deterrence," pp. 31–51 in Gary L. Guertner, Robert Haffa, Jr., and George Quester (eds.), *Conventional Forces and the Future of Deterrence*. Carlisle Barracks, Pa.: U.S. Army War College.

Quinn, Jane Bryant. (2002) "Iraq: It's the Oil, Stupid," *Newsweek* (September 30): 43.

Ray, James Lee. (1995) *Democracy and International Conflict: An Evaluation of the Democratic Peace Proposition*. Columbia: University of South Carolina Press.

Raymond, Gregory A. (1999) "Necessity in Foreign Policy," *Political Science Quarterly* 113 (Winter): 673–688.

———. (1994) "Democracies, Disputes, and Third-Party Intermediaries," *Journal of Conflict Resolution* 38 (March): 24–42.

Redfield, Robert. (1962) *Human Nature and the Study of Society*, vol. 1. Chicago: University of Illinois Press.

Regan, Patrick M. (1994) *Organizing Societies for War: The Process and Consequences of Societal Militarization*. Westport, Conn.: Praeger.

Reid, T. R. (1998) "Feeding the Planet," *National Geographic* 194 (October): 56–74.

Reinares, Fernando. (2002) "The Empire Rarely Strikes Back," *Foreign Policy* (January/February): 92–94.

Reinicke, Wolfgang H. (1997) "Global Public Policy," *Foreign Affairs* 76 (November/December): 127–138.

Rieff, David. (1999) "The Precarious Triumph of Human Rights," *New York Times Magazine* (August 8): 36–41.

Riggs, Robert E., and Jack C. Plano. (1994) *The United Nations*, 2nd ed. Belmont, Calif.: Wadsworth.

Riker, William H. (1962) *The Theory of Political Coalitions*. New Haven, Conn.: Yale University Press.

Rosecrance, Richard. (1999) *The Rise of the Virtual State*. New York: Basic Books.

———. (1992) "A New Concert of Powers," *Foreign Affairs* 71 (Spring): 64–82.

———. (1986) *The Rise of the Trading State: Commerce and Conquest in the Modern World*. New York: Basic Books.

Rosenau, James N., and Mary Durfee. (1995) *Thinking Theory Thoroughly: Coherent Approaches to an Incoherent World*. Boulder, Colo.: Westview.

Rosset, Peter. (1999) "Biotechnology Won't Feed the World," *International Herald Tribune* (September 2): 8.

Rostow, W. W. (1960) *The Stages of Economic Growth*. Cambridge, Eng.: Cambridge University Press.

Rothgeb, John M., Jr. (1993) *Defining Power: Influence and Force in the Contemporary International System*. New York: St. Martin's.

Rummel, Rudolph J. (1994) *Death by Government*. New Brunswick, N.J.: Transaction Books.

Runyan, Curtis. (1999) "NGOs Proliferate World Wide," pp. 144–145 in Lester R. Brown, et al. (eds.), *Vital Signs 1999*. New York: Norton.

Russett, Bruce. (2001) "How Democracy, Interdependence, and International Organizations Create a System for Peace," pp. 232–242 in Charles W. Kegley, Jr. and Eugene Wittkopf (eds.), *The Global Agenda*, 6th ed. Boston: McGraw-Hill.

Russett, Bruce, and John Oneal. (2001) *Triangulating Peace: Democracy, Interdependence, and International Organizations*. New York: Norton.

Sagan, Carl, and Richard Turco. (1993) "Nuclear Winter in the Post-Cold War Era," *Journal of Peace Research* 30 (November): 369–373.

Samin, Amir. (1976) *Unequal Development*. New York: Monthly Review Press.

Samuelson, Robert J. (2002a) " 'Digital Divide' Facing Poor Looks Like Fiction." (Columbia, S.C.) *The State* (April 3): A13.

———. (2002b) "The New Coin of the Realm," *Newsweek* (January 7): 38.

———. (2001) "The Spirit of Capitalism," *Foreign Affairs* 80 (January/February): 205–211.

Saurin, Julian. (2000) "Globalization, Poverty, and the Promises of Modernity," pp. 204–229 in Sarah Owen Vanderslvis and Paris Yeros (eds.), *Poverty in World Politics*. New York: St. Martin's.

Schelling, Thomas C. (1966) *Arms and Influence*. New Haven: Yale University Press.

Schroeder, Paul W. (1989) "The Nineteenth Century System: Balance of Power or Political Equilibrium?" *Review of International Studies* 15 (April): 135–153.

Schulz, William F. (2001) *In Our Own Best Interest: How Defending Human Rights Benefits Us All*. Boston: Beacon Press.

Schwenniger, Sherle R. (2004) "America's 'Suez Moment,'" *The Atlantic* 293 (January/February): 129–130.

Seck, Manadon Manosour. (1999) "Shrinking Forests," *Christian Science Monitor* (May 3): 9.

Shannon, Thomas Richard. (1989) *An Introduction to the World-System Perspective*. Boulder, Colo.: Westview Press.

Shultz, Richard H., Jr., and William J. Olson. (1994) *Ethnic and Religious Conflict*. Washington, D.C.: National Strategy Information Center.

Simon, Herbert A. (1957) *Models of Man*. New York: Wiley.

Simonis, Udo Ernst and Tanja Brühl. (2002) "World Ecology—Structures and Trends," pp. 97–124 in Paul Kennedy, Dirk Messner, and Franz Nuscheler (eds.), *Global Trends and Global Governance*. London: Pluto Press.

Singer, Hans W., and Javed A. Ansari. (1988) *Rich and Poor Countries*, 4th ed. London: Unwin Hyman.

Singer, J. David. (1991) "Peace in the Global System," pp. 56–84 in Charles W. Kegley, Jr. (ed.), *The Long Postwar Peace*. New York: HarperCollins.

Singer, Max, and Aaron Wildavsky. (1993) *The Real World Order: Zones of Peace/Zones of Turmoil.* Chatham, N.J.: Chatham House.

Sivard, Ruth Leger. (1996) *World Military and Social Expenditures 1996.* Washington, D.C.: World Priorities.

———. (1993) *World Military and Social Expenditures 1993.* Washington, D.C.: World Priorities.

———. (1991) *World Military and Social Expenditures 1991.* Washington, D.C.: World Priorities.

———. (1982) *World Military and Social Expenditures 1982.* Leesburg, Va.: World Priorities.

Siverson, Randolph M., and Harvey Starr. (1991) *The Diffusion of War: A Study of Opportunity and Willingness.* Ann Arbor: University of Michigan Press.

Sklair, Leslie. (1991) *Sociology of the Global System.* Baltimore: Johns Hopkins University Press.

Slaughter, Anne-Marie. (1997) "The Real New World Order," *Foreign Affairs* 76 (September–October): 183–197.

Slomanson, William R. (2003) *Fundamental Perspectives on International Law,* 4th ed. Belmont: Wadsworth.

Small, Melvin, and J. David Singer. (1982) *Resort to Arms: International and Civil Wars, 1816–1980.* Beverly Hills, Calif.: Sage.

Smith, Jackie, and Timothy Patrick Moran. (2001) "WTO 101: Myths about the World Trade Organization," pp. 68–71 in Robert J. Griffiths (ed.), *Developing World 01/02,* Guilford, Conn.: Dushkin/McGraw-Hill.

Smith, Steve. (1997) "Bridging the Gap: Social Constructivism," pp. 183–187 in John Baylis and Steve Smith (eds.), *The Globalization of World Politics.* New York: Oxford University Press.

Snyder, Jack. (1984) "The Security Dilemma in Alliances," *World Politics* 36 (July): 461–495.

Snyder, Glenn H., and Paul Diesing. (1977) *Conflict among Nations.* Princeton, N.J.: Princeton University Press.

Somit, Albert. (1990) "Humans, Chimps, and Bonobos: The Biological Bases of Aggression, War, and Peacemaking," *Journal of Conflict Resolution* 34 (September): 553–582.

Soroos, Marvin S. (2001) "The Tragedy of the Commons in Global Perspective," pp. 485–499 in Charles W. Kegley, Jr. and Eugene R. Wittkopf (eds.), *The Global Agenda,* 6th ed. Boston: McGraw-Hill.

———. (1999) "Global Institutions and the Environment: An Evolutionary Prespective," pp. 27–51 in Norman J. Vig and Regina S. Axelrod (eds.), *The Global Environment: Institutions, Law, and Policy.* Washington, D.C.: CQ Press.

Spero, Joan E., and Jeffrey A. Hart. (1997) *The Politics of International Economic Relations,* 5th ed. New York: St. Martin's.

Speth, James Gustave. (1999) "Debt Relief, Yes, but Development Aid as Well," *International Herald Tribune* (May 7): 6.

Sprout, Harold, and Margaret Sprout. (1965) *The Ecological Perspective on Human Affairs.* Princeton: Princeton University Press.

Spykman, Nicholas. (1944) *Geography of Peace.* New York: Harcourt Brace.

Srodes, James. (2001) "Importing Economic Muscle," *World Trade* 14 (June): 13–15.

Starr, Harvey. (1978) " 'Opportunity' and 'Willingness' as Ordering Concepts in the Study of War," *International Interactions* 4: 363–387.

State of Indigenous People. (2002) Olympia, Wash.: Center for World Indigenous Studies. www.soroptimisi.org.

State of the World. (2002) Worldwatch Institute. New York: Norton.

Stephenson, Carolyn M. (2000) "NGOs and the Principal Organs of the United Nations," pp. 270–294 in Paul Taylor and R. J. Groom (eds.), *The United Nations at the Millennium.* London: Continuum.

Stock, Thomas, and Anna De Geer. (1995) "Chemical and Biological Weapons, pp. 337–57 in the Stockholm International Peace Research Institute. *SIPRI Yearbook 1995.* New York Oxford University Press.

Stockholm International Peace Research Institute (SIPRI). (2002) *SIPRI Yearbook 2002.* New York: Oxford University Press.

———. (2001) *SIPRI Yearbook 2001.* New York: Oxford University Press.

———. (1999) *SIPRI Yearbook 1999.* New York: Oxford University Press.

Stokes, Bruce. (2000) "The Protectionist Myth," *Foreign Policy* 117 (Winter): 88–102.

Stopford, John. (2001) "Multinational Corporations," pp. 72–77 in Robert J. Griffiths (ed.), *Developing World 01/02.* Guilford, Conn.: Dushkin/McGraw-Hill.

Stott, Philip. (2002) "Cold Comfort for 'Global Warming,' " *Wall Street Journal* (March 25): A18.

Thakur, Ramesh, and Steve Lee. (2000) "Defining New Goals for Diplomacy in the Twenty-First Century," *International Herald Tribune* (January 19): 8.

Thompson, Kenneth W. (1953) "Collective Security Reexamined," *American Political Science Review* 47 (September): 753–772.

Thompson, William R. (1988) *On Global War: Historical-Structural Approaches to World Politics.* Columbia: University of South Carolina Press.

Thurow, Lester C. (1999) *Building Wealth: The New Rules for Individuals, Companies, and Nations in a Knowledge-Based Economy.* New York: HarperCollins.

———. (1998) "The American Economy in the Next Century," *Harvard International Review* 20 (Winter): 54–59.

Tickner, J. Ann. (2002) *Gendering World Politics.* New York: Columbia University Press.

———. (1988) "Hans Morgenthau's Principles of Political Realism: A Feminist Reformulation," *Millennium* 17 (3): 429–440.

Tillema, Herbert K. (2001) *Overt Military Intervention in the Cold War Era*. Columbia: University of South Carolina Press.

———. (1994) "Cold War Alliance and Overt Military Intervention, 1945–1991," *International Interactions* 20 (No. 3): 249–278.

Timmerman, Kenneth. (1991) *The Death Lobby: How the West Armed Iraq*. Boston: Houghton Mifflin.

Todaro, Michael P. (2000) *Economic Development*, 7th ed. Reading, Mass.: Addison-Wesley.

Toner, Robin. (2002) "FBI Agent Gives Her Blunt Assessment" (Columbia, S.C.) *The State* (June 7): A5.

Tuchman, Barbara W. (1962) *The Guns of August*. New York: Dell.

Turk, Danilo. (2001) "Genocide," p. 316 in Joel Krieger (ed.), *The Oxford Companion to Politics of the World*, 2nd ed. New York: Oxford University Press.

Tyler, Patrik E. (2001) "Seeing Profits, Russia Prepared to Become World's Nuclear Waste Dump," *International Herald Tribune* (May 28): 5.

United Nations Development Programme (UNDP). (2002) *Human Development Report 2002*. New York: Oxford University Press.

———. (2001) *Human Development Report 2001*. New York: Oxford University Press.

———. (1999) *Human Development Report 1999*. New York: Oxford University Press.

———. (1997) *Human Development Report 1997*. New York: Oxford University Press.

———. (1995) *Human Development Report 1995*. New York: Oxford University Press.

United Nations Environment Programme (UNEP). (2002) *Global Environment Outlook*. New York: Oxford University Press.

United Nations Population Division (UNPD). (2001) *World Population Prospects*. New York: United Nations.

Urquhart, Brian. (2001) "Mrs. Roosevelt's Revolution," *New York Review of Books* 49 (April 26): 32–34.

U.S. ACDA (Arms Control and Disarmament Agency). (1997) *World Military Expenditures and Arms Transfers*. Washington, D.C.: U.S. Government Printing Office.

Van Evera, Stephen. (1999) *Causes of War*. Ithaca, N.Y.: Cornell University Press.

———. (1997) *Guide to Methods for Students of Political Science*. Ithaca, N.Y.: Cornell University Press.

———. (1994) "Hypotheses on Nationalism and War," *International Security* 18 (Spring): 5–39.

———. (1990–91) "Primed for Peace: Europe after the Cold War," *International Security* 15 (Winter): 7–57.

Vasquez, John A. (ed.). (2000) *What Do We Know About War?* Lanham, Md.: Rowman & Littlefield.

———. (1998) *The Power of Power Politics: From Classical Realism to Neotraditionalism*. Cambridge, Eng.: Cambridge University Press.

———. (1993) *The War Puzzle*. Cambridge, Eng.: Cambridge University Press.

———. (1986) "Capability, Types of War, and Peace," *Western Political Quarterly* 39 (June): 313–327.

Vasquez, John A., and Colin Elman (eds.). (2003) *Realism and the Balancing of Power: A New Debate*. Upper Saddle River, N.J.: Prentice Hall.

Verba, Sidney. (1969) "Assumptions of Rationality and Non-Rationality in Models of the International System," pp. 217–231 in James N. Rosenau (ed.), *International Politics and Foreign Policy*. New York: Free Press.

Vital Signs 2002. (2002) *Vital Signs 2002: The Trends That Are Shaping Our Future*. New York: Norton, for the Worldwatch Institute.

Vital Signs 1999. (1999) *Vital Signs 1999*. New York: Norton.

Wallace, Michael D. (1973) "Alliance Polarization, Cross-Cutting, and International War, 1815–1964: A Measurement Procedure and Some Preliminary Evidence," *Journal of Conflict Resolution* 17 (December): 575–604.

Wallensteen, Peter, and Margareta Sollenberg. (2001) "Armed Conflict 1989–2000." *Journal of Peace Research* 38 (September): 629–644.

Wallerstein, Immanuel. (1988) *The Modern World-System III: The Second Era of Great Expansion of the Capitalist World-System, 1730–1840*. San Diego: Academic Press.

Walters, Robert S., and David H. Blake. (1992) *The Politics of Global Economic Relations*, 4th ed. Englewood Cliffs, N.J.: Prentice Hall.

Waltz, Kenneth N. (1979) *Theory of International Politics*. Reading, Mass.: Addison-Wesley.

Wattenberg, Ben J. (2002) "Over-population Turns Out to Be Overhyped," *Wall Street Journal* (March 4): 10.

Wayman, Frank. (1985) "Bipolarity, Multipolarity, and the Threat of War," pp. 115–144 in Alan Ned Sabrosky (ed.), *Polarity and War*. Boulder, Colo.: Westview.

Weart, Spencer R. (1994) "Peace among Democratic and Oligarchic Republics," *Journal of Peace Research* 31 (August): 299–316.

Wendt, Alexander. (2000) *Social Theory of International Politics*. Cambridge: Cambridge University Press.

———. (1995) "Constructing International Politics," *International Security* 20 (Summer): 71–81.

Wendzel, Robert L. (1980) *International Relations: A Policymaker Focus*. New York: Wiley.

White, Donald W. (1998) "Mutable Destiny: The End of the American Century?" *Harvard International Review* 20 (Winter): 42–47.

White, Ralph K. (1990) "Why Aggressors Lose," *Political Psychology* 11 (June): 227–242.

Williamson, Samuel R., Jr. (1988) "The Origins of World War I," pp. 225–248 in Robert I. Rotberg and

Theodore K. Rabb (eds.), *The Origins and Prevention of Major Wars*. Cambridge: Cambridge University Press.

Wilmer, Franke. (2000) "Women, the State and War: Feminist Incursions into World Politics," pp. 385–395 in Richard W. Mansbach and Edward Rhodes (eds.), *Global Politics in a Changing World*. Boston: Houghton Mifflin.

———. (1993) *The Indigenous Voice in World Politics*. Newbury Park, Calif.: Sage.

Wilson, James Q. (1993) *The Moral Sense*. New York: Free Press.

Wittkopf, Eugene R., Charles W. Kegley, Jr., and James M. Scott. (2003) *American Foreign Policy*, 6th ed. Belmont, Calif.: Wadsworth.

Wohlforth, William C. (1999) "The Stability of a Unipolar World," *International Security* 24 (Summer): 5–41.

Wolfers, Arnold. (1962) *Discord and Collaboration*. Baltimore: Johns Hopkins University Press.

Wolfers, Arnold, and Laurence W. Martin (eds.). (1956) *The Anglo-American Tradition in Foreign Affairs*. New York: Oxford University Press.

Woodward, Bob. (2004) *Plan of Attack*. New York: Simon & Schuster.

———. (2002) *Bush At War*. New York: Simon & Schuster.

World Bank. (2002a) *World Bank Atlas*. Washington, D.C.: World Bank.

———. (2002b) *World Development Indicators 2002*. Washington, D.C.: World Bank.

———. (2001) *World Development Report 2000/2001*. New York: Oxford University Press.

———. (2000) *World Development Report 1999/2000*. New York: Oxford University Press.

Wright, Quincy. (1942) *A Study of War*. Chicago: University of Chicago Press.

Yearbook of International Organizations, 1993/1994. (1993) vol. 1. Munich: K. G. Sauer.

Zacher, Mark W., and Richard A. Matthew. (1995) "Liberal International Theory: Common Threads, Divergent Strands," pp. 107–149 in Charles W. Kegley, Jr. (ed.), *Controversies in International Relations Theory*. New York: St. Martin's.

Zakaria, Fareed. (2002) "The Trouble with Being the World's Only Superpower," *New Yorker* (October 14 and 21): 72–81.

Zinnes, Dina A., and Jonathan Wilkenfeld. (1971) "An Analysis of Foreign Conflict Behavior of Nations," pp. 167–213 in Wolfram F. Handieder (ed.), *Comparative Foreign Policy*. New York: McKay.

Credits

This page constitutes an extension of the copyright page. We have made every effort to trace the ownership of all copyrighted material and to secure permission from copyright holders. In the event of any question arising as to the use of any material, we will be pleased to make the necessary corrections in future printings. Thanks are due to the following authors, publishers, and agents for permission to use the material indicated.

Chapter 1. 6: Photo Courtesy of the U.S. Army/Staff Sgt. Klaus Baesu **6:** © Werner Forman/Art Resource, NY, British Museum, London, Great Britain **8:** © AP/Wide World Photos

Chapter 2. 25: Isaac Fuller, Burghley House Collection, Lincolnshire, UK/Bridgeman Art Library **25:** © Scala/Art Resource, NY **28:** The Granger Collection, NY **28:** © Bettmann/CORBIS

Chapter 3. 45: Courtesy of the White House/Getty Images

Chapter 4. 66: © AP/Wide World Photos **75:** © Topham/Image Works **83:** © Stephen Shaver/AFP/Getty Images

Chapter 5. 97: © Bettmann/CORBIS **97:** © Bettmann/CORBIS **113:** © Robert Nickelsberg/Getty Images

Chapter 6. 127: © Beth A. Keiser/AP/Wide World Photos

Chapter 7. 152: © Chris Hondros/Getty Images **152:** © Les Stone/Zuma **157:** U.S. Army/AP/Wide World Photos **157:** © Hutton Archive/Getty Images **165:** © AP/Wide World Photos **169:** © AP/Wide World Photos

Chapter 8. 183: © NASM/SYGMA/CORBIS **186:** © Bernard Hermann/Liaison Agency/Getty Images

Chapter 9. 207: The Granger Collection, NY **212:** © AP/Wide World Photos **218:** © Claro Cortes IV/Reuters/CORBIS **219:** © Reuters/Archive Photos/CORBIS **221:** © Andreas Stringlos/AFP/Getty Images

Chapter 10. 227: © Reuters/Getty Images **231:** © Erich Lessing/ Art Resource, NY/ Stedelijk Museum "Het Prinsenhof", Delft, The Netherlands **237:** © Kathy Willens/AP/Wide World Photos **237:** © Matthieu Polak/Sygma/CORBIS **237:** © P.F. Gero/Paul F. Gero Photography **237:** © Reuters/Rubin Sprich/Archive Photos/Corbis **237:** © Sygma/CORBIS **237:** © Vienna Report/Sygma/CORBIS **237:** ©William Campbell **244:** © Boris Grdanski/AP/Wide World Photos

Chapter 11. 256: © Saleh RiFai/AP/Wide World Photos **257:** © Sally Wiener Grotta/ The Stock Market/CORBIS **261:** © Eraldo Peres/AP/Wide World Photos **266:** © Frank Fournier/ Contact Press Images

Chapter 12. 293: © Anja Niedringhaus/EPA/AFP/Getty Images **294:** © Eric Feferberg/AFP/Getty Images

Chapter 13. 314: © Graeme Ewens/Panos Pictures **317:** © 2001, The Washington Post, reprinted with permission. Photo by Lucian Perkins. **321:** © AFP Photo/Getty Images **322:** Piers Benatar/Panos Pictures

Chapter 14. 329: © Sherwin Castro/AP/Wide World Photos **338:** © Robert Harbison/The Christian Science Monitor/Getty Images **339:** © Isabelle Rouvillois/AFP/Getty Images **342:** © Yanin Arthus Bertrand/CORBIS **347:** © Greenpeace/Daniel Beltra

Index

Note: Page numbers followed by a t *indicate tables.*